S0-BDG-922

Development Economics

Development Economics

A Framework for Analysis and Policy

R. M. Sundrum
Australian National University

JOHN WILEY & SONS
Chichester · New York · Brisbane · Toronto · Singapore

Library of Congress Cataloging in Publication Data:

Sundrum, R. M.
Development economics.

Includes index.
1. Economic development. I. Title.
HD82.S8538 338.9 82-7066
AACR2

ISBN 0 471 10366 7 (cloth)
ISBN 0 471 10464 7 (paper)

British Library Cataloguing in Publication Data:

Sundrum, R. M.
Development economics.
1. Underdeveloped areas — Economic conditions
I. Title
330.9172′4 MC59.7

ISBN 0 471 10366 7 (cloth)
ISBN 0 471 10464 7 (paper)

Phototypeset by Dobbie Typesetting Service, Plymouth, Devon, England
and printed by Pitman Press, Ltd., Bath, Avon, England

To

A. D.

in loving memory

and

H.W.A. and D.M.B.

with deep gratitude

Contents

PART IV. THE FINANCING OF DEVELOPMENT

Preface

So large has the literature on economic development become in the past decade or two that yet another book requires justification. The justification for the present book is that over three decades of development efforts have failed to make a significant impact on the living standards of hundreds of millions of poverty-stricken people in the less-developed countries of the world. Therefore, this book attempts to present a new view of the problems of these countries through the prism of a more precise definition of the concept of development, one that gets away from those of GNP growth and equity of distribution which have dominated the literature. This new definition of development is used to re-examine some of the standard analyses of topics such as production, trade and distribution, and their policy implications. In a book of this size, it has not been possible to discuss all these problems, and the appropriate policies to tackle them, in much detail, but it is hoped that the approach suggested here may provide a useful framework for others wishing to study them further, especially in the context of particular countries.

The present book assumes that readers are already familiar with the basic ideas of economics, such as may have been acquired in the first or second year at university. It is therefore offered in the first place to students at the post-graduate or advanced undergraduate levels intending to specialize in the study of development. It is also offered to those professional economists whose work concentrates on particular aspects of the development process as a brief conspectus of the subject as a whole, so that they can then place their special interests in a wider perspective. Above all, it is hoped that the work will be found useful by those who have to make and execute policies relating to economic development—the political leaders and the economic administrators—and interested members of the general public. It is in the hope of making it intelligible to this audience that all essentially technical arguments of a mathematical or statistical nature have been omitted or left with only brief references to the sources where they are more fully discussed.

This book has been a long time in the writing as I searched for a useful framework for the study of development, both as a teacher and a researcher in universities and various international development agencies. It therefore bears the mark of my debt to a long list of writers on the subject, a debt which can only be acknowledged by the references to their work. Some debts, however, are so great that they have to be acknowledged here. I could not have written this book anywhere but in the Department of Economics of the Research School of Pacific Studies, Australian National University, which provided me both with excellent facilities for studying the literature and the opportunity of observing economic change in a number of less-developed countries of the Asia–Pacific region at first hand. Constant discussion with my colleagues in this department greatly advanced my understanding of the subject. Mr David Butt encouraged and advised me from the very beginning of the project. He, Professor H. W. Arndt, Dr Anne Booth, Dr D. P. Chaudhri, Mrs Ruth Daroesman and an anonymous referee read and commented on the whole or parts of the book, some in several versions. Although I have not always understood or followed their advice, and although I am solely responsible for all the errors that remain here, they have contributed to whatever merits there are in this work, and I am deeply grateful to all of them.

February 1982 R. M. SUNDRUM

PART I

Developed and Less-Developed Countries

CHAPTER 1

Introduction

1.1 Alternative approaches to development
1.2 Alternative strategies of development
1.3 The contrast between developed and less-developed countries
1.4 The concept of development
1.5 Growth and distribution at a low level of development
1.6 The role of government
1.7 Limitations of the study

It is a remarkable feature of the world today that the human race is so sharply divided into two groups of countries, one comprising less than a third of the world's population living in great material affluence and the other comprising people living in great poverty who have experienced little, if any, improvement over time. There have always been rich and poor countries in the world but never before modern times has the gap between them been so great in magnitude and so persistent over several decades.

This division of the world into two groups of countries differing so widely in their economic circumstances is the *raison d'être* of development economics. This branch of economics seeks answers to the questions: What are the differences between the two groups of countries? How have they come about, and in particular, why have the forces which eradicated mass poverty in some countries not done so in others? What policies can governments of countries still ridden with such poverty follow to deal with this problem? This book attempts to deal with these questions from the point of view of economics.

For a number of reasons, this problem has attracted world attention only since World War II. First, there has been greater awareness; because of greater facilities for travel and communication, the people of the developed countries (hereafter referred to as DCs) have become more aware of abject poverty in the less-developed countries (hereafter referred to as LDCs), while people of the LDCs could see for themselves the higher standard of living in the DCs and aspired to the same. Second, there was greater political willingness to tackle the problem. It was a time when LDCs, one after the other, became independent of Western political domination and when new national governments came to power in the LDCs with the promise of promoting development, and put this objective at the top of their policy agenda. At the same time, the DCs undertook an international responsibility to assist the LDCs in their development efforts, partly out of a genuine humanitarian interest and partly to seek greater influence among the LDCs which had now attained political power in international relations far outweighing their economic strength. Finally, there was a new confidence that the poverty of LDCs was not an immutable fact but something which could be remedied by deliberate policies, as shown by the experience of countries such as Japan and the Soviet Union, the 'late-comers' where the efforts of their governments played a significant part in promoting development in an historically short period.

Since the problem of development came to the forefront of attention, there has been a large and growing literature on the subject. But in spite of the efforts of policy-makers and the researches of economists for over three decades, there has been little change in the conditions of life for the mass of the people in most LDCs. Therefore, it is time to re-examine some of the basic principles underlying the professional study of the development problem and the practical policies of governments. This is the object of the present book.

By way of introduction, this chapter begins with the main features of the standard approaches to the subject in much of the extant literature (Section 1.1) and presents an outline of the main argument of the present work in later sections.

1.1 Alternative Approaches to Development

The extant literature on development can be broadly classified into four categories. First, there is a class of books of a highly descriptive nature. Some of this work is presented in books with titles such as 'The Economic Development' of this country or that. Other studies deal with all or large groups of LDCs and consist of international compilations of data from these countries, especially of a statistical nature. The steady accumulation of such data, mostly inspired by the United Nations, has been a valuable contribution; as a result, we have now become more aware of at least some aspects of economic life of the greater part of mankind living in the LDCs. Without such knowledge of the actual situation of these countries, it would be futile to understand the problems facing them or to design policies for their solution. Therefore, an attempt is made in the present work to summarize some of these data all too briefly, but hopefully in sufficient detail to indicate the dimensions of the problem.

But description alone is not sufficient either for analysis or for policy. It has to be supplemented by a theoretical model or framework which can explain how the prevailing conditions have come about and which can then be used to design appropriate policies. Of course, even the act of description, the choice of things to be described, already implies an underlying model which determines what is relevant and what is not, but in most studies which are either frankly descriptive or which rely on simple statistical analyses of data, the underlying model is often left implicit. This is particularly the case with a second category of studies which search for 'patterns of development', i.e. empirical regularities in international cross-section and historical data. The underlying assumption is that all the countries included in the particular samples studied belong to the same universe, so that their behaviour can be studied by a single model revealed by the cross-section pattern. In particular, it is assumed that the current experience and the probable future prospects of LDCs will follow the historical pattern of the DCs. Apart from this basic assumption, these studies relate the 'patterns of development' primarily to the level of per capita income according to rather simple functional forms. The underlying model therefore tends to treat the process of development mainly in terms of the growth of per capita income.

A more theoretical approach is taken in the third group of studies consisting mainly of the application of neo-classical economics to the development problem. The typical procedure is to start with certain assumptions about economic behaviour, taken practically as axioms, and to work out their consequences for analysis and policy, often by highly sophisticated mathematical techniques in a parody of the method of the so-called exact sciences. Three of these assumptions are particularly important. One is the assumption of maximizing behaviour, i.e. the assumption that individuals are constantly and efficiently maximizing their satisfactions as consumers and their profits as producers. Hence, economics has even been defined as the study of maximizing behaviour (Samuelson, 1947, chapter 3). Sometimes this assumption is taken as an *a priori* axiom; in the words of the great mathematician, Euler, writing in a more devout age,

> Since the fabric of the world is the most perfect and was established by the wisest Creator, nothing happens in this world in which some reason of maximum or minimum would not come to light. (cited in Polya, 1954, p.121)

A detailed criticism of this assumption is given in Butt (1978).

The second main assumption of the neo-classical approach is that markets work impersonally, that any person can enter any market to sell the goods and services he produces and to buy the goods and services he needs on the same terms as any other person. This means that in any region there is a single market for each good and each service which brings together all buyers and sellers in that region, so that the same price rules all over the market.

The third assumption is that prices in individual markets are so highly flexible that they speedily adjust to equilibrate supply and demand. It follows, then, that the prices observed at any time may be taken to be at, or rapidly tending towards, their equilibrium levels. (For a modern criticism of this assumption, see, for example, Barro and Grossman, 1976)

The neo-classical approach also identifies the process of development with the growth of per capita income and seeks to explain this process on the basis of the above assumptions. The theory is then used to explain how resources are allocated to various uses, how the quantum of these resources increases over time, and how such increases in productive resources lead to growth of national incomes, according to various theories of growth. The logical consequence of the above assumptions is that all resources are fully utilized and 'optimally' allocated to various uses, i.e. so as to maximize the aggregate value of the production of goods and services, weighted by their respective market prices, taken as representing their values to consumers and their costs to producers. Further, there is also generally an assumption of constant returns to scale in each line of production, partly because of its mathematical convenience in separating questions of factor proportions from those of scale, and partly because it enables the marginal productivity principle of the pricing of factors of production to be applied to all factors. The result of all these assumptions is that the level of income in a country is explained by its endowment of various factors of production, such as land, labour and capital; the poverty of countries is explained by their small factor endowment relative to their population, and the growth of incomes of such countries is explained by the increase of their factor endowments, especially stock of capital.

It is also recognized that the relation between outputs and inputs of production depends on the state of technology in each country, and hence that the growth of aggregate output also depends on the rate of technological progress. In the earliest growth theories, such technological progress was assumed to occur exogenously, like 'manna falling from heaven'; since then, there has been more emphasis on technological progress as an endogenous process with laws of its own, derived largely from the experience of DCs. In many of these studies, however, the rate of technological progress is ultimately resolved into the inputs of various factors of production.

The neo-classical approach, and the assumptions on which it is based, were evolved mainly in the study of the developed market economies (hereafter referred to as DMEs) and have then been applied also to the study of LDCs. But many of these assumptions and concepts are not applicable to the LDCs because of their lower level of development, and applying them to the LDCs amounts indeed to assuming away the problem of development. It is therefore a principal objective of the present work to modify the conclusions of this approach to make them more appropriate for the study of the development problem.

Even within DMEs, there is increasing controversy over some of the basic assumptions and conclusions of this approach, regarding such issues as how competitive markets are; how efficiently they attain equilibrium of supply and demand, and achieve full utilization of resources, especially labour; how significant are economies of scale; and how satisfactory the resulting allocation of resources and distribution of income are from a social, as distinct from a private, point of view. As a result, there have been significant theoretical revisions of this approach. (For many of these innovations, see Cornwall, 1977) Some of the ideas are also relevant for LDCs and will therefore be used in the present work to modify the neo-classical approach to the development problem.

A different approach is taken in the fourth category of works, whose main inspiration comes from Marx. According to this approach, economic processes are not determined by the price system, with markets functioning in the efficient and impersonal manner assumed in neo-classical theory, but rather through the struggle between different social classes for control of the economic surplus. The main argument has been summarized by Wilber and Jameson (1979, p.19) as follows:

> The economic or social surplus is viewed as a residual—that which remains after necessary consumption has been subtracted from total output. Political economists argue that control of this economic surplus determines the nature of the development process. If a landed aristocracy controls the surplus, you will get one style of development; if the middle class controls it, then you will get a different style. The degree of foreign control of the surplus will shape the strategy of development.

In Marx's own analysis, which focussed on the capitalist system, a key element is the exploitation of labour by capitalists, who invest the surplus so acquired in the expansion of productive capacity:

> The bourgeoisie, during its rule of scarce one hundred years, has created more massive and more colossal productive forces than have all preceding generations together. (Marx and Engels, 1848, cited in Schumpeter, 1943, p.7)

Marx therefore believed in the role of capitalism as a means of expanding productive capacity and was particularly critical of 'utopian socialists' wishing to introduce socialist measures prematurely. As Robinson, J. (1962, p.46) put it,

> the misery of being exploited by capitalists is nothing compared to the misery of not being exploited at all.

Relying on his materialist interpretation of history, Marx himself had a vision of a continuous movement from a state of underdevelopment to a state of development in all countries. Hence his statement that,

> The country that is more developed industrially only shows, to the less-developed, the image of its own future. (Marx, 1969 edition, p.92)

As the countries of Europe were advancing industrially, they established a new pattern of trade with other countries, mostly in the tropics, which were under their colonial domination. Many writers have argued that the gains from such trade were very unequally distributed between the two groups of countries, especially because of a long-term tendency for the terms of trade to move against the LDCs. This pattern of trade became significant only after the middle of the nineteenth century and therefore Marx himself did not go deeply into the effects of such trade. But many writers in this category have extended his approach to study these effects, in the process reaching some conclusions sharply diverging from Marx himself.

The main concept of these writers is that of 'dependency' i.e. the view that LDCs have become increasingly dependent on the DCs for their economic growth, even after achieving political independence. Such dependency is due to the fact that economic events in LDCs are manipulated for their own benefit by powerful interests in DCs, sometimes assisted by 'comprador' elements in LDCs who get a share of the profits. As a consequence, many of these writers conclude that 'underdevelopment' was not an initial state of affairs in LDCs but one brought about by the development of the DCs. The dependency theorists, however, differ quite sharply among themselves in their explanations of this process. Some writers follow Marx quite closely in linking it to the working of merchant capital as distinct from industrial capital (see e.g. Kay, 1975). Some see it mainly as a result of political factors (see, especially, Frank, 1967). Some writers seek to explain the process by modifying the classical theories of trade and development (see especially Emmanuel, 1972). One of the important issues in the controversy is the extent to which the dependency relationship is due to internal factors in LDCs and the extent to which it is due to external factors in the economic relationships between DCs and LDCs.

The writers in this category have brought out some important factors affecting the development process and we must take account of them. However, most of them rely heavily on political factors and relationships in their analysis. Such political factors are certainly important but there are few commanding hypotheses of political science that can be applied to them, and it will take us too far outside our scope to consider them in any great detail. Therefore the present work is mainly concerned with an economic analysis of the development problem. It is a basic tenet of the 'political economy' approach that economic and political factors cannot be separated in this fashion, but this position is only valid when economic analysis is viewed narrowly in neo-classical terms based on the impersonal working of competitive markets. In fact, political and other factors influence economic variables and relationships in significant ways. What is needed, therefore, is to modify the neo-classical model of impersonal markets. When this is done, it is possible to separate the study of the economic variables and relationships involved from the study of the political factors influencing them, so that the two sets of factors can be studied more efficiently by division of labour among specialists in various branches of social science. For example, much of the economic content of the dependency theories is derived from the 'structuralist' theories evolved mainly in a Latin American context, which can be studied by economic analysis, once it is extended beyond its neo-classical limits.

With the experience of the past three decades, we can now see that these four approaches all have something to contribute to our understanding of the development process, but each has also some weaknesses that must be remedied. The object of the present work is to produce a synthesis of the valid elements from each of these approaches. In pursuing this objective, we shall be specially concerned to provide a new framework for policy as a basis for the practical efforts of governments of the countries concerned to promote the development of LDCs more successfully than in the past. For this purpose, it is useful to consider the policy implications of the various approaches distinguished above. Some of these implications will be discussed with respect to particular topics in the later chapters dealing with them. Here we shall briefly review some general features of the broad strategy of development implicit in each of the above approaches.

1.2 Alternative Strategies of Development

The approach based on the 'patterns of development' which occurred in the past and which is revealed by international cross-section and time-series data leads to what may be described as the 'imitative strategy', i.e. a strategy in which the LDCs recapitulate the historical experience of the DCs which have successfully attained development. In a sense, the LDCs of today are seeking to develop their economies and in particular to overcome their mass poverty as the DCs have done and must therefore learn from the historical experience of the DCs. Mass poverty has afflicted the bulk of mankind throughout its history; it has been a part of man's struggle with nature. Therefore, from a historical point of view, the real question is not why so many people are poor but rather how the people of a relatively small group of countries have managed to escape this fate. It might therefore seem at first that the appropriate strategy for LDCs is to recapitulate the historical experience of the DCs. However, there are many weaknesses in such an imitative strategy, which suggest that the past experience of DCs has to be modified before it can be used to formulate a development strategy for the LDCs in the future.

In the first place, the past experience of development was one shared by a limited group of countries which had already many social, cultural and political factors in common, so that their development was shaped by these factors. To imitate all these features is to confuse development with 'westernization', which may be neither necessary nor desirable. Second, the imitative strategy depends crucially on the assumption that there is only one route to development, that followed by DCs in the past. This assumption is made explicitly in Marxist and other stage theories; it is also made implicitly in the statistical approach of deriving this route from the cross-section growth patterns among countries at different levels of development. But even among countries which have achieved development in the past, there were significant differences in the paths they followed, depending on the level of backwardness from which they started. Hence, in adopting an imitative strategy, there is the problem of which of these paths to imitate.

Third, even to the extent that DCs followed the same route to development, it was not necessarily an optimal one for them. To repeat that process is to repeat its mistakes as well, like the proverbial Chinese farmer who burnt down a pig shed every time he wanted roast pork, because that was how he first discovered roast pork. Some of the earliest countries to achieve development did not do so by deliberate policies; it has even been described as an 'absent-minded' process (Singh, S. K., 1975, p.xviii). As a result, their development was a rather leisurely process, whereas LDCs are anxious to achieve their development more rapidly. Also, there was much poverty and inequality of income distribution until a rather late stage in the historical experience of many DCs, which LDCs wish to avoid in their own future development.

Even if the historical route to development had been an optimal one, it does not follow that the same path would also be optimal for LDCs in the future because conditions have changed so much, and the contemporary LDCs face a completely different situation both regarding the options available to them and their ability to choose among them. On the one hand, the technological progress that has already occurred in the DCs presents the LDCs with a greater range of techniques which was not available to the DCs when they embarked upon their development. While some of these techniques may not be suitable for the LDCs, others will make their development task easier. On the other hand, the DCs started their development when there were few countries more developed than themselves, while the LDCs now face a world in which they have to deal with a larger number of economically powerful countries at a much higher level of development. This situation offers LDCs some advantages, because the existence of more developed countries provides large markets in which to sell their products and buy their requirements, and because the DCs can assist the LDCs in various financial and technical ways. But there are also some disadvantages in such dependence because the superior economic power of the DCs has a great influence on economic conditions in LDCs and diverts scarce human and material resources from the LDCs.

As a result of the special circumstances which attended the development of the DCs, many historical generalizations derived from their experience do not apply to the same degree in the LDCs and cannot therefore be relied upon to the same extent in formulating future policy. For example, one of the best-founded generalizations in the historical experience of DCs is the theory of demographic transition, according to which death rates, and with a time lag, birth rates declined in the course of economic growth. In the recent experience of LDCs, however, death rates have fallen sharply, even faster than in DCs, without much acceleration of economic growth rates, but birth rates have persisted at their traditional high levels. Another such generalization is that economic growth in the DCs was accompanied by a steady decline in the proportion of the labour force engaged in agriculture; the recent experience of many LDCs indicates little change in this proportion. Yet a third example is that in most DCs, economic growth was so closely linked with the growth of their foreign trade that trade was looked upon as the engine of growth; in contrast, the rapid growth of exports of some LDCs in the nineteenth century failed to produce sustained economic growth. Many of the economic and social processes which accompanied development in the DCs were, at least in some degree, in balance with each other, but in the LDCs, they are substantially out of phase with each other, giving rise to most of their economic and social problems. Because of all such differences, an appropriate strategy for LDCs in the future must be designed anew, taking some features of the historical experience of the DCs and modifying others, on the basis of an explicit theory of development.

The neo-classical approach leads to what may be called a growth strategy because it is based on factors stressed in the theories of growth. It is a strategy which relies mainly on increases in the quantum of productive resources, especially capital, relative to population, and on the allocation of these resources so as to maximize the national output in each short period, such as would be brought about by efficient competitive markets. It is recognized that markets in LDCs do not quite conform to the neo-classical model but such divergences are mainly attributed to interventions by governments. Therefore, the main policy implication of this approach is that governments refrain from such interventions, except in a few cases involving externalities, imperfect competition, etc. This approach also calls for efforts by governments to reduce the rate of population growth in LDCs by such methods as family-planning campaigns. It also calls for financial and technical assistance from DCs to supplement the capital stock and to hasten technical progress in the LDCs.

This strategy also suffers from a number of limitations. Historically, it now appears that increases in the stock of productive resources in relation to population played a relatively small part in the growth of incomes in the DCs. Therefore, attempts to increase incomes and reduce poverty in the LDCs only by increasing the stock of productive resources will take an unduly long time. Apart from the increases in productive resources, the improvement in the general standard of living in the DCs was made possible by other basic changes in their economies. In the rest of this book, the term 'development' will be used to describe these changes, particularly to distinguish it from the term 'growth' which will be used to describe the effects on the national income flowing from increases in the stock of productive resources. (The distinction is spelt out in more detail in Chapter 5.) It is especially with regard to their development defined in this way that the LDCs are at a lower level than the DCs. It is mainly because of the lower level of development in the LDCs that many of the policies of the growth strategy are not likely to be effective in these countries. For example, quite apart from government interventions, markets in LDCs do not function efficiently because of the lower level of development and hence fail to make full use of the existing resources. Therefore, even if all government interventions were removed, these markets will not function to produce rapid increases of national income as assumed in neo-classical theory. Also with the low level of development prevailing in LDCs, the unrestricted play of market forces will lead to growing inequality of income distribution. Further, under these conditions, programmes such as family-planning campaigns alone are unlikely to have a significant effect on the rate of population growth. Finally, under the same conditions, LDCs are unable to absorb fully any financial or technical aid that may be provided by DCs. (These arguments are discussed in more detail in Part III of this book.)

The policy implications of the writers following the political economy approach are not always clear, partly because of the great diversity among them. To the extent that they attribute underdevelopment or the slow pace of development in LDCs to the capitalist mode of production based on private property, it would seem that the policy implication is the abolition of private property rights in all productive assets and the State operation of all production. More often, this policy implication seems to be confined to asset redistribution applied especially to agricultural land. Sometimes, it seems to be implied that such land reform policies should be combined with a collectivist system of agriculture. Also to the extent that the underdevelopment of LDCs is attributed to their economic relationships with DCs, the policy implication seems to be one of autarky and isolation from the world economy. Such changes involving the expropriation of powerful vested interests cannot be brought about peacefully; hence the frequent call for revolutionary methods to attain these objectives.

In this approach, the case for such policies is ultimately based on a political analysis. Regarding the prevailing situation in LDCs, it assumes a distribution of political power among various sections of society based on their ownership of various productive assets and particular ways in which the exercise of such political power affects the economic situation. Regarding the outcome of the revolutionary changes proposed, it also assumes particular forms of behaviour on the part of the highly centralized political systems that may result. This is a complex subject in which there are few reliable generalizations. It involves profound questions of the balance between any economic advantages that may result from these policies and the costs in terms of individual liberty that may be involved. These are questions which must ultimately be resolved by the people of each country and on which economists as economists have little to contribute. The present work is therefore confined to the study of the development problem in a mixed economy, the system which has been adopted by most LDCs. It is the system in which a large part of the economy is in the private sector and is subject to various types of regulation by the public sector. The main policy issues to be considered, therefore, concern the role of governments in promoting development in such economies.

One important problem that still remains is whether the policy recommendations derived by economists will in fact be followed by governments, and indeed whether under prevailing political conditions, they *can* be followed. On the one hand, economists generally have been most naïve in assuming determinate behaviour on the part of individuals in the market place and unlimited free will on the part of governments in making policy, so that all that is needed is for economic advisers to whisper discreetly into ministerial ears the exact solutions to all economic problems. On the other hand, political economists have been dogmatic in assuming that the behaviour of governments is also highly deterministic and inexorably influenced in particular directions by socal and economic circumstances beyond their control. The position taken in the present work is the intermediate one that while there are significant political constraints on governments, they also have some degree of manoeuvrability in policy-making. Within these limits, their policies can be improved by a closer study of the economic issues involved and by a widespread understanding of these issues among the general public. The role of economists therefore lies in extending the range of options that are available to governments in their search for faster development of the LDCs. It is to this task that the present work is addressed. In particular, it seeks to sharpen the concept of a development strategy, as distinct from the imitative and growth strategies which have dominated the literature so far. The following sections outline the main argument of the book and describe its organization.

1.3 The Contrast between Developed and Less-Developed Countries

In Chapters 2–4, we consider the ways in which LDCs differ from DCs. Chapter 2 deals with the static aspect of these differences, i.e. the differences that may be observed at a point of time. It deals with the level and structure of economic activities in the two groups of countries at the latest date for which a comprehensive set of statistical data is available. In most approaches to development, the main emphasis is placed on the difference in per capita income between DCs and LDCs, i.e. LDCs are considered as just poorer versions of DCs. There is indeed a great difference in per capita income but the two groups of countries also differ in many other ways and to such a great extent that the difference between them must be considered a qualitative, rather than just a quantitative, one. An important consequence is that theoretical models evolved for the study of DCs are not equally applicable to LDCs, and statistical techniques applied to both groups of countries taken together may not be useful to reveal relationships obtaining within each group.

Chapter 3 deals with the dynamic aspect of the differences between DCs and LDCs. It does so by comparing the changes that have taken place in these countries in the past two or three decades, the period since World War II. It is there shown that, in some respects, there was rapid economic progress in both groups of countries, especially regarding the growth of the national product. Many writers have taken this fact as a sign that the LDCs are converging to the position of DCs but here again there is a qualitative difference. In the DCs, economic growth was self-sustained, depending primarily on internal factors of investment, technological progress and economic management. There was rapid growth of trade among these countries, which also contributed to their growth, mainly because this trade consisted largely of manufactures. In contrast, the growth of national incomes in LDCs was mainly due to external factors, especially the expansion of their trade with DCs. Hence, the economic growth of LDCs was derived from that of the DCs. To a large extent, the growth of LDC trade was based on the exploitation of natural resource endowments. A relatively few LDCs were able to expand their exports of manufactures to DCs. Hence, there was great variation in growth rates among the poor countries, mainly due to differences in their natural resource endowments and the extent of their participation in the growth of world trade. Further, although the LDCs on the average had high rates of growth of national incomes in this period, they also experienced high rates of population growth. Therefore, there has been little improvement in per capita income or the structure of their economies in the post-war period.

The causes of the great difference in the general standard of living between DCs and LDCs must therefore be traced back beyond the recent period to the historical experience of the two groups of countries covering a much earlier period. This is the subject of Chapter 4. This chapter describes how the process, which Kuznets (1966) has described as 'modern economic growth', emerged first in Britain in the late eighteenth century and then spread by a process of diffusion to other countries in Europe, North America, Australia and New Zealand, Japan and the Soviet Union. This process of diffusion was not just a matter of the 'late-comers' simply imitating the forerunners, for there were systematic differences depending on the level of backwardness from which they started. But in spite of the fact that many other countries, especially those in the tropics, were in close economic contact with the countries experiencing modern economic growth in this period, the diffusion of this process did not reach the tropical countries. The division of the world into two sharply contrasting groups of countries must ultimately be traced to this fact, for the countries where the diffusion occurred are the DCs and those where it did not reach are the LDCs of today. Instead of the diffusion of modern economic growth, the economic history of most LDCs was shaped by the pattern of the trade which emerged between them and the DCs. Therefore, the central problem of development economics is to understand the nature of the process which has transformed the DCs in the past, why it has not occurred in the LDCs and what may be done to promote it in the future.

1.4 The Concept of Development

Part II of the book is concerned with the concept of development and of development policies. Economists often use the term development interchangeably with the term growth. This usage has led to a confusion of two distinct processes and to a neglect of some crucial factors which led to the great transformation which occurred in the DCs in the past two centuries and which underlies the contrast between DCs and LDCs today. In much of the literature on the subject, DCs and LDCs are distinguished simply as the rich and the poor countries, i.e. on the basis of their per capita incomes, and the economic progress of the DCs in the past two centuries primarily as one of economic growth, i.e. the growth of per capita income. These differences and changes are then explained by a growth theory model based on factor endowments and technological progress. Such a model, however, is not sufficient to explain the great differences between DCs and LDCs and the rapid progress of DCs in the past. Instead, it is a central proposition of this work that a more significant explanation lies in differences and changes in the modes of economic behaviour of individuals in their production activities and in their economic relationships. In the LDCs, a traditional mode of behaviour largely based on customary rules has survived among a large section of the population, hindering the speedy adoption of new technologies as they become available, while in the DCs, this has been replaced by a different kind of economic behaviour in which individuals are more aware of, and have greater access to, such new technologies, and are induced to take advantage of their possibilities through the working of market forces. Therefore, this change in the mode of behaviour is taken as the definition of the concept of development in Chapter 5, sharply distinguished from the process, described as growth in modern usage, where the growth of incomes is based on increases in the stock of productive resources and on technological progress.

Having defined development in this way, we then consider the policies by which it may be advanced in the LDCs. These policies are broadly divided into three categories, namely education dealing with the human aspect, infrastructure dealing with the physical aspect, and institutions dealing with the working of economic institutions, especially goods and factor markets. These components of development and the policies relating to them individually are discussed in Chapters 6–8, but some general features common to all of them are described in Chapter 5. In most countries, these three components of the development process as we have defined it are the special responsibility of governments and were in fact included by Adam Smith in his list of the 'Duties of the Sovereign'. Secondly, they are generally of the nature of 'permissive' factors, necessary but not sufficient conditions for rapid economic growth. And finally, improvements in them will generally take a long time to achieve and to have significant effects on growth of incomes. These special features of the key components of the development process have some important implications for policy. In the DCs, they were improved gradually over a long period of time, and generally in response to the demand for them. But in the LDCs which aim to promote development more rapidly, they have to be provided ahead of demand. Hence, policy relating to them cannot be based on an imitative strategy.

Further, because of their permissive nature, the expansion of education and infrastructure cannot be based on a comparison of their costs and benefits in terms of growth of national incomes in the short or medium term periods. Thus, policies relating to them cannot be based on what we have described as a growth strategy. Instead, they must be based on long-term final targets in each case. Short-term policies relating to them must then be geared to attain these final targets as efficiently as possible taking account of their internal relationships, instead of adjusting these policies to the current state of the rest of the economy. Policies relating to these factors must then be combined with other policies which adjust the rest of the economy to make full use of the improvements in education, infrastructure and institutions as they occur. This strategy is explained in more detail in connection with each of the development factors described above.

Chapter 6 describes the low level of education in LDCs compared with the DCs in spite of a rapid expansion in the post-war period. This expansion has been brought about mainly in response to the growth of private demand for education. The private demand for education expanded most rapidly at the tertiary level and the rapid expansion at this level was accompanied by a drastic decline in the quality of education. The private demand for education, which influenced the pattern of educational expansion, was mostly influenced by the persistence of large income differentials between workers of different educational categories. As a result of this structure of incomes, the growth in the number of graduates, especially at the higher levels of education, has not been absorbed in the economy, leading to the phenomenon of educated unemployment and thus frustrating the private demand for education. An alternative strategy in which educational development contributes more fully to growth is to expand education to attain certain long-term final targets of quantity and quality at the different levels as rapidly as possible, ahead of demand if necessary, and to adjust the demand for the graduates to balance the growing supply.

The nature of modern infrastructure is discussed in Chapter 7 together with a comparison of the levels and growth of infrastructural facilities in DCs and LDCs. A certain amount of transport and marketing infrastructure was built up in LDCs in colonial times, mainly to promote their foreign trade. Similarly, there has been some expansion of transport and power infrastructure in the post-war period primarily to serve the industrial sector and the major urban centres. The present levels of infrastructure remain inadequate to promote growth in the rest of the economy. An alternative strategy of building infrastructure ahead of demand oriented towards certain final targets is illustrated by an application to urbanization.

One of the main obstacles to development in LDCs is the nature of the prevailing economic institutions, particularly those governing the commodity and factor markets. These are discussed in Chapter 8. In consequence, the supply and demand for many important goods and services are highly inelastic, and their prices highly inflexible. Further, many markets are highly fragmented by the lack of adequate transport and communications infrastructure, and by powerful social and political factors which restrict access to these markets for large sections of the population. To promote more rapid growth, these market institutions must be improved so as to extend the economic options open to individuals and to give them more freedom to choose among such options. The advantages of such free markets have been considered in neo-classical theory to lie mainly in their static allocative efficiency, but in fact they are far more important because of their dynamic creative functions as explained in this chapter.

1.5 Growth and Distribution at a Low Level of Development

The policies discussed in Part II of the book will take a long time to bring about a high level of development in the LDCs. In order to achieve a rapid rise in the general standard of living in the intervening period, the LDCs must also consider policies relating to growth and distribution. The discussion of these policies in the literature has generally assumed a high level of development, such as that which obtains in the DCs. We must therefore consider the modifications needed to apply them at the lower level of development which will continue to obtain in the LDCs in the intervening period. This is the task of the chapters in Part III of the book. The issues involved are discussed under three headings, namely production, international trade and the distribution of income.

Chapter 9 deals with the analysis of production. It discusses the limitations of the production function approach and examines the role of population growth and capital accumulation. It also extends this approach to take account of technological progress, increasing returns and the role of demand. Policies relating to production are then discussed in Chapter 10. It considers how the techniques of production and the composition of output according to major sectors of the economy may be chosen so as to promote more rapid long-term growth, and how government policies relating to development measures should be allocated to these sectors in order to induce such choices by the private sector.

The nature of the international trade of LDCs is described in Chapter 11, together with the theories which explain such trade. The dominant neo-classical theory of the subject, in assuming efficient international markets in commodities and immobility of factors of production between countries, emphasizes the role of factor endowments to the neglect of levels of technology and modes of behaviour. This theory is therefore modified to take account of the levels and changes in technology, the international mobility of factors, increasing returns to scale, and the role of demand. Various policy issues relating to trade are then discussed in Chapter 12. They relate to the role of technical progress in the primary product exports of LDCs, to the choice of manufactures to protect, the methods of dealing with balance of payments problems, and with measures to stabilize the prices of, and foreign exchange earnings from, LDC exports.

Chapter 13 describes the distribution of income in LDCs. Much of the existing literature is limited to static analysis and the application of trends observed in the historical experience of DCs to the future prospects of LDCs. In contrast, an attempt is made in this chapter to identify some long-term dynamic tendencies in the distribution of income, and to distinguish between the classical determinants based on the amount and distribution of productive assets on the one hand and the nature of the development process involving education, infrastructure and institutions on the other. Chapter 14 then examines how the distribution of income may be influenced by price, production, employment and redistributive policies.

1.6 The Role of Government

The long-term task of development, and short-term policies for growth and distribution while LDCs are still at a low level of development, both impose a heavy burden on the State. How governments can make their efforts more efficient by a system of planning is discussed in Chapter 15. It is there argued that for this purpose, planning must consist of commitments to future action, and must therefore be confined, in mixed economies, to the activities within the control of governments. Some of the most important measures needed for development are of this type, and indeed are activities which only governments can undertake. Especially with regard to these activities, it is argued that planning must be extended over a longer period than is usually the case and must be formulated to a greater extent in real terms rather than in the more usual financial terms. Some policies relating to other functions of government, such as the monetary and the fiscal system, are also discussed in Chapter 15.

Finally Chapter 16 discusses the role that the affluent countries can play by their aid in promoting development. It discusses the factors which have influenced the volume, forms, terms and the distribution of aid in the past. Where it has not been granted simply as an instrument of foreign policy, it has been used to supplement the savings of LDCs following what has been described above as the growth strategy. Following the analysis of the present study, a case is made for adjusting aid policy so that it is more directly addressed to the development needs of the LDCs.

1.7 Limitations of the Study

It has already been pointed out that this book is confined to the study of development policies in LDCs with mixed economies. The nature of the problem and of the policies needed has been studied on the basis of as much empirical data as are available, rather than on the basis of theoretical analysis using conveniently chosen assumptions. However, in order to keep the discussion to a reasonable size, it has been mostly carried out in terms of the average conditions prevailing in LDCs as a group. This approach has been followed in order to sharpen the concept of development and of the policies needed for it, by a comparison of LDCs as a whole with DCs as a whole. However, LDCs differ greatly among themselves. Therefore, the particulars of development policy for individual LDCs must be further elaborated by a more detailed consideration of the ways in which individual LDCs differ from the average situation of all LDCs.

Another limitation of the work is that the nation-state has been taken as the unit of study. The main reason is that most of the data are available only for these units. It is also because the nation state is the logical unit of study for many aspects of government policy. But there are disadvantages in this approach. First, it treats all countries on an equal footing, whereas in fact they differ greatly in many significant ways—in size, in history, in endowments and in the effectiveness of their governments in formulating and implementing national policies. Second, there are great variations within individual countries so that policies for some regions may not be the same as for other regions. Finally, it is not always the policies of the central government which are important for development, but also the policies of lower levels of government.

CHAPTER 2

The Structure of Less-Developed Countries

In this chapter, we consider the differences between DCs and LDCs as they appeared at the end of the 1970s, the latest period for which a reasonably full complement of statistical data is available. These data give, as it were, a snapshot picture of the two groups of countries in which all movement beyond a year is frozen; they are therefore primarily concerned with the differences in the levels and the structures of their economies. Because countries vary so much in their populations, most of the statistical tables give the number of countries in each category as well as their populations. Section 2.1 discusses the classification of countries into DCs and LDCs. Sections 2.2–4 then summarize the differences between these groups of countries regarding demographic features, labour force and employment, and national product. Other differences between the two groups of countries are described in later chapters but in order to bring out the great contrast between the two groups of countries, Section 2.5 brings together summary data on a large number of variables; they show that the two groups of countries differ markedly not only in their per capita incomes but also in many other variables. The contrast beween the groups of countries is so marked as to constitute a qualitative difference between them.

2.1 Classification of Countries

There is a great deal of controversy over the concept of development, whether it is primarily an economic one, and if so, which economic aspects are the most relevant. It is very common to use per capita income as the criterion for distinguishing LDCs from DCs, and to identify the LDCs as the poor countries, but it is the central thesis of the present study that while underdevelopment is the main cause of the poverty of nations, it should be distinguished from poverty as such. However, while there is controversy over the criterion to be used, there is very little disagreement about the classification of countries into the developed and less-developed categories. There are remarkably few, e.g. Argentina, Chile, Uruguay, Israel, some south European countries, and Taiwan, South Korea, Hong Kong and Singapore, sometimes known as the 'Gang of Four', which are described by some as developed and by others as less-developed, or put into an intermediate category. For our present purpose of studying the problem of development in some generality rather than in particular countries, the discussion is not much affected by the classification of these few countries. Therefore, at least to start with, until we define the concept of development in Chapter 5, we shall follow the near unanimity observed in the literature and classify countries according to their generally accepted reputation; therefore all countries of Europe (except Turkey) and North America, the three countries of temperate South America (Argentina, Chile and Uruguay), Israel, South Africa, Japan, Australia and New Zealand, and the countries of the East European bloc are considered as DCs and the rest as LDCs.

One feature that strikes us immediately in this classification is that the LDCs are situated in the tropical regions of the world, so that LDCs are often described simply as tropical countries. This correlation is not perfect because some groups of people within the tropical countries share many characteristics with the people of the DCs, but the broad relationship has led some writers to argue that climate must have something to do with development and that the tropical countries are less-developed simply because it is too hot in these countries; e.g. Myrdal (1968, Vol.I, p.677) says,

> This cannot be entirely an accident of history, but must have to do with some special handicaps, directly or indirectly related to climate, faced by countries in the tropical and subtropical zones.

Similar views have been expressed by Bauer (1971), and Kamarck (1977) has written an entire book on the effect of climate on economic development. However, it is argued below (Section 4.4) that the observed correlation between climate and the location of LDCs is indeed a historical accident, and not in itself a cause of their underdeveloped status.

2.2 Demographic Features

The territorial extent of individual nation states, in terms of which the present study is conducted, is a political phenomenon resulting from the accidents of history. However, the resulting population sizes, their densities and distribution have important consequences for the working of their national economies, the ways different policies operate and the choice of their

Table 2.1 Distribution of countries by population size, 1979. (Population in millions; number of countries in brackets)

		LDCs			
Population size	DCs	Total	Africa and Middle East	Latin America	Asia
Very large (over 100)	603 (3)	1883 (4)	—	117 (1)	1767 (3)
Large (50–100)	227 (4)	370 (5)	83 (1)	66 (1)	222 (3)
Medium (25–50)	128 (4)	383 (11)	179 (5)	26 (1)	178 (5)
Small (5–25)	215 (17)	377 (38)	244 (25)	67 (7)	67 (6)
Very small (below 5)	22 (6)	81 (30)	47 (17)	24 (8)	11 (5)
Total	1196 (34)	3094 (88)	552 (48)	300 (18)	2244 (22)

Source: World Bank, *World Development Report, 1981*

development strategies. Hence, we consider some of these demographic features. The first aspect to be considered is the size of population. Table 2.1 shows the size distribution of DCs and LDCs according to their 1979 populations as estimated by the World Bank; it covers all countries with populations over one million. DCs and LDCs occur in all size classes and in roughly the same proportions; among LDCs, the large countries are mostly in Asia, while most countries of Africa and Latin America are small. Size of population is, therefore, not a feature that distinguishes DCs from LDCs.

LDCs, taken together, have a population density (persons per square kilometre) of 44, more than double the average of 20 for DCs. However, there is great variation among countries in each category, as shown in Table 2.2. Most DCs have high population densities; the average for these countries is brought down mainly by the low density of the two continental countries, the United States and the Soviet Union. Most LDCs in Africa and Latin America have low densities, but the average for all LDCs is raised by a few large countries in Asia with high densities. Therefore, population density is also not a significant feature differentiating LDCs from DCs.

Table 2.2 Distribution of countries by population density, 1979. (Population in millions; number of countries in brackets)

		LDCs			
Density	DCs	Total	Africa and Middle East	Latin America	Asia
Over 200	267 (6)	1806 (13)	3 (1)	13 (4)	1790 (8)
100–200	150 (8)	207 (7)	9 (2)	5 (1)	193 (4)
50–100	161 (7)	346 (8)	141 (4)	17 (2)	188 (2)
25–50	3 (1)	309 (24)	182 (17)	77 (3)	50 (4)
Below 25	616 (12)	427 (36)	217 (24)	187 (8)	23 (4)
Average Density	20	44	17	18	105

Source: World Bank, *World Development Report, 1981*

Turning to population growth, while the rates of population growth in DCs are fairly uniform at about one per cent per annum, or less, there is much greater variation among LDCs as shown in Table 2.3

Table 2.3 Distribution of LDC populations by annual rates of population growth 1970–79

Annual rate of population growth (percentage)	Number of countries	Population (millions)
Below 2	12	1055
2–2.5	23	1167
2.5–3	32	540
3 and over	21	333
Total	88	3094

Source: World Bank, *World Development Report, 1981*

Most LDCs have high rates of population growth; the large population of countries with rates below 2 per cent per annum is mainly due to the inclusion of China, with an estimated rate of 1.9. The annual growth of population can be analysed into birth and death rates and rates of international migration; for most countries the last factor is insignificant. In DCs, the birth rate is mostly between 10 and 20 per thousand, and the death rate around 10 per thousand. The position of LDCs is shown in Table 2.4.

Table 2.4 Distribution of LDC populations by birth and death rates, 1979. (Population in millions; number of countries in brackets)

Death rate per thousand	Birth rate per thousand: Below 30	30–35	35–40	40 & Over	Total
Below 10	1169 (11)	140 (6)	147 (7)	10 (2)	1467 (26)
10–15	—	50 (2)	891 (5)	250 (18)	1192 (25)
15–20	—	—	3 (1)	309 (18)	312 (19)
20 & Over	—	—	—	124 (18)	124 (18)
Total	1169 (11)	190 (8)	1041 (13)	693 (56)	3094 (88)

Source: World Bank, *World Development Report, 1981*

Most LDCs have reduced their death rates to below 15 per thousand, but with the important exception of China with an estimated birth rate of 18 per thousand, most LDCs have high birth rates of over 35 per thousand. Hence, it has been pointed out that

> It seems that at present no social or economic indicator separates countries as clearly into two sharply differentiated groups as does the measure of fertility. (United Nations, 1963, p.137)

Table 2.4 also shows a tendency for high birth rates to be correlated with high death rates.

Another important difference between DCs and LDCs is in the level of urbanization, i.e. the proportion of the population living in urban areas (Table 2.5). The DCs generally are highly urbanized. The average level of urbanization of LDCs is very low, but some countries, e.g. Brazil, Mexico and the smaller LDCs are as highly urbanized as the DCs.

Table 2.5 Distribution of LDC populations by level of urbanization. (Population in millions; number of countries in brackets)

Percentage of population in urban areas	DCs		
	DMEs	CPCs	LDCs
Below 10			40 (6)
10–20			1287 (18)
20–30			1086 (18)
30–40	10 (1)		134 (13)
40–50	22 (1)	22 (1)	139 (9)
50–60	50 (5)	46 (2)	109 (11)
60–70	71 (3)	288 (3)	235 (6)
70–80	453 (6)	17 (1)	41 (3)
80 & Over	217 (11)		23 (4)
Total	823 (27)	373 (7)	3094 (88)
Average level of urbanization	77	64	25

Source: World Bank, *World Development Report, 1981*
Note: CPC = centrally planned countries

2.3 Labour Force and Employment

The labour force of a country is its economically active population. Estimates of the labour force are derived from population censuses and labour force surveys, but there is considerable variation in concepts and definitions, especially in the classification of female workers in LDCs. In recent censuses, most countries have followed United Nations recommendations based on the 'labour force' approach, which classifies as economically active all persons who worked, or were seeking work, for pay or profit, during a relatively short period, such as a week. This approach, evolved in the DCs, where the concept of economic activity is well established, is not very suitable for LDCs, where there is no sharp distinction between individuals working for pay or profit and those doing other kinds of economic activity such as work in subsistence or household enterprises. Further, there is in LDCs great seasonal variation in economic activity, because much of it occurs in the agricultural sector; e.g. the percentage of the population of working age in the labour force in the Philippines in 1968, as estimated by the labour force approach, varied from 64.7 in May to 51.2 in October. Subject to these problems of definition,

Table 2.6 shows the difference between DCs and LDCs in their labour force participation rates, i.e. the proportion of total population in the labour force.

Table 2.6 Labour force participation rates, 1970

Countries and factors	Males	Females	Total
LDCs	53.6	26.4	39.8
DCs	57.2	33.2	44.7
Difference	−3.6	−6.8	−4.9
due to age and sex distribution	−8.4	−4.3	−6.4
due to socio-economic factors	+4.8	−2.5	+1.5

Source: I.L.O. *Labour Force Projections, 1971.*

Note: The two components of the difference in overall activity rates are calculated by the equation

$$\Sigma pr - \Sigma PR = \Sigma \tfrac{1}{2}(r_i + R_i)(p_i - P_i) \quad \text{(due to age-distribution)}$$
$$+ \Sigma \tfrac{1}{2}(p_i + P_i)(r_i - R_i) \quad \text{(due to socio-economic factors)}$$

where p_i is the proportion of population in ith age–sex group and r_i the age and sex-specific participation rates in LDCs, and P_i and R_i are the corresponding values in DCs.

The overall participation rates for both males and females are lower in the LDCs than in the DCs. These rates depend partly on the age distribution and partly on the socio-economic factors affecting age-specific participation rates. Because the LDCs have a larger proportion of their population below working age, the effect of the age distribution is to reduce the overall rates in LDCs below those of the DCs. This effect is offset to some extent by the socio-economic factors in the case of males, and enhanced in the case of females.

The employment status of workers also differs considerably between DCs and LDCs, as shown in Table 2.7.

Table 2.7 Labour force by employment status, c.1970. (Percentages)

	Males		Females	
Employment status	DCs	LDCs	DCs	LDCs
Self-employed	16.2	44.5	7.8	29.0
Employees	79.6	41.5	78.2	40.7
Unpaid family workers	2.4	12.4	12.1	27.9
Others	1.8	1.6	1.9	2.4
Total	100.0	100.0	100.0	100.0

Source: I.L.O. *Yearbook of Labour Statistics, 1975*

Most workers in DCs are wage employees; this category is much smaller in LDCs. A high proportion of workers in LDCs are self-employed, especially among males, and unpaid family workers, especially among females.

The main difference in employment between DCs and LDCs is in the distribution of the labour force among the three major sectors of the economy, as shown in Table 2.8. This table shows the enormous difference between DMEs and LDCs in the agricultural share of the labour force, leading to a corresponding difference in the shares of the other two sectors. There are, however, quite large variations within each group of countries, as shown in Table 2.9 for the agricultural sector.

Table 2.8 Distribution of labour force by sectors, 1979. (Weighted averages: percentages)

Sector	DMEs	LDCs
Agriculture	8.9	64.5
Industry	36.9	15.9
Services	54.2	19.6
Total	100.0	100.0

Source: World Bank, *World Development Report, 1981*

Table 2.9 Distribution of population by percentage of labour in agriculture, 1979. (Population in millions, number of countries in brackets)

Percentage of labour force in agriculture	DMEs	LDCs
Below 10	494 (15)	9 (3)
10–20	248 (7)	18 (3)
20–30	21 (2)	44 (5)
30–40	60 (3)	159 (9)
40–50		221 (7)
50–60		499 (17)
60–70		81 (9)
70–80		1917 (15)
80 & over		147 (20)
Total	823 (27)	3094 (88)

Source: World Bank, *World Development Report, 1981*

2.4 National Product

The most commonly used measure of the economic level of a country is its per capita national income, i.e. the per capita value of the total income accruing to the residents of a country. This total income is the value of production and net income from abroad. Production is mostly valued at market prices or at factor cost, i.e. net of indirect taxes; goods and services provided by government which do not enter the market are generally valued at the costs incurred in producing them. For the national income, the output has to be valued net of depreciation, but as depreciation estimates are generally not available, the measure often used is the Gross National Product (GNP). For making international comparisons, GNP estimates are converted to US dollars on the basis of official exchange rates. Table 2.10 shows the distribution of population according to per capita GNP as estimated for 1979 by the World Bank.

Table 2.10 Distribution of population by per capita GNP, 1979. (Population in millions, number of countries in brackets)

Per capita GNP (US $)	DMEs	CPCs	LDCs
Below 250			949 (17)
250–500			1404 (26)
500–1000			254 (16)
1000–2500	102 (6)	22 (1)	451 (22)
2500–5000	53 (4)	319 (4)	23 (4)
5000 & Over	668 (17)	32 (2)	13 (3)
Total	823 (27)	373 (7)	3094 (88)
Average	7770	4090	510

Source: World Bank, *World Development Report, 1981*

There are a number of problems in using per capita national income as an index of relative economic level. Firstly, there is the question of statistical reliability. The data from the LDCs are much less reliable, especially as much of their production does not enter into the market and is consumed by the producers themselves in the subsistence sector. Then, there is the problem that many valuable services and benefits, e.g. housekeeping and leisure are not included and many disamenities such as pollution and congestion are not allowed for in the national income while many items included in the national income estimates are not valuable in themselves but are only of an instrumental nature, such as police and defence services. An attempt has been made to allow for these factors in a new measure of economic welfare by Nordhaus and Tobin (1972); in the estimate for the United States for 1965, it was found that the value of non-market activity was about half of GNP, that the value of leisure should be put as about equal to GNP, and that about a fifth of the value of GNP should be subtracted as cost of various disamenities and instrumental outputs.

There are other problems in using national income statistics for making international comparisons. One of them is the index-number problem which arises because the comparison between quantity indices depends on the price weights used. There is generally a negative correlation between relative quantity differences and relative price differences. Therefore, if a rich country's price weights are used for the comparison, the extent of its superiority over a poor country is less than if the poor country's weights had been used; this effect is known as the 'Gerschenkron effect' (see Samuelson, 1974, p.596).

Another problem in making international comparisons arises because the official exchange rates often used for converting values from one currency to another may not be an equilibrium rate, and even if it is, the equilibrium rate relates only to the goods and services which enter into international trade and does not take account of the vast bulk of goods and services which do not. This problem is particularly serious in the comparison of LDCs with DCs, because the deviation of the official exchange rates from the purchasing power parity of currencies is greater in such comparisons than in comparing countries with similar income levels. A comprehensive study of the purchasing power parity of a few selected countries has been made by Kravis *et al.* (1975, 1978); when the results of this study are applied to 36 LDCs, it is found that their average per capita income at official exchange rates underestimated the value at purchasing power parities by about 60 per cent (Ahluwalia *et al.*, 1979). Hence, the fifteenfold difference between DMEs and LDCs as a whole shown in Table 2.10 becomes much smaller in purchasing-power terms. However, even when this deviation is allowed for, there is a great difference between the standard of living of DCs and that of a large part of the population of LDCs; e.g. the per capita income of India which was one-fiftieth of that of the United States at the official exchange rate is still only one-fourteenth in terms of purchasing power parity.

While the national income measure is subject to many limitations when used for comparing the standard of living of different countries, it is more useful for comparing the structure of their economies. This is shown most conveniently by the sectoral origin of the Gross Domestic Product (GDP) in Table 2.11.

Table 2.11 Composition of GDP by sectors, 1979
(Weighted averages: percentage)

Sector	DMEs	LDCs
Agriculture	4.5	22.8
Industry	37.1	38.9
Services	58.4	38.3
Total	100.0	100.0

Source: World Bank, *World Development Report, 1981*

The sectoral composition of output is fairly uniform among the DMEs, but there is great variation among the LDCs, as shown in Table 2.12.

Given the distribution of the labour force in the various sectors (Table 2.8) and the distribution of GDP in these sectors (Table 2.11), we can derive the relative productivities of labour in each sector. The results will not be very precise because the classification of labour into the three sectors does not generally correspond exactly with the allocation of GDP to these sectors. A rough comparison is shown in Table 2.13 opposite.

Table 2.12 Distribution of LDC populations by sectoral share of major sectors, 1979. (Population in millions; number of countries in brackets)

Percentage of sectoral share	Countries with given share of GDP in:		
	Agriculture	Industry	Services
Below 10	84 (14)	27 (3)	—
10–20	319 (16)	327 (20)	124 (11)
20–30	391 (17)	1025 (32)	1034 (8)
30–40	1953 (18)	527 (20)	1112 (17)
40–50	170 (12)	1087 (6)	571 (33)
50 & Over	177 (11)	110 (7)	254 (19)
Total	3094 (88)	3094 (88)	3094 (88)

Source: World Bank, *World Development Report, 1981*

Table 2.13 Indices of labour productivity by sector, 1979. (Percentage)

Sector	Productivity in each sector relative to average		Productivity in LDCs relative to DMEs
	DMEs	LDCs	DMEs
Agriculture	51	35	4.5
Industry	101	245	16.0
Services	108	195	11.9
Total	100	100	6.6

Source: Tables 2.8 and 2.11 above

Both in DMEs and in LDCs, the productivity of labour in agriculture is lower than in other sectors. As between DMEs and LDCs, the gap in labour productivity is greatest in agriculture. The low productivity of labour in agriculture is one of the most crucial factors affecting the level and structure of LDC economies compared with DMEs. Because of this low productivity, a large proportion of the labour force has to be engaged in the agricultural sector to produce food for the population. Hence only small proportions of the labour force are engaged in the non-agricultural sectors. Because such a large proportion of the labour force works at a low productivity, the per capita income itself is low. The gap in labour productivity in the other sectors is also large, but smaller than in agriculture. Therefore, although only a small proportion of the labour force is engaged in the non-agricultural sectors, they have a larger share of total output.

The national income accounts can also be used to compare the pattern of expenditure as shown in Table 2.14. In spite of the big difference between DMEs and LDCs in their average incomes and sectoral composition of output, the pattern of expenditure is very similar; the major difference is that LDCs

Table 2.14 Patterns of expenditure, 1979

Countries	Percentage of GDP spent on:				
	Consumption		Gross domestic investment	Exports	Imports
	Public	Private			
DMEs	17	61	23	19	−20
LDCs	12	63	26	19	−20
(a) Low income	11	66	26	11	−14
(b) Middle income	12	63	26	21	−22
(c) Oil exporters	22	27	28	65	−42

Source: World Bank, *World Development Report, 1981*

spend less on public consumption and more on investment. The pattern shown in the above table, however, is considerably affected by the conditions of recession prevailing in the DMEs at the time, reflected in their lower share of investment.

2.5 The Contrast Between DCs and LDCs

So far we have been considering the major differences between DCs and LDCs in their demographic features, labour force and employment, and national product. They also differ in many other respects which are discussed in more detail in later chapters. But to highlight the contrast between the two groups of countries, Table 2.15 brings together summary data on a large numbers of variables for which fairly comprehensive data for the period around 1970 have been compiled from U.N. statistical sources by the United Nations Research Institute for Social Development (UNRISD). The table shows the average values of these variables for LDCs (shown as M_1) and for DCs (shown as M_2).

The table also shows the extent to which each variable discriminates between the two groups of countries; for each variable, a critical value was calculated which separates LDCs from DCs most sharply, and the discriminating power of each variable, i.e. the percentage of all countries which are correctly assigned to the two groups by that variable, is shown under the value of D. Most of the variables are found to have a high discriminating power, i.e. it is found that the two groups of countries differ sharply with respect to most of the variables. Such sharp differences with respect to so many variables suggest that the difference between the two groups of countries should be considered one of kind rather than of degree. This contrast is also shown by the fact that the statistical distributions of certain variables show a distinct bi-modality, i.e. they have two points of concentration at which frequencies (the number of countries with certain values of the variables) are higher than at neighbouring values. Figure 2.1 shows the bi-modality of the distribution of 125 countries according to the gross reproduction rate. In Figure 2.2, the distribution by the percentage of the male labour force engaged in non-agricultural activity is

Table 2.15 The contrast between DCs and LDCs

Variable	Average for LDCs M_1	Average for DCs M_2	Dis-crimi-nating power D	Corre-lation of per capita income C
I. *Demographic and health variables.*				
1. Infant mortality rate	99	28	85	−0.71
2. Life expectancy: both sexes	54	70	89	0.71
3. males	53	67	86	0.69
4. females	56	73	92	0.72
5. Gross reproduction rate	2.9	1.3	96	−0.73
6. Birth rate	41	19	94	−0.75
7. Death rate	14	10	68	−0.45
8. Population growth rate: 1960–70 (%)	2.6	1.1	93	−0.54
9. Percentage of population in urban areas	29	61	85	0.15
10. Percentage of population in cities	18	36	78	0.80
11. Population (000) per doctor	15.6	0.78	96	−0.41
12. Population per hospital bed	790	140	99	−0.41
II. *Educational variables.*				
1. Adult literacy (%)	52	97	95	0.69
2. 6–11 population in schools (percentage)	59	92	83	0·54
3. 12–17 population in schools (percentage)	37	77	90	0.78
4. Enrolment ratio: levels I and II	41	73	88	0.74
5. 15–19 population in vocational schools (%)	3.1	26.5	95	0.77
6. Enrolment ratio: level III	2.1	9.0	89	0.84
7. Female percentage of Level I enrolment	39	49	81	0.49
8. Pupil–teacher ratio: level I	39	25	90	−0.51
9. Newspaper circulation per 1000 population	41	243	89	0.82
10. Apparent newspaper consumption: kg per capita	1.6	16	85	0.83
III. *Labour force variables*				
1. Per cent of labour force in: agriculture (ISIC 1) (males only)	55.8	17.8	91	0.15
2. utilities & transport (ISIC 4, 7)	4.1	7.4	93	0.65
3. transport (ISIC 7)	3.6	6.3	89	0.61
4. manufacturing (ISIC 3)	11.5	26.8	91	0.67
5. professional & related occupations (ISCO 0–1)	4.7	10.1	81	0.86
6. Wages & salaries of employees as per cent of national income	38	55	82	0.70
IV. *Energy and transport variables*				
1. Per capita apparent consumption of electricity (kWh)	265	3351	93	0.85
2. Per capita apparent consumption of energy (kg coal equivalent)	386	3818	94	0.89
3. Railway traffic—passenger km per capita	64	711	93	0.55
4. Passenger cars per 1000 people	12.6	139	92	0.95

Table 2.15 The contrast between DCs and LDCs (cont'd)

Variable	M_1	M_2	D	C
5. Passenger cars & commercial vehicles per 1000 people	17.7	190	92	0.95
6. Domestic mail per 1000 people	7.4	139	92	0.94
7. Telephones per 1000 people	1.5	20.4	88	0.94
8. Radio receivers per 1000 people	85	311	86	0.77
9. TV receivers per 1000 people	20	181	91	0.93
V. *Production variables*				
1. GDP per capita (US $) at: official exchange rates	315	1933	92	1.00
2. at: purchasing power parity	578	2862	96	0.98
3. Percentage of GDP: industry	22.2	33.4	82	0.47
4. Percentage of GDP: manufacturing	13.7	29.2	94	0.67
5. Percentage of GDP: agriculture	29.3	11.1	79	−0.66
6. Agricultural output (US $) per male worker	678	4568	93	0.92
7. Apparent consumption of fertilizers: kg per hectare	36.5	232	81	0.74
8. kg per male worker	78	1661	93	0.81
9. Apparent consumption of steel: kg per capita	28	365	93	0.90
10. Apparent consumption of cement: kg per capita	113	411	91	0.53
VI. *Food consumption variables*				
1. Apparent daily consumption per capita: calories	2240	3070	96	0.74
2. protein	58	92	74	0.69
3. animal protein	15.6	48.4	96	0.82
4. Calories from cereals and starchy roots as percentage of total calories	62	39	86	−0.79

Source: United Nations Research Institute for Social Development, *Research Data Bank for Development Indicators*, Vol.I. 1976

shown together for all countries (a) and separately for the two groups of countries (b). These figures show the number of countries at various levels, but countries vary greatly in size. Therefore, it is also useful to consider the distribution of populations at various values of some variables. An example is shown in Figure 2.3 for the variation according to per capita income. (For other examples, see United Nations 1963, pp.135–6; also Brown, 1975) Such bi-modal distributions arise from the combination of two distinct unimodal distributions and suggest that they describe samples from different universes and that the region between the two groups is an unstable area with a high probability of transition to one or the other of the extreme cases.

The tendency for observations to fall into two such distinct groups has been described as the 'double-clustering' tendency. As a result of this tendency, we generally get a high correlation between pairs of variables when both groups are combined, due to the high inter-class correlation between clusters. This is particularly the case when per capita income is correlated with other variables;

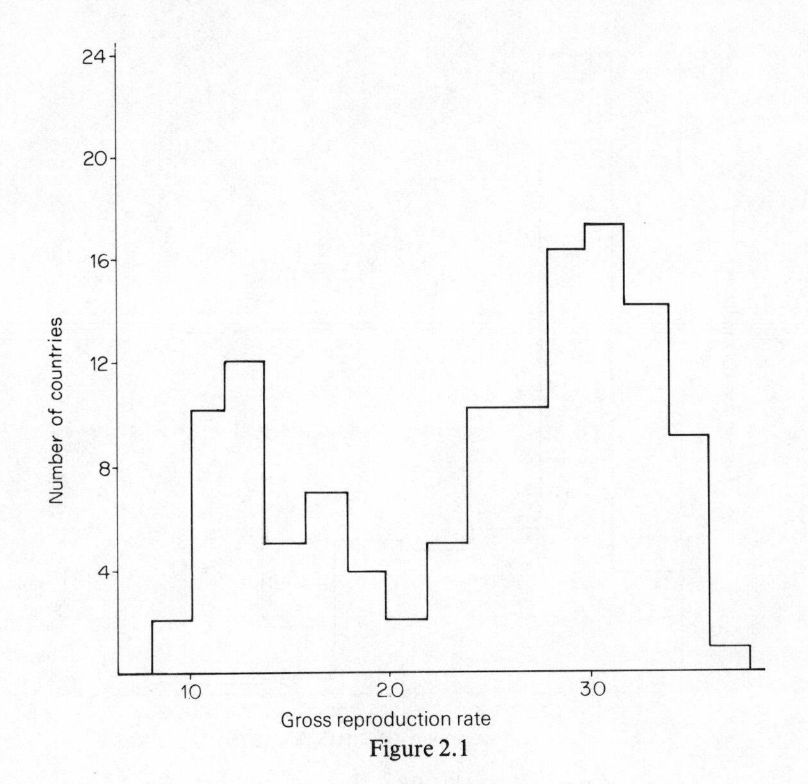

Figure 2.1

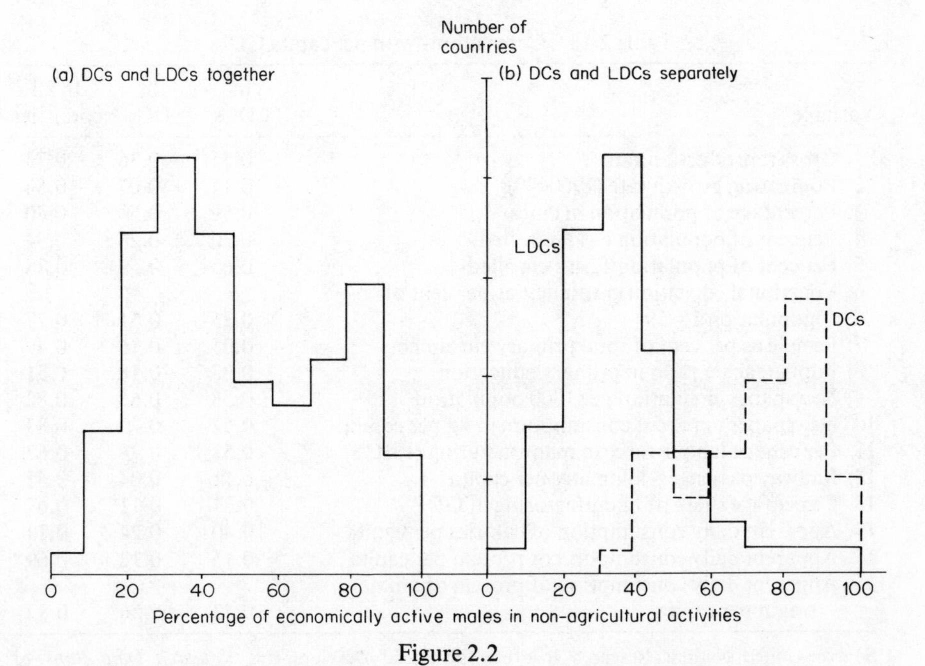

Figure 2.2

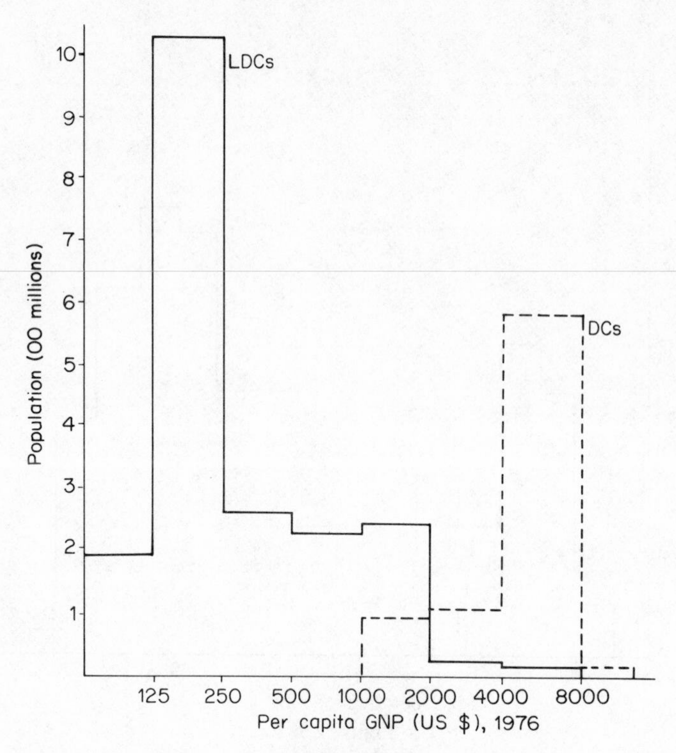

Figure 2.3

Table 2.16 Correlations with per capita GDP

Variable	In LDCs	In DCs	In all countries
1. Gross reproduction rate	−0.55	−0.36	−0.73
2. Population growth rate (1960–70)	0.11	0.07	−0.54
3. Percentage of population in cities	0.59	0.50	0.80
4. Per cent of population 6–11 enrolled	0.20	0.26	0.54
5. Per cent of population 12–17 enrolled	0.65	0.59	0.78
6. Vocational education enrolment as per cent of population 15–19	0.35	0.51	0.77
7. Female as per cent of total primary enrolment	0.35	0.16	0.49
8. Pupil–teacher ratio in primary education	−0.28	−0.18	−0.51
9. Newspaper circulation per 1000 population	0.58	0.66	0.82
10. Newspaper apparent consumption in kg per capita	0.52	0.70	0.83
11. Per cent of labour force in manufacturing (ISIC 3)	0.51	0.28	0.67
12. Railway passenger–kilometre per capita	−0.11	0.04	0.55
13. Percentage share of manufacturing in GDP	0.27	0.11	0.67
14. Apparent daily consumption of calories per capita	0.40	0.24	0.74
15. Apparent daily consumption of protein per capita	0.15	0.12	0.69
16. Apparent daily consumption of protein of animal origin per capita	0.43	0.56	0.82

Source: United Nations Research Institute for Social Development, *Research Data Bank of Development Indicators*, Vol.I. 1976

values of such correlations (for all countries taken together) with the variables listed in Table 2.15 are shown under the column headed *C*. The correlations become much smaller when calculated within each of the two groups. Some values for a smaller list of variables with per capita income are shown in Table 2.16. Hence, correlations from data from a combination of DCs and LDCs are often misleading as an indication of relationships within each group.

CHAPTER 3

Recent Changes in Less-Developed Countries

3.1 Growth of population and labour force
3.2 Growth of national and per capita product
3.3 Structural changes of the economy

In Chapter 2, we compared the levels of a number of variables in LDCs and DCs; it was a comparison between two snapshot pictures and concentrated on the structural differences between two groups of countries. In the present chapter, we compare the changes that have taken place in the LDCs since World War II with those that took place in the DCs both in that period and in their historical past; the objective now will be to describe the dynamic working of the economic system in these countries.

The period covered is particularly interesting as it was a period of rapid change in the world economy. Many of the DCs started the period with vigorous efforts to reconstruct their war-damaged economies. In the DMEs, new techniques of macro-economic management were evolved to promote economic growth as a major policy objective. This was accompanied by a substantial liberalization of trade policies, leading to a great expansion of world trade. This was also the period in which most LDCs achieved independence from colonial status and the new national governments of these countries started with deliberate policies to promote their development high on their policy agenda. The LDCs were greatly affected by the rapid growth of the DCs and the expansion of world trade. There was also the new phenomenon of a flow of international aid to the LDCs and the establishment of new international agencies, such as the World Bank, the International Monetary Fund and other agencies of the United Nations Organization, aimed to assist the LDCs in their development. From the mid-1960s onwards, there was increasing concern about whether the world's stock of non-renewable and other exhaustible resources would allow the rapid economic growth, especially of the DCs, to continue, and in view of the increasing costs of pollution, congestion and social tensions, even whether it was desirable. In the early 1970s, all countries were seriously affected by the sharp rise in oil prices brought about by the concerted action of the oil-producing and -exporting countries (OPEC). The DMEs then went into a period of sharp recession, rapid inflation and severe problems of balance of payments, from which they have been recovering only gradually. It is against these significant changes in the world economic setting that we consider the dynamics of economic change in the LDCs in the past three decades.

Many special aspects of these changes are discussed in later chapters dealing with those aspects. But to set the stage for the later discussion, the present chapter deals with some of the major changes that have taken place in LDCs in the post-war period, namely, growth of population and labour force (Section 3.1); growth of national product and per capita product (Section 3.2); and structural changes of the economy (Section 3.3).

3.1 Growth of Population and Labour Force

One of the most dramatic changes that occurred in the LDCs in the post-war period was a great increase, amounting to a veritable explosion, of population. The magnitude of these changes is summarized in Table 3.1.

Over the past three decades, the population of LDCs has almost doubled, while that of the DCs has increased by little more than a third. While population growth rate in DCs has been declining continuously and rapidly from its already low level in 1950, in LDCs it started above 2 per cent per annum and increased until 1965 and has been declining very slowly since then. While the decline in population growth in DCs was due to a declining birth rate with a fairly stable death rate, the high rates of population growth in LDCs were due to a dramatic fall—by nearly half in three decades—in the death rate, while birth rates were high and declined very slowly.

As measures of fertility and mortality, these birth and death rates are, of course, much influenced by the age distribution. It is therefore useful to look also at the life expectation at birth and the reproduction rates which are measures of mortality and fertility unaffected by the age distribution. Some estimates are shown in Table 3.2.

The expectation of life at birth has continued to increase in the DCs; this increase is not reflected in death rates because of the ageing of their populations. In the LDCs, life expectation at birth increased nearly twice as fast in the past three decades; in their case, the effect on the death rate was accentuated by changes in the age distribution. The death rates in the two groups of countries are currently quite similar; this is because of the difference in their age distributions. In fact, there is a considerable difference in their life expectations at birth, indicating that there is a considerable potential in LDCs for further declines in mortality and hence, unless offset by corresponding declines in fertility, for continued high rates of population growth. The proportionate difference in fertility as measured by the gross reproduction rate

Table 3.1 Demographic changes in DCs and LDCs, 1950–80

Period	DCs	LDCs	World
(a) *Population (millions)*			
1950	832	1681	2513
1955	887	1858	2745
1960	945	2082	3027
1965	1003	2341	3344
1970	1050	2628	3678
1975	1093	2940	4033
1980 (p)	1131	3284	4415
(b) *Rates of Population Growth (annual percent)*			
1950–55	1.29	2.02	1.78
1955–60	1.27	2.30	1.98
1960–65	1.20	2.37	2.01
1965–70	0.92	2.34	1.92
1970–75	0.81	2.27	1.86
1975–80 (p)	0.69	2.24	1.83
(c) *Birth Rates (per thousand)*			
1950–55	22.9	42.1	35.6
1955–60	21.9	40.9	34.6
1960–65	20.3	40.0	34.0
1965–70	18.1	38.4	32.1
1970–75	16.7	35.5	30.3
1975–80 (p)	15.6	33.6	28.9
(d) *Death Rates (per thousand)*			
1950–55	10.1	23.3	18.8
1955–60	9.3	19.9	16.4
1960–65	9.0	16.8	14.4
1965–70	9.1	15.5	13.5
1970–75	9.2	13.2	12.0
1975–80 (p)	9.4	12.0	11.3

Source: United Nations, *The World Population Situation in 1979.* (p) provisional estimates

Table 3.2 Expectation of life at birth and reproduction rates

Measures		DCs	LDCs	World
Life expectation at birth:				
1950–55	Males	63.1	41.7	46.2
	Females	67.3	43.5	48.5
	Both	65.2	42.6	47.4
1975–80	Males	68.3	54.1	56.1
	Females	75.5	56.2	59.0
	Both	71.9	55.2	57.6
Gross Reproduction Rates, *1975–80*		0.99	2.31	1.96
Net Reproduction Rate, *1975–80* (a)		1.06	1.93	1.68

Source: United Nations, *The World Population Situation in 1979*; (a) from United Nations, *Selected World Demographic Indicators by Countries 1950–2000* (U.N. Population Division, 1975)

is even greater than that in the birth rates. While fertility in the DCs, as measured by the net reproduction rate, is just above replacement levels, it is nearly double that level in the LDCs.

The magnitude of the population explosion in LDCs in this period can be better appreciated by comparing it with the historical rates of population growth, shown in Table 3.3.

Table 3.3 Annual rates of population growth, 1750–1950 (per cent)

Period	DCs	LDCs	World
1750–1800	0.4	0.4	0.4
1800–1850	0.7	0.5	0.5
1850–1900	1.0	0.3	0.5
1900–1950	0.8	0.9	0.8

Source: Durand, 1967, Vol.III, p.137.

The DCs had experienced an acceleration of population growth in their historical past, as death rates declined faster and ahead of the decline in birth rates, but it was nowhere near the rate of population growth of the LDCs in the past three decades. The recent changes in birth and death rates of LDCs are compared with the historical experience of the DCs in Fig. 3.1.

One of the most important consequences of rapid population growth for the LDCs was the growth of the labour force, summarized in Table 3.4.

Table 3.4 Annual growth rates of labour force (per cent)

Period	DCs	LDCs	Total
1950–55	1.18	1.89	1.63
1955–60	0.95	2.09	1.69
1960–65	1.07	1.66	1.46
1965–70	0.92	1.90	1.57
1970–75	1.28	1.97	1.75
1975–80 (p)	1.11	2.03	1.75

Source: I.L.O., *Labour Force 1950–2000*, Vol.V.
(p) projections.

As with population growth, the labour force in LDCs has also grown at about double the rate in DCs. While the rate of population growth in LDCs peaked in the mid-1960s, the effect on labour-force growth appears with a lag of 15 to 20 years and is currently still increasing, although population growth rates are beginning to decline. The growth of the labour force is determined not only by the growth of population, but also by changes in age distribution and by the socio-economic factors affecting age-specific activity rates. The relative contributions of these factors are roughly quantified in Table 3.5.

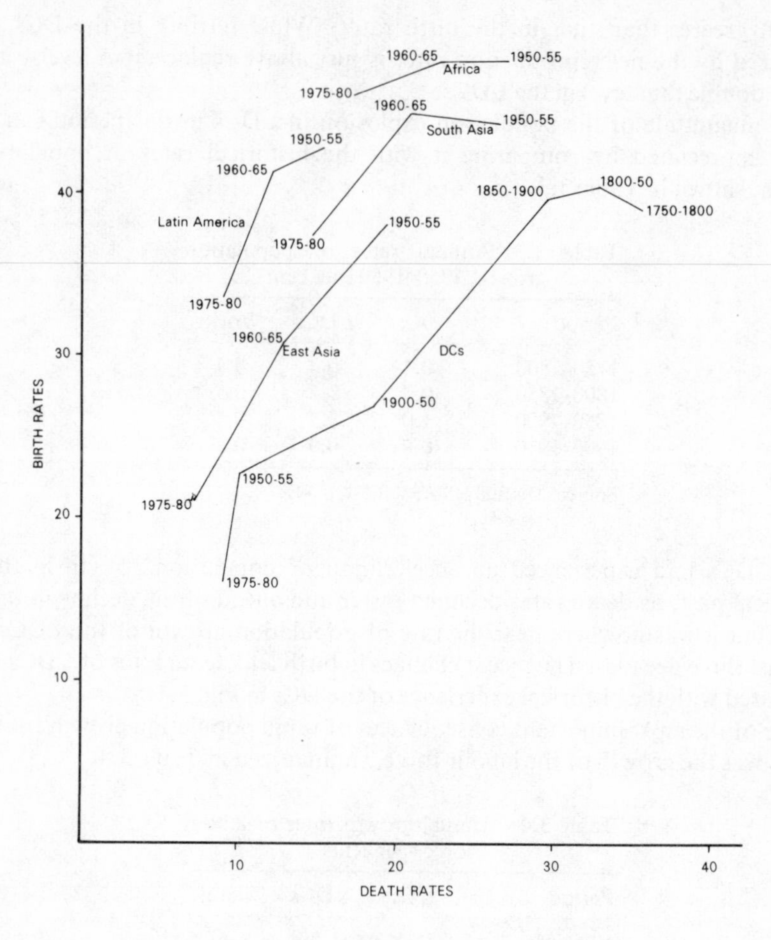

Figure 3.1

In all cases, the growth of population is the major factor in the growth of the labour force. The effects of changes in age distribution have generally been negative in the early post-war decades but they became positive in the last decade as the increase in the numbers born in the immediate post-war years moved into the working age groups. Socio-economic factors led to a decline in the male working force both in DCs and in LDCs, mainly due to later entry and earlier retirement from the labour force, but in the case of females, they led to an increase in the DCs and a decrease in the LDCs; the increased labour-force participation of women in the DCs was partly due to the decline in fertility and partly to the influence of women's liberation movements. While the socio-economic factors were quite significant in the DCs in comparison with the demographic factors, they were much weaker in the LDCs, where the rapid growth of population has led to large increases in the labour force.

Table 3.5 Demographic and socio-economic factors in growth of labour force. (millions)

Country/sex/period		Growth of labour force	Due to: Population growth	Age distribution	Socio-economic factors
DCs	*Males*				
	1950–60	22.8	36.7	− 3.2	−10.7
	1960–70	20.9	31.6	+ 5.1	−15.8
	1970–80	34.7	28.3	+13.9	− 7.5
	Females				
	1950–60	21.5	19.1	− 5.7	+ 8.1
	1960–70	25.2	17.9	− 0.2	+ 7.5
	1970–80	27.1	16.1	+ 4.7	+ 6.3
LDCs	*Males*				
	1950–60	71.1	109.1	−16.4	−21.6
	1960–70	109.1	145.2	− 5.5	−30.6
	1970–80	155.9	179.5	+ 9.7	−33.3
	Females				
	1950–60	81.8	45.2	+36.6	0
	1960–70	55.9	72.7	0	−16.8
	1970–80	68.1	89.5	+ 5.8	−27.2

Source: Calculated from data of I.L.O., *Labour Force 1950–2000*

3.2 Growth of National and Per Capita Product

We next consider the growth of gross product; the available data are summarized in Table 3.6.

The DMEs experienced high rates of growth throughout the 1950s and 1960s, but these rates fell quite sharply in the 1970s. The CPCs started with a high rate of growth in the 1950s, faster than the DMEs; then the rate of growth dropped in the 1960s to below the rate in the DMEs, but rose to a much higher rate in the 1970s. The most interesting observation that has come as a welcome surprise to many economists is that the LDCs grew so fast throughout the post-war period, after their relative stagnation in pre-war periods. In the post-war period, the growth rate of LDCs was not only higher than the contemporary growth rate of DMEs but was also considerably higher than the historical experience of the DCs shown in Table 3.7.

After a long period of stagnation before World War II, the rate of growth achieved by the LDCs, so much faster than even the growth of DMEs in their historical past, is a remarkable feature of the post-war period. It has therefore been widely acclaimed as a sign of their development. However, there are two qualifications to be made. One is that much of the accelerated growth of GDP of this period was eaten up by the unprecedented growth of population that occurred at the same time. Therefore, the growth of per capita national

Table 3.6 Annual percentage rates of growth of total and per capita GDP (unweighted averages)

Countries		1950–59[a]	1960–69[a]	1970–79[b]
DMEs:	GDP	4.7	5.2	3.4
	per capita	3.6	4.1	2.4
CPCs:	GDP	6.0[c]	4.4[c]	6.1
	per capita	—	—	5.5
LDCs:	GDP	4.7	5.6	4.5
	per capita	2.3	3.0	1.8

Sources: (a) Yotopoulos and Nugent, 1976, p.5; (b) World Bank, *Development Report, 1981*, (c) World Bank, *World Tables, 1976*.

Table 3.7 Historical growth rates of DCs

Country	Period	Rate of growth (percentages)
England & Wales—UK	1780–1881	2.5
	1855/9–1957/9	2.0
France	1841/50–1960/2	1.9
Germany/W. Germany	1851/5–1871/5	1.6
	1871/5–1960/2	2.8
Netherlands	1900/4–1960/2	2.6
Switzerland	1890/9–1957/9	2.3
Denmark	1870/4–1960/2	2.8
Norway	1865/74–1960/2	2.6
Sweden	1861/5–1960/2	3.2
Italy	1861/5–1898/1902	0.9
	1898/1902–1960/2	2.4
USA	1839–1960/2	3.6
Australia	1861/5–1959/60	3.0
European Russia/USSR	1860–1913	2.7
	1913–1928	0.5
	1928–1958	4.4
Japan	1879/81–1959/61	3.6

Source: Kuznets, 1966, Table 2.5, pp.64–5.

income in the LDCs was very modest, being less than half the growth rate of GDP in most cases. Among the 81 LDCs for which estimates are given in the *World Development Report, 1979* for the period 1960–77, apart from some oil-exporting countries, only four countries—Taiwan, South Korea, Hong Kong and Singapore—had annual growth rates of per capita income over 6 per cent, because these were the countries in which fast growth of GDP was combined with a sharp fall in population growth rates. For most LDCs, the rate of growth of per capita GDP was too low to make a significant impact on the standard of living of the mass of the population. It is an indication of the extent to which they have not been able to make full use of their development opportunities.

The second important qualification is that the growth performance of LDCs was very uneven. The extent to which these variations in growth rates were associated with various factors, as measured by the correlation coefficient, is summarized in Table 3.8.

Table 3.8 Factors associated with GDP growth rates in LDCs

Correlation coefficient of GDP growth rates with:	1960–70	1970–79
Population	−0.23	0.07
Initial per capita GDP	0.29	−0.01
Growth rate of previous decade	0.37	0.10
Investment Ratio	0.39	0.40
Growth rate of investment	0.67	0.71
Growth rate of exports	0.64	0.62

Source: calculated from data of World Bank, *World Tables 1976* (for 1960–70) and *World Development Report, 1981* (for 1970–79)

In the 1960s, the rate of growth was generally higher among the smaller countries. The situation has been described as follows:

Most of the high growth countries were relatively small. Of the twenty-nine countries achieving a rate of growth of six per cent a year or more, only a fifth had a gross product of $3 billion in 1967 (Mexico, Iran, Israel, South Korea, Saudi Arabia and Thailand). The largest high-growth country in Africa was the Libyan Arab Republic with a 1967 gross product of just over $2 billion. (United Nations, *World Economic Survey, 1971*, pp.9–10)

In contrast, the larger countries had some of the lowest growth rates. The position changes in the 1970s when there was no correlation between population and GDP growth rates. Growth rates in the 1960s were also associated with initial income levels, the richer countries growing faster, but again in the 1970s, there was little correlation between growth rates and income levels. Yet another difference between the two decades is that there was a stronger correlation with the growth rates of the preceding decade in the 1960s than in the 1970s. In these respects, the position in the 1970s was that more rapid growth spread to some of the large poor LDCs.

With regard to the above factors, there appears to have been a change from the 1960s to the 1970s. But with respect to some other factors, the same relationships appear to have held in both decades. Growth rates were positively correlated with investment ratios; this is in accordance with the role generally attributed to capital in promoting growth. But rates of growth of income were even more strongly correlated with rates of growth of investment, suggesting that rapid growth of incomes may also have led to rapid growth of investment. Particularly significant is the high correlation between growth of GDP and growth of exports. In some countries, rapid growth occurred in the exports of manufactures and services, as in the case of Taiwan, South Korea,

Hong Kong and Singapore, but in most cases, where exports grew rapidly, they consisted of natural resource products. The position in the 1960s has been described as follows:

> Except in the case of Mexico, where the expansionary force was largely internally generated, the countries achieving the highest growth rates in the 1960s received much of their impetus from external demand. In many instances, this came from the exploitation of a mineral resource: petroleum, bauxite and alumina, iron ore, phosphate, copper. (*United Nations, World Economic Survey*, 1971, p.10)

(For an analysis of the relationship between export growth and income growth, see Section 11.3(a)).

3.3 Structural Changes of the Economy

The economic growth of LDCs in the post-war period was accompanied by a certain amount of structural change, i.e. changes in the allocation of the labour force and composition of output in various sectors. Table 3.9 summarizes the changes in the sectoral allocation of the labour force.

Table 3.9 Sectoral allocation of labour force (per cent)

Countries/Year		Agriculture	Industry	Services
LDCs:	1950	79.5	8.4	12.1
	1960	72.9	12.7	14.4
	1970	66.6	15.9	17.5
	1980	64.5	15.9	19.6
DCs:	1880	56.2	24.2	19.6
	1900	48.1	28.7	23.3
	1920	39.9	31.3	28.9
	1930	35.9	31.2	32.9
	1950	37.6	30.4	32.0
	1960	28.1	34.6	37.3
	1970	18.3	37.6	44.1
	1979	8.9	36.9	54.2

Sources: 1950–70, I.L.O., *Labour Force 1950–2000*; 1979, World Bank, *World Development Report 1981*; 1880–1930, Bairoch and Limber (1968)

In the LDCs, there was a decline in the share of agriculture and an increase in the shares of the other sectors; this is the pattern observed in the historical experience of DCs also. The data are illustrated diagrammatically in Figure 3.2 by the method of triangular coordinates; in this diagram, the three sides of the triangle represent the three sectors and the allocation of labour to a particular sector is represented by the perpendicular distance of a point within the triangle to the side representing that sector. We then see that the LDCs now have a higher share of the labour force in agriculture than the DCs had even a century ago, and that the recent movement in the sectoral allocation of labour is at a rather slow rate compared with the historical experience of the DCs.

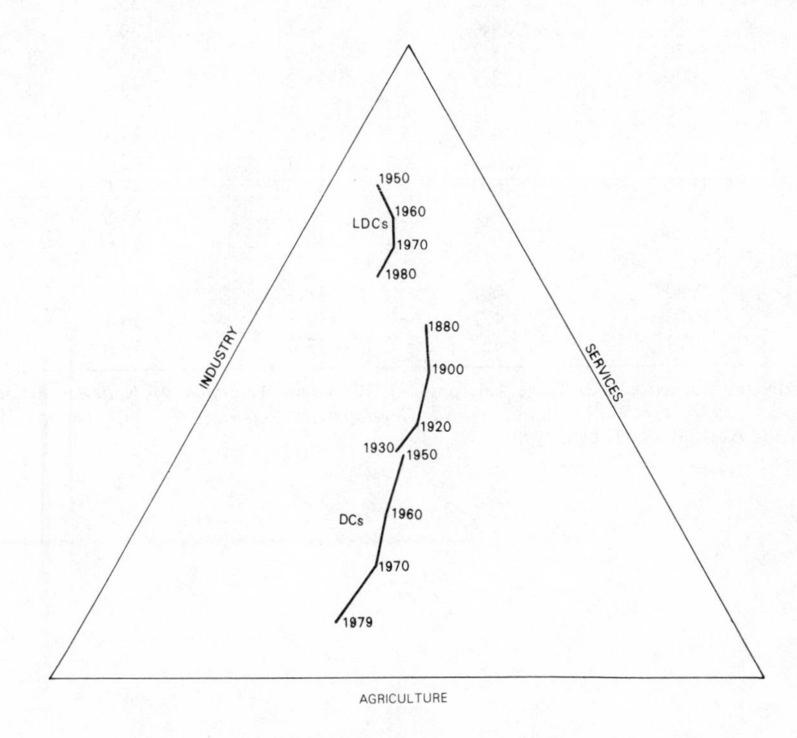

Figure 3.2 Allocation of labour force

The changes in the sectoral composition of output are summarized in Table 3.10 and illustrated in Figure 3.3 by the same method of triangular coordinates. Again we see that recent changes in the sectoral composition of output in LDCs have followed the historical experience of DCs but slightly faster than in the case of labour allocation.

One of the significant structural changes that occurred in the LDCs in the post-war period was a high rate of urbanization. This is shown by the increase in the urban ratio, i.e. the percentage of total population living in urban areas (Table 3.11). Urbanization in LDCs is much lower than in the DCs but has been increasing rapidly. Table 3.12 shows the rate of growth of total and of urban population. It shows that, in both groups of countries, the urban population has been growing at about twice the rate of total population. This suggests that the rapid urbanization of LDCs is related to the acceleration of population growth, rather than to the structural changes going on in the economy.

Table 3.10 Sectoral composition of GDP (per cent)

Countries/year		Agriculture	Industry	Services
LDCs:	1950/2[a]	39.2	25.7	35.1
	1960/2[a]	34.4	30.8	34.8
	1970[b]	28.2	33.4	38.3
	1979[c]	22.8	38.9	38.3
DMEs:	1870[d]	34.4	26.5	39.1
	1890[d]	30.1	27.1	42.8
	1910[d]	26.0	31.0	43.0
	1930[d]	17.1	33.0	49.9
	1950[d]	16.0	40.0	44.0
	1960[e]	6.4	41.1	52.5
	1970[e]	4.2	39.7	56.1
	1979[c]	4.0	37.0	59.0

Sources: (a) Kuznets, 1972, Table 1.6, pp.42–3; (b) U.N., *Yearbook of National Accounts Statistics, 1972*; (c) World Bank, *World Development Report, 1981*; (d) Temin, 1967; (e) World Bank, *World Tables, 1980*

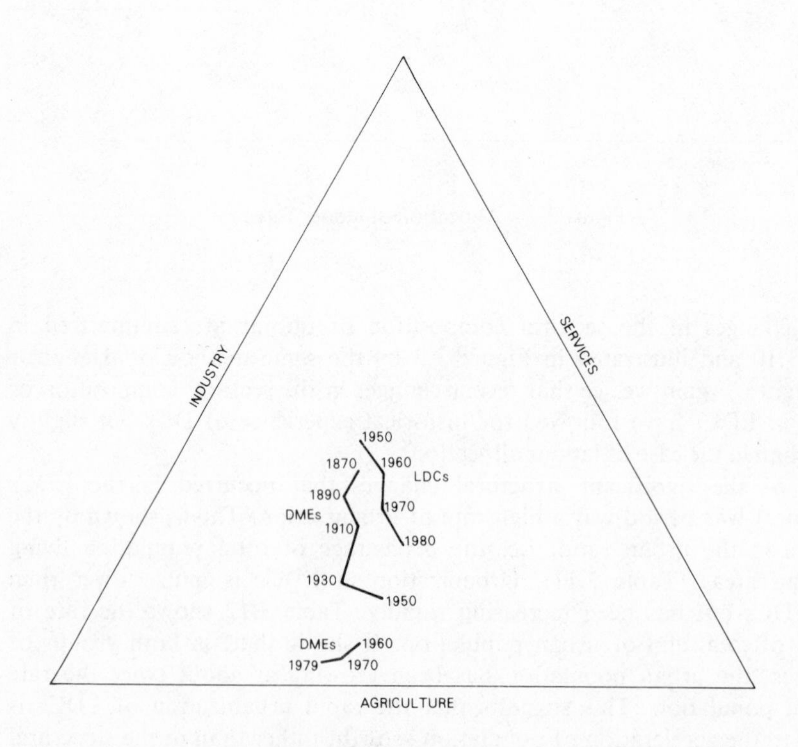

Figure 3.3 Sectoral composition of GDP

Table 3.11 Urban ratio (per cent)

Year	LDCs	DCs	World
1800		(7.6)	3.0
1850		(15.1)	6.4
1900		(26.4)	13.6
1950	16.7	52.5	28.9
1960	21.9	58.7	33.9
1970	25.8	64.7	37.5
1980 (p)	30.5	70.2	41.3

Sources: For 1800–1900, Davis, 1972, Vol.II, Table 13, p.51; For 1950–1980, U.N., *World Population Trends and Policies* 1979, Vol.I; (p) projections made in 1979. Figures in brackets are rough estimates.

Table 3.12 Annual rates of growth of total and urban populations (per cent)

Period		DCs	LDCs	World
1950–60	Total	0.99	2.16	1.88
	Urban	2.47	4.79	3.41
1960–70	Total	1.06	2.36	1.96
	Urban	2.07	4.02	2.95
1970–80	Total	0.75	2.25	1.84
	Urban	1.72	4.09	2.93

The growth of urban population in any period can be analysed into three components, namely, natural increase of urban population, rural-urban migration, and the reclassification of rural areas into urban areas during the period considered. Data are not available for many countries to estimate the last two components separately; they are therefore combined in Table 3.13. We see that rural–urban migration and natural increase contributed in about equal measure to the growth of urban population in both groups of countries.

To summarize the main results of the changes in the post-war period described in this chapter, the changes in LDCs have been in the same direction

Table 3.13 Components of urban population growth (annual percentage rates of growth)

Countries/period		Rate of growth of urban population	Due to natural increase	Due to rural–urban migration
DCs:	1960	2.35	1.12	1.23
	1970–75	1.74	0.87	0.90
LDCs:	1960	4.55	2.25	2.30
	1970–75	4.11	2.41	1.86

Sources: For 1960, U.N., *The Population Debate* (1975) p.185; For 1970–75, U.N., *World Population Trends and Policies, 1977* p.117.

as the historical experience of the DCs but with some significant differences in the speed of these changes. There have been rapid declines in death rates but much slower declines in birth rates, leading to a greater acceleration in population growth than that experienced by the DCs. The growth of national product in LDCs has been, on the average, at least as rapid as in the DCs in the same period and faster than in their historical experience, but because of the population explosion in LDCs, the growth of per capita income starting from a low base has been more modest and has not had a significant impact on the living standards of the mass of the population. Further, growth rates have varied greatly among individual LDCs and have been mainly influenced by external factors associated with the expansion of world trade in this period, whereas growth in the DCs has been due much more to internal factors. To explore the causes of these differences in the factors influencing growth in the two groups of countries we now turn to a study of the historical background.

CHAPTER 4

The Historical Background

The data presented in Chapter 2 showed the low level of economic activity in LDCs compared with DCs during the past decade, and an economic structure adjusted to that low level. In Chapter 3, we saw that, although the LDCs had on average grown as fast as the DCs in the post-war period, it was so nearly offset by the acceleration of their population growth that it did not make a significant impact on the standard of living of the mass of their population. The difference between DCs and LDCs is therefore the outcome of differences in their previous historical experience and can only be fully understood by considering that history. This is the purpose of the present chapter.

Economic development viewed as the long history of man's struggle with nature commenced in certain tropical countries, which are now among the LDCs, and spread to other countries. It gave rise to an organization of production and a pattern of society which became rooted in certain traditional ways of life (Section 4.1). Then, there occurred in Britain, about two centuries ago, a revolutionary change in methods of production and social organization which transformed the economy; it is described as modern economic growth (Section 4.2). Section 4.3 describes how this type of growth spread by a diffusion process to other countries which have become the DCs of today, and Section 4.4 explains how this diffusion process stopped short of reaching other countries, which are now the LDCs. Finally, the effects of the modern economic growth of the DCs on the LDCs are summarized in Section 4.5.

4.1 Early History

In the earliest stages of economic development, man's capacity for contending with nature was small, and physical causes were most powerful in influencing the growth of civilization in certain favoured spots. These favoured spots were the regions with warm climates where the necessities of clothing and shelter were small. Within these climatic regions, the valleys of the great rivers of the Middle East, Asia and Latin America were especially favoured by being provided with an adequate water supply which periodically replenished the fertility of the soil and afforded an easy means of communication. It was in such places that around 6000 B.C., food production came to supersede the previous food-gathering stage and

> the appearance of an established food-producing settled village type of economy seems to have come into being with relative (even revolutionary) suddenness. (Braidwood, 1952, p.5)

With this development, economic activities became a social phenomenon, an interaction among people living in groups. This led to a further development—the establishment of elaborate systems of irrigation covering vast areas;

> to make a large-scale irrigation system efficient, a considerable amount of social control, a sense of land law and riparian rights, perhaps even a maintainance agency and police force must have been available as well as technological know how. (Braidwood, 1952, p.39)

This was the first great economic revolution—an agricultural revolution—in man's control over nature, and gave rise to the great civilizations of ancient times.

The improvement of agricultural productivity meant an increase of population in these favoured places. Hitherto fertility was high and unchecked but mortality was also high. After the first agricultural revolution, mortality declined; even though the margin for growth was still small, but when stretched over centuries, it gave rise to the large populations of countries like India and China. The growth of population was subject to long cycles of growth and decline, corresponding to the rise and fall of great empires. To these societies, it was a matter of survival to maintain high levels of fertility, but they also evolved elaborate rules about marriage, child-bearing and abstinence to keep fertility below the biologically maximum level, rules which still prevail as part of traditional values and customs in LDCs.

Even with this development, the quantity of food that each family could grow was little more than was needed for its own consumption; therefore, most of the population was engaged in agriculture. But the small surplus that existed gave rise to a variety of non-agricultural occupations for people who managed to exact the surplus from the farmers. The principal index of the strength of an economy, which survived down to the time of the Physiocratic economists, was the taxable surplus of the agricultural sector. This was mainly reflected in the splendour of royal courts, the size of their armies, and the building of vast temples and monuments and a few great cities. There were also significant advances in the arts, in science and mathematics, and in philosophy, which spread to the whole world so slowly that their origins are largely forgotten.

Economic activities of these early societies were highly organized, on the basis of rigid customary laws which individuals had to obey, rather than on the basis of a market economy (Hicks, 1969, Chapter 2). The traditional customs were mainly oriented towards the preservation of society as a whole from the disasters to which it was prone; in return, there was social concern for alleviating distress on the part of any of its members rather than for the success of particular enterprising individuals. Superimposed on the customary economy, there was a command economy, based on feudal landlords, a priestly order or a strong military authority. Sometimes this command society became an empire in which a central court ruled vast areas through a bureaucracy. Much of ancient history was the story of the rise and fall of such empires.

In societies organized on the basis of custom and command, there was little room for technological change. The main object of their organization was the maintenance of social stability and many features of these societies, especially their division into classes and castes, served this object. Arrangements which started out as a way of preserving a technology evolved over a long period became in course of time the means of stifling change, so that these societies became stationary states. As Adam Smith (1776, p.106) was to remark,

> China seems to have been long stationary, and had probably long ago acquired that full complement of riches that is consistent with the nature of its laws and institutions.

The prospect of change depended on the rise of a market economy. In the ancient societies, there was a certain amount of trade but under the primitive conditions of transport, it was confined to luxury goods, goods of small bulk and high value.

> The quantitative significance of these luxury trades turns out to be remarkably small when one thinks of the romance and blood and misery which have been attached to them. (Lewis, 1978, p.143)

A significant development was the emergence of the craftsman who produced manufactures, not for a master as in the command economy but for the market.

The further development of the mercantile economy took place through the city states of Europe.

> The fact that European civilisation has passed through a city-state phase is the principal key to the divergence between the history of Europe and the history of Asia. The city state of Europe is a gift of the Mediterranean. (Hicks, 1969, p.38)

The rise of the city state led to an increase in international trade. The leadership in international trade moved from the Mediterranean city states to other countries—Spain, Portugal, Holland, France and Britain—as these countries progressed in the science of navigation and their naval command of the sea. In their hands, improvements in the weapons of war, geographical discoveries in the New World and of new sea routes to the Old and the need to establish and protect trading posts abroad led to the colonization of many tropical countries by European powers.

This expansion of international trade brought European countries in close contact with the tropical countries, some of which had developed over longer periods of civilization and whose skills were viewed with admiration and envy. There was little difference in standards of living between the European and tropical countries; if anything, the difference was often in favour of the tropical countries. While the expansion of trade brought many new products to Europe, it also created a ferment in the European countries to produce goods to be exchanged for these products. In fact, what was prized most by the European powers was the inflow of precious metals obtained from the tropical countries by pillage or colonial exactions and by trade; this inflow of precious metals, used as the basis of money supply, may have led to an increase in economic activity. Economic policy became governed by the mercantilist philosophy which laid down an elaborate system of restrictions especially on import trade.

The economic and social organization of production, evolved over a long period of time, has remained as a traditional force among most peoples living in the tropical countries of the world. But a small group of countries broke away from this traditional system, because of a remarkable development which occurred during the middle of the eighteenth century.

4.2 Modern Economic Growth: The Origins

At that time, there occurred in Britain a major breakthrough from an agrarian handicraft economy to one dominated by industry and mechanization. This was the Industrial Revolution. It was 'Prometheus unbound'.

> in the span of scarce two lifetimes, [it] transformed the life of Western man, the nature of his society and his relationship to the other peoples of the world. The heart of the Industrial Revolution was an inter-related succession of technological changes. The material advances took place in three areas: (1) there was a substitution of mechanical devices for human skills; (2) inanimate power—in particular, steam—took the place of human and animal strength; (3) there was a marked improvement in the getting and working of raw materials, especially in what are known as the metallurgical and chemical industries. (Landes, 1969, pp.1–2)

These changes in industrial technology were at the heart of a larger, more complex, process, which Kuznets has described as modern economic growth. It was a single long drawn-out process;

> there was an addition to the stock of human knowledge so major that its exploitation

and utilisation absorbed the energies of human societies and their growth for a period long enough to constitute an epoch in human history. (Kuznets, 1966, p.2)

The first century of modern economic growth was dominated by a spate of inventions in manufacturing industry, especially in the fields of textiles, iron and steam engines. Cotton textiles had previously been imported from India which held a position of primacy because of the skill of her craftsmen, especially in using cotton as warp in making cloth. The control of such textile imports under the reigning mercantilist philosophy posed an import substitution challenge which British inventors finally solved by matching with machines the deftness of Indian hands (Rostow, 1975). The mechanized techniques then spread to other industries. The need for machines promoted the metallurgical industry and the need for power to run these machines led to the development of steam power. In turn, the precision made possible by mechanical methods introduced the era of interchangeable parts, which increased the scale of production and the role of specialization. The stage was set for the triumph of the factory system with its mass employment of labour working to the rhythm of machines over the handicraft system of independent craftsmen.

To begin with, the inventions were made by practical men of affairs, in the form of small improvements to old ideas. Many of the mechanical devices had been invented earlier in other countries merely as objects of amusements, but the social conditions of Britain were more propitious for their application to economic production. In course of time, further inventions depended on a conscious and systematic application of basic scientific principles.

Whereas any intelligent and observant person with a stroke of genius could invent the steam engine or the flying shuttle or the hot blast, innovation after 1880 for the most part needed something more than genius. It required scientific knowledge to develop electrical machinery, organic chemicals or workable internal combustion engines. To put the matter differently, academic science contributed next to nothing to the industrial revolution, and did not become entwined with industrial progress until after 1880. (Lewis, 1978, p.129)

The application of the new techniques was accompanied by a high rate of investment. Capital accumulation is therefore often thought of as the driving force of the system. But it was the profitability of the technology that induced the accumulation of capital. The process of economic expansion that took place may therefore be likened to a race in which capital accumulation was constantly trying to catch up with technological progress. There was also a rapid increase in population but this did not pose any handicap when the rate of economic growth was so rapid. Unlike the present situation in LDCs the rapid growth of population was even looked upon with approval, for it kept up the spirits of entrepreneurs.

The changes involved in modern economic growth were not only technological; their exploitation required 'much social invention' as well. Under the pressure of the technological progress, there were major changes in the economic institutions of society. The forces released by the new inventions could not operate under the restrictions imposed by the previous mercantilist philosophy. The rise of classical economics in Britain paved the way for a new freedom for the individual in economics affairs, whose result was 'to multiply the points of creativity' (Landes, 1969, p.19; see also Section 5.1 below).

4.3 Modern Economic Growth: The Diffusion

Modern economic growth began in Britain in the middle of the eighteenth century. It then spread to other countries of Europe and to European settlements overseas in North America and Australasia. The beginning of modern economic growth is sometimes explained in terms of a stages theory, i.e. the theory that there is a uniform sequence of stages of growth which each country can go through. But, in historical fact, the changes associated with modern economic growth were initially brought about by a process of diffusion of the new technology and the associated institutions, first developed in Britain, and then adapted and further developed by the imitating countries. The diffusion process was due partly to the actions taken by the governments and partly to the efforts of individuals.

The role of governments was mainly to ensure greater freedom for the efforts of individuals adopting the new technology for industrial production and to provide the infrastructure and institutions needed for that purpose. The governments in some countries, especially in western Europe, responded in this way very quickly and modern economic growth was established in these countries without much delay. In other countries, in south and east Europe, the

> governments long continued to be dominated by backward landed aristocracies, hostile in spirit to industrialisation, which menaced their political power and threatened to deprive them of their labour force. (Lewis, 1978, p.167)

and modern economic growth was delayed much longer.

The speed with which modern economic growth was diffused from country to country varied with the extent of economic contact. The early history of modern economic growth is full of references to the international economic influences in these countries. A particularly significant factor was the movement of people rather than the movement of goods or capital (Arndt, 1954), most significantly the movement of fifty million people out of Europe (Lewis, 1978a, p.14). In the early stages, the technology to be borrowed was relatively simple and was easily diffused by the migration of skilled workers from the more advanced to the less advanced of these countries.

As in Britain, the onset of modern economic growth in the other countries to which it spread occurred as a sharp discontinuity in economic trends. Hence, this stage has been described as a 'take-off' by Rostow (1960) and as a 'great 'spurt' by Gerschenkron (1962). The take-off concept was defined in terms of the growth of the economy as a whole, but according to Gerschenkron, the discontinuity was mainly in industrial production. While the take-off was considered as one of five stages of growth—a 'definite pentametric rhythm'—which occurred in a definite sequence, Gerschenkron has shown that the spurt in industrial production occurred in countries at different levels of backwardness and was influenced by that factor. The historical experience of European industrialization was that the more backward an economy at the time of the great spurt,

(i) the sharper the initial 'kink' in the curve of industrial output and the more sustained was the following great spurt of industrialization;
(ii) the greater was the stress on producers' goods as against consumers' goods;
(iii) the larger was the scale of industrial plant and enterprise;
(iv) the greater was the pressure upon the levels of consumption of the population;
(v) the less active was the role performed by agriculture as a market for industrial goods and as an area of increasing productivity of labour, and
(vi) the more active—up to a point—the role of banks, and beyond that point, the role of the state—as a promoter of industrial development.

(Gerschenkron, 1962, pp.53–4).

One important difference between Britain and other countries to which modern economic growth spread was that Britain was the leader in industrialization and other countries had to promote their industries in the face of competition of imports from Britain. Therefore, the governments of the late-comers to industrialization adopted various protectionist measures to promote their nascent industries. It was therefore not an accident that the case for tariff protection, especially the infant industry argument, was advanced by economists of the late-industrializing countries, such as List in Germany and Hamilton in the United States, while the classical economists of Britain were preaching the virtues of free trade.

The next major step was the diffusion of modern economic growth to Japan, a country outside the mainstream of European culture, at the time of the Meiji Restoration of 1871, when the country was opened up to the outside world. The industrialization of Japan was achieved, not so much by the migration of European workers to that country, but by the Japanese workers who had travelled to the more advanced countries in a deliberate strategy of imitation of the new technology. Further, Japan could not, under the peace terms imposed by the American forces, rely on protectionist policies to promote its new industries. She achieved this instead by a remarkable collaboration of the State and corporate business, which has survived to the present day. Almost every modern Japanese industry owed its establishment to State initiative. In the late nineteenth century, the government carried out half the investment in the country (Lockwood, 1954). There were other differences; e.g. unlike Britain and other European countries, the landlords of Japan played a significant part in industrial investments and have therefore been described as 'dualistic landlords' (Fei and Ranis, 1964).

There was some diffusion of modern economic growth to Russia before World War I along the same pattern as to other countries of Europe. A great spurt in industry occurred in that country in the period 1890–1914 but this was not sustained during World War I and the disturbed conditions following the Revolution of 1917. The industrialization of Russia was resumed after the Soviet government was well established, but this time under central planning in a series of Five Year Plans. Even then, in the early stages, it was based on extensive borrowing of technology from the western countries.

In countries which had an adequate level of agricultural productivity, modern economic growth would have spread under the influence of market forces, especially in the early days when the gap between the advanced and the backward countries was relatively small. But even countries with an initial disadvantage could have overcome it by pursuing a more active policy to promote modern economic growth, as Japan was able to do. In other countries, as Lewis (1967a, pp.145–6) has said,

> when all is said in extenuation, including the smallness of the agricultural surplus, a failure of will remained. The tropical countries and the backward countries of Europe shared a common obstacle: reactionary landed aristocracies more interested in tribute than in growth; vested interests more interested in cheap imports than in industrialization; governments steeped in *laissez-faire* or positively hostile to domestic manufacturing for reasons of imperial power or agricultural domination.

In this failure of will, the fact that most of the tropical countries were under the colonial domination of European powers played a crucial role. The early phase of colonialism was a grim record of loot and disorganization but this was before modern economic growth was well established in the DCs and before cheap transport had brought all countries into close economic contact. Thereafter, the colonial governments, acting primarily in the interests of the people of the metropolitan countries, failed to diffuse modern economic growth in the tropical countries, but instead encouraged these countries to follow the trade option, discussed in the following section.

4.4 Modern Economic Growth: The Limit of Diffusion

After modern economic growth spread from Britain to Europe and European settlements overseas and then to Japan and Russia, its further diffusion came to a stop. From a long-term historical perspective, this is the main reason for the division of the world today between DCs to which modern economic growth diffused and LDCs to which it did not. Thereafter, a central question of development economics is why this type of growth did not diffuse to the present-day LDCs. In answering this question, Lewis (1976a, p.152) has pointed out that,

> The industrial revolution in north-west Europe and the United States offered the rest of the world not one opportunity but two; an opportunity to follow the example by

applying the new technology and new systems of organisation in agriculture and industry; and an opportunity to trade. The fundamental weakness of the tropical countries was that they concentrated on the trade option instead of taking up the challenge to revolutionise their agricultural and industrial technologies.

In this present section, we shall consider why LDCs failed to choose the option to follow the example of the DCs and in the next, we consider why the trade option they followed did not lead to faster development.

The failure of modern economic growth to diffuse to the LDCs is most often explained by the absence of certain 'pre-requisites' in these countries. These pre-requisites are usually defined as a higher level of income to begin with, a more conscious control of fertility, a more equal distribution of income, a higher rate of saving, a more favourable attitude to science, etc. Rostow (1960, p.17) actually speaks of the small group of countries that experienced take-off as 'in a sense, born free'. But even among these 'free born' countries there were many which were backward in respect of the 'pre-requisites' listed above and used various devices to substitute for the missing 'pre-requisites' so that as Gerschenkron (1963, p.166) says,

> what passes in modern discussion under the name of pre-conditions (such as the emergence of entrepreneurs, investment in fixed and working capital or employment of hired labour) is not in the nature of pre-conditions at all but the very stuff economic development or industrialisation is made of and that what is looked for to serve as a pre-requisite or a cause of industrial development comes into being as its effect.

A more significant factor than those which have usually been considered as the pre-conditions for the discussion of modern economic growth was the level of agricultural productivity. It was in this respect that there was a great difference between Europe and the tropical countries, a difference which had a number of effects. First, the low agricultural productivity of the tropics inhibited the diffusion of modern economic growth because it limited the market for industrial goods (see Section 9.6 for an analysis). Secondly, it also affected the movement of people between countries. As was pointed out in the last section, one of the means by which modern economic growth was diffused to many DCs was the movement of people from the more advanced countries, taking with them the new techniques and the new institutions. Most of this migration was to the temperate countries which have now become DCs. This was partly because the temperate countries were less densely populated and could therefore absorb more immigration compared with the tropics. But a more important reason was the high productivity of labour in agriculture in the temperate countries which could support a European wage level while the much lower agricultural productivity of the tropics meant a wage level which could only attract migration from such poor and overpopulated countries as India and China (Lewis, 1978a, pp.14–16). In the case of Japan, there was little immigration from Europe but there was a rapid increase of agricultural productivity on the one hand and a substantial flow of Japanese people to Europe who brought back the new techniques to Japan.

4.5 The Trade Option of the LDCs

Instead of following the example of modern economic growth which was being established in the DCs, the LDCs chose to follow what Lewis (1976a) has termed the 'trade option'. There were a number of reasons for this. First was the revolutionary change in ocean transport which halved transport costs in the second half of the nineteenth century. Second was the growing demand for tropical products resulting from the growth of incomes and industrial production in the DCs. Third was the pattern of development in the tropical countries by their colonial governments acting in the interests of the metropolitan countries. This was partly the result of the free trade regimes established by the colonial governments, especially between each metropolitan country and its tropical colonies, with the support of the prevailing economic philosophy of the times. It was also partly due to the role of colonial governments in developing institutions and infrastructure in their tropical dependencies for the specific purpose of promoting exports of primary products. (A comparative study of the colonial experience of ten countries, using econometric techniques and concentrating particularly on the impact of government, has been made by Birnberg and Resnick, 1975).

The result of following the trade option has been described by Lewis (1969, 1976a, 1978a Chapter 7). Between 1883 and 1913, world trade in primary products grew at 3.1 per cent per annum in real terms, i.e. at about 80 per cent of the growth of industrial production in the DCs. Some countries achieved even more spectacular growth of their exports; e.g. under the influence of growing world trade 'Burma emerged with break-neck speed to become the world's largest exporter of rice' (Bernardelli, 1952). The growth of exports was reflected in correspondingly high growth rates of national income; this was the historical parallel of the experience of LDCs since World War II.

The rapid growth of exports of primary products by the tropical countries was associated with a number of circumstances which affected their economic growth. First the growth of these exports was brought about by a concentration of infrastructure and institutions in the export sector; hence the provision of these facilities for the development of the domestic economy of the tropical colonies was neglected. Second, the increased production of most primary products for export was not based on an improvement of technology but rather on the 'vent for surplus' provided by trade using hitherto under-utilized resources of land, natural resources and labour (Myint, 1958; see also Chapter 10 below). Third, the economic growth that the tropical countries achieved by the rapid growth of their exports was dependent on economic growth in the DCs, which provided the demand for these exports; hence this growth was not self-sustained and slackened when the industrial countries went into a prolonged depression in the 1930s. Fourth, the terms of trade of the tropical countries deteriorated because of their failure to increase productivity in food (see Section 10.3 below for an analysis of this aspect) so that in spite of the rapid growth of exports in real terms, their purchasing power in terms of imports grew more slowly. Fifth, the tropical countries generally had surpluses in their trade balances, which were either used to pay for the changes of colonial government (see Ganguli, 1965, for a study of the Indian 'drain theory') or accumulated in the metropolitan countries. Finally, to the extent that the exports were used to buy imports, these imports were in the form of manufactures from the more advanced industrial countries, which further hindered the industrial development of the tropical countries.

Because of these consequences of the 'trade option', the LDCs emerged into independence as underdeveloped countries in spite of trade with the developed world. This has led to some writers of the so-called 'dependency' school to argue that economic underdevelopment in today's LDCs is due to their economic contact with the DCs i.e. that there has been a process of progressive underdevelopment in the LDCs as *a consequence of* the process of development in the DCs (e.g. Frank, 1967). This view has been summarized by Wilber and Jameson (1979, p.26) thus:

> The simplest way to understand the meaning of underdevelopment in dependency theory is to see it as a process whereby an underdeveloped country, characterised by subsistence agriculture and domestic production, progressively becomes integrated as a dependency into the world market through trade or investment. Its production becomes geared to the demands of the world market and particularly of the developed countries, with a consequent lack of integration between the parts of the domestic economy. Thus both agriculture and industry become export oriented.

In fact, however, the idea of economic dependency originated in the temperate countries of European settlement, which have now become some of the richest countries of the world. This has led Lewis (1976a, p.150) to argue that 'it was not dependency that made [the tropical countries] poor. If dependency made the temperate settlements among the richest countries in the world, why would it have made the tropics poor?' The poverty of the LDCs at present is not the result of the trade option alone, but of this trade option combined with internal factors which were responsible for the failure of modern economic growth to diffuse to these countries. In order to study the nature of these factors, we consider the concept of development in more detail in the next chapter.

PART II

Development: Concept and Policies

CHAPTER 5

The Concept of Development

The last three chapters were mainly descriptive and provided a general account of the present state and recent trends in the economic conditions of LDCs compared with DCs along with an historical account of the division of the world into two such widely differing groups of countries. The later chapters of this book aim to provide a framework for policy to deal with the economic problems of LDCs, especially those which have opted for a system of mixed economy. This framework is based on a sharp distinction between policies to promote development on the one hand and policies to promote growth and improve income distribution on the other. For this purpose, Section 5.1 introduces a definition of the concept of development. It is then argued that development so defined can be advanced in the LDCs by policies to expand education and infrastructure and to improve the economic institutions of LDCs. Some general features of these policies are discussed in Sections 5.2 to 5.4, and the broad strategy of development to which they lead is discussed in Section 5.5.

The concepts of growth and development are often confused with each other but many writers have also attempted to draw a distinction between them. Appendix 5.1 gives a review of the discussion of these concepts in the literature. One of the main problems of LDCs is the persistence of mass poverty, but this problem and the policies needed to deal with it have been neglected because of the confusion between the concepts of growth and development. Especially to blame has been the tendency to describe the economic conditions of countries in terms of aggregate statistics of production. Speaking as recently as 1950, Viner (1953, p.100) claimed:

> Were I to insist, however, that the reduction of mass poverty be made a crucial test of the realisation of economic development, I would be separating myself from the whole body of literature in this field. In all the literature on economic development, I have not found a single instance where statistical data in terms of aggregates and of averages have not been treated as providing adequate tests of the degree of achievement of economic development. I know, moreover, of no country which regards itself as underdeveloped which provides itself with the statistical data necessary for the discovery of whether or not growth in aggregate national wealth and in per capita income are associated with decrease in the absolute or even relative extent to which crushing poverty prevails.

What is needed therefore is an alternative measure of development which focusses on the circumstances of the individual human beings involved. Some considerations leading towards such a measure are discussed in Appendix 5.2 to this chapter.

5.1 An Interpretation of Development

While there is considerable controversy over the concept of development which differentiates DCs from LDCs, there is near unanimity about which countries are developed and which are not. It has been said that development is like a giraffe, difficult to define but easy to recognize. It is therefore tempting to define the concept by the equation:

development = developed country *minus* less-developed country

i.e. to define development as the sum of all the differences between the two groups of countries. But among all these differences, some are *causal* in the sense that they have led to affluence in the DCs and poverty in the LDCs, while others are only *consequential* and result from differences in levels of economic well-being. Policies which seek to remove the consequential differences without dealing with the causal ones will not advance development in the LDCs. Much of the controversy over the development concept revolves around which of the differences between DCs and LDCs should be identified as causal factors crucial to development.

If we contemplate the present differences between DCs and LDCs and the differences in their recent histories at a somewhat superficial level, it is easy to assign two main causes: the higher level of investment in DCs over many decades and the vigorous adoption of improved scientific technologies, which contrast with the relatively static production methods in LDCs. But we have to go deeper to find more fundamental causes which will in turn explain these superficial differences. At this deeper level, various possibilities have been advanced. Some have sought the fundamental explanation in differences in natural resources, some in climate, some even in racial characteristics. None of these is satisfactory. A far more convincing explanation lies in the gradual emergence in the now developed countries of a profound change in the economic psychology and the mode of behaviour of the bulk of the population. It is this change which characterized the beginnings of modern economic growth described in the last chapter.

This change has been described by Hicks (1977, p.182) as 'the emergence of economic man'. It was described in more detail by Marshall (1961, p.5) thus:

> The economic conditions of modern life, though more complex, are in many ways more definite than those of earlier times. Business is more clearly marked off from other concerns, the rights of individuals as against others and as against the community are more sharply defined; and above all the emancipation from custom, and the growth of free activity, of constant forethought and restless enterprise, have given a new precision and a new prominence to the causes that govern the relative values of different things and different kinds of labour . . . There is no one term that will express these characteristics adequately. They are . . . a certain independence and habit of forecasting the future and of shaping one's course with reference to distant aims.

As there is no established term in the literature to describe the emergence of such behaviour, we shall appropriate the term development to describe it.

According to this view, the essential difference between DCs and LDCs lies in the attitudes and behaviour of people in their economic activities. In the LDCs, the economic behaviour that characterized early history has survived to a great extent. It is dominated by custom and tradition evolved over long periods of time. On the one hand, the technology of production was embodied in the customs relating to productive activities and served to transmit the technology from generation to generation. On the other hand, customs also governed the relations among individuals and the organization of society into rigid social classes corresponding to their roles in productive activity. In this way, customary rules of great binding force served to keep society stable during periods when technology was relatively constant. By the same token, they also obstructed the adoption of new technology when it became available.

In the countries which have now become DCs, this customary behaviour has given way to what Marshall described as the conditions of modern life. Various aspects of this change have been described as the growth of individualism, capitalism, the rise of the market (Hicks, 1977), the technological revolution, etc. The essential characteristic of this change was a break-up of the social barriers which confined the individual to a particular economic role in society and freed the individual to experiment with new ideas and new techniques of production as they became available with the advance of science. More and more production flowed through the impersonal working of markets and there was an increase in specialization. The new freedom encouraged individuals to make their own decisions about alternative courses of action and to take a longer view in doing so.

This view of the difference in modes of individual economic behaviour as the essential difference between DCs and LDCs and as the essential part of the change which occurred in the DCs and led to their present state of material affluence does not find a prominent place in current discussions of development. The main reason is that these discussions are dominated by neo-classical economic theory, which derives its central assumptions from the relatively recent conditions of the DCs, if not from an axiomatic view of human behaviour, rather than from an historical perspective of their evolution in the past two centuries. In applying these assumptions to the LDCs also, the theory assumes away this difference in modes of behaviour.

For example, the assumption of maximizing behaviour ignores the extent to which people in LDCs are influenced by tradition and typically limited in their knowledge of technological possibilities, in their willingness to undertake the risks involved in adopting them, and in the time horizon within which they make their choices. When western people first came into contact with the people of the tropical countries, they tended to attribute differences in behaviour and values to climatological differences between regions and even racial differences between peoples; this means that policy efforts to change traditional behaviour in LDCs will have no effect. Nowadays, it is more common to deny that there are such differences in behaviour. Some authors (e.g. Bauer and Yamey, 1957; Schultz, 1964; and Yotopoulos and Nugent, 1976) have deduced maximizing behaviour from the efficiency with which resources are allocated in traditional systems of production. It is true that resources are often quite efficiently allocated in some traditional systems, but this is the result of trial and error over long periods of time rather than of maximizing behaviour on the part of individuals. The real test is the extent to which individuals are able and willing to adopt new techniques of production rapidly; it is here that behaviour in LDCs has been most deficient. Similarly, the other assumption of the efficient working of market forces ignores the extent to which markets in LDCs are highly fragmented by a severe lack of modern infrastructure on the one hand and various institutional obstacles to market access for many sections of the people on the other, and hence fail to utilize existing resources, especially labour, more fully. The result of these basic assumptions of neo-classical economics is to focus the explanation of poverty in the LDCs on their factor endowments, i.e. on the hypothesis that people are 'poor but efficient' rather than on the differences in the modes of behaviour, especially in the adoption of new and more productive techniques of production.

The difference in modes of behaviour is not something which is fixed permanently in the characteristics of the people or the location of the two groups of countries. What we have described as traditional behaviour was widespread in the presently developed countries in their early history. In recent times, in the countries which are on the whole less-developed, many people have adopted more modern behaviour. Modes of behaviour, therefore, change over time. The speed with which modern behaviour is adopted by large sections of the people can be accelerated in a number of ways. These measures may be broadly classified into three categories. First, there are measures to promote greater knowledge of the economic and technical opportunities available to individuals and more favourable attitudes to exploiting these opportunities; this is the task of education. Second, there is the physical infrastructure needed to promote the use of modern techniques and the cheap mobility of people, ideas and goods in order to realize and maintain the active innovative motivation of the educated individual. Third, there are the economic institutions of modern societies which offer individuals the incentives to invent and utilize new techniques of production and to enter into new types of specialization by fuller access to market opportunities irrespective of race, caste or class.

These measures are discussed in more detail in Chapters 6–8. It is there pointed out that the present endowment of educated people, infrastructure and economic institutions is very low in the LDCs compared with the DCs. A rapid increase in this endowment will affect economic growth in these countries by influencing the economic behaviour of their people in their productive activities and economic relationships. It is therefore convenient to distinguish them from ways of increasing aggregate production by growth in the stock of productive resources. As we have defined development in terms of modern behaviour, these measures to promote such behaviour may be described as development policies. Some general features of the relationship between these policies and the growth of production are discussed in Sections 5.2–4, and their implications for a broad strategy of development are drawn in Section 5.5.

5.2 'Duties of the Sovereign'

The first main feature of the way these development policies affect growth of production is through the externalities involved in them. For example, the presence of an educated person in a society makes a difference to the whole society; hence the benefits that a society derives from the education of a large proportion of its members are greater than the sum of the benefits that each person derives from his or her education. (See Chaudhri, 1968, for a method of calculating such externalities and the evidence from India.) These externalities are even more obvious in the case of infrastructure and institutional improvements.

It is because of such externalities that these measures were included by Adam Smith (1776, p.214) in his list of the 'Duties of the Sovereign':

> The third and last duty of the sovereign or commonwealth is that of erecting and maintaining those public institutions and those public works which, though they may be in the highest degree advantageous to a great society, are, however, of such a nature, that the profit could never repay the expence to any individual or small number of individuals, and which it therefore cannot be expected that any individual or small number of individuals should erect or maintain.

To stress the importance of this duty, Marshall (1925, p.338) applied to the State the slogan that Adam Smith had applied to the people:

A new emphasis is given to the watchword *Laissez faire*: Let everyone work with all his might; and most of all let the Government arouse itself to do that work which is vital and which none but the Government can do efficiently. For instance, public authorities are just beginning to awake to the urgency of their duties with regard to mapping out in advance the ground plans on which cities should expand—a task more vital to the health and happiness of coming generations than any other which can be accomplished by authority with so little trouble, while private effort is powerless for it. So I cry, '*Laissez faire*—let the State be up and doing'.

Because of their externalities, these measures have become the responsibility of governments. Though originally emerging without much effort or encouragement from the State, education and infrastructure have gradually become almost entirely its exclusive preserve. In the case of free economic institutions, the State in LDCs has often acted to inhibit their emergence or to wreck them after they have appeared; the State can therefore promote such institutions by refraining from such adverse interventions. In some cases, it can also take positive efforts to promote such institutions.

5.3 Development Policies as Long-Term Factors

The second main feature of development policies is the period over which they affect economic growth. When the stock of productive resources, such as land, labour and capital, is increased, the effects on the national product are felt in the relatively short period of a few years. But in the case of the development measures described above, it takes a much longer period, to be measured in decades rather than years, for their full effects to be felt. This is because they operate mainly through changes in the modes of economic behaviour of individuals, which are subject to a strong element of inertia. By the time a person reaches adult age, his mode of behaviour is largely fixed. Further, the future mode of behaviour of children is determined to a great extent by the ideas which they receive from their parents in the course of family life. Therefore, significant changes in modes of behaviour have to be introduced to people at a relatively young age outside their family life, and will affect economic growth only when they themselves reach adult working ages. The more strongly traditional modes of behaviour are entrenched in a society, the longer it will take to bring about modern behaviour on a large scale and thereby to influence economic growth.

In the case of the western countries, the beginnings of modern economic behaviour were built up over a very long period, dating back to their Renaissance, involving the gradual spread of modern scientific ideas. In most of these countries, the spread of a modern approach to economic life was not the result of deliberate policies of their governments but of private interest and initiative. Even after these countries embarked upon their modern economic growth and made a break with past trends of economic stagnation, the pursuit of development policies by their governments was mainly in response to the demand for them, as determined by the rate of economic growth. Even by the second half of the nineteenth century 'the rate of growth of the industrial core was low by modern standards' (Lewis, 1978, p.135), per capita income growth being only about one and a half per cent per annum. This was because new technologies had to be invented in these countries, and the rate of growth was ultimately constrained by the rate of such technological progress.

The LDCs at present have a much greater backlog of technological progress to catch up with. They must increase their capacity to exploit these technological opportunities. This they can do by adopting development policies which influence their modes of economic behaviour. Indeed they can move much faster than the DCs did in the early stages of their growth by a more deliberate pursuit of development policies rather than by following an imitative strategy. Even so, the full effects of such policies will only appear in the longer term of at least two or three decades.

5.4 Development Policies as Permissive Factors

While it is quite widely recognized nowadays that the development policies described above are the responsibility of governments, there is less agreement on the strategy that governments should follow in implementing these policies because of differing views of the relationship between these policies and economic growth. One approach that is implicit in the practice of some governments and the writings of some economists is to treat these measures as matters of 'social' rather than 'economic' development; with a higher priority assigned to what is considered as economic development, the resources allocated to social development are generally determined as a residual. Because of the chronic financial stringency facing LDC governments, this has led to a relatively slow implementation of development policies as defined in Section 5.1.

Another approach is to assume that the rate of growth of incomes is determined by other factors, such as the growth in the stock of productive resources, but that certain quantities of development factors are 'required' to achieve this rate of growth. Hence, the development factors are treated as 'missing components' for a given rate of growth, rather than as ways of influencing the rate of growth itself. The difference has been explained by Myint (1965, pp.210–1) for the case of education as follows:

> Only in so far as we can assume that the rate of economic growth is given from outside can we treat the role of the educational system passively as a supplier of this missing component required to sustain a given target rate of economic development. On the one hand, we may look upon the educational system as playing a passive role, trying to supply the different types of skilled manpower which will be required by a *given* pattern and rate of economic growth. On the other hand, we may look upon the education system as playing an active role, trying to transform the economic structure to accelerate the rate of economic growth.

Yet another approach is based on the assumption that development policies affect economic growth through the amount of productive resources used in implementing these policies, just as productive resources are used in directly productive activities. The allocation of resources for development policies is then determined by the techniques of cost–benefit analysis; for example, resources are to be allocated so as to equate the rates of return to investment in all uses including both development activities and directly productive activities. This is a case of applying a growth strategy to development problems. In practice, in applying the techniques of cost–benefit analysis to development activities, the benefits are often estimated without taking full account of the externalities and the long gestation periods involved. Further, this approach does not fully take account of the indirect way in which development activities affect economic growth. Development policies are provided by governments, while, in mixed economies, the productive activities they assist are largely carried out in the private sector. The contribution of the development activities to growth of incomes is essentially of a permissive nature. As explained by Kuznets (1973, p.247), modern economic growth is ultimately based on

> advancing technology and the institutional and ideological adjustments that it demands. Advancing technology is the *permissive* source of economic growth, but it is only a potential, a necessary condition, in itself not sufficient.

Because of the permissive nature of development measures, the most appropriate strategy for using these measures deliberately to promote growth is to implement them ahead of demand. Some general aspects of such a strategy are worked out in the next section.

5.5 A Strategy for Development Policies

In such an alternative strategy, we note first that the more widely these development measures are spread among the population and influence their economic behaviour, the greater will be the effect on growth and the wider the distribution of the benefits from growth. Therefore, the ultimate targets of the strategy should be to expand education and infrastructure and to improve economic institutions so that these facilities are available to all members of society. For example, one of these targets may be defined as the provision of education to all members of society to the fullest extent that each can absorb it. Another target would be to provide modern infrastructure, such as transport, communications and power, so that it is available to all members of the population and all sectors of the economy. Finally, all members of society should have access to modern economic institutions, especially to efficient markets for all goods and services.

The qualitative aspects of these targets may vary a great deal, but as far as their quantitative aspects are concerned, the targets are essentially finite, in contrast to people's objectives in terms of their income and expenditure levels. In the case of these latter, people's aspirations are constantly being pushed upwards as individuals seek to improve their position relative to others. (See Hirsch, 1977, for an excellent discussion of this tendency.) But in the case of the development measures, the targets for government action can be defined in finite terms and hence planned for in their totality.

When development measures are implemented in response to the demand for them, the rate at which they are implemented will be limited by past trends of growth or other factors affecting growth. But in the alternative strategy of providing them ahead of demand, they may be implemented as rapidly as governments are able to mobilize the financial and administrative resources needed. The pursuit of development measures on this strategy will be independent of the prevailing trends and at the same time have their full effect in raising the rates of growth in the future, and hence in raising the standard of living of the mass of the population to a desired level in a much shorter period.

However, even the most rapid implementation of these measures to reach the ultimate targets laid down above will take a considerable period of time. This is partly because of the large gap between these targets and the present low level of the development activities in the LDCs. It is also partly because the development measures themselves are time-consuming. Hence these policies are eminently suitable for long-term planning. (See Chapter 15 for a discussion of planning techniques.)

Given the targets to be achieved in the relatively long period, we must next consider the method of implementing them in each successive short period. Some of the approaches to this problem relate the implementation of these measures in each short period to the economic conditions prevailing in that short period in the rest of the economy. In the alternative strategy of implementing these measures as rapidly as possible, the short-term policy is determined by working backwards from the final targets laid down above, on the basis of the technical relationships that have to be maintained within each system of development measures. Some applications are illustrated in the following chapters.

Generally, the above approach to short-term policy will mean that the provision of development measures may be greater than can be fully absorbed by the rest of the economy at present rates. The clearest example of this situation is open unemployment at some higher levels of education. Under such conditions, rather than slowing down the implementation of the development measures to suit the prevailing conditions in the rest of the economy, a more appropriate strategy is to adopt other policies to adjust the rest of the economy to the rate at which the development measures are implemented, as far as this is possible.

This approach to the provision of development measures will make great demands on the resources of LDCs, especially the financial resources of governments. LDCs can therefore be greatly helped to follow this approach by the flow of more aid from the DCs specifically addressed to provision of these development measures. But even when LDC governments are assisted by more generous financial aid, their efforts to implement development measures will be constrained by other facts, such as, for example, their administrative capacity. If, as a result, LDCs are unable to implement these development measures throughout the economy and for all the people, we must consider the priorities they must assign to different sectors of the economy and to different sections of the population in phasing their development efforts in each successive short period. Some suggestions are made in Part III of this book based on the role of the various sectors of the economy in the growth process and the distribution of income among various sections of the population.

Appendix 5.1
Alternative Interpretations of Development

The term development is most frequently used to refer to the level of per capita national income, and its growth over time. To a considerable extent, this is due to the ready availability of statistical estimates of national income of varying degrees of reliability for a large number of countries. This tendency is deeply rooted in the literature, since it was first introduced by the classical economists as a measure of economic performance. Many authors use the terms growth and development interchangeably. For example, the *Encylopaedia of the Social Sciences* says, under the heading 'Economic Development' simply 'See Economic Growth'. Sometimes, the terms are distinguished only on the basis of geography; e.g. Maddison (1970, p.15) says, 'the raising of income levels is generally called economic growth in rich countries, and in poor countries it is called "economic development".' In terms of the definition proposed in Section 5.1, however, it was in the historical experience of the rich countries that development occurred, and led to the rapid growth of their incomes rather than in the contemporary poor countries.

In some versions, it is recognized that DCs and LDCs differ not only in the levels of their per capita incomes but also in the structure of their economies. However, it is then assumed that structural transformation is so tightly linked with growth of incomes that the latter can be identified with development. For example, Reynolds (1977, p.4) says:

> If one observes a sustained rise in per capita output, one can infer a number of other structural changes, including growing commercialisation of production, gradual improvement of markets, shifts in the composition of output by sector of origin, and a rise in savings and investment as a percentage of gross national product (GNP). The significance of rising per capita income is not just that it connotes the possibility of a rise in living standards, but also that it stands as a proxy for many associated aspects of economic change.

Although there is some relationship between some of these structural changes and the growth of per capita income, it is shown in Chapter 9 that it is not as strong a link as the above argument would imply.

Another persistent theme in the literature has been to take self-sustaining growth as the characteristic difference between DCs and LDCs, and hence to define development in terms of self-sustaining growth. In the words of Rostow (1960, p.7) speaking of countries which have become developed,

> Growth becomes its normal condition. Compound interest becomes built, as it were, into its habits and institutional structure.

Or as Millikan (1970, p.8) put it,

> The most important feature of the more developed countries, which distinguishes them from the less-developed ones, is not their relative affluence but rather the fact that they have exhibited over a period of several decades a capacity for sustained, built-in and reasonably steady annual growth in economic output per head of the population, amounting to two or three percentage points per year.

Self-sustaining growth is indeed a characteristic that distinguishes the DCs from the LDCs but what matters from a policy point of view is the cause of such growth, how it may be brought about in the LDCs, rather than just the statistical fact. We have argued in this chapter that the basic cause of self-sustaining growth is development as we have defined it, because it internalizes the engine of growth. But it is sometimes attributed to the efficiency with which resources are allocated to different uses, compared with the norm of competitive markets. Hence, for example, it has been claimed that

> Many problems in development can be reduced to misallocation problems in one form or another, and the development economist is concerned with devising feasible programs for improving allocation. Development occurs when misallocations are eliminated. (Neher, 1971, p.81)

If this is meant to refer to the allocation of directly productive resources to different sectors of production, it is not obvious that there is much difference between DCs and LDCs. Further, the costs of such misallocations, i.e. the difference between the actual national income and what would result under a competitive allocation, are quite small (Harberger, 1959) and anyway, improving resource allocation at any time will only have a once-over effect. Therefore, misallocations in this sense cannot explain the great contrast between DCs and LDCs.

More often, self-sustaining growth is attributed to a country's ability to save a sufficiently high proportion of its national income. Thus, the Pearson Commission (1969, p.125) interpreted the condition for self-sustaining growth as follows:

> The developing countries should generally become independent of the need for aid on concessional terms as soon as they can do without reducing their rate of growth below the six per cent level.

However, as argued in Chapter 9 below, the constraint on growth is not so much the rate of domestic savings as the productivity of capital; with more productive use of capital as a result of a higher level of development, funds for investment would be more readily available both from domestic and foreign sources.

In the pre-war literature on colonial policy and in the development literature of the early post-war years, the concept of development was applied to the physical natural resources of the poor countries. The process was interpreted to mean one of developing these recourses. (For a comparison of this transitive use of the verb 'develop' with its intransitive use by Hegel and Marx, see Arndt, 1981.) This interpretation has since proved awkward, because many poor countries did not have much natural resources, while countries which were already rich, such as the United States or Australia, would have to be counted as underdeveloped because their vast resources have not been fully exploited. Hence, Myint (1954) made a sharp distinction between the underdevelopment of physical resources on the one hand and the economic (as distinct from the cultural) backwardness of people, on the other. Nowadays, the rapid increase of national income in countries with generous natural resource endowments has been described as 'growth without development' (Clower *et al.*, 1966).

In the more recent literature on development, there has been a tendency to consider a more equal distribution of income, not only as one means of eradicating mass poverty, but as the definition of development itself. This view has been put most emphatically by Seers (1969) thus:

> The questions to ask about a country's development are therefore: what has been happening to poverty? What has been happening to unemployment? What has been happening to inequality? If all three of these have declined from high levels, then beyond doubt, this has been a period of development for the country concerned.

In Chapter 14, we will argue that a reduction of inequality by itself will have little effect on the extent of poverty in most LDCs. It will also be argued (Section 13.5) that there is no simple relationship between poverty and unemployment.

The authors whose views were summarized above have generally been inclined to interpret development or the difference between DCs and LDCs, in terms of growth of national income or some part of it, or in terms of distribution. Others, however, have distinguished two types of factors involved in economic progress quite sharply, as we have done ourselves in Section 5.2 above. The earliest is, of course, the statement of Adam Smith himself (1776, p.106) in his description of China:

> In a country which had acquired that full complement of riches which the nature of its soil and climate, and its situation with respect to other countries, allowed it to acquire; which could therefore advance no further . . . both the wages of labour and the profits of stock would probably be very low . . . Perhaps no country has yet arrived at this degree of opulence. China seems to have been long stationary, and had probably long ago acquired that full complement of riches that is consistent with the nature of its laws

and institutions. But this complement may be much inferior to what, with other laws and institutions, the nature of its soil, climate and situation might admit of.

Here a distinction is made between riches due to a country's 'laws and institutions' and its 'soil, climate and situation' which corresponds to the distinction we have made between development and growth in the light of modern economic conditions.

More recently, Singer and Ansari (1977, pp.40–47) say:

The developing countries are not all poor countries, though the overwhelming majority of them certainly are. We must carefully avoid, therefore, using the increase in per capita income as an *identification* of development. This would be an extremely narrow view. Development consists of much more than an increase in per capita income; it is desired for many and complex reasons of which the increase in per capita income is merely one. An increase in per capita income, reflecting an increase in production, in many ways is merely the end product of factors or forces, which cause economic development, rather than its cause or essence . . . The Third World countries . . . cannot overcome the problem of underdevelopment as long as efforts are not made to bridge the technological gap which separates them from the richer countries, whatever the short-run windfall gains that may occur.

Similarly, Lewis (1970, pp.5, 26) has commented on recent events as follows:

The prosperity of the underdeveloped countries is still peripheral to that of the industrial world, whereas in a developed country, the engine of growth is internal . . . In the language now sometimes used, the less-developed countries have *grown* remarkably over the last twenty years but their *development* is less impressive. Output has grown mainly in response to export demand, but the capacity to generate self-sustaining growth, influenced but not wholly determined by external factors, is still far off.

Kindleberger (1965, p.3) has suggested that the two terms be used to describe different processes thus:

Growth and development are often used synonymously in economic discussion and this usage is entirely acceptable. But where two words exist, there is point in seeking to draw a distinction between them. Implicit in general usage, and explicit in what follows, economic growth means more output and economic development implies both more output and changes in the technical and institutional arrangements by which it is produced. Growth may well imply not only more output, but also more inputs and more efficiency, i.e. an increase in output per unit of input. Development goes beyond these to imply changes in the structure of outputs and in the allocation of inputs by sectors. By analogy with the human being, to stress growth involves focusing on height or weight, while to emphasize development draws attention to the change in functional capacity—in physical coordination, for example, or learning capacity.

This distinction is well established in biological studies; for example according to Lowrey (1978, p.11):

The terms *growth* and *development* are often used interchangeably, and it is certainly true that each depends on the other for fruition. In the normal child each parallels the other, and any separation would be an artificial one. For convenience, however, we may distinguish between them. We restrict, when possible, the term *growth* to mean an increase in physical size of the whole or any of its parts. Growth, therefore, may be measured in terms of inches or centimetres and pounds or kilograms. It can be measured also in terms of metabolic balance, i.e. the retention of calcium and nitrogen by the body. *Development* is used to indicate an increase in skill and complexity of function. The individual develops neuromuscular control, he develops dexterity and he develops character. Maturation and differentiation are frequently used as synonyms for development. Used in this sense, it is evident that development is related to growth but is not the same.

On this analogy, to treat an LDC as simply a country with a low per capita income, as is done by those who identify development with growth, is to make the same mistake as to treat a child simply as a small adult.

A distinction between growth and development closely related to that of Section 5.2 was used by Schumpeter as the central point of his study of the historical experience of DCs. First, he makes a distinction between internal and external factors:

By 'development', therefore, we shall understand only such changes in economic life as are not forced upon it from without, but arise by its own initiative, from within. (Schumpeter, 1934, p.13)

Thus, he rules out from the concept of development the sort of changes that result from a country's external trade. Then, Schumpeter distinguishes the internal factors according to whether they refer just to an increase in the quantity of directly productive resources or whether they refer to a more productive use of a given quantity of resources.

We shall designate by the term growth, changes in population and in the sum total of savings plus accumulation. (Schumpeter, 1939, Vol.I, p.83)

Nor will the mere growth of the economy, as shown by the growth of population and wealth, be designated here as a process of development. (Schumpeter, 1934, p.63)

The slow and continuous increase in time of the national supply of productive means and of savings is obviously an important factor in explaining the course of economic history through centuries, but it is completely overshadowed by the fact that development consists primarily in employing existing resources in a different way, in doing new things with them, irrespective of whether these resources increase or not. In the treatment of shorter epochs, this is even true in a more tangible sense. Different methods of employment, and not savings and increases in the available quantity of labour, have changed the face of the economic world in the last fifty years. The increase of population especially but also of the sources from which savings can be made, was first made possible in large measure through the different employment of their existing means. (Schumpeter, 1934, p.68)

The essence of economic development consists in a *different* employment of *existing* services of labour and land. (Schumpeter, 1934, p.95)

[It] involves the setting up of a new production function. (Schumpeter, 1939, Vol.I, p.87)

Appendix 5.2
Towards a Measure of Development

One reason why the concepts of growth and development are so often confused with each other is that the same measure—the national income—is used for calibrating both processes, often simply because national income estimates are readily available for a large number of countries and have by now become widely understood.

In recent years, this measure has come under increasing criticism as an index of development. One of the main grounds for criticism is that it takes no account of the distribution of income. Therefore, attempts have been made to construct measures of growth taking account of distribution. An example is the suggestion of Chenery *et al.* (1974, p.39; see also I.L.O. 1972, p.106). In this proposal, they first calculate the growth rates g_i of incomes accruing to different income classes ($i = 1, 2, \ldots, k$). Then they point out that the growth rate G of total income is a weighted average of the growth rates of incomes of the various classes:

$$G = \Sigma w_i g_i, \qquad \text{(A5.2.1)}$$

where w_i is the proportion of total income initially accruing to the ith class, i.e. this measure gives more weight to the income growth of the richer classes. They therefore suggest using other measures giving a different set of weights to the income-growth rates of the various groups. One possibility is the set of equal weights. Then the overall growth rate becomes

$$G_e = \frac{1}{k}\Sigma g_i. \qquad \text{(A5.2.2)}$$

This measure can also be written as

$$1 + G_e = \frac{(1 + G)}{k}\sum\frac{(w_i')}{w_i}, \qquad \text{(A5.2.3)}$$

where w_i' is the share of the ith group in total income at the end of the period. This expression shows that the new index is a measure of both the growth of income and the change in distribution. It must be noted, however, that it is more sensitive to the changes in distribution than to the inequality at any point of time. It is easy to see from the above equations that if the incomes of all groups change at the same rate, i.e. if all g_is are equal, then $G_e = G$, i.e. the two indices coincide, however unequal the distribution of income may be.

In this approach, the weight given to the growth and the distribution aspects is somewhat haphazard, being the mathematical consequence of the weights given to the income-growth rates of the various groups. A better procedure of getting a composite index of the two objects, growth and distribution, may be to measure them separately and then combine them with weights chosen deliberately to reflect the importance attached to the two objectives from the social point of view.

However satisfactory or unsatisfactory may be such measures of the growth of a country and of changes in its income distribution, they are clearly unrelated to the concept of development as we have interpreted it. Development in our sense is not promptly reflected in the increase of national income. Economic growth is concerned with changes in the output of goods and services valued at certain prices; it is therefore measured by a monetary index, such as the national income. Development, on the other hand, is concerned with the attitudes and abilities of people, as influenced by education, access to infrastructure and the nature of institutions, for which there are no monetary measurements. Therefore, some writers have tried to devise a non-monetary index to measure development (e.g. Divatia and Bhatt, 1968; Adelman and Morris, 1971; McGranahan, D. V., *et al.*, 1972). The typical approach followed by these writers is to take a number of non-monetary indicators, such as educational stocks and flows, fertility and mortality rates, availability of physical and social infrastructure, etc., and compress them by various multivariate statistical techniques into a single composite index of development. The methods used are mainly chosen for their statistical convenience, such as e.g. the assumption of linear relationships and of equal weights. The resulting index is difficult to interpret or apply in practice.

Therefore, an alternative approach to the measurement of development may be defined as follows. The concept of development to which we have been led by the argument of this chapter is the pervasiveness of modern economic behaviour and the ability of people to absorb modern technology, based on education, infrastructure and institutions. On this view, a society can be considered more developed, the higher the education of its members, the greater the supply of infrastructure and the better its economic institutions for encouraging modern technology. Therefore, an appropriate measure of development is the proportion of the population of a country which has an adequate access to education, modern infrastructure and efficient institutions. A similar measure is already in vogue in the form of the proportion of the labour force in 'modern occupations' (Boserup, 1970, p.178). To calculate the measure suggested above, we must have certain norms by which to classify people according to whether or not they have adequate access to the various elements of development. There are no such norms widely accepted at present and even more important, there are not sufficient data for many countries, but once the merits of this measure of development are recognized, it will not be difficult to agree on some norms and to get the required data.

The conceptual basis of this measure of development is a very simple one, that can be widely understood by all persons concerned with development, though there are serious problems of quantifying it. By stressing the characteristics of people rather than the number of dollars worth of output, it helps to differentiate the concept of development sharply from that of growth. It also offers a ready guide to policies: development plans can set their targets in terms of this measure rather than in rates of growth of national income, which may not be entirely within the power of planning agencies to achieve. With targets set in the new form suggested above, policy makers have an additional principle for the allocation of public resources for promoting development. They can do this by estimating how different allocations will affect this measure of development. One advantage of the proposed measure is that, as its maximum is 100 per cent, it brings out the nature of development as a finite process unlike the growth process which can go on endlessly. Thus planners will be encouraged to take a total view of development and adopt appropriate long-term plans for its achievement.

CHAPTER 6

Education

The activities that governments can undertake to promote development, as defined in the last chapter, may be broadly divided into three components, namely, those dealing with the human agents, broadly described as education; those dealing with some physical aids to production, i.e. infrastructure, and those dealing with the economic institutions of society. The present chapter deals with the first of these, education.

The stock of knowledge in a society is embodied in its people and has to be transmitted from generation to generation. In the process, the stock of knowledge must also be increased in order to expand man's understanding of the world he lives in and to control the forces of nature to satisfy his wants more fully. This is the task of education. It is accomplished by schooling for young people and by training in the methods of production for older people.

Historically, there was little education for the mass of the people, except for some folklore passed on by word of mouth from parents to children. Most people entered the labour force at a very early age and learnt the arts of production from their parents mostly by imitation, so that they followed the occupations of their parents and there was little change in methods of production over long periods of time. Such education as there was consisted mostly of religious education, confined to a small section of the population, who were then venerated as the custodians of learning. In some countries, a minimum of literacy was also imparted to young people in the religious institutions of the country.

When modern economic growth began in the DCs, it involved innovations in many fields of production. To begin with, the innovations were made by practical men but as time went on, they were based on a systematic and conscious application of scientific principles. In order to promote this process, a modern system of education was introduced to impart a high level of literacy, numeracy and the basic elements of a scientific approach to natural and social phenomena to people at the age when their learning capacity was highest, and when their basic attitudes to life and work were being formed. The growth of such a modern system of education in the DCs was gradual, but after a long period of time it spread, until almost the entire population of primary and secondary school ages is now receiving universal and compulsory education in these countries.

In the LDCs colonized by western powers, the modern system of education was introduced to a small fraction of the population, primarily to serve the needs of public administration and a small enclave of modern sector establishments, especially those engaged in foreign trade. Therefore, at the time of their independence after World War II, most LDCs had only a low level of education on the average, much lower than that in the DCs. Since then, the educational systems of LDCs have been expanded rapidly by the newly established national governments. The nature of this expansion is discussed in Section 6.1; the next two sections deal with its causes and consequences; the final section is devoted to some issues of educational policy.

6.1 The Expansion of Education in LDCs

The extent of education in a country may be measured in two ways: one, the stock concept, is the level of educational attainment of the adult population, usually taken as 15 years and over, and the other, the flow concept, the rate at which young people go through the educational system, usually measured by enrolment ratios, i.e. the proportion of the population of various school-going ages enrolled in different levels of the educational system.

Among the stock measures of the educational level of a country, the most basic is the proportion of the population which is literate, i.e. can read and write. In 1960, it was estimated that the literacy rate among adults in LDCs was about 33 per cent; the rate had increased to about 55 per cent by 1976 (World Bank, *World Development Report, 1981*). The progress, however, was very unevenly distributed. For example, it was particularly low in the South Asian countries, having increased only from 22 to 26 in Bangladesh, from 28 to 36 in India, and from 15 to 24 in Pakistan.

The other stock measure of educational level is the average number of years of schooling received by the adult population. Most of the present population of DCs have gone through a period in which there was almost universal education up to the secondary level; therefore, the mean years of schooling in these countries must be above, say, 10 years. Comprehensive data are not available for the LDCs. The data for some Asian countries are summarized in Table 6.1.

Table 6.1 shows that even in countries like the Philippines and Sri Lanka, which had a tradition of high levels of education among LDCs, the stock of education is well below that in DCs. The position is much worse in other

Table 6.1 Means years of schooling in some Asian countries

Country/year	Males	Females	Total
Indonesia (1971)			
(population 10 years and over)			
National	3.3	2.1	2.5
Urban	5.1	3.6	4.4
Rural	2.9	1.8	2.3
India (1971)			
(population 10 years and over)			
National	2.4	1.0	1.7
Urban	4.6	2.6	3.7
Rural	1.8	0.6	1.2
Philippines (1971)			
(heads of households)			6.2
Sri Lanka (1969/70)			
National			
Urban	5.8	5.1	5.4
Rural & Estates	6.6	5.9	6.3
By age group:	5.7	4.9	5.2
5–14	4.8	4.8	4.8
15–19	6.9	6.7	6.8
20–24	7.2	6.7	6.9
25–34	6.8	5.8	6.3
35–44	6.1	4.3	5.2
45–54	5.7	3.5	4.7
55–69	5.4	3.2	4.4
60 & over	4.6	2.3	3.6

Source: National Censuses and Surveys

countries. In most countries, the position in rural areas is much lower than in urban areas, and the position of females worse than that of males. The data from Sri Lanka on educational level by age shows the way educational level has been increasing over time.

We next consider some measures of the flow of young people through the various levels of the educational system. The growth of enrolments in the post-war period is summarized in Table 6.2.

In the DCs, most children of primary-school age were already enrolled at the beginning of this period; therefore the slow growth of enrolments was almost entirely due to the slackening of population growth; enrolments grew faster at other levels, especially at the tertiary level as the DCs continued to upgrade their educational levels. Enrolments at all levels increased rapidly in the LDCs, but to see how far this was due to the rapid growth of their populations, we must look at the enrolment ratios (Table 6.3).

This table shows a much less impressive achievement in raising enrolment ratios, especially at the lower levels of education. Therefore, most of the increase in enrolments was due to the increase in population. The fastest increase in enrolment ratios occurred at the tertiary level.

Table 6.2 Growth of enrolments (annual percentage rates)

Countries/period		Primary	Secondary	Tertiary	Total
DCs:	1950–60	1.0	4.9	5.9	2.2
	1960–65	1.5	6.5	9.2	3.3
	1965–70	0.7	2.3	7.2	1.7
	1970–76	−1.3	2.5	5.3	0.6
	1960–76	0.2	3.7	7.1	1.8
LDCs:	1950–60	6.2	9.3	8.3	6.7
	1960–65	6.4	10.4	12.0	7.2
	1965–70	4.2	7.9	11.6	5.1
	1970–76	4.1	5.6	8.0	4.5
	1960–76	4.8	7.8	10.4	5.5

Source: UNESCO, *Statistical Yearbook*, 1971, 1978–79.

Table 6.3 Enrolment ratios by age groups (percentages)

	Age-groups			
Period	6–11	12–17	18–23	6–23
(a) DCs				
1960	90.8	73.0	15.1	62.0
1975	93.4	84.5	29.6	69.2
(b) LDCs				
1960	46.8	21.6	3.6	26.6
1965	54.6	27.9	5.2	32.7
1970	57.8	31.7	7.2	35.9
1975	61.8	35.3	9.0	38.7

Source: UNESCO, *Statistical Yearbook, 1978–79*

6.2 Causes of Educational Expansion

Soon after national governments took power in the LDCs after World War II, there was much talk of expanding education as a means of promoting development. A number of other objectives were added, such as national integration, social development and greater equality. Solemn conferences of government leaders and educational experts were convened by UNESCO to set ambitious targets for educational expansion. Countries such as India even put the target of universal primary education to be achieved within ten years of independence as a directive for state action in the constitution itself.

The actual pattern of educational expansion, however, turned out to be determined, not so much by the active policies of governments, but rather by their passive response to the growth of private demand. There was a strong and insistent demand for education by private individuals simply because they could see that persons with higher levels of education earned more than those with lower levels. Table 6.4 shows the relationship observed in Indonesia and Table 6.5 summarizes some data from the Philippines.

Table 6.4 Per capita household expenditures by education of head of household, Indonesia, 1976 (Rp 000 per month)

Education of head of household	Urban	Rural	Total
No school	3.72	2.37	3.16
Less than primary	3.92	2.98	3.09
Primary	4.37	3.23	3.51
Less than junior high	4.79	3.56	4.00
Junior high	5.12	3.96	4.53
Less than senior high	5.56	3.95	4.93
Senior high	6.55	4.62	5.60
Less than academy or university	9.10	5.64	8.31
Academy or university	11.32	5.62	10.21
Not stated	4.43	3.87	3.92
Total	4.84	3.16	3.44

Source: Sundrum and Booth, 1980, Table 20, p.478.

Table 6.5 Household income and mean years of education of head of household, Philippines, 1971

Income of household (pesos)	Mean years of education of head of household
Below 500	4.1
500–999	4.4
1000–1499	4.7
1500–1999	5.1
2000–2499	5.5
2500–2999	6.0
3000–3999	6.8
4000–4999	6.8
5000–5999	7.4
6000–7999	9.0
8000–9999	9.3
10000–14999	10.4
15000–19999	11.2
20000 & Over	10.2
Total	6.2

Source: Philippines Bureau of Census and Statistics, *Family Income and Expenditure, 1971*

The universality of this association between education and earnings has been claimed as 'one of the most striking findings of modern social science' (Blaug, 1974, p.27). Governments simply tried to follow a policy, sometimes described as the 'social demand approach', of providing places in schools and universities for all those who were qualified and sought admission: 'if the truth were told, nine-tenths of educational planning around the world is of this type, despite the lip-service to the more sophisticated varieties of education as investment in economic growth!' (Bereday and Lauwerys, 1967, p.85).

The personal economic advantage that individuals derive from education may be summarized by the concept of the private rate of return to education, i.e. the rate of interest at which it would just pay individuals to borrow funds for educational expenses; some estimates of the average rates of return are shown in Table 6.6.

Table 6.6 Average private rates of return to education (per cent)

Countries	Secondary education	Tertiary education
DCs	11.3	12.7
LDCs	21.8	25.0

Source: Psacharapoulos, 1973, Table 4.1, p.62

The main reason why these rates are so much higher in LDCs, about double those in DCs, is the large differential in the earnings of different educational groups, summarized in Table 6.7.

Table 6.7 Ratio of average annual earnings

Countries	Primary/ none	Secondary/ primary	Higher/ secondary
USA, Canada, UK, France, Netherlands, Norway	n.a.	1.4	1.7
Israel, Greece, Mexico, Chile, Colombia	2.4	1.9	1.8
Malaysia, Philippines, Ghana, S. Korea, Kenya, Uganda, Nigeria, India	2.4	2.4	2.7

Source: Psacharapoulos, 1973, Table 8.4, p.132.

The large income differentials between educational categories in LDCs were initially due to the fact that educated workers were so scarce in these countries relative to demand and because the demand was partly met by expatriates from the metropolitan countries. Thus, the differentials should have declined with the educational expansion in the LDCs. However, this process has been very slow. One reason is that the more educated workers are mostly employed in the public sector, where their salaries are in the nature of 'administered prices' kept at a high level because of their greater political strength in influencing government decisions. Another reason is that the salaries of the most highly educated workers in LDCs are kept close to the incomes they can earn by migrating to DCs, whereas the incomes of the less educated who do not enjoy such international mobility are tied to the average incomes of the LDCs. Hence, there is a greater spread of incomes, as illustrated in Figure 6.1, where the Roman figures stand for educational categories, I for the highest and IV for the lowest.

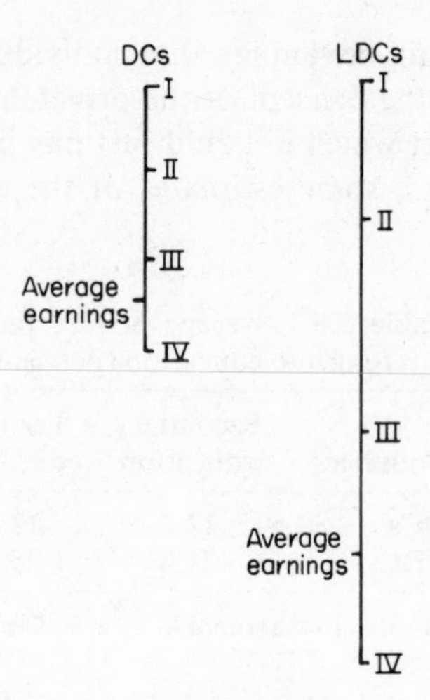

Figure 6.1

Apart from the earnings differential between educational categories of the labour force, another factor which influences the private rate of return to education is the extent to which the costs of education are borne by the State. In 1975, it was estimated that public expenditure on education as a percentage of GDP was 6.0 in DCs and 3.9 in LDCs. (UNESCO, *Statistical Yearbook*, 1978–79) The difference may be analysed into three factors: (i) the difference in age distribution affecting the proportion of the population which is of school-going age; (ii) enrolment ratios, the extent to which the population of school-going age is actually enrolled; and (iii) the unit costs of education at the various levels relative to per capita income. Table 6.8 shows the influence of these factors on the public expenditure on education as a percentage of GDP. The quantitative importance of the three factors is derived in Table 6.9.

There is no difference due to the difference in age distribution; the lower percentage of the population at the primary school age in DCs is just about balanced by the higher percentage at the higher levels. The lower enrolment ratios in LDCs contribute to most of the difference between DCs and LDCs in the costs of education. It is noteworthy that the higher unit costs in LDCs contribute so significantly to the public costs of education in these countries. These unit costs also reflect the salary differentials between educational categories, as they result from the higher salary levels of teachers at the upper levels.

The fact that a large part of the cost of education is borne by the State in most LDCs, especially at the higher levels, has raised the private rate of return to education at those levels. But the more important factor is still the large income differentials. This is illustrated by the great demand for education in a country like the Philippines, where a much higher proportion of the costs of secondary and tertiary education is borne by the private sector.

The influence of earnings differentials on the private demand for education

Table 6.8 Public expenditure on education, 1975

Level of education	Percentage of population at each age	Enrolment ratios	Enrolments as percentage of population	Unit costs as percentage of per capita GDP	Total costs as percentage of GDP
(a) DCs					
Primary	9.93	118.6	11.78	21	2.5
Secondary	10.55	66.8	7.05	31	2.2
Tertiary	10.13	23.8	2.41	54	1.3
				Total	6.0
(b) LDCs					
Primary	11.44	75.9	8.68	23	2.0
Secondary	9.81	25.8	2.53	47	1.2
Tertiary	8.57	4.9	0.42	167	0.7
				Total	3.9

Source: UNESCO, *Statistical Yearbook*, 1978–79; Unit costs estimated.

Table 6.9 Factors affecting public expenditure on education in DCs and LDCs, 1975

Factor	Effect
Public education expenditures as percentage of GDP in DCs:	6.0
Difference due to:	
age distribution in LDCs	−0.0
lower enrolment ratios in LDCs	−3.2
higher unit costs in LDCs	+1.1
Public Educational Expenditures as percentage of GDP in LDCs:	=3.9

Source: Table 6.8 above.

has been the main cause of the pattern of educational expansion in LDCs. These differentials are greatest at the tertiary level, and private demand for education has increased most rapidly at that level. Because governments have responded mainly to private demand, places at the tertiary level have expanded fastest (Table 6.3), and because unit costs are so much higher at this level (Table 6.8), there were less resources available for primary education, where the expansion of facilities was slowest. A similar relationship also applies to the case of vocational education. Because graduates with general education earned higher incomes than those with vocational education, there was little private demand for vocational education. Therefore, although governments were interested in providing for vocational education, these facilities were under-utilized, while there was increasing pressure on the facilities for general education. Foster (1966) has provided an analysis of this 'vocational school fallacy'.

6.3 Consequences of Educational Expansion

The educational expansion which occurred in LDCs was due to individuals seeking economic advancement through education induced by the large income differentials between educational categories of the labour force. But in the event, these differentials proved to be 'false signals', for although they have remained large, employment prospects at these income levels did not keep pace with the educational expansion. The typical position in south-east Asian countries has been described by Myint (1962, p.230) thus:

> In the first phase after independence, where the jobs vacated by foreigners have to be filled and where there is a redistribution of the available jobs between the expatriates and the nationals, these expectations [of employment at high salaries] can be realised to some extent. When all these jobs have been filled, it became evident that no country can go on providing a larger and larger proportion of its population with many times its present per capita income unless there is a rapid expansion of its total national income. But the overcrowding of the universities by lowering the standard of efficiency and competence of its educated class, may reduce the possibility of such a rapid expansion in national income—rapid enough to absorb the expanding stream of graduates from the universities.

The failure of employment opportunities to expand at the same rate as educational expansion has resulted in the phenomenon of 'educated unemployment'. Surveys from many LDCs show unemployment rates generally increasing with the level of education up to a point, usually around the upper secondary level, and declining thereafter. A clear example is provided by the data from the Philippines (Table 6.10).

Generally speaking, because educational opportunities were expanded in LDCs so recently, the younger population is more highly educated than the older. Therefore, to some extent, workers with more education have a higher unemployment rate than those with less because they are younger and are seeking their first jobs. But the tendency for unemployment rates to increase with the level of education also exists for people in each age group. Therefore, it is sometimes argued that educational expansion in LDCs has been too rapid for the educated to be absorbed into productive employment.

However, much of the educated unemployment in LDCs has arisen because educated workers have high expectations about the sort of jobs suited to their qualifications, based on the experience of earlier generations, and because they can better afford to be unemployed due to the support they get from their more affluent families. Their unemployment is therefore to a considerable extent voluntary and of the same type as unemployment among rural migrants to urban areas (Section 7.4 below). The decision to seek a higher level of education is based, not on the earnings actually received when employed, but on the expected earnings, i.e. the actual earnings multiplied by the probability of getting employed. So long as the private costs of education are low, and so long as earnings differentials are high, the expected earnings at higher levels of

Table 6.10 Unemployment rates by education: Philippines, 1965

Educational level	Unemployment rate (%)		
	Urban	Rural	Total
No school	6.1	2.3	2.8
Elementary school grades:			
1	4.5	2.1	2.3
2	7.6	2.5	3.4
3	8.8	2.5	3.6
4	8.1	3.5	4.4
5	9.6	3.4	4.7
6–7	11.4	6.9	8.3
High school grades:			
1	14.3	4.7	9.1
2	14.2	2.2	8.3
3	16.4	6.3	11.2
4	12.8	9.4	11.4
University grades:			
1	20.0	5.5	16.4
2	13.3	5.5	11.6
3	15.0	22.0	16.9
4	6.8	4.6	6.1
5	3.9	—	3.8
Total	10.7	4.1	6.2

Source: *Philippine Labour Force Survey, October 1965*

education are sufficiently large to make the investment in education appear profitable. This is one reason why the private demand for education has remained high in the presence of educated unemployment.

There is, however, another reason. When there are large numbers of applicants for a limited number of jobs, employers use the level of education as a way of screening applicants and rationing the limited employment opportunities to those with higher paper qualifications. The steady upgrading of the educational requirements for jobs and the corresponding devaluation of educational qualifications leads to a further increase in the demand for education, as people seek more education to increase their chances of employment.

The paradox of the situation is that the worse the educated unemployment situation gets and the more useless educational certificates become, the *stronger* grows the pressure for an expansion of educational facilities. (Dore, 1976, p.4)

The situation in which students flock into schools and universities, not so much for education, in the sense of seeking knowledge for its own sake and for exercising the mind, but rather to get a qualification for various well-paid jobs, has been described by Dore as 'the diploma disease'. As a result of the quantitative expansion of educational facilities, by which governments responded to the growth of private demand, there was a drastic decline in the quality of education.

> Enrolments throughout the developing world have shown a rapid increase. Crash courses for teacher training, supplementation by untrained teachers, double shift use of schools, grants and subsidies to self-help schools, increases in class size, occasionally, in the more boldly experimental countries, the use of student monitors to help teach— numerous are the devices that have been resorted to in order to meet the rising level of demand for schooling. (Dore, 1976, p.4)

Most of the financial resources available to the educational system were spent on expanding the number of places in schools and universities rather than on textbooks, library and laboratory facilities. Unlike the DCs where there was already a large stock of well-qualified people who could be drawn into an expanding educational system, the LDCs had fewer qualified people and had to staff their educational expansion with under-qualified teachers. The problem was compounded by the fact that salaries offered to teachers did not keep pace with those of people with similar qualifications in other occupations (Sen, 1970). Once under-qualified staff were appointed, they continued to serve their whole working lives with a minimum of 'refresher' courses, teaching a whole generation of students. The decline in the quality of education without much change in the structure of salaries meant, in turn, that employment opportunities in the private sector did not expand as rapidly as they might have done, because these opportunities depended on the productivity of workers, rather than the paper qualifications which sufficed in the public sector. Hence, the problem of educated unemployment was further accentuated.

The decline in the quality of education was particularly true of the public sector of the educational system in most countries. A higher quality of education was provided by the private educational sector to the children of the more affluent families who could afford the greater cost, especially in the urban areas. The result was that the education system, once looked upon as the main instrument of equalization, became instead the main source of growing inequality, as the children of richer families in the urban areas received a bigger share of the available educational facilities, especially those of a higher quality. Because of this, and because of the better home backgrounds provided by their more educated parents, they got the best jobs available.

6.4 Educational Policy

In the last two sections, we saw, first, that there was a great increase in the private demand for education as students flocked into schools and universities seeking their personal economic advancement through education. This increase in private demand was motivated by the large income differentials between educational categories, differentials which declined very slowly over time. Secondly, governments' role was a passive political response to this growth of private demand. As a result, there was a considerable expansion of the educational systems in LDCs.

> The world's bureaucracies are littered with development plans gone awry, with targets unfulfilled. But not many educational plans fall in that category. Their targets—at least the targets for secondary expansion—are much more likely to be overfulfilled than underfulfilled. (Dore, 1976, p.3)

The result was that the rapidly increased output of the educational system could not be absorbed into employment at the prevailing salary structures, giving rise to the problem of educated unemployment. The problem was exacerbated by the decline in quality that accompanied the quantitative expansion of the education system. This process reflects the educational policy that was actually followed in the LDCs. We turn now to the theory of educational policy that was evolved in the literature.

Economists were quick to see the importance of education in the post-war period.

> The economists had just 'discovered' education. In the first decade of development thinking—the decade which followed the Asian wave of independence—the emphasis had been all on the lack of physical capital. Capital was the missing factor which outside aid donors could supply to create the impetus for self-sustained development. But soon it was apparent that physical capital was not enough. Capital given to Europe under the Marshall Plan, capital given to Japan to restore its devastated industries, proved productive because those countries had people with the knowledge necessary to make it productive. Similar investment in an Indonesia or Burma, which lacked the engineers and managers and technicians of the richer countries, failed to produce the same results. And so economists discovered—or actually rediscovered, because Adam Smith had never overlooked the point—the importance of complementary human factors, of 'investment in human resources'. (Dore, 1976, p.1)

The result was a remarkable blossoming of the subject of 'economics of education'.

> In the 1950s and 1960s, economists were thick on the ground in every ministry of education in every capital city of Asia, Africa and Latin America. Those were the days when all the indications pointed towards the rapid expansion of educational systems at all levels and when economists were welcomed for producing new arguments to support an educational inflation that was, anyway, desired on political grounds. What did it matter that manpower forecasting was crude and that cost-benefit analysis was based on rather implausible assumptions, when, in fact, they led to answers that called for still more education? (Blaug, 1979, p.73)

In this section, we summarize the various approaches recommended by economists, point out some of their weaknesses, and then offer an alternative approach to educational policy as an instrument of development.

One of the earliest approaches to get off the ground was that based on an imitative strategy. By considering the growth of enrolment ratios in DCs in the course of their economic growth, Harbison and Myers (1964) laid down educational targets for countries based on their level of development, measured by their per capita national incomes (Table 6.11). But the DCs achieved their development over a long period and this development was not initially based on their educational progress. Therefore, their experience is not particularly suitable as an example for LDCs if they wish to develop more

Table 6.11 Enrolment targets

Targets	Level of development: I	II	III	IV
Per capita GNP (US $)	84	182	380	1100
Primary enrolment ratio (unadjusted)	22	42	62	73
Primary and secondary enrolment ratio (adjusted)	20	45	66	89
Secondary enrolment ratio (adjusted)	2.7	12	27	59
Tertiary enrolment ratio	0.15	1.6	5	11

Source: Harbison and Myers, 1964, Table 2, p.38

rapidly by deliberately using education as an instrument of development policy. As Dore (1976, pp.7–8) says,

> In this, as in so many other ways, the process of development in a country which starts deliberately modernising in the mid-twentieth century is very different from the process of less deliberate development the rich countries experienced in the nineteenth century.

Another approach that was developed in the early post-war phase was based on the idea that the educational system should be expanded to meet the 'manpower requirements' of a target rate of growth of national income. The calculation of these requirements was based on a long chain of argument (Parnes, 1962; for an application of the method to Indian educational planning, see Government of India Ministry of Education, 1966, Chapter 5). First, the target growth rate of national income is laid down; from this are derived the growth rates of various sectors implied by some estimates of income elasticities of demand and input–output matrices. The growth rate of output of each sector is then translated into the manpower requirements in various industrial, occupational and educational categories. Once these have been calculated, it is a simple matter to derive the targets for expansion of the various levels of the educational system.

The manpower requirements approach is a policy of adapting the educational system to the expected growth of the economy. In doing this, it assumes a large number of coefficients to be rigidly fixed in a highly deterministic way to the growth of income, leaving little room for alternative strategies of growth. The coefficients required for the calculation of manpower requirements are usually derived from the experience of more developed countries. As LDCs are particularly deficient in their stock of high-level manpower compared with more developed countries, the usual conclusion is to recommend a higher rate of expansion at the tertiary level. Such recommendations are usually valid only for relatively short periods in the future, because it is only for such periods that targets for income growth rates can be laid down with any confidence and the values of the various coefficients assumed to be constant. But educational planning cannot be done for such short periods, because of the important interactions between different parts of the educational system; any increase of enrolments at one level in one period will mean an increase of enrolments at the higher level in the next period. An increase of enrolments at any level means that there should be prior training of teachers required at that level and the building of schools and provision of books and equipment. These relationships are very important if the quality of education is to be maintained or improved. It is the neglect of these relationships that has lowered the quality of education in LDCs in the past. The most important weakness of this approach is that

> The role of the educational system is to perform the passive function of filling the gap in the skilled manpower requirements, to achieve the target rate of growth as distinct from the active function of raising the possible rate of growth. (Myint, 1969, p.261)

Sometimes a macro-economic approach is used to estimate the manpower requirements to be supplied by the educational system; for an example, see Tinbergen and Bos (1964). This approach has been described and criticized by Dore (1976, p.87) as follows:

> Regression analysis offered a possible solution to the estimation problem. If you take a hundred countries and chart the relationship between level of GNP and primary and secondary and tertiary enrolments, you can arrive at a formula which offers the best possible means of guessing a country's level of GNP if all you know about it is its school enrolments. If you stand this formula on its head and make the whopping assumption that *grosso modo* all countries (even if they do locate themselves very untidily around the assumed trend line) are *essentially* following the same growth pattern, with some just having got a little bit further along than others, then you can say how many per cent primary, say, or secondary enrolments are likely to increase for a given percentage increase in income level (*provided that* the various forces which hitherto have operated to produce the historical trend line discovered by the analysis continue to exercise their determining influence). If, then, your economic plan tells you how fast GNP will grow, then you know how fast to expect *enrolments* to grow too. Well, not actually *expect*, since there were supposed to be planners in charge of the matter—how fast to *make* enrolments to grow—on the curious, and rather Taoist, assumption that the aim of good planning should be to achieve a consonance with the underlying forces of History —a daring *non sequitur* of enormous subsequent influence. (italics in original)

To many economists, the greatest defect of the manpower-requirements approach was its neglect of the costs and benefits of education. Therefore, they developed a highly sophisticated application of cost–benefit analysis to educational planning. The central proposition of this approach is that resources should be applied to education and other sectors, and within the educational system to various levels of education, so as to maximize the benefits from a given total outlay. From this is derived the rule that the optimum allocation is one which equalizes the rate of return to all investments (e.g. Blaug *et al.*, 1969). The dominance of this approach in the development literature is a major victory for economists against the traditional approach which resisted the application of capital theory to human beings; as a result, education has become human capital. This sounds very persuasive in theory, but it raises a number of problems in its practical application.

In Sections 6.2 and 6.3, we saw the problems that have arisen in LDCs as a result of the educational system responding to demand as determined by the private rates of return. In applying the cost–benefit approach to social policy in this area, it is recognized that what is relevant is the social rate of return to education. However, in practice, the only adjustment that is made to the private rates of return to reflect the social point of view is on the cost side, i.e. the social rates of return to education are calculated to take account, not only of the costs incurred by private individuals, but also those incurred by the State. The result is that the social rates of return are lower than the private rates; sometimes it turns out that the social rates of return to education are even lower than those of investment in physical capital (Harberger, 1966). Further, as public expenditures are a higher proportion of total costs at the higher levels of education, the social rates of return at these levels are reduced to a greater extent at these levels than at lower levels of education. Therefore, the usual recommendation of this approach is for faster expansion at the primary level. A fairly typical example of social rates of return to education derived in this way is given by some estimates for India (Table 6.12).

Table 6.12 Social and private rates of return to education in urban India, males, 1960 (per cent)

	Rates of return	
Level of education	Social	Private
Primary over none	13.7	16.5
Middle school over primary	12.4	14.0
Matriculation over middle school	9.1	10.4
College over matriculation	7.4	8.7
Matriculation over none	12.2	14.7
College over none	10.3	12.3
Engineering degree over none	12.3	15.2

Source: Blaug *et al.*, 1969, pp.218–9.

In most practical applications, the rate of return approach to educational planning does not make any adjustment to the private rates on the benefit side, and identifies the social benefits of education with the private benefits which individuals derive from their education in the form of higher personal earnings. But for a number of reasons, these private earnings are not satisfactory measures of the social benefits of education. In the first place, the higher earnings of the more educated workers are not only due to their education, but due to their innate abilities as well as their better connections in securing jobs. Second, the differences in individuals earnings do not reflect differences in marginal products to the employers. This is particularly the case when the employer is the public sector, because there is no market price for the output of this sector and because public sector salaries are not determined by market forces but rather are administered prices. Because the public sector is the major employer of educated workers in LDCs, the structure of salaries in the public sector dominates that of the private sector also. Third, the benefit that an individual worker or his employer derives from education, as measured by the difference it makes to his earnings, does not take account of the externalities of education, the benefits that the community as a whole derives from having a more educated labour force. As Marshall (1961, Vol.I, p.216) pointed out a long time ago, 'the wisdom of expanding public and private funds in education is not to be measured by its direct fruits alone.' Finally, in deriving its policy conclusions about the numbers of students to be enrolled in the educational system at any time, the rate of return approach assumes that the salary structure observed at the point of time will remain constant and applicable to the earnings of these students throughout their working lives.

Another limitation of the rate of return approach is that, because it takes the total amount of resources available in any short period and the salary structures prevailing in that period as given and poses the problem as one of the optimum allocation of these resources to alternative uses, its policy conclusions are only applicable to such short periods. But educational development should be planned over the long term; because of the tight relationships between different parts of the educational system, long-term planning is necessary in order to maintain the quality of education. Long-term planning is also necessary because decisions made in a short period have significant effects in the future; for example, increased capital expenditures in building schools in one period will entail increased levels of current expenditure in the future. Therefore, a series of short-term policy decisions may not yield the best solution over the long term. Further, by reducing the resources needed for various types of investment to a common denominator in financial terms, this approach treats the resources needed for educational expansion as of the same type as those needed for other investments. But the resources needed for educational expansion are essentially the human beings, those who receive education and those who provide it, and are of a different category from the resources needed for other investments, say, in physical capital. It is only at the level of the government budget that allocating more funds to education competes with funds needed elsewhere. But rather than take the amount of budgetary resources as given, the role of government financial policy should be to mobilize the real resources needed for various types of development activities, including measures to influence the salary structures which have a significant effect on the costs of educational development.

Perhaps the most serious weakness of applying cost–benefit analysis to education is that it assumes that there is a rigid relationship between education and total output such as that involved in a production function between the amount of directly productive resources and total output. This is a relationship that is involved in the concept of growth rather than of development, as we have distinguished the two concepts. A high level of education among the population is necessary for the running of a modern economy, as shown by the difference between DCs and LDCs. It is sometimes argued that the high level of education in DCs is partly due to the fact that they can afford more education as a consumer good rather than as a producer good but it is not possible to separate these effects. As far as growth is concerned, education is a permissive, rather than a causal, factor. How far education promotes growth depends on many other circumstances, such as the prevailing institutions, the levels of infrastructure and the growth of directly productive resources. For example, at the micro-economic level, it is widely recognized that most productive skills are learnt on the job, but an individual's ability to benefit from such training depends on the level of his education. Hence, the effect of education on productivity depends on the opportunities for on-the-job training. As a result, 'an extraordinary variety of manpower structures are compatible with identical levels and rate of growth of national income.' (Ahmed and Blaug, 1973, p.16)

In the light of the weaknesses of the various approaches described above, we can formulate an alternative approach to educational policy as an instrument of development as follows. In this approach, education is to be desired because it increases people's knowledge and changes their attitudes, and thus increases their ability to absorb new technology. As this ability is crucial to the development of the LDCs, the ultimate objective of educational policy in these countries should be that of a fully educated society, i.e. one in which every person receives as much education as he or she is capable of absorbing. This certainly involves universal education of 8 to 10 years duration between the ages of 6 and 15 when children's learning capacity is high. Beyond that, those with the aptitude continue to receive general education, while others are provided with technical or vocational education or enter the labour force and get on-the-job training to improve their productive skills. This target can be expressed in stock terms as the proportions of the labour force with various educational attainments or more conveniently in flow terms as the enrolment ratios and rates of transfer from one level of education to the next. However, planners should try not only to increase quantity but should seek to maintain high standards as well. Such a target for educational policy means that it can only be achieved in the long run. This is in contrast to the other approaches which plan in terms of short-term targets; a succession of such short-term targets is unduly influenced by the initial conditions of income and employment, whereas educational progress should be used to change these conditions. Using a short-term approach, an LDC may never attain the final objective of a fully educated society. In the alternative approach proposed here, the corresponding targets for each short-term period are derived by working backwards from the final long-term target. Then, the task of educational development can be viewed as a whole and planned accordingly. The advantage is that we can better take account of the internal relationships between different parts of the educational system. When these internal relationships are taken into account, there is a maximum rate at which the educational system can be expanded towards the final objective without risk of lowering the quality of education. If education is to be an instrument of development, the policy in each period should be to attain this maximum rate of expansion of the educational system.

When the educational policy is based on such a final objective to be attained at a pace determined only by the constraints within the educational system, there remains the problem of the relationship between the educational system and the rest of the economy. As we have seen, the other approaches described above solve this problem by accepting a given rate of growth of the economy and adjusting the rate and pattern of educational expansion to this rate of economic growth, partly by adjusting the resources allocated to education and partly by adjusting its output in terms of graduates. In contrast, in the alternative approach considered here, the problem has to be solved by adjusting the economy to the educational system as it is expanded towards its final objective as rapidly as possible. On the one hand, it is the function of short-term fiscal policy to mobilize the real resources needed for educational development. On the other hand, measures must be taken to utilize in productive employment the expanding stream of graduates of the educational system. The most important of these measures is a reform of the salary structure, which the governments of LDCs are in a commanding position to do. In this process, there may be some educated unemployment but such unemployment is itself a part of the adjustment process. That is why Lewis (1968, p.137) has argued that 'one ought to produce more educated people than can be absorbed at current prices, because the alteration in current prices which this forces is a necessary part of the process of economic development.' The adjustment process will be difficult, but the real challenge to governments in promoting development lies in the way they confront and deal with these difficulties, rather than adopting the expedient policy of following the course of private demand.

CHAPTER 7

Infrastructure

7.1 Characteristics of Infrastructure

Infrastructure is part of the capital stock of a country. It is also described as 'social overhead capital' to distinguish it from 'directly productive capital'. A very elaborate theory of capital has been developed by economists but it deals mostly with directly productive capital; in contrast, the theory of social overhead capital has been largely neglected, with the exception of the comprehensive study by Youngson (1967). There is not even a clear definition of the concept of infrastructure; in fact, Hirschman (1958, p.83) once suggested the best way to define it was as all those things for which the World Bank provides assistance, just as behavioural science research consists of anything that is supported by the Ford Foundation. In formulating a theory of infrastructure, the central issues are to decide what constitutes infrastructure, whether it should be provided by the State or by private producers in response to market forces, and to the extent that it has to be provided by the State, what principles should guide the State in providing various elements of infrastructure.

In practice, infrastructure refers to such services to producers as transport and communications, power, water supply, irrigation and drainage systems. But as Youngson (1967, p.68) says, 'The correct conclusion is that overhead capital is not a *set of things*, but a *set of properties*.' The most important property of infrastructure is that it is a source of external economies. It is for this reason that Adam Smith included the provision of infrastructure among the 'Duties of the Sovereign' (see Section 5.2). Once a road is constructed, it benefits all persons located on its route. Once a power transmission system is built, it can be used to deliver power to all persons within reach of the system. In the theory of public expenditure, goods are classified either as 'private goods' or as 'public goods'; private goods are those which, the more one person consumes them, the less there is for others to enjoy, while in the case of public goods, a given quantity of such goods may enter into the consumption of many individuals, so that the consumption by one person will not reduce the consumption by others (see Samuelson, 1954, 1969; also Atkinson and Stiglitz, 1980, Chapter 18). Infrastructure therefore belongs to the category of public goods. As explained in the theory of public expenditure, if the allocation of resources between private goods and public goods were to be determined by a market in the same way as the allocation among private goods, the output of public goods will be less than optimal. This is one reason why the output of public goods, like infrastructure, has to be determined by the State.

Another characteristic of social overhead capital, noted by Nurkse (1952, p.268) is that it consists of 'large and costly installations'. One consequence is that such installations may be beyond the capacity of individuals or small groups to establish. A more serious consequence is that the use of such installations will be subject to decreasing costs. Under these conditions, prices determined by marginal costs in a competitive private industry will not cover costs. Without State intervention, the industry will tend to become a monopoly and the supply will be less than optimal.

While their externalities and decreasing costs indicate the need for some form of State provision or State regulation of private supply, infrastructure has a third characteristic which makes it even more necessary for provision by public agency. As Youngson (1967, p.71) puts it (with special reference to education, but also applicable to infrastructure):

> it is a matter of facilitating the evolution of new ideas, of new combinations of the factors of production. It is, indeed, a matter of promoting innovation; and it is the peculiar quality of innovation that it makes nonsense of average calculations of future benefits. It is at this point that the idea of external economies meets that of Schumpeterian innovation. *Overhead capital is facilitating investment which promotes innovation.*

This role of infrastructure is particularly important for the development of LDCs because infrastructure makes it possible for producers to use modern technology. By introducing modern technology to producers, infrastructural expansion stimulates directly productive activities. Speaking of transport, Owen (1964, p.196) says,

> Economic justification of transport expenditures can be measured in part by increased production from reductions in transport cost and improvements in service for traffic already moving. But an additional measure is the volume of new production created by

activities that greater mobility makes possible. In judging the desirability of improved transport, newly generated traffic may be the most important factor as well as the most difficult to estimate.

The role of infrastructure in stimulating directly productive activities by a large number of producers is not something which can be appreciated by private entrepreneurs; therefore, it constitutes another reason, perhaps the most important reason, why its expansion in LDCs is a special responsibility of the State.

The various characteristics of infrastructure noted above are particularly important in the case of power, transport and communications. The levels and growth of such infrastructure in the post-war period are described in the following section.

7.2 Levels and Growth of Infrastructure

Table 7.1 summarizes the difference between DCs and LDCs in the levels of power and transport infrastructure. The table shows how poorly the LDCs are supplied with these types of infrastructure compared with the DCs.

Table 7.1 Levels of power and transport infrastructure

Infrastructure	DCs	LDCs
Energy consumption per capita (kg of coal equivalent), 1979[a]	5950	680
Electricity: installed capacity (kw per 1000 population), 1977[b]	1334	73
Electricity: consumption (kwh per annum per capita), 1977[b]	5049	247
Road mileage: 1975–76[c]		
(a) km per 1000 population	31.7	3.8
(b) km per 1000 km^2	921	151
(c) km per population distance[d]	90	19
Railway mileage: 1975–76[c]		
(a) km per 1000 population	0.9	0.2
(b) km per 1000 km^2	51.0	10.3
(c) km per population distance[d]	5.51	1.24
Telephones per 1000 population	308	8.6

Sources: (a) World Bank, *World Development Report, 1981*; (b) United Nations, *Statistical Yearbook*, 1978; (c) The Economist, *The World in Figures*, 1980; (d) Population distance is defined as the distance between a person and his nearest neighbour when population is evenly distributed over a given area and is measured by $\sqrt{(A/P)}$, where A is the area in km^2 and P is population.

The present position is the result of nearly three decades in which the LDCs have been trying to improve their infrastructural position. The growth of infrastructure in the post-war period is summarized in Table 7.2 for some cases.

Power and transport and communications facilities expanded more rapidly in LDCs than in DCs but the difference in growth rates was quite small, little

Table 7.2 Growth of electricity and telephones (annual percentage rates)

Infrastructure	DCs	LDCs
Electricity: installed capacity (kw)		
1955–65	7.9	10.2
1965–77	6.6	9.1
Electricity: consumption (kwh)		
1956–66	7.7	11.4
1966–77	6.2	9.1
Telephones		
1956–66	6.3	8.8
1966–77	6.4	10.7

Source: United Nations *Statistical Yearbook*, 1970, 1978.

more than the difference in population growth rates. Therefore, there is little change in the relative positions of the two groups of countries. In order to understand the reasons for this result, we consider alternative strategies that governments have followed or might follow in expanding infrastructure.

7.3 Alternative Strategies for Infrastructure

The policies of governments in providing infrastructure may be classified under two distinct strategies. One is the strategy of responding to demand, i.e. providing infrastructure for which a demand already exists or can be clearly foreseen. The other is the strategy of providing infrastructure ahead of demand.

The strategy of providing infrastructure in response to the demand for it has played the major role in the historical experience of DCs. In those countries, the advent of modern economic growth meant an increase in directly productive activities stimulated by technological progress and institutional changes, which in turn created a demand for infrastructure. The governments of these countries then played a passive role of providing infrastructure to meet this demand. Such a policy, followed over a long period of time, led to the present substantial levels of infrastructure in those countries.

In the post-war period, the LDCs have also generally been following the strategy of responding to demand. For example, as a result of the industrialization policies followed by these countries, there was a growth of modern industry and of urbanization which increased the demand for electric power, transport and various facilities for the growing urban populations. Similarly, the spread of the new high-yielding varieties of seed created a demand for electricity in rural areas to provide power for pumps for irrigation. As a result, capacity for generating and transmitting electric power was expanded but with a time lag behind the growth of demand, so that there was a chronic shortage of power. In contrast, the persistence of traditional technology in other sectors of the economy has meant a weak demand for modern infrastructure and hence a slow expansion of such facilities.

The strategy of providing infrastructure in response to demand underlies some of the project appraisal methods practised by national planning offices and by national and international aid agencies such as the World Bank. In these methods, demand is projected on the basis of a target rate of growth of income or by the extrapolation of past trends, and the decision whether or not to implement an infrastructural project is made by comparing the rate of return to investment derived from such a projection of demand with some estimate of the cost of capital to the country; the opportunity cost of capital is usually estimated by the returns expected in directly productive activities. If there is already a strong demand which is not yet satisfied, the rate of return will be high and the project is considered to be justified. But if there is little demand to begin with, the project will be rejected because the rate of return from it will be too low.

If infrastructure is expanded only in response to demand, it has the advantage that the infrastructural needs of a country can be judged on a project-by-project basis by the above methods. But this approach has some disadvantages. Infrastructure will be provided only to meet the requirements of current rates of growth rather than as the means of accelerating these rates of growth. Further, the expansion of infrastructure will be determined from a short-term point of view because demand can be reliably forecast only for relatively short periods. When individual projects are decided upon such short-term considerations, their over-all structure may not be efficient because the interrelations among these projects may tend to be neglected. This is a particularly serious problem for transport infrastructure, where it leads to serious lack of coordination among different types of transport facilities such as road, rail and waterways. Hence, Owen (1964, p.197) has argued that:

> Establishing the need for transport investment has become more and more dependent on the presentation of elaborate analyses of project costs and benefits. This process has facilitated the task of decision-making, but there are two dangers in the current trend. One is that concentration on individual projects can limit economic perspectives and defeat the objective of developing an integrated transport network. Second, the concentration on project proposals has led to meticulous and time-consuming study of details, the validity of which may depend on broad underlying assumptions that depend primarily on good judgment. If the now affluent countries had put their faith exclusively in benefit–cost ratios, it is not altogether clear that they would have achieved their present state of development.

As against this approach, the strategy of building infrastructure ahead of demand relies on the role of infrastructure in stimulating the demand for it. This alternative strategy has been strongly advocated by Nurkse, who is mostly known for his advocacy of the balanced growth doctrine in other respects. According to him,

> Public overhead investment creates investment opportunities in directly productive activities. These two categories (overhead investment and direct investment) are

complementary, and the relationship between them is a vertical relationship in the sense of the traditional theory of capital. Overhead investment lays down the essential framework for miscellaneous economic activity. It represents a non-specific, initiatory, pioneering type of investment. Overhead capital may have to be built ahead of demand. Since it provides inducements for directly productive investments, it tends eventually to create its own demand. A structure of public overheads causes economic activity to grow up around it and creates in this way an increasingly full and profitable demand for the services which it provides . . . Projects of this sort are not built to meet an existing need but to create one. (Nurkse, 1961, pp.75–7)

In a poor country, an overhead capital structure may not initially have enough work to do to justify its existence and can then justify itself only by faith in the future. (Nurkse, 1952, p.152)

In the case of transport infrastructure, the difference between the two approaches has been explained by Owen (1964, p.53) thus:

Traffic projections are too often based on what may be expected to happen rather than on what can be made to happen. The first approach is guessing the future while the second is planning it.

Or, as Lewis (1966, p.27) says,

development planning begins not by projecting consumer demands but by seeking the most fruitful production possibilities.

In one important case, the strategy of building infrastructure ahead of demand was followed in the historical experience of LDCs. This was the policy followed by colonial governments of promoting exports of primary products from LDCs to DCs through the provision of transport infrastructure to serve the export trade. This approach was an important factor in the expansion of the primary product exports of LDCs in the nineteenth and early twentieth centuries. This experience has been described as the 'colonial pattern of development' (Birnberg and Resnick, 1975). The transport infrastructure built in this way was mainly designed to link the export-producing areas within LDCs with their ports from which the produce was exported. Therefore, this transport system played little part in promoting internal trade or in production for domestic consumption.

The main advantage of the strategy of building infrastructure ahead of demand is that it will then play an active role in promoting faster growth, by enabling the country to absorb new technology more rapidly. The expansion of infrastructure by itself will not produce growth; in that sense, it is only a permissive factor. It will stimulate growth by increasing the profitability of directly productive investment, especially those using new techniques of production, thereby stimulating a larger volume of investment in directly productive activities.

The strategy of building infrastructure ahead of demand has been rejected by Hirschman (1958) in favour of a demand approach to economic development. He argues that LDCs tend to invest too much in power and transport infrastructure ahead of demand and too little in directly productive activities; he therefore favours a policy of building factories first and then letting the pressure of excess demand and public opinion break the resulting bottlenecks in infrastructure, on the argument that

> strong pressures are felt by public authorities 'to do something' and since the desire for political survival is at least as strong a motive as the desire to realise a profit, we may ordinarily expect some corrective action to be taken. (Hirschmann, 1958, pp.63–4)

Apart from being 'a very impressionistic way of treating political factors' as Myint (1960, p.129) pointed out in his review, this argument assumes that government policies can stimulate directly productive investments without providing the infrastructure for them, whereas, according to Nurkse's approach, directly productive activities are constrained by the lack of infrastructure, and the role of building infrastructure ahead of demand is precisely to stimulate such activities.

The two strategies of providing infrastructure also differ in their effects on income distribution. An active demand for infrastructure will usually come from people who are already in the modern sector of LDCs and who are therefore likely to be better off than those in the rest of the economy. If infrastructure is supplied only to meet an actual or foreseeable demand, it will exclusively benefit such people and hence worsen the distribution of income. But in the strategy of building infrastructure ahead of demand, policy can be used to stimulate directly productive activities of the poorer sections of the population by providing infrastructure for such activities, and hence to improve the distribution of income.

In the strategy of building infrastructure ahead of demand, the guiding principle is that all sections of the population and all parts of the country should eventually have access to modern infrastructure. In applying this principle, the unit of planning should not be the individual project but rather the whole system of each type of infrastructure. In this way, the type and amount of infrastructure to be provided in any given short period is determined, not only by the demand that is foreseen in that period, but also by the extent to which it fits in with all other projects to be constructed in the future. This approach will then enable planners to design the overall pattern of infrastructure more efficiently by taking more account of the technical interrelationships between different parts of each type of infrastructure. For example, just as different parts of the educational system have to be planned to support each other, transport infrastructure has to be planned on a long-term basis to secure the best coordination of its various parts. Similarly, power infrastructure has to be planned to coordinate different sources of power, such as coal, oil, hydro-electricity and nuclear energy.

The target of providing infrastructure to all sections of the people and all parts of the country will take a long period to achieve. Therefore, in the course of progressing towards this final objective, infrastructural expansion should be phased in accordance with the preferred strategy of growth. For example, a higher priority can be given to infrastructure serving the agricultural sector, in cases where this sector is lagging behind and constraining the growth of other sectors (see Sections 10.5 and 10.6 below). Similarly, a higher priority can be given to infrastructure serving particular groups of people who are lagging behind others. Infrastructure itself may be highly capital-intensive but it can be used to stimulate labour-intensive methods in other activities in countries faced with a serious problem of unemployment.

7.4 Pricing of Infrastructural Services

Building infrastructure ahead of demand will stimulate the demand for it in the long run, but in the short period there will be excess capacity and therefore every effort must be made to ensure that demand increases as rapidly as possible to match increases in supply. In most cases, the availability of infrastructure will stimulate the use of it, and it will not be necessary to keep the costs to users low, especially because these costs are usually quite small compared with the profitability of its use by individual producers. But in some cases, pricing policies may also be used to stimulate demand. The problem of infrastructure pricing most discussed in the literature arises from the externality aspect that has been described as the 'non-excludability' characteristic of public goods (see e.g. Musgrave, 1969, p.127). This means that persons using such public goods cannot be charged on the basis of the benefits they individually derive, because once the infrastructure exists, particular users cannot be excluded from it without high costs. The difficulty, however, is greatly exaggerated. Generally, even though it may be expensive or impossible to exclude particular individuals from the use of infrastructure, it will be possible to exclude certain identifiable groups. Thus, car-owners are a group who derive a special benefit from the use of roads, for which they can be charged a fee. The difference in the benefits which individual car owners derive is less than the difference in the benefits accruing to owners as a group and to those who do not own cars.

A more serious problem is that of determining the level of fees to be charged for the use of infrastructure, because these cannot be based on any observable market behaviour. If infrastructure is provided to meet an existing demand, it may be possible to charge fees corresponding to the benefits received by broad groups of people using these facilities. If, instead, infrastructure is provided to stimulate demand, the main principle should be to ensure maximum utilization of such infrastructure, and the costs of providing the infrastructure should be recouped as fully as possible from those benefitting from its use. In the early stages when there is excess capacity of the infrastructure built ahead of demand, the fees for their use may be kept low in order to stimulate the demand, but in the later stages, when demand has been built up, the fees may be raised corresponding to the benefits derived. This is the same as the policy of monopolists using 'loss leaders' in order to build up demand (see e.g. Allen, 1938, p.362).

In practice, governments tend to charge very low fees for the infrastructural services they provide. This may be partly due to the political power of vested interests benefitting most from these services. One result is that the revenues of governments do not increase rapidly enough to expand infrastructure even further in the future.

7.5 Urbanization

The strategies discussed above have a special application to urbanization in LDCs, because the growth of cities is so heavily dependent on the provision of infrastructure. In the past, the provision of urban infrastructure has been in response to the demand created by the rate of urbanization. But in the future, it is possible to use the provision of infrastructure as a means of influencing the pace and pattern of urbanization.

Urbanization policy in LDCs has to take account of two considerations pulling in opposite directions. On the one hand, as we saw in Chapter 2, the LDCs have a low urban ratio, so that they do not have the full benefits of urbanization in the development of new ideas, the changing of traditional attitudes, and the performance of those services which are most conveniently located in urban areas. On this consideration, they need a rapid growth in the number and population of their urban areas. On the other hand, as we saw in Chapter 3, the urban population of LDCs has been growing rapidly and this growth has led to severe congestion of urban facilities and widespread poverty in urban areas because employment opportunities have not expanded as rapidly as the urban labour force. Hence, it is often recommended that the pace of urbanization should be reduced, even though the urban ratio is still very low. In order to resolve this conflict, LDCs must adjust their urban infrastructure policies to influence not only the pace of urbanization but also its pattern.

There are two types of explanations for the pace of urbanization—one stressing the pull of urban areas and the other the push from rural areas. The pull of urban areas is often supposed to be the result of sociological and other factors, such as the attraction of city lights. In contrast, Harris and Todaro (1970) have pointed out the importance of economic factors. According to their theory, urban wages are institutionally fixed at a level higher than rural labour incomes leading to an influx of rural migrants faster than the growth of urban employment opportunities. The rate of such migration is governed by the difference between rural incomes and the *expected* urban wage, i.e. the urban wage multiplied by the probability of getting urban employment at that wage, this probability being determined by the rate of urban employment. Such migration tends to go on until rural labour incomes are equal to the expected urban wage, at which point there is an equilibrium amount of unemployment in urban areas.

The 'push' explanation focusses on the limited ability of the rural areas to absorb the natural increase of population into productive employment. To see this relationship, let the total population be P, of which a proportion u is in urban areas, and let the rate of natural increase be n. Then, if the fraction of the natural increase in rural areas which can be absorbed into productive employment in those areas is b, the rate of growth of urban population r is given by

$$r = \frac{n(1 - b)}{u} + bn. \tag{7.5.1}$$

For example, if a country has reached the limit of its cultivable land and cannot absorb any increase in population in its rural areas, i.e. if $b=0$ and $n=0.03$, then $r=0.06$ when $u=0.5$ but it is equal to 0.15 when $u=0.2$; that is, urban population has to increase much faster to absorb the natural increase if the urban ratio is low as in LDCs than if it is high as in the DCs (Lewis, 1978, p.240).

In determining urban infrastructural policy, therefore, LDCs must make a deliberate choice of the desired rate of urbanization rather than leave it to the outcome of demographic forces or to the institutional forces determining urban wages. In order to influence the rate of urbanization, they must on the one hand seek to reduce the wage disparity between urban and rural areas so that it does not lead to excessive migration, and on the other hand, they must raise the proportion of the natural increase of population that can be accommodated in the rural areas by a faster rate of agricultural development. In making these decisions, the objective is not necessarily to reduce rural–urban migration to a minimum, for a certain amount of urbanization is necessary and desirable even for the purpose of promoting agricultural development.

But even with policies to reduce the present high rate of urbanization in LDCs, the rates that can be achieved are likely to be high because they are influenced to a great extent by the high rates of population growth. Therefore, LDCs must also consider the pattern of urbanization. In the experience of DCs, which dominates the world picture, urban places vary in size, such that there is a systematic pattern in the size distribution of these places, known as the rank order law. According to this law, when urban places are ranked according to their size, the total populaton of all urban places in each rank increases quite systematically. This can be seen most clearly in Table 7.3.

In this pattern, when the range of each class is halved from one rank to the next, the number of urban places tends to double fairly regularly, and the total population in each class tends to be fairly constant, except at the two extremes. The pattern is not just a coincidence but reflects the economic functions of towns of different sizes. The smallest towns perform various urban services for

Table 7.3 Number and population of urban places by size, 1960

Size (thousands)	Number	Percentage of world population
Over 12 800	1	0.5
6 400–12 800	6	1.6
3 200–6 400	14	2.2
1 600–3 200	42	3.0
800–1 600	93	3.4
400–800	163	3.0
200–400	340	3.1
100–200	641	3.0
50–100	1 295	3.0
25–50	2 571	3.0
12.5–25	4 952	2.9
6.25–12.5	9 118	2.7
Less than 6.25	12 351	1.6

Source: Davis, 1972, Table 9, p.37, and Table 11, p.39.

immediate rural hinterlands and hence a large number of them are needed. The most important of these services is the marketing function; these towns act as the centre at which the produce of the surrounding rural areas is assembled in the first instance for wider distribution and from which the rural areas are supplied with their requirements of various manufactures. Larger towns also have a marketing function in further combining the produce assembled in the smaller towns for distribution over longer distances. In addition, they are also the centres of industrial production. Hence, the number of these larger towns is less than that of the smaller towns. The biggest cities may also have a large share of industrial activities; in addition, they are the administrative, political and cultural centres for the whole country, and so there are fewer of them (Johnson, E. A. G., 1970, pp.19–20, and Chapter 3).

The pattern described by the rank order law, however, is particularly true for DCs; it applies to the world scene because the vast majority of urban places are in the DCs. It is much less valid in the LDCs, in which the principal or capital city tends to have a disproportionately large share of urban population and to be several times larger than the next two or three cities. This characteristic is known as 'urban primacy'. There are a number of factors which lead to urban primacy, such as the overall urban ratio and the country's dependence on foreign trade; but one of the main factors is the size of the country. Hence, in comparing DCs and LDCs, we must allow for the size of the country; this is illustrated in Table 7.4 in terms of a four-city index of primacy (ratio of the population of the largest city to the combined population of the next three cities) for countries of different sizes. When the few cases of large countries are excluded, urban primacy is more pronounced in LDCs than in DCs. The table shows that urban primacy tends to increase as we move from large to small countries.

Another way to describe urban primacy is to take the percentage of the urban population of a country residing in its largest city, a measure which can be calculated for more countries. This measure shows even more clearly the greater extent of urban primacy in LDCs (Table 7.5).

Table 7.4 Four-city index of primacy, c. 1970

Size of country (millions of population)	DCs	LDCs
Very large (over 100)	1.09	0.82
Large (50–100)	1.59	0.85
Medium (25–50)	0.80	1.90
Small (5–25)	1.27	1.92
Very small (below 5)	1.77	—
Total	1.33	1.70

Source: Davis, 1972, Table 8, pp.244–6.

Table 7.5 Percentage of urban population residing in principal city, 1970

Size of country (millions of population)	DCs	LDCs
Large (over 100)	9	13
Large and medium (25–100)	18	29
Small (5–25)	24	37
Very small (below 5)	35	52
Total	23	41

Source: Davis, 1969, Table A, pp.57–82, and Table E, pp.163–232.

Urban primacy is accentuated further by a tendency for the large urban places (cities with population over 100 000) to grow much more rapidly than smaller towns, especially in LDCs (Table 7.6).

The high and growing degree of urban primacy, especially in LDCs, is the result of a government policy of expanding infrastructural facilities in response to demand. In the initial stage, the large cities are relatively better endowed with these facilities. Further, the cost of these facilities is highly subsidized to users. Hence, a great share of industrial investment is attracted to the larger centres rather than to the smaller towns. Such investment in turn attracts migration from rural areas and smaller towns, so that smaller towns grow more slowly or even decline. On the other hand, the increasing congestion in the main urban centres makes governments allocate much of their resources to expand infrastructure in those areas further. In contrast, the neglect of smaller towns makes them less able to serve their rural hinterlands

Table 7.6 Growth of city and town population (decimal growth rates)

Period	DCs Cities	DCs Towns	LDCs Cities	LDCs Towns
1920–30	28.9	16.1	42.9	23.6
1930–40	22.8	23.5	54.6	25.3
1940–50	12.9	13.0	64.4	29.0
1950–60	33.8	23.9	77.2	42.0
1960–70	32.3	19.5	60.3	44.7

Sources: For 1920–60, U.N. *Growth of the World's Urban and Rural Populations*, 1969, Table 50, p.118.
For 1960–70, Davis, 1969, Table A, pp.57–82.

and to stimulate economic growth there. Hence, urbanization is caught in a vicious circle of increasing primacy.

The second strategy of building ahead of demand will start with the planning of urbanization as a whole with special attention to establishing a more appropriate pattern of urbanization. This will involve the deliberate creation of smaller towns to fit in with a preferred pattern. Because the growth of towns depends so heavily on infrastructural facilities, such as transport, power and water supply, and the availability of educational opportunities and urban amenities, for which government has the major responsibility, government has a great opportunity to influence the pattern of urbanization by its infrastructural strategy. Government can also influence the pattern of urbanization by more actively using price policy, e.g. by subsidizing infrastructure in the newly established smaller towns to attract investment and migration and by raising the fees charged in the already established large cities to discourage further concentration of industries and migration there. When small towns are built up on this strategy, they will not only stimulate economic growth in their hinterlands but also stem the flow of migration to the large cities, and hence lead to a more appropriate pattern of urbanization.

CHAPTER 8

Economic Institutions

8.1 Institutions and Economic Growth

In the case of a single individual or household isolated from others, all the benefits of their actions accrue to themselves and they can plan their actions so as to maximize these benefits. The same may even be true of a collectivized economy in which a central authority has complete control over the actions of all its members; such a central authority can, in principle, determine the behaviour of its members so as to maximize the welfare of the whole society. But in the case of a country which has opted for a mixed economy, many economic decisions are made by persons on the basis of their individual costs and benefits; then these decisions may not necessarily bring about the maximum economic advancement that society as a whole is capable of. How far such individual decisions do so depends on the institutions through which economic activities are organized. As North and Thomas (1973, pp.1–2) argue,

> In the past, most economic historians have heralded technological change as the major source of Western economic growth; indeed European economic history pivots around the industrial revolution. More recently, others have stressed investment in human capital as the major source of growth. Still more currently, scholars have begun to explore the growth effects of the reduction in costs of market information. There can be no doubt that each of these elements has contributed notably to growth in output. So have economies of scale, based on production for larger and larger markets . . . [These elements] reflect what economic historians and economists have almost universally cited as determinants of economic growth in their diagnoses of the past performance of economies. Yet the explanation clearly has a hole in it. We are left

wondering: if all that is required for economic growth is investment and innovation, why have some societies missed this desirable outcome. The factors we have listed (innovation, economies of scale, capital accumulation, etc.) are not causes of growth; they are growth. Growth will simply not occur unless the existing economic organization is efficient. Individuals must be lured by incentives to undertake the socially desirable activities.

Efficient economic organization is the key to growth; the development of an efficient economic organization in Western Europe accounts for the rise of the West. Efficient organization entails the establishment of industrial arrangements and property rights that create an incentive to channel individual economic effort into activities that bring the private rate of return close to the social rate of return.

In this chapter, we consider the various institutions through which economic activities are organized in societies, interpreting institutions broadly to refer to established values, practices, rules of conduct and generally accepted norms. Such institutions affect economic growth in two ways. One way is that the prevailing institutions must be such that people desire economic growth and are willing to make the required effort. Lewis (1955, chapter 2) has described this aspect as the 'will to economize'; it is discussed in Section 8.2 below. Further, the institutions must be such as to reward these efforts; as Lewis (1955, p.57) puts it,

Institutions promote or restrict growth according to the protection they accord to effort, according to the opportunities they provide for specialisation, and according to the freedom of manoeuvre they permit.

The ways in which institutions reward the efforts needed for growth may conveniently be divided into those concerning property rights and the legal protection of these rights on the one hand and those relating to the performance of markets on the other; these are discussed in Sections 8.3 and 8.4 respectively.

The later sections are mainly concerned with how these institutions affect economic growth. Before going on to those topics, we have also to consider how these institutions have come about, and why they differ from country to country. Until recently, the study of institutions was neglected by economists and was mostly carried on by other social scientists, such as sociologists, anthropologists and political scientists, but they have generally been concerned with various institutions for their own sake rather than their interaction with economic growth. More recently studies have shown, however, that these institutions are not rigidly determined by a society's culture, race, geography or other exogenous factors, but are influenced by economic growth itself. Therefore, in the course of time, there is a cumulative interaction between institutions and economic growth. Lewis (1955, p.143) has argued:

It is easy to see why there are these cumulative processes. The continuance of a social institution in a particular form depends upon its convenience, upon belief in its rectitude, and upon force. If growth begins to occur, all these sanctions are eroded. The

> institution ceases to be convenient, because it stands in the way of opportunities for economic advancement. Priests, lawyers, economists and other philosophers, who used to justify it in terms of their various dogmas, begin to reject the old dogmas, and to replace them by new dogmas more appropriate to the changing situation . . . . In the same way, when growth stops, the institutions which suited an expanding economy are no longer appropriate. People cease to believe in them; the priests, the lawyers, the economists and the philosophers turn against them, and the powerful groups who favour the *status quo* are able to enforce changes unfavourable to economic growth.

However, the interaction between institutions and economic growth is a slow process that has taken a long period of time in the past. For example, North and Thomas (1973) trace the evolution of property rights in western Europe from the tenth century onwards until they led to modern economic growth in Britain in the eighteenth century. Many of the institutions of LDCs which now hinder economic growth were evolved over a long period of time to suit conditions of economic stagnation; as new opportunities for growth appear, these institutions are themselves undergoing change, but the process is a slow one. The challenge to policy is therefore to hasten this process of institutional change, thereby allowing LDCs to exploit their growth opportunities more fully.

8.2 The Will to Economize

Neo-classical economics assumes that all persons are constantly and efficiently engaged in maximizing their individual welfare. In fact, however, while most people prefer more of a good to less, they rarely act with sufficient knowledge and calculation to maximize their advantage with the cold precision assumed in the theory (for a comprehensive critique, see Butt, 1978). At the same time, it is unrealistic to argue, as some writers have done, that the people of LDCs place a low value on material gains, i.e. that they lack the will to economize, and that this attitude is a major cause of slow economic growth in LDCs. (See Boeke, 1953 for a statement of this argument with special reference to Indonesia; for a critique of Boeke's arguments see Higgins, 1956.) The people of LDCs appear at first sight to be other-worldly, to venerate the ascetic life of renunciation, and to value non-economic objectives such as status and prestige. These attitudes, however, are the results of long periods of economic stagnation, and resignation to poverty (see e.g. Galbraith, 1980, Chapter 4). Under these conditions, there is little change in the total welfare of society as a whole, and the gains of one individual are usually at the expense of others. This is one of the principal reasons why religious and moral codes were developed to check the acquisitive instinct. Apart from this, what appears to be lack of desire for goods is often due to limited horizons, limited goods to enjoy, lack of knowledge and sheer habit and taboos.

A more stringent test of the will to economize is to see what happens when people face new opportunities and new incentives. Here also, many observed patterns of behaviour have been used to argue that the will to economize is limited because people do not make the effort to seize these opportunities and respond to these incentives. It is possible, however, to explain these patterns of behaviour by the inadequacy of the incentives. The point may be illustrated by a few examples.

An example that has been frequently cited from the historical experience of LDCs was the difficulty experienced by modern sector enterprises such as mines and plantations in getting wage labour. This used to be explained by the argument that workers placed a low value on material gain and a high value on leisure, leading to the theory of the backward-bending supply curve of labour. It is more likely, however, that this was due to the low level of wages offered compared with the profitability of own-account work in peasant cultivation, as Myint (1964) suggests, or to the lack of commodities on which to spend cash incomes, as suggested by Lewis (1955, p.30). Therefore, colonial governments imposed various types of tax to be paid in cash in order to induce workers to accept wage employment. In recent times, with further growth of population and greater opportunities to purchase goods, the numbers seeking wage employment in the modern sector far exceed the demand.

A second example is the reluctance of higher social groups to do manual work, often cited as a case of non-economic attitudes. Lewis (1955, p.45) has offered the alternative explanation that this attitude emerged under conditions of over-population as a moral duty on the part of the better-off to provide as much employment as possible to those who were not so well off.

A third example is the treatment of cattle. The case most often cited is the Hindu veneration of the cow as a sacred animal and the ban on cow slaughter for meat, which was thought to lead to a non-economic use of cattle in countries such as India. However, a deeper analysis has shown that this could be explained by the importance of the use of cattle for draft purposes in the technology prevailing in early times. Although the religious dogmas have survived to modern times, as technology changes, actual practice is also in a process of change and there is a more rational adjustment of cattle populations to actual economic needs (see Raj, 1969; Vaidyanathan *et al.*, 1979).

A final example that may be considered is the fact that the people of LDCs are not prone to take risks and to experiment with new techniques and new productive activities. The explanation is not so much the lack of desire for more material gain but rather the low level of income, barely above subsistence level. At such income levels, any failure would spell serious disaster for a household, so that it is unwilling to take risks in new activities, unless there is a good prospect of large gains. Such prospects were extremely limited in the past, but where more productive technologies have appeared in recent times, they tend to be adopted, initially by small numbers, and later by more people as their success is demonstrated.

If the will to economize is really absent or limited, then there is little chance of promoting rapid growth in the LDCs by government policies. But most indications of a limited desire for growth are really due to lack of knowledge, force of custom and tradition, and lack of profitable new technologies. As these conditions change, the values governing people's behaviour also change, but they do so very slowly. The changes usually start with small groups inbred with a spirit of adventure, often those who have recently migrated from another region or country. The process can be greatly accelerated by rapid expansion of education and technological progress. The problems of inducing faster growth in the LDCs lie, not so much in the failure of the will to economize, but rather in the weakness of the institutions which reward the efforts needed for growth, a problem that is examined in the following sections.

8.3 Property Rights

In order to induce people to make the necessary efforts to promote economic growth, they must be assured an adequate reward for these efforts. In so far as economic growth depends on the quantity and quality of productive resources, the extent to which people make the effort to maintain, improve and accumulate such resources depends on the security of their property rights. Capitalist societies are distinguished from socialist societies in that the former recognize, while the latter do not, the rights of private property in the factors of production. But even in capitalist societies and mixed economies, there are great differences in the nature and security of property rights.

In the early stages of civilization, an individual's right to property depended on his own ability to defend his possession against others. In course of time, there evolved in the western countries the concept of property rights which were protected by society as a whole. In recounting the long historical process, North and Thomas (1973, pp.8, 157–8) say,

> The creating, specifying and enacting of such property rights are costly, in a degree affected by the state of technology and organization. As the potential grows for private gains to exceed transaction costs, efforts will be made to establish such property rights. Governments take over the protection and enforcement of property rights because they can do so at a lower cost than private volunteer groups. However, the fiscal needs of government may induce the protection of certain property rights which hinder rather than promote growth; therefore we have no guarantee that productive institutional arrangements will emerge.
>
> [By the eighteenth century] a structure of property rights had developed in the Netherlands and England which provided the incentives necessary for sustained growth. . . . International competition provided a powerful incentive for other countries to adapt their institutional structures to provide equal incentives for economic growth and the spread of the 'industrial revolution'. Success has been a consequence of the reorganization of property rights in those countries. The failures—the Iberian Peninsula in the history of the Western World, and much of Latin America, Asia and Africa in our times—have been a consequence of inefficient economic organization.

There is little new about the conclusion. Karl Marx and Adam Smith both subscribed to this view. They both saw successful growth as dependent on the development of efficient property rights. However, Marx failed to recognize that there is nothing inevitable about economic growth and Smith did not tell us how to ensure an efficient government that will devise and maintain a set of property rights that assures sustained economic growth.

We have therefore to consider the differences in the evolution of property rights in countries which have achieved rapid economic growth and in those which have not, and the policies that the latter might pursue in this regard.

In general, the experience of the western countries has been that as a factor of production became scarce, property rights in that factor became more sharply defined. This means that individuals could count more confidently on the returns from such resources and hence, by using the scarce resources more productively for their own benefit, would also promote economic growth in their societies. Thus, in the earliest phase, when land was abundant relative to labour, there was little private property in land, and most land was available for communal use. It was labour which was scarce, giving rise to property rights in labour in the form of slavery in some societies and virtual property rights exercised by feudal overlords over the labour of serfs and villeins in others. It was only as labour became more plentiful that it was cheaper to hire free and willing workers for wages.

The next phase was thus one in which, with population growth, it was land which became scarce relative to labour. This led to more sharply defined rights to private property in land, and the taking over into private ownership of land which had hitherto been used communally and cultivated by collectively determined methods. This change led to an advance in agricultural development with more productive use of land, amounting to what is often described as an agricultural revolution. As these countries began to industrialize, property rights in industrial capital came to be more sharply defined to ensure its productive use. This phase also gave rise to new types of property rights in various intangible assets, such as patents and financial assets.

The institutions of private property were evolved in the western countries over a long period, even before their modern economic growth began. It was largely a process induced by changes both in the demand for and supply of institutional change (see Ruttan, 1978, for a review of these factors). In the LDCs, however, many of these forms of property rights together with other forms of commercialization were introduced more abruptly by the western powers which had colonized these countries, suddenly replacing earlier indigenous systems. Myrdal (1970, p.215) describes the transition as follows:

> Generally speaking, the pressure to introduce a Western form of ownership of land, the partial monetization of certain economic relations, the spur by these two changes to moneylending, the internal migrations, the influx of 'oriental aliens' in some countries, and the superimposition of a colonial administration that aimed mainly at collecting taxes and maintaining peace and order resulted in a weakening and in some areas the virtual breakdown of the indigenous system of rights and obligations, laws, and procedures.

In retrospect, the introduction of a foreign system of property rights in that way and at that time may have been premature. One reason was simply that the institutional, especially legal, framework of these property rights was not fully understood by most of the people, especially the large population who had little education. Another reason was that the new system disrupted the earlier institutions based on a more complex balance of rights and obligations and offered a new set of rights that was unfair, and felt to be unfair. Small groups of people who understood the new system better were able to take undue advantage to enrich themselves at the expense of others. A third reason was that the efficiency of a system of property rights depended ultimately on the legal framework. To be efficient, the legal framework must be predictable, uniform in application to all persons, capable of speedy adjudication, and seen to be fair. In many LDCs, these conditions are not fulfilled. Myrdal (1970, Chapter 7) has described these countries as 'soft states' because of a general state of social indiscipline, weakness in law observance and enforcement, and widespread corruption in public life. These may all be seen as a premature and artificial hastening of the progression from status to contract which occurred in a slow but orderly fashion in the western countries and which was forced on the colonial countries before the people were ready for it.

In formulating the development policies relating to property rights, the LDCs have to make a number of decisions, such as the type of assets in which to recognize rights of private property and those to be reserved for public ownership, what type of private property rights to recognize, and how they may be exercised. So far, we have been discussing property rights as if they represented a simple concept of ownership. In fact, it consists of a bundle of particular rights, each with a wide spectrum of gradations. One of these rights is the power to use property to produce income. Another is the right to the income from the property, whoever manages it. Initially these rights are exercised together. From a social point of view, the right to the income is the reward for the efficient management which makes productive use of the property. But the two rights are separable and, with the managerial revolution in the large modern corporation, have increasingly become separated. This has expanded the policy options available to governments. As Lewis (1969a, p.64) says:

> The separation between management and ownership is one of the striking features of the large modern corporation. One does not any longer have to choose between private management of private property and public management of public property. One can also have public management of private property. This in one sense, is what nationalisation comes to; the assets belong to the public in the legal sense, but they are matched by an equal amount of private wealth, since the original assets are acquired by paying compensation, and new assets are financed by borrowing from the private sector. The fourth alternative, private management of public property, meets the socialist requirement that it brakes the growth of private wealth, and ensures at the same time such virtues as private management may have.

In choosing from these options, government must lay down clear-cut principles, such as the type of industries affected, the conditions under which some will be nationalized and the terms in which it will be done, rather than decide individual cases arbitrarily. The potential threat of nationalization is a powerful disincentive to investment.

One of the most important issues facing LDCs, especially those with an acute scarcity of land relative to population, is land reform, i.e. the expropriation of land from large owners and its redistribution to others. The case for land reform is often based on a sentiment for equality. It must also be considered from the point of view of the efficient use of land. Thus, there is a case for land reform if the large owners are less efficient in the use of land than small owners. At the present stage of development in many LDCs, farm sizes resulting from land reform will be small because a large proportion of the population is still engaged in agriculture. But in course of time, as labour moves to other sectors, and as the productivity of labour in agriculture rises, farm sizes must expand. Therefore, the rights conferred by land reform must be defined carefully to permit this trend.

8.4 The Performance of Markets

(a) The Institution of Free Markets

In broad historical perspective, one of the main features of economic development is the steady progress from subsistence to specialization, from individual households producing all their requirements to the system of a large number of producers each producing a different commodity and exchanging their products. A high degree of specialization, such as that characterizing the DCs, depends on the functioning of free and efficient markets. Markets have existed from time immemorial but it was only since the eighteenth century that a system of markets was established in western Europe, free from excessive government intervention and open to all persons.

The advocacy of market freedom from State interference was, of course, the central theme of classical economics, but it must be remembered, as Hutchinson (1978, p.22) points out, that Adam Smith

> valued economic freedoms not mainly or simply because he believed that they promoted a more rapid growth of GNP but for *their own sake*.

The point is further clarified by Stigler (1975, pp.40, 50–1)

> Smith based his proposals for economic policy upon two main positions. Smith's first basis for his economic policies was his belief in the efficiency of the system of natural liberty. The second foundation of Smith's strong preference for private economic activity was that he deeply distrusted the state. This distrust, I must emphasize, was primarily a distrust of the motives rather than the competence of the state. Smith makes very little of inept governmental conduct—indeed he clearly believes that as far as inefficiency is concerned, the joint stock companies and even more the universities are worse offenders than the state. His real complaint against the state is that it is the creature of organized, articulate, self-serving groups—above all, the merchants and manufacturers. The legislative is directed less often by an extended view of the common good than by the clamorous importunity of partial interests. . . . To the extent that theory was guiding [economists], surely it was a theory of government rather than of economics.

The system of free enterprise, however, turned out to be one of the major sources of economic growth. The effects have been described by Landes (1969, p.19) thus:

The scope of private economic activity was far larger in western Europe than in other parts of the world and grew as the economy itself grew and opened up new areas of enterprise untrammeled by rule or custom. The trend was self-reinforcing; those economies grew fastest that were freest. This is not to imply that state enterprise or control is intrinsically inferior to private enterprise; simply that, given the state of knowledge in pre-industrial Europe, the private sector was in a better position to judge economic opportunity and allocate resources efficiently. Even more important, perhaps, was the impulse given thereby to innovation; in an age when the nature and direction of technological opportunity were far less obvious than now, the multiplication of points of creativity was a great advantage.

The role that free markets played in promoting economic growth in the historical experience of DCs was essentially dynamic and this was well appreciated by the classical economists. As O'Brien (1975, pp.54–4) says,

It is perhaps ironic that a dynamic view of economic phenomena, taken for granted in the classical writings, disappeared from view with the marginal revolution of the 1980s and had to be rediscovered by Schumpeter, Galbraith and others in our times. . . . The view of the allocative process which is contained in Book I of the *Wealth of Nations* or in Book I of J. S. Mill's *Principles* is a view of the mechanism of allocation taking place within a framework of changing technology and changing resources. To anyone living through one of the greatest explosions of economic growth in the history of mankind, such a view was the one most likely to make sense. It was because of the dynamic nature of this competition that owners of capital were able to exploit *new* profit opportunities, sell *new* commodities, obtain supplies from *new* sources, and sell in *new* markets.

Kaldor (1972) has therefore made a sharp distinction between the *creative* and the *allocative* functions of markets. The allocative function, on which neoclassical economics has focussed its attention, is concerned with the allocation of a given stock of resources to satisfy tastes and preferences as fully as possible; it is a static function. In contrast, the creative function of markets is to transmit impulses to economic change, and to encourage entrepreneurs to produce new commodities and use new techniques at their own risk; then the impersonal forces of market competition select the more efficient producers and techniques, and thus promote growth.

(b) Market Performance in LDCs

In the DMEs, the performance of markets has become very efficient in bringing together large numbers of producers and consumers from various parts of the world and thus promoting a high degree of specialization. Neoclassical economics has mostly evolved from the study of these DMEs. Therefore, in its application to LDCs, this approach also tends to assume the functioning of efficient markets, subject only to government interventions, and has concentrated on the effects of such interventions. In fact, however, the efficiency of market performance in the LDCs is limited in many ways.

First, there is only a limited participation in market activities. One reason is the small scale of production, especially in the agricultural sector; thus, for example, each agricultural household produces such a small quantity of food that most of it is consumed by the household and does not enter into the market at all. Another reason is the acute shortage of transport and communications infrastructure, so that it is not possible or profitable for persons in one region to sell to, or buy from, persons in other regions. This explains why there is little trade between regions in such basic commodities as food, and why there are large regional price disparities (e.g. Arndt and Sundrum, 1975) and why levels of food consumption among different regions are highly correlated with levels of production (see e.g. United Nations, 1975; Hasan, 1976). Yet another reason is the lack of knowledge of market opportunities due to the low level of education. The increase in the degree of market participation, in the course of transition from subsistence to commercial farming, is a slow process (for a study of the various stages of this process, see Fisk, 1975).

Next, there is the problem that even when people participate in market activities, the prices at which they do so tend to be determined by custom and tradition; two well-known examples are the prohibition against charging interest on loans and the fixing of wages for harvesting labour as a traditional proportion of output independently of the number of workers employed. These prices do not respond to the forces of supply and demand. Some recent studies have shown that even in the DMEs, many prices tend to be rigid (see Section 9.9) but in the LDCs, prices often tend to reflect some concept of the 'just price' that may have prevailed over long periods of time (Polanyi, 1958).

In the DMEs, an important characteristic of markets is that they function impersonally and are no respector of persons. This enables all people to have equal access to market opportunities and to specialize according to their abilities. In the LDCs, the movement from status to contract is still incomplete, and access to markets still depends on status and personal circumstance. With the high degree of social stratification prevailing in these countries, markets are also highly segmented.

In LDCs, the weaknesses of market performance are most severe in the case of factor markets. When the ownership of the factors of production is distributed in such a way that the owners are not able to use them fully themselves, a more productive use can be achieved if there is an active market in the factors or their services. Such markets are very inefficient in the LDCs.

In the case of land, Lewis (1955, p.91) has argued that

> there is probably no country in the world where land is bought and sold solely for its value as a factor of production, and no country where non-economic factors do not frustrate schemes which would otherwise increase output.

These non-economic considerations are particularly important in the LDCs, where much land is held for reasons of prestige and status. The result is that large numbers of people hold and operate small pieces of land. One of the most serious consequences of the lack of land markets in LDCs is that even small holdings are divided into a large number of parcels. For example, the average holding was divided into 2.7 parcels in Indonesia in 1973 (Booth and Sundrum, 1976, Table 12) and into 5.7 parcels in India in 1960–1 (Minhas, 1974, p.403). Countries such as India have tried to consolidate these parcels by administrative action. A more efficient method would be to promote an active land market, so that small parcels could be exchanged for each other at their market values. The main problem is that these parcels vary greatly in quality and location. A useful step towards this goal would be to develop the land to reduce such variations.

There is a more active market in land leases. In some Asian countries, e.g. Pakistan and the Philippines, a considerable proportion of operated land is leased in. There are, however, wide variations in the terms of such leases, such as fixed rents or share cropping, depending on the relative bargaining strength of owners and tenants. There is also a tendency for land to be leased to the large rather than small farmers; in the case of India, Raj (1970) found little difference between the inequality of operated and owned holdings.

There are also serious problems in the labour markets of LDCs. To begin with, the market for wage labour is small, and a high proportion of the labour force consists of workers on their own account. This is because agricultural activity is carried on in such small farms that most of the work is done by family labour, and there is only a small industrial sector. With the growth of population, increasing numbers are seeking wage employment, especially women previously engaged in household enterprises and young workers. One of the most serious problems facing LDCs is the inability of the labour market to absorb the increasing numbers of those seeking wage employment. This is partly due to the slow growth in the demand for wage labour, but it is also due to the institutional weakness of the labour market. One problem is that the concepts of labour force participation and of employment and unemployment are ill-defined in the transitional state of these economies. Thus, by the usual labour force criteria, the unemployment rate is usually found to be small. Hence, statisticians have tended to use a poverty criterion to estimate that up to 25 per cent of the labour force is unemployed or unproductively employed (see e.g. I.L.O., 1974, p.7).

The other problem is that the labour market is highly segmented, with different wage rates and different levels of absorption of labour in the various segments. This is, of course, partly due to differences in the quality of labour, especially differences in ability and educational qualifications. The wage differentials between labour of different educational qualifications are very high, higher than the costs of education. This is partly because the wage levels are dominated by the public service salary structures and partly because of the imperfection of the capital market, in which young workers cannot borrow for educational investment at the prevailing interest rate.

But the market for the same quality of labour, especially unskilled labour, is also highly segmented. First, there is the sharp distinction between the urban and rural markets for wage labour, with urban wages being distinctly higher than rural labour incomes, mainly for institutional reasons. This wage disparity induces a steady migration of labour from rural to urban areas, but because of the high costs of movement and lack of information about employment opportunities, the rate of migration is too small to reduce the wage disparity or to make a dent in the levels of rural unemployment and underemployment. But even this relatively low rate of migration leads to high rates of growth or urban population because of its small base (see Section 7.4 above).

The labour market within each of these areas is also highly segmented. In the urban areas, a privileged minority, especially those with some education and political influence, get employed at wages set by administrative decision rather than market forces. The large-scale, capital-intensive, modern sector, also offers a limited amount of employment at relatively high wages. Most of the urban wage employment is in the small-scale sector; because this sector is sharply separated from the others, there is little competition between these segments, and employers in the small-scale segment can exercise considerable monopsony power to keep wages low. The rest of the urban labour force works on its own account in the 'informal sector' where there is considerable ease of entry for those with small amounts of capital and where an intermediate technology is used to produce output for the lower income groups of the urban population (for more details of this sector, see I.L.O., 1972, Chapter 13). There is a considerable amount of visible unemployment in urban areas, but this may be considered largely voluntary, as argued in the Harris–Todaro theory (see Section 7.4 above).

The labour that is not absorbed in the urban areas is then thrown on the rural labour market as a kind of residual. There is little regular wage employment in the rural areas, most of the regular work being done by family labour on small farms. Especially in the densely populated LDCs, there is a large proportion of workers seeking wage employment but not getting it, both because the demand for labour is not wage-elastic and because wages are fixed above equilibrium levels, partly for institutional reasons, such as traditional and customary practices, and partly at their efficiency maximizing levels (see Bliss and Stern, 1978, for a fuller discussion of this aspect). The limited amount of available regular employment is rationed out to workers on the basis of various forms of stratification, such as caste, class, access to own assets, etc. (see Beteille, 1969 and Stoler, 1977, for evidence on India and Java). The rest of the rural labour force gets only casual employment in peak seasons and suffers from severe underemployment for the rest of the year, maintaining themselves with own account work at low levels of productivity. (See White, B., 1976, for a discussion of patterns of labour allocation among low income rural households in rural Java).

Under these circumstances, a useful policy approach is to provide public sector employment at wages corresponding to a minimum standard of living; this policy is already being followed in some countries, for example, the Employment Guarantee Scheme in some states of India (see Dandekar and Sathe, 1980) and the *kabupaten* programme in Indonesia (see de Wit, 1973). Quite apart from providing employment for the underemployed, it also improves the working of the labour market in the rural areas by introducing more competition and raising wages for the poorest workers. To have this effect, however, these schemes must be greatly expanded. In the urban areas, the main problem is the low wages of those employed in the small-scale segment of the labour market; to the extent that this is due to the monopoly power of employers, measures such as minimum wages may raise wage levels without reducing employment.

(c) The Capital Market

The capital market is so important that we discuss it here in more detail. In traditional economies, the investor and the saver are often the same person, and most investment is financed by own savings. Such lending as there was was mainly for immediate consumption to persons in distress rather than for investment; hence there was a general disapproval of, and even a ban against, charging interest on loans and, when allowed, the accumulation of interest was restricted. The financing of investment by own savings greatly limited its volume and reduced its efficiency. Persons who have savings may not know of, or be able to undertake, the most productive investments, and often sink their savings into acquiring existing capital and land, thus bidding up their prices. Persons who can undertake highly productive investments may not be able to finance them with their own savings. The problem is further compounded by the fact that savings are made by a large number of persons in small amounts each and for short periods of time, while many new production possibilities require investment in large amounts for long periods. There are also wide disparities in the productivity of investments in different sectors and regions of traditional economies, but the savings of each region are usually invested in that region rather than allocated among all regions according to the returns.

The DMEs have overcome these problems by developing various types of financial assets and financial institutions dealing in such assets. The growth of such financial intermediaries helps to mobilize more resources and allocate them more productively. For increasing such financial intermediation, the most important requirement is the easy marketability of financial assets. An important advance in DCs towards this end was the development of joint stock corporations with limited liability. The financing of investment through financial assets was very important in the early stages of growth of the DCs and, although large corporate enterprises rely heavily on undistributed profits for their expansion, is still important at present.

A convenient measure of financial development suggested by Goldsmith (1969) is the financial intermediation ratio (FIR) defined as the ratio of total financial assets to national wealth. In the 1960s, this ratio was well above 1 in the advanced developed countries such as Great Britain, United States and Japan, and slightly below 1 in countries such as Germany, France, Belgium, Norway and Australia. Even in the more advanced of the LDCs, such as Venezuela, Mexico and India, the ratio was only about 0.4. Another measure is the ratio of money (including demand and time deposits) to national income; in 1970, this ratio was around 0.60 in the DMEs compared with an average of only about 0.25 in eleven semi-industrialized LDCs (McKinnon, 1973, Chapter 8).

At a higher level of development, the financial system of a country consists of a large variety of financial institutions specializing in different types of financial assets according to their risk, maturity and yield. In the initial stages, the role of the banking system was very important with a significant difference in two groups of countries. In some countries, such as Britain and the United States, there was an early development of the stock exchange and other institutions dealing in securities for financing long-term investment; therefore the banking system tended to specialize in short-term credit, for working capital. In France, Germany and other European countries which were late-comers to industrialization, the lack of the securities market led to the banking system playing a greater role in providing long-term capital. Schumpeter (1934) therefore assigned a key role to banks in the development process and Gerschenkron (1962, p.12) speaks of their 'truly momentous role [as] specific instruments of industrialisation in a backward country'.

Two approaches may be distinguished in policies for financial development (Patrick, 1966). One is to follow the historical experience of the DCs in which financial institutions were evolved in the private sector in response to the demand for them; this demand-following approach, however, is a slow process because the demand at a low level of development is inadequate to induce the growth of financial institutions, and can only expand with the growth of such institutions. Therefore, countries anxious to force the pace of economic growth have to follow the other supply-leading approach of setting up financial institutions ahead of the demand for them.

The supply-leading approach has in fact been followed in many LDCs. They have set up a number of new institutions to provide capital for productive investment. For example, with the help of the World Bank, many countries have set up development banks. There are, however, a number of problems. In setting up such new institutions, the LDCs have often tended to imitate the model of the DCs too closely, without consideration of the circumstances prevailing in their own countries. For example, one of the rules guiding ordinary banking is to insist on borrowers having a debt–equity ratio below some maximum level. This rule was based on the situation in countries with a highly developed capital market through which enterprises could finance their equity capital. In the LDCs, where enterprises cannot raise long-term capital in this way, a more appropriate rule would be to ensure that the borrower stakes a sufficient amount of his own capital, not in relation to the total size of the project, but in relation to his own personal wealth.

Another problem in LDCs imitating the procedures of the DCs is the high transaction costs involved. High transaction costs are the main reason for the fragmentation of LDC capital and credit markets. In most of these countries, it is a complex and time-consuming task for savers to make deposits in the major banks; therefore special institutions must be developed to tap small savings at low administrative cost and less inconvenience to depositors. There are also high costs of administration and of default, especially in making small loans, if decisions are highly centralized; these can be avoided by greater decentralization of lending decisions to local managers who know their clients and their economic circumstances better (see Bhatt, 1978).

In the early stages when only a few new financial institutions can be set up, it is inevitable that there will be some dualism between the organized and the unorganized money markets. The problem, however, is that the organized capital market initially serves the modern and industrial sectors of the economy, providing them with cheap credit, and after the needs of these sectors are met, progress in extending the institutions to other sectors is slow. Some writers (e.g. Shaw, 1973; McKinnon, 1973) have described this situation as 'financial repression' and have argued that interest rates should be raised in order to mobilize more savings and allocate them more efficiently. A more effective approach would be to extend the new financial institutions more rapidly to all sectors of the economy; in doing so, they should not imitate the practice of DCs completely but seek to modify them especially by reducing transaction costs, e.g. by greater decentralization. It may also be necessary to combine technical advice with credit (see Bhatt, 1978).

A particularly serious problem exists in the agricultural sector of LDCs, which depends greatly on capital for its development. The capital needs of this sector are mostly provided by the unorganized money market with a substantial monopolistic element. There has been an increase in the supply of institutional credit to this sector in the last two decades by the expansion of rural lending institutions such as village banks and cooperative credit societies, but the progress in the volume of institutional credit and the reduction in the cost of borrowing has been slow (Tun Wai, 1977). What is required is a faster expansion in the supply of institutional credit to this sector in order to overcome the weaknesses of the unorganized money market.

PART III

Growth and Distribution at a Low Level of Development

CHAPTER 9

Production: Analysis

Part II of the book was concerned with an interpretation of the concept of development and the long-term policies needed to promote development in the LDCs. Part III is concerned with how growth and distribution are affected by the low level of development in the LDCs at present and with policies to deal with them until these countries become more developed. The subject is discussed under three topics, namely, production, international trade and income distribution. Each topic is discussed in a pair of chapters, one dealing with analysis and the other with policy. The present chapter deals with the analysis of the level, structure and growth of production. It starts with a critical review of the main approaches followed in the literature and discusses some important factors which have generally been neglected in these approaches.

9.1 The Level and Growth of Production

The widespread poverty in LDCs as reflected in the low standard of living of the mass of the population is ultimately due to the low levels of production per head of population in these countries. Some of the data on the levels and growth of production in LDCs were given in Chapters 2 and 3, and compared with the position in DCs. It was there shown that the rate of growth of aggregate production in the LDCs in the post-war period was quite high, comparable to that in the DCs in the same period, and higher than that in the historical experience of the DCs. But this growth of aggregate output has not raised the general standard of living significantly, because it was offset by an unprecedented rate of population growth.

It was also shown that the structure of the economy in LDCs was dominated by the agricultural or primary production sector, which produced a large part of the total output and employed a large part of the labour force. The average productivity of labour in this sector was lower than in other sectors, and the gap between DCs and LDCs was greatest in this sector. There was some structural transformation, i.e. a decline in the role of the primary sector and an increase in that of the secondary, industrial, sector but, for the average of all LDCs, the change was relatively small, especially in comparison with the corresponding changes in the historical experience of DCs.

This pattern reflects the average experience of all LDCs, but because of their greater weight in numbers, it is dominated by the experience of the large LDCs. There have been some significant exceptions to this general pattern. Those which were earliest to show exceptionally high rates of growth and structural transformation in the post-war period were Taiwan, South Korea, Hong Kong and Singapore, relatively small countries and city-states, known as the 'Gang of Four'. Since then, a number of other countries have also shown a similar performance. Reynolds (1977) has identified 15 cases, which best merit the description of 'developing' countries, for special study. In the present chapter, we seek explanations for the low level and slow growth of production and the agriculture-dominated structure of the economy in the LDCs, with such few exceptions.

9.2 The Production Function Approach

The standard explanation, that most frequently followed by economists, is the 'production function' approach. Although it has been most fully elaborated by neo-classical economists, it is also implicit in much of the Marxist literature. According to this approach, the aggregate output of a country is determined by its endowment of various factors of production. In the ultimate analysis, these factors are reduced to three, classified according to their supply characteristics: land, 'the original and indestructible properties of the soil', whose supply is fixed; capital, 'the produced means of production', whose supply is constantly augmented by investment, generally assumed to be influenced by economic considerations; and labour, whose supply is mainly governed by population growth, which is sometimes assumed to be determined by economic factors and sometimes by other, exogenous, factors.

Neo-classical economic theory then shows how a free enterprise system working through competitive market forces brings about a maximum of aggregate output for a given stock of these factors of production. To be more precise, it shows that aggregate output is maximized in the sense of 'Pareto optimality', i.e. that the resource allocation at an equilibrium position cannot be altered to benefit any member of the economy without hurting some others.

Therefore, aggregate output is maximized at the equilibrium position only for the particular way the factors of production are distributed among the population to begin with. The stock of productive resources and its distribution among the population then determine the structure of output by the laws of supply and demand. The theory then goes on to show how increases in the stock of these resources, especially capital and labour, lead to growth of aggregate output over time. The variation of per capita income then depends on the race between capital accumulation and population growth. The rate of capital accumulation depends on the savings ratio, the proportion of income that is saved and invested, which is generally assumed to be determined by the levels of income. Economic growth is also influenced by technological progress either occurring exogenously or under the influence of market forces.

Although this approach gives us some useful insights in some limited contexts, it is not completely satisfactory as an explanation of the level and growth of production in LDCs at present or the historical growth of production in DCs. The main reason is that it is based on assumptions implying a high level of development. It assumes that markets function impersonally so that all individuals have equal access to them, whereas in fact markets at a low level of development are highly segmented regionally and by the rigid division of society into distinct social classes. It assumes that these markets function efficiently to equilibrate supply and demand for goods and services, so that all resources are fully utilized, whereas many of the resources of LDCs, especially labour, are seriously under-utilized. It assumes maximizing behaviour on the part of individuals who are then highly responsive to economic incentives, so that the price system leads to the efficient allocation of resources consistent with people's tastes and preferences. Individuals in LDCs may respond to economic incentives regarding some of their short-term decisions but much less regarding their longer-term decisions. Thus, in some respects, resources are allocated quite efficiently in LDCs according to the prevailing technology, but this is the result of trial and error over long periods in which this technology has remained stationary. Individuals in LDCs have been much less responsive in adopting new techniques of production. Hence, the underlying assumptions of the production function approach do not reflect the dominant modes of behaviour at the low levels of development prevailing in LDCs; that is why the concepts of growth and development were sharply distinguished in Chapter 5.

The production function approach has been evolved with particular reference to the DMEs. But even in these countries, it neglects some important factors. It is a highly static theory because it assumes that prices adjust rapidly to changes in supply and demand, and hence that resources are allocated efficiently to maximize output at any time for the stock of resources existing at that time, thereby neglecting some dynamic factors. It generally assumes constant returns to scale in each line of production, whereas increasing returns, especially in manufacturing industry, have been an important source of growth. Even in DMEs, prices in some important markets are not sufficiently flexible to bring about equilibrium, especially in the labour market, so that levels of employment are determined by demand factors, often at below full employment levels.

In the rest of this chapter, we shall consider some important factors determining the level and growth of production, especially in LDCs, which have been neglected in the production function approach. Before doing so, we shall consider another approach which is also prominent in the literature.

9.3 The 'Patterns of Development' Approach

In this approach, the basic assumption is that there is a single pattern of economic progress that all countries must follow, with some countries lagging behind others. The past experience of the 'advanced' countries is then used to explain the present trends in the lagging or 'backward' countries. This approach underlies, implicitly or explicitly, a number of theories which differ in many other respects. Some of these theories, known as 'stages of growth theories' aim to explain broad aspects of the economy as a whole. Marx's theory of the succession of feudalism, various phases of capitalism, and socialism is an example of this approach. In his version, he also attempted a logical justification of this sequence and applied it to predict future trends in the DCs, but his prophecies in this regard have failed to materialize. Another example is Rostow's (1960) theory of the five stages of growth, including in particular, the 'take-off' stage which has often been used to separate developed from less-developed countries. These stage theories have mostly been derived from the past experience of the relatively few countries which have already achieved a high level of development, but in spite of the long period of contact between these countries and others which are at a low level of development, there is little sign that the latter will inevitably follow the same pattern.

There are a number of other theories based on this approach which deal with particular aspects of the economy. Some examples, mentioned in Section 1.2, are the demographic transition theory, the theory of foreign trade as an 'engine of growth', and the theory that the agricultural share of the labour force will decline over time as incomes rise. These are historical generalizations which cannot lightly be applied to the present situation in LDCs or their future prospects. In order to do so, they must first be explained in terms of more basic factors which are likely to hold more widely. The demographic transition theory is examined in Section 9.4 below; the role of foreign trade is considered in Chapter 11. Here we shall analyse the factors affecting the agricultural share of the labour force in more detail, in terms of supply and demand factors, in order to see how far past experience can be applied to the future.

The historical experience in this regard has been described by a number of writers (Fisher, 1935; Clark, 1940; Kuznets, 1957). The theoretical explanation takes one of two forms. One theory is the demand explanation based on income elasticities of demand. According to Engel's law, the income elasticity of demand for food, the principal product of the agricultural sector, is typically less than unity, i.e. the proportion of expenditure on food declines as income rises; the theory then uses this relationship to explain the decline in the agricultural share of the labour force. The theory does not explain the growth of income but only its effect on agriculture. The other theory is based on supply factors. It argues that in the early stages of growth, the productivity of labour in agriculture is low, so that each worker in agriculture produces little more than the food requirement of himself and his family; therefore most of the labour force is engaged in agriculture. As the productivity of labour in agriculture increases, more and more labour is released from agriculture to other sectors. Except for the concept of 'food requirements' this explanation does not take account of demand factors. In historical fact, it is obvious that both demand and supply factors have played a part. The combination of these factors then explains the changes in agriculture's share of both income and employment.

For example, it can be shown that, in a closed economy with full employment of labour and constant relative prices, the agricultural share of labour is governed by the formula

$$\lambda_a' - \lambda_a = \frac{\lambda_a \lambda_b (R_b \epsilon_a - R_a \epsilon_b)}{\lambda_a \epsilon_a (1 + R_b) + \lambda_b \epsilon_b (1 + R_a)}, \qquad (9.3.1)$$

where R_i is the rate of growth of labour productivity, ϵ_i is the income elasticity of demand, λ_i is the initial and λ_i' the final share of the labour force, in sector i ($i = a$ for agriculture, $= b$ for other sectors). Hence the condition for the agricultural share of the labour force to decrease or increase over time takes the simple form

$$\lambda_a' \lesseqgtr \lambda_a \text{ according as } \frac{R_a}{R_b} \gtrless \frac{\epsilon_a}{\epsilon_b}, \qquad (9.3.2)$$

i.e. according as the ratio of the growth rates of labour productivity in the agricultural and non-agricultural sectors representing the supply factors is greater or less than the ratio of the respective income-elasticities of demand. (See Booth and Sundrum, 1982, for the derivation and some applications to DCs and LDCs). The result shows that it is not possible to derive any conclusion just from the information that $R_a > 0$ and $\epsilon_a < 1$; the actual outcome depends on the ratios of the productivity growth rates and the income elasticities of demand. The ratio of income elasticities is generally less than unity. Therefore, for the agricultural share of labour to decline, it is not necessary that the ratio of productivity growth rates be greater than unity; it is sufficient if it is greater than the ratio of income elasticities. This condition was satisfied in the historical experience of DCs and is also likely to be satisfied in LDCs in the long run, but may or may not be satisfied in particular short periods. The condition (9.3.2) has to be modified to take account of other factors, such as the effect of international trade and changes in relative prices, but these effects do not appear to have been very significant in the historical experience of DCs.

The historical generalization relates the agricultural share of the labour force to the growth of income which is left unexplained. But in the present analysis, the overall rate of growth of income, R_e, can be explained by the demand and supply factors as follows:

$$R_e = \frac{\lambda_a R_a(1 + R_b) + \lambda_b R_b(1 + R_a)}{\lambda_a \epsilon_a(1 + R_b) + \lambda_b R_b(1 + R_a)}, \qquad (9.3.3)$$

or

$$R_e = (k_a R_a + k_b R_b) + \frac{(\lambda_a' - \lambda_a)(q_a' - q_b')}{\lambda_a q_a + \lambda_b q_b}, \qquad (9.3.4)$$

where k_i is the initial share of output, and q_i and q_i' are the initial and final products of labour, in the ith sector. Equation (9.3.4) shows that the growth of income cannot be taken simply as the weighted average of the productivity growth in the two sectors, shown by the first term, as is often assumed, but depends also on the re-allocation of labour between the sectors, as shown by the second term. The relation between the growth of income and the agricultural share of the labour force must be analysed in terms of such supply and demand factors, rather than just by applying an historical generalization.

There is another group of studies following this approach, in which the 'patterns of development' are derived, not so much from the long-term historical experience of countries, but rather from a cross-section of the more recent and relatively short-period experience of countries at various levels of development. The typical procedure is to derive various statistical relationships by fitting regression equations to international cross-section data from as many countries as possible. These studies also suffer from the basic weakness of assuming that the experience of all countries conforms to a single universal law. Another theoretical weakness of most such statistical studies is the assumption that the variables studied are closely related to income level, which is most often chosen as the explanatory variable. Apart from these theoretical limitations, there are also a number of statistical weaknesses in many of these studies.

The regressions in these studies often give a good fit to the data, as indicated by high R^2 and t-values, but the fact that a statistical relationship fits the data of a particular sample closely is not sufficient evidence of the same regularity in the universe from which the sample is drawn. For example, we can always improve the goodness of fit of the relationship between variables by choosing a sufficiently complex functional form. (See Jeffreys, 1973, pp.61–2 for a mathematical exposition.) In practice, however, many of these statistical exercises are based on very simple functional forms, often just linear relationships; such simple forms cannot reflect turning points and threshold phenomena which may exist. (For an ingenious method of using segments of linear relationships to detect threshold effects, see Encarnacion, 1974). Even when a multiple regression equation has a high degree of statistical explanation, the explanatory variables have a tendency to 'cling together', i.e. to have a high degree of 'multi-collinearity', so that we cannot rely on individual regression coefficients. Further, the fact that there is a strong relationship between two variables does not indicate the direction of causation between them.

In most applications to development studies, the main reason for the high degree of statistical explanation of regression equations is the tendency for 'double clustering' of the data, i.e. the tendency of points representing such data to fall into two distinct clusters, one for DCs and another for LDCs, because of the great contrast between them in many variables. The difference between these two groups of variables is often greater than the variation within each of them. (Some examples were given in Chapter 2.) Then, the goodness of fit of relationships in the data from both groups of countries is mostly due to inter-class correlation rather than intra-class correlation, and the same relationship will have a much poorer fit to the data of each group taken separately and provide a much weaker explanation.

These problems may be illustrated by Chenery and Syrquin's (1975, p.38) results from applying this method to explain the relative shares of the primary sector (P) and the industrial sector (M) from international cross-section data for the period around 1965. Their regression equations, adjusted for a population of 10 million and a capital inflow of 2 per cent of GDP, are as follows:

$$P = \underset{}{1.955} - \underset{(17.2)}{0.456\,(\ln Y)} + \underset{(12.3)}{0.028\,(\ln Y)^2} \qquad (R^2 = 0.75)$$

$$M = -0.456 + \underset{(8.3)}{1.581\,(\ln Y)} - \underset{(3.8)}{0.006\,(\ln Y)^2} \qquad (R^2 = 0.71)$$

where Y is per capita income in US dollars, ln stands for natural logarithms, and t-values are shown in parentheses below the regression coefficients. These equations show the primary share as a decreasing, and the secondary share as an increasing, function of per capita income but the per capita income may itself be influenced by the shares of the various sectors. The R^2 and t-values are quite high in these regressions fitted to the data of all countries taken together but drop quite sharply when computed separately for rich (mostly developed) countries and for poor (mostly less-developed) countries. The results with the same values of population and capital inflow rates are as follows (Chenery and Syrquin, 1975, pp.113–14):

Rich countries

$$P = 1.943 - \underset{(3.5)}{0.450\,(\ln Y)} + \underset{(2.9)}{0.027\,(\ln Y)^2} \qquad (R^2 = 0.61)$$

$$M = -2.759 + \underset{(5.4)}{0.855\,(\ln Y)} - \underset{(5.1)}{0.058\,(\ln Y)^2} \qquad (R^2 = 0.39)$$

Poor countries

$$P = 2.038 - \underset{(7.2)}{0.483} (\ln Y) + \underset{(4.7)}{0.030} (\ln Y)^2 \qquad (R^2 = 0.63)$$

$$M = -0.411 + \underset{(3.5)}{0.149} (\ln Y) - \underset{(1.5)}{0.006} (\ln Y)^2 \qquad (R^2 = 0.49)$$

Thus we see that although there is not much difference between rich and poor countries in the case of the primary share, the results for the industrial share are quite different, the regression coefficients for the poor countries being much smaller than for the rich countries, and the degree of explanation and the significance of the coefficients are also lower.

Part of the difference between DCs and LDCs is, of course, due to the difference in their trade patterns. Therefore, Chenery and Syrquin (1975, pp.210–11) have extended their statistical analysis to include some trade variables. From their data for around 1965 (pp.192–4), the exports of primary products (E_p), of manufactures (E_m) and of services (E_s) as a proportion of GDP of DCs and LDCs are as in Table 9.1.

Table 9.1 Export ratios by sectors: *DCs* and *LDCs* around 1965

Export ratios	DCs	LDCs
E_p	0.0544	0.1480
E_m	0.1044	0.0146
E_s	0.0598	0.0376

Table 9.2 Actual and predicted shares of sectors in GDP

	Average shares in GDP			
	LDCs		DCs	
	Actual	Predicted	Actual	Predicted
Agriculture	0.368	0.335	0.136	0.095
Industry	0.167	0.199	0.365	0.355
Utilities	0.066	0.087	0.105	0.126
Services	0.389	0.379	0.396	0.424

Using these average values and taking average per capita income as US $1200 for DCs and US $200 for LDCs, the actual shares of the various sectors and the shares predicted by the regression equations are as in Table 9.2.

Thus, we see that, even taking account of trade variables, these regression equations in terms of per capita income tend to overestimate the industrial share in LDCs and conversely in DCs, and to underestimate the primary share in both groups.

9.4 Population and Economic Growth

As pointed out in Chapters 2 and 3, the feature which most sharply distinguishes LDCs from DCs is the level of fertility. The persistence of high fertility combined with a dramatic fall in mortality has led to a high rate of population growth, unprecedented in the historical experience of DCs, and has eaten up the benefits of the acceleration of economic growth in the post-war period. In the present section, we consider the determinants and consequences of these population trends.

In classical economics, population growth was assumed to be strongly influenced by economic factors. According to this theory, the standard of living of the working classes depended on the size of the wage fund in relation to population size. Population increased when wages rose above the subsistence level and decreased when they fell below the subsistence level, though it was not always made clear whether the effect operated through the birth rate or the death rate. Therefore, an increase in the wage fund led to an increase in population numbers; because of this relationship, a rise in population was even welcomed as a sign of progress. From this relationship, it followed that population always tended to the size at which the standard of living of workers was at the subsistence level. This law of population, combined with the law of diminishing returns, then led eventually to the classical stationary state.

In the event, this forecast of population growth did not materialize in the historical experience of DCs. With the onset of modern economic growth, there was first a fall in the death rate but this was not primarily due to economic factors. Three different factors—the improvement in food supply, improvement in public health and advances in medical science, and the extension of medical services to all sections of the community—have been identified, each accounting for a fall of about 10 points from an initial death rate of around 40 per thousand. Therefore,

> the truth is rather that that part of the fall in the death rate which is due to medical improvements is even more spectacular than that part which is due to improvements in food supply. (Lewis, 1955, p.307)

The fall in the death rate in the DCs was, however, accompanied by a fall in the birth rate with varying time lags in different countries. The rate of population growth rose sharply during this time lag and later fell to a low level when birth rates declined to the same low levels as death rates.

This experience of DCs gave rise to the theory of demographic transition (see e.g. Notestein, 1945; United Nations, 1973). According to this theory, birth and death rates are initially high and almost equal, with little or no population growth. Then, in the course of development, these vital rates decline, with birth rates lagging behind death rates, leading to a rapid growth of population. Finally, birth rates decline to nearly the same levels as death rates, and population once again becomes relatively stable. In effect, what the theory does is to transform the statistical history of vital rates in DCs into a causal theory, by re-labelling the time axis with something called 'development'. In some versions, such development is measured in terms of per capita income; the theory then states that population growth is an increasing function of per capita income up to a point and a decreasing function thereafter. In other versions, transition theorists have come up with an embarrassingly long list of factors, such as urbanization, industrialization, spread of education, decline of the extended family system, reduction of infant mortality, improvements in contraceptive technology, etc.; it has also been argued (e.g. by Demeny, 1968) that a small family norm spread over Europe along cultural, even linguistic, lines.

In the post-war period, there was a sharp decline in mortality in the LDCs but the decline in fertility has been confined to a few countries. A rapid decline of fertility was first experienced in Taiwan, South Korea, Hong Kong and Singapore. Since then, a number of other countries have also experienced significant fertility declines. Many of these countries are small island communities (see Kirk, 1971). A considerable decline has also been reported from China, and in parts of other large countries, such as Kerala in India, Bali in Indonesia, and Chiengmai in Thailand. Apart from these cases, fertility has remained at a high level in most LDCs, and combined with the dramatic fall in mortality has caused a population explosion. The expectation of demographic transition theory that the factors which reduce death rates would also reduce birth rates has not been fulfilled.

To explain the actual experience, we must distinguish between, on the one hand, the actions of governments and other official agencies, pursuing various programmes of modernization and, on the other hand, those of private individuals responding to changes in their personal economic and social circumstances, and note that official actions can influence death rates to a great extent while fertility behaviour depends mainly on individuals. The rapid decline of mortality in LDCs was mainly due to official actions in controlling widespread diseases such as malaria, smallpox and cholera by public health measures and improvements in medical services. Infant and child mortality, and deaths due to diseases such as tuberculosis, depend on individual circumstances to a greater extent and have persisted at higher levels, varying quite sharply with the economic and social conditions of the families concerned.

There is a great deal of controversy about the factors affecting fertility. Some authors have attempted to identify these factors by statistical regression techniques. These techniques are subject to the same weaknesses in this case as when used in the search for 'patterns of development' (see Section 9.3 above; see also Keyfitz, 1975). To cite an example, Heer (1966) took a sample of 41 countries including both DCs and LDCs, and derived the following regression equation:

$$\begin{array}{lllllll} B = 81.7 + & 0.008Y - & 0.094E + & 0.553M - & 0.080D + & 11.55G, & (R^2 = 0.62) \\ & (0.6) & (1.5) & (2.4) & (1.3) & (1.8) & \end{array}$$

where Y = per capita income; E = an index of education; M = infant mortality rate; D = population density; G = growth rate of energy consumption, and B = birth rate per thousand. The most significant variable is infant mortality with a positive effect; this has been explained by parents' seeking a particular family size, so that the number of births is reduced when infant mortality declines. But both high birth rates and high infant mortality rates in LDCs may be due to traditional attitudes and behaviour, and it is even possible that the causal connection is from high birth rates in LDCs to high infant mortality rather than the other way about. The regression shows that education has a negative effect on birth rates but income has a positive effect; these coefficients are not significant and are subject to a high multicollinearity between education and income. The high degree of statistical explanation shown by R^2 is mainly due to a 'double clustering' tendency. When the same regression is calculated separately for DCs and LDCs, we get

DCs

$$\underset{}{B} = 57.5 + \underset{(1.2)}{0.008Y} + \underset{(6.1)}{0.003E} + \underset{(0.7)}{0.197M} - \underset{(1.0)}{0.044D} + \underset{(1.0)}{12.59G} \qquad (R^2 = 0.29)$$

LDCs

$$B = 160.7 + \underset{(0.6)}{0.030\,Y} - \underset{(0.3)}{0.011E} - \underset{(0.1)}{0.004M} - \underset{(1.1)}{0.130D} - \underset{(0.6)}{4.44G} \qquad (R^2 = 0.21)$$

Within each group of countries, the regression has little explanatory power. The infant mortality variable becomes very insignificant. The coefficients of some other variables even change signs. (For other examples of the use of such techniques, see Sundrum, 1976.) A particular weakness of such regressions is that, being linear, they cannot identify possible threshold effects.

A recent trend in the literature is to apply the neo-classical assumption of maximizing behaviour to fertility decisions also. This approach tries to explain the persistence of high fertility in LDCs by such micro-economic considerations as the value of children—their economic benefits to parents in the form of help in parents' productive activities and in the form of support in the parents' old age (see e.g. Schultz, 1973; Kuznets, 1975), or, as Caldwell (1976) has summarized them, in terms of the inter-generational flow of resources.

In a careful restatement of the demographic transition theory, Coale (1973) has distinguished three pre-conditions for fertility decline: (a) whether fertility decisions are brought within the calculus of conscious choice; (b) whether individual couples perceive any economic and social advantages from reduced fertility; and (c) whether there is widespread knowledge of, and willingness to use, effective contraceptive techniques. The first condition is particularly important; it is a part of the difference between modern and traditional behaviour, which we have argued is the main element in development. In the case of fertility, a distinction has been made between 'natural' and 'controlled' fertility, according to whether there is conscious decision making or not

(Henry, 1961). Natural fertility does not mean fertility at a biologically maximum level, for there may be social forces relating to family life and child-bearing practices which keep fertility below that level; similarly controlled fertility does not necessarily mean low fertility, for communities who have the means of control may nevertheless desire and achieve large families. It is only when fertility is controlled that economic and other factors play a role. An important stage of demographic transition, therefore, is the change from natural to controlled fertility. When such a change occurs, it is likely to be sudden and lead to rapid fertility decline thereafter.

We now consider the relationship between population growth and economic growth. Some authors have stressed the effect of economic conditions on population growth. For example, the classical economists believed that population always tended to the size at which the standard of living of the masses was at the subsistence level. In some versions of the demographic transition theory, the rate of population growth increased with per capita income up to a point and decreased thereafter. Other authors have stressed the effect of population growth on economic conditions. These authors generally conclude that the faster the growth of population, the slower the growth of per capita income, but these conclusions are often based on highly simplified economic–demographic models following the production function approach. The prototype of these models is that constructed for India by Coale and Hoover (1958). Although these models are quite elaborate on the demographic side, allowing for the effects of population growth on the labour force through changes in the age distribution, they are rather simple in dealing with the economic relationships. They tend to use production functions, such as the Cobb–Douglas, in which output is a function of labour and capital. Further, they either assume that the savings ratio is constant or determined by per capita income. Hence, their conclusion that the rate of growth of per capita income varies inversely with the rate of population growth follows from the assumptions built into their models. (For a critical review, see Arthur and McNicoll, 1975.)

For a deeper understanding of the relationship between population and economic growth, we must also take account of changes in the techniques of production. For example, Boserup (1965) has shown how increasing population pressure has led to greater intensity of land cultivation and helped to maintain the standard of food consumption of growing populations. Further, the relationship between population and economic growth depends on the extent to which both variables are influenced by the level of development. As Kuznets (cited in Ohlin, G., 1967, p.55) has argued,

> A high birth rate may be far more important as a sign of the traditional patterns of behaviour with all that this betokens, than as a source of demand for higher capital formation proportions.

The difference in population densities or growth rates accounts for only a small part of the difference in living standards between DCs and LDCs. A much greater part is due to the difference in levels of development, as defined in Chapter 5, which at the same time accounts for the difference in fertility levels and hence in population growth rates.

9.5 Savings and Growth

The production function approach explains the level and growth of production mainly in terms of the factors of production. Of these, the supply of land is assumed to be fixed, and the growth of population assumed to be either exogenous or determined by the level of income. Therefore, both neo-classical and Marxist economists have placed their main emphasis on capital accumulation as the engine of economic growth. Investment in a country may be financed either by domestic savings or foreign capital inflow; most writers have concentrated on domestic savings. The present section deals with the relationship between savings and growth.

An increase in the capital stock is certainly needed to promote growth of production. We must, however, distinguish between two processes—capital widening and capital deepening. Capital widening refers to the case where capital increases at the same rate as labour, so that the capital–labour ratio is constant and hence, in the absence of technological progress, per capita output also remains constant. Using the Marxist model of an economy divided into two sectors, one producing a consumer good and the other a capital good, the so-called modern theory of growth has been concerned with the conditions of 'dynamic stability', under which a constant rate of saving will lead only to a widening of capital, i.e. to a rate of capital accumulation equal to an exogenous fixed rate of growth of labour. When these conditions are satisfied in the long run, the rate of saving has no effect on the rate of growth of total production but only on the level of the constant size of per capita output. These conditions of dynamic stability depend on such 'casual properties of technology' (Solow, 1962, p.48) as factor-intensities in the two sectors or elasticities of factor substitution. (For references and a summary of results, see Stiglitz and Uzawa, 1969, pp.406–7.) The theory is based on the usually neo-classical assumptions of constant returns to scale, full employment of capital and labour, and efficient competitive markets. In this approach, the whole brunt of the explanation of rising per capita income is thrown on technological progress. (For a more detailed critique, see Cornwall, 1977, Chapter 3.)

Most writers on development economics have been concerned with capital deepening, i.e. a rise in the capital–output ratio, and have therefore concentrated on the rate of saving as an important determinant of the rate of growth. In the words of Lewis (1955, p.226),

> The central problem in the theory of growth is to understand the process by which a community is converted from being a 5 per cent to a 12 per cent saver—with all the changes in attitudes, in institutions and in techniques which accompany this conversion.

The most common assumption is that the saving rate depends on the level of per capita income. Such an assumption then leads to a vicious cycle: LDCs save little because they are poor, and they remain poor because they save little. Many statistical studies have tried to show the effect of income level on the saving rate; all these efforts suffer from the usual weaknesses of cross-section analyses. For example, Chenery and Syrquin (1975, p.30) derived the following results from a cross-section regression analysis of international data of around 1965:

$$S = \underset{(5.8)}{-0.340} + \underset{(5.7)}{0.115}\,(\ln Y) - \underset{(3.6)}{0.006}\,(\ln Y)^2 + \underset{(9.2)}{0.051}\,(\ln N) - \underset{(6.9)}{0.007}\,(\ln N)^2 \qquad R^2 = 0.32$$

$$S = \underset{(5.2)}{-0.199} + \underset{(7.0)}{0.093}\,(\ln Y) - \underset{(4.3)}{0.005}\,(\ln Y)^2 + \underset{(5.5)}{0.020}\,(\ln N) - \underset{(4.6)}{0.003}\,(\ln N)^2 - \underset{(43.7)}{0.832}F \qquad R^2 = 0.71$$

where S = saving rate; Y = per capita GDP, N = population, F = capital inflow, ln = natural logarithm, and the figures in brackets under the regression coefficients are their t-values. Although the t-values are high, the first equation has low explanatory power. The second equation, which adds capital inflow as a proportion of GDP, has a higher degree of explanation and shows that such capital inflow has a negative effect on savings. But the results are drastically altered when this regression is computed separately for rich and poor countries (Chenery and Syrquin, 1975, pp.110–11):

Rich countries

$$S = \underset{(0.6)}{0.301} + \underset{(1.1)}{0.146}\,(\ln Y) - \underset{(1.1)}{0.010}\,(\ln Y)^2 + \underset{(1.5)}{0.016}\,(\ln N) - \underset{(1.4)}{0.003}\,(\ln N)^2 - \underset{(18.83)}{0.857}F \qquad R^2 = 0.59$$

Poor countries

$$S = \underset{(2.3)}{-0.178} - \underset{(2.0)}{0.060}\,(\ln Y) + \underset{(3.5)}{0.010}\,(\ln Y)^2 + \underset{(4.7)}{0.019}\,(\ln N) - \underset{(3.2)}{0.003}\,(\ln N)^2 - \underset{(139.3)}{0.836}F \qquad R^2 = 0.70$$

Then, we see that the income variable becomes much less significant and there is a considerable difference between the two equations; in fact, the income coefficient for the poor countries becomes negative.

A more important influence on the rate of saving is the distribution of income, especially between wages and profit, because a higher proportion is assumed to be saved out of profit incomes. This relationship is the basic feature of the dualistic models of growth (Lewis, 1954, 1958, 1972, 1979). In contrast to the modern theory of growth which divides the economy into a sector producing consumer goods and another producing capital goods, the dualistic theory divides the economy into a modern or capitalist sector which uses capital and hires labour to make a profit, and a traditional or subsistence sector with surplus labour, i.e. a stock of labour whose marginal product is less than the wage ruling in the modern sector. The main object of the theory is to show how the rate of saving increases with the share of profit as the modern sector expands.

The conclusions of the model depend on two assumptions, one concerning the supply of labour and the other concerning saving out of profit incomes. The modern theory of growth assumes that there is an inelastic supply of labour at any time and that the existing capital stock determines the wage according to the marginal product of labour. In contrast, the dualistic theory assumes an 'unlimited supply of labour', i.e. a highly elastic supply of labour to the modern sector at an institutionally fixed wage, and the stock of capital determines employment. Using some plausible values of the parameters, Singh, S. K. (1975, p.39) shows that

> the rate of growth under a surplus labour situation would be twice as fast as the rate of growth under the neo-classical situation of full employment. The difference then is clearly not marginal.

Most of the controversy over the dualistic theory has been concerned with the assumption about labour supply, so much so that Lewis (1972, p.77) has ruefully remarked that

> It was probably a mistake to mention marginal productivity at all, since this has merely led to an irrelevant and intemperate controversy.

More important for the application to LDCs is the assumption about capitalists' saving behaviour. Lewis based his model on European experience, where a high rate of saving out of rising profit incomes in an expanding modern sector led to a rise in the overall saving ratio. As Keynes (1919, p.18) pointed out

> Europe was so organized socially and economically as to secure the maximum accumulation of capital. While there was some continuous improvement in the daily condition of the mass of the population, society was so framed as to throw a great part of the increased income into the control of the class least likely to consume it . . . Herein lay in fact the main justification of the capitalist system. If the rich had spent their new wealth on their own enjoyment, the world would long ago have found such a regime intolerable.

In the historical experience of LDCs, however, the rich appear to have increased their consumption with growth of income. Even when they saved a large proportion, they have preferred to invest these savings in the DCs. In the post-war period, some countries also registered a sharp rise in the saving ratio, especially India in the late 1970s, but much of it was invested in financial assets and durable consumer goods, such as residential houses, so that the modern sector did not expand rapidly. Hence, Singh, S. K. (1975, p.236) has concluded that

> When we come to testing we find the dualistic models as a whole falsified. This is so most clearly with respect to saving and investment behaviour, which Lewis justly thought to be the central feature of the phenomenon of development.

Rather than the factors discussed above, the main influence on the rate of saving is probably the profitability of investment in new technology, and the efficiency of institutions, such as the capital markets, which enable people to invest profitably. As Lewis (1978, p.155) himself has remarked elsewhere,

> not having new technology to invest in shows up as a low propensity to save. Underdeveloped countries have plenty of rich people who have traditionally spent their incomes on hordes of servants, courtiers, armies and entertainers. Saving is a function of the opportunity to invest.

Bauer and Yamey (1957, p.127) have therefore suggested that, because of this influence on saving,

> It is often nearer the truth to say that capital is created in the process of development than that development is a function of capital accumulation.

9.6 Investment and Growth

Capital accumulation leads to growth of production in a number of ways. We have already referred to capital-widening, the case where capital is expanded in proportion to other factors of production, especially labour, and does not involve any change in techniques or rise in per capita output, and to capital-deepening, an increase in capital per unit of other factors, which involves a change in the methods of production and an increase in output per worker. The latter process has been a significant source of the economic growth of the DCs. In what is known as the Austrian theory, the process of capital-deepening is interpreted as the use of more and more roundabout methods of production, as increases in the 'period of production', so that capital is a form of stored up labour. But an increase in capital per worker also results from 'automation', a substitution of capital for labour, mainly as a source of power and for the simpler manual tasks. An important use of capital is to increase the production of goods requiring a large amount of capital, the 'capital-intensive' goods. The consumption of such goods generally increases with the growth of income; this is yet another way in which capital accumulation promotes growth of incomes. Hawtrey (1937) has described this process as 'capital-thickening'.

Although the increase in capital stock takes a variety of forms, the most popular growth models used for planning purposes assume a constant capital–output ratio. This assumption is often made because of its mathematical convenience, as in the Harrod–Domar models; then the growth rate varies proportionately with the saving ratio. This assumption is also made because it is believed to be a 'stylized fact' of the historical experience of the DCs. In fact, however, the capital–output ratio has varied greatly in the course of this experience. As Bicanic (1962) has argued, the capital–output ratio was initially low, then increased to a high level in the second stage, and declined to a relatively stable medium level only in the third and final stage.

> The second stage can . . . be described more realistically as a painful process of creeping over the threshold of economic growth rather than an elegant 'take-off' which does not adequately convey the difficulty and intensity of the problem of this stage of economic growth. In one word, infrastructure of the national economy is taking place. This shows an increase in the capital coefficient from 2 or 2.5 to 4 or even 6. (Bicanic, 1962, pp.19–20)

The role of capital invested in infrastructure is particularly important. The extent to which increases in directly productive capital raises output depends on the amount of social overhead capital. Therefore, as argued in Horvat's (1958) theory of the 'optimum rate of investment', the productivity of a given amount of investment depends on the way it is distributed between directly productive activities and social overhead capital. The productivity of capital also depends on other factors, such as the quality of the labour force and the overall organization of economic activity, in short the level of development. This relationship underlies the concept of the 'absorptive capacity for capital' (Adler, 1965; Kalecki, 1976, p.71). The low level of development in LDCs reduces their ability to use capital productively, and the profitability of investment is below what it would be at a higher level of development.

An important question concerning the effects of capital accumulation on economic growth is the way capital is allocated to different sectors of the economy. Many important aspects of this process have been studied with great insight in Butt's theory of the mechanization process (Butt, 1960). Unlike the modern theory of growth in which the output of a single composite consumer good varies continuously with the amount of capital used, Butt's theory brings out the role of capital by making a sharp distinction between two kinds of techniques, one a handicraft technique which uses only labour and the other a mechanized technique which uses both labour and capital. The physical productivity of capital in each of a number of sectors is given by the extent to which a unit of capital increases output as compared with the corresponding handicraft technique; it is convenient to call this quantity the rate of return to capital in that sector. As capital accumulates, the rate of profit declines. The mechanized technique is introduced into a sector when the rate of profit declines to the level of the rate of return in that sector. This means that the various sectors are mechanized in a particular sequence, the sequence in which they are arranged in descending order of their respective rates of return. The pattern is illustrated in Figure 9.1, where S_i is the rate of return to capital in the ith sector and r_t is the rate of profit at time t.

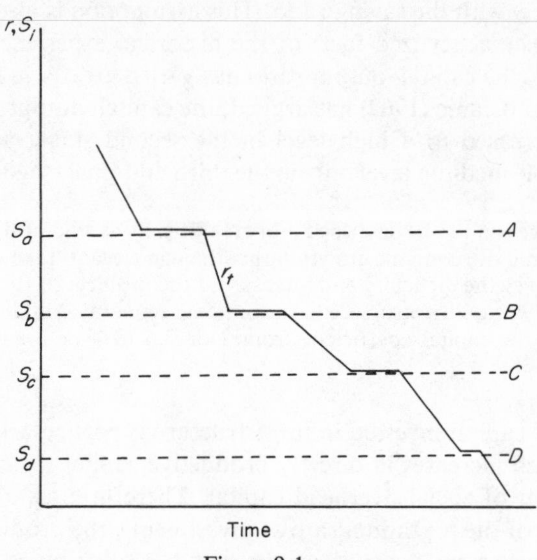

Figure 9.1

Each sector has to wait its turn for mechanization. The mechanization of each sector occurs in two phases: phase I in which both handicraft and mechanized techniques are in use, the price of the product is constant and the rate of profit equals the rate of return in that sector, and phase II in which the sector is fully mechanized, its product price falls, and the rate of profit falls below the rate of return of capital in that sector; then the margin of mechanization moves to the next sector in the sequence of mechanization. In Figure 9.1 the horizontal sections of the r_t curve represent phase I and the downward-sloping sections phase II of the various sectors.

There are a number of possible outcomes depending on the relationship between the rate of capital accumulation and the rate of population growth. So long as the capital stock grows faster than population, the process of mechanization moves forward until the rate of profit declines to zero—the 'euthanasia of the rentier'—and accumulation ceases in an 'exhausted state'. Accumulation may also cease if the rate of profit is too low to induce saving—the case of exhaustion through improvidence—or if capitalist consumption has reached a satiety point. If wage earners also save and their consumption also reaches satiety, we have the Ramsey case of universal bliss. If, at any time, the rate of capital accumulation equals the rate of population growth, we have

Marshall's case of an expanding stationary state. If population grows faster than capital, there may be a retrogression of the mechanization process.

A particularly important sector is agriculture, for in this sector land, which is fixed in supply, is an essential factor of production. For this sector, the role of capital is brought out by distinguishing between a peasant technique using labour and land, and a mechanized farming technique using land, labour and capital. With peasant techniques only, the case analysed by Ricardo in his 'magnificent dynamics', increasing population pressure leads to a succession of peasant techniques with a steadily increasing labour-intensity of peasant cultivation and a rising rent of land. As the rate of return to capital in the mechanized farming technique depends on the labour-intensity of the prevailing peasant technique, and the corresponding rent of land, it is more convenient to measure the labour-intensity of peasant cultivation in the horizontal axis; then the curve showing the rate of return is not a horizontal line as for other sectors but a curve as shown in Figure 9.2.

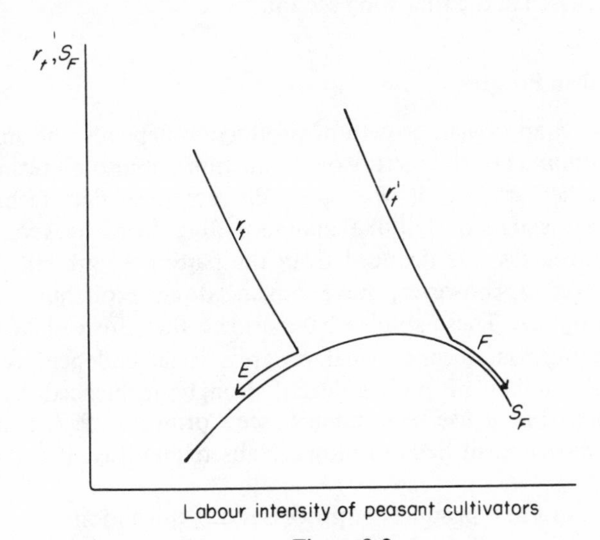

Figure 9.2

The agricultural sector will be mechanized when the rate of profit declines to the level of the rate of return to the mechanized farming techniques. The longer this stage is delayed, the greater the chance that the mechanized technique will be labour-saving; it is even possible that the mechanized technique will also be land-using compared with the prevailing peasant techniques. There are two possibilities for the course of events in phase I of the mechanization of this sector. If the sector begins its mechanization at an early stage in the process of growing population pressure, then further movement will be along the arrow marked *E*, and increased investment in agriculture will reduce the price of food and the rent of land; this is the route that was followed by the DCs. But if the mechanization of agriculture occurs at a late stage, further movement may be along the arrow marked F, in which increased investment will increase the rent of land and the price of food. This is analogous to Ricardo's famous problem of machinery, in which investment in machinery is profitable to the individual investor but reduces total output. (For a fuller exposition of the mechanization process, see Sundrum, 1978, 1981).

The above analysis has concentrated on how capital accumulation leads to a substitution of a given set of mechanized techniques for a given set of handicraft and peasant techniques. Historically, however, the contribution of increases in the stock of capital to economic growth has been relatively small. (For some statistical estimates, see Abramovitz, 1956; and Solow, 1957.) The main contribution of investment has been as a vehicle of technological progress. This process has been described as 'learning by doing' (Arrow, 1962) and has been formulated in terms of a 'technical progress function' by Kaldor (1957, 1961; see also Eltis, 1971). Some factors affecting technological progress are discussed in the following section.

9.7 Technological Progress

In the neo-classical approach, growth of production depends not only on the increase in the amounts of the factors of production but also on technological progress. In earlier studies, it was generally assumed that technological progress occurred exogenously, like manna falling from heaven, and the nature of such progress was deduced from the pattern of growth that took place. Recent studies, however, have advanced an economic theory of technological progress. These studies have argued that, instead of being an exogenous phenomenon, technological progress is an endogenous process, consisting of a number of phases, each strongly influenced by various economic factors. (For a useful summary, see Cornwall, 1977, Chapter 6.) Four phases have been identified as follows (Nabseth and Ray, 1974, p.4):

(a) the discovery of new products or processes, i.e. 'inventions';
(b) the development of inventions into commercially feasible and profitable techniques, i.e. 'innovations';
(c) the modification of innovations in the course of actual production, i.e. the 'learning process'; and
(d) the spread of profitable innovations among firms in an industry and among countries, i.e. 'diffusion'.

The endogenous aspect of technological progress was first stressed by Schmookler (1966) by observing a high correlation between the numbers of patented inventions in various US industries and the amounts of investment outlays in these industries. He concluded that

> the amount of invention is governed by the size of the market . . . A million dollars

> spent on one kind of good is likely to induce as much invention as the same sum spent on any other good. (Schmookler, 1966, p.172)

This conclusion was then extended to the relationship between innovations and the expenditures on research and development (R & D). In some cases, the relationships found have been used to calculate rates of return to R & D expenditures, following Griliches' (1957) classic study of hybrid corn in the period 1910–55.

Another endogenous relationship was also derived regarding the process of diffusion. According to this argument, there was an inverse relationship between the 'technology gap' of a country from the industrial leader (e.g. the United States) and the rate at which new technology diffused from the leading to the imitating country (see e.g. Nabseth and Ray, 1974). In this process, the borrowing country not only acquired knowledge of new products and processes but also had the additional advantage of greater flexibility in the innovations it chose to imitate.

According to these theories of the determinants of technological progress, it would seem that the LDCs as late-comers have a great advantage in borrowing technology from the more advanced countries. But the studies referred to have all been based on the experience of DCs. These countries have all achieved a high level of scientific development; they have large numbers of highly educated and trained workers; they have large enterprises able to initiate and finance research and development. Therefore, there is little variation among them with regard to the supply factors involved in technological progress; hence these studies have been able to derive strong relationships between the rate of technological progress and the demand for innovations. But in considering the application of these theories to LDCs, we must take account of the great differences between the DCs and the LDCs in the supply of the factors affecting technological progress. On the supply side, new inventions depend on scientific breakthroughs, which have a life of their own (see Rosenberg, 1974), but are also influenced by the existing stock of scientific and technological manpower. In the case of different industries within an advanced country there is a correlation between innovations and R & D expenditures, because these industries have roughly equal access to the same body of scientific knowledge and personnel. But as between countries with differing scientific resources,

> there is no observed correlation between the proportion of national resources devoted to R & D and rates of growth of productivity. (O.E.C.D., 1971, p.20)

The same is also true of the diffusion process. In order to get the benefit of late-comers, a country must be above some threshold level of technology. Gomulka (1971) has therefore argued, using differences in per capita incomes as a measure of technology gaps, that maximum benefits from borrowing technologies occur when per capita incomes in the imitating country vary from one-tenth to one half that of the industrial leader. (cited in Cornwall, 1977, p.111n).

But, of course, the relative income level is a poor measure of the technology gap between DCs and LDCs; the gap really depends much more on the stock of scientific knowledge and the organization of economic activity.

9.8 Increasing Returns

Most theories of growth are based on production functions with constant returns to scale. This is often because of the sheer mathematical convenience of linear homogeneous functions, which enable theorists to separate questions of scale from questions of factor proportions. It is also because of the theoretical advantage of being able to explain the distribution of the product among the factors of production according to the marginal productivity theory, due to the Euler's theorem property of linear homogeneous production functions. The process of growth is then described as a succession of equilibrium positions, i.e. as an exercise in comparative statics. In fact, however, there are significant economies of scale in production and the extent to which such economies are exploited has been a significant factor in the growth experience of individual countries. In order to understand this phenomenon, our theory must be essentially dynamic, i.e. one in which disequilibrium at a point of time provides the motive force for the forward movement of the system over time (Young, 1928).

Economies of scale may be classified in several ways (Arndt, 1955). One is the distinction between internal and external economies. Internal economies are those arising within firms, as they expand in size, due to the spreading of indivisible overhead costs over a larger output, specialization of staff, economies in use of materials, use of different techniques at different scales of production, and marketing and financial economies (see, e.g., Robinson, E. A. G., 1953; for some estimates of their magnitude, see United Nations, 1964, and Pratten, 1971). Recent studies have shown that such economies are closely related to size of plants within firms (for an analysis, see Grubel and Lloyd, 1975, Chapter 6). External economies are those which depend on the size of an industry as a whole and arise from such factors as intensity of competition, localization of firms, special markets for products and skilled labour, and the establishment of specialist journals, etc. (for an extensive description, see Marshall, 1961, Book IV, Chapters X–XIII).

Economies of scale have also been distinguished according to whether they are static or dynamic. In the usual statements of this distinction, static economies of scale may be represented by a curve of unit costs of production which falls as output increases, and dynamic economies of scale by a fall of the curve itself over time; these economies are called internal when they are a function of output of a firm and external when they are a function of the total output of all firms in an industry. It is this view of dynamic economies of scale which fails to bring out their great importance for the growth process, for it makes them tantamount to technological progress as a function of time. A further distinction is therefore made by Corden (1974, p.250)

> The average costs of a firm are assumed to fall the longer its output has continued; it learns from experience. This is to be distinguished not only from costs falling with scale of output in the static sense but also from costs falling over time for exogenous reasons.

However, most discussions of dynamic economies make them depend on time, e.g. 'as time passes the costs of the firms in the industry fall' (Corden, 1974, p.259) or relate them to such factors as labour training, knowledge diffusion, creation of goodwill and a favourable climate, which do not depend in an essential way on the increase of output over time.

Adam Smith's well known illustration of economies of scale—the pin factory—is concerned with static economies. As Young (1928, pp.530–1) has pointed out

> It is generally agreed that Adam Smith, when he suggested that the division of labour leads to inventions because workmen engaged in specialized routine operations come to see better ways of accomplishing the same results, missed the main point. The important thing, of course, is that with division of labour a group of complex processes is transformed into a succession of simpler processes, some of which, at least, lend themselves to the use of machinery. . . . The principal economies which manifest themselves in increasing returns are the economies of capitalistic or roundabout methods of production . . . The economies of roundabout methods, even more than the economies of other forms of the division of labour, depend upon the extent of the market.

It is in this way that increasing output and technological progress are closely intertwined to produce truly dynamic economies of scale. Further, the pervasiveness of increasing returns in the modern industrial economy is

> not to be discerned adequately by observing the effects of variations in the size of an individual firm or of a particular industry, for the progressive division and specialisation of industries is an essential part of the process by which increasing returns are realised. (Young, 1928, p.539)

Dynamic economies are therefore best described, not by expressing unit costs as a function of output or as a function of output and time, but by expressing the rate of growth of productivity as a function of the rate of growth of output. This relationship in the case of the manufacturing sector is known as Verdoorn's law; it shows that in the recent experience of DMEs, a one per cent increase in the growth rate of output was accompanied by increases of over half per cent in the growth rates of productivity. (For some estimates of this relationship, see Cornwall, 1977, Table 7.2, p.127 and Table 8.4, p.149.)

The relationship between increasing returns and economic growth is a two-way relationship. The effect of growth on increasing returns is that expressed in Adam Smith's famous dictum that division of labour is limited by the extent of the market; this draws attention to the fact that when economic growth occurs due to such factors as capital accumulation or technological progress, or when the market is extended by trade, countries enjoy economies of scale. This is the basis used to measure the component of growth due to economies of scale in DMEs (see e.g. Denison, 1967, and Denison and Chung, 1976). But there is also another relationship, which Young (1928, p.534) has described thus:

> An increase in the supply of one commodity *is* an increase in the demand for other commodities, and it must be supposed that every increase in demand will evoke an increase in supply . . . Even in a stationary population and in the absence of new discoveries in pure or applied science there are no limits to the process of expansion except the limits beyond which demand is not elastic and returns do not increase.

It is in this sense that Rostow (1975, p.16) described the historical experience of DCs as 'an explosive interaction between cost-reducing innovations and elastic demand embraced by the case of increasing returns.'

Finally, the interaction between economies of scale and other growth factors is a cumulative one:

> Change becomes progressive and propagates itself in a cumulative way . . . No analysis of the forces making for economic equilibrium, forces which we might say are tangential at any moment of time, will serve to illumine this field for movements away from equilibrium, departures from previous trends, are characteristic of it . . . the counter forces which are continually defeating the forces which make for economic equilibrium are more pervasive and more deeply rooted in the constitution of the modern economic system then we commonly realise. (Young, 1928, pp.528, 533)

This interaction is an example of 'circular cumulative causation' (originally suggested by Myrdal, 1968, Vol.III, p.1843). According to this principle, any initial growth of output will lead to cost reductions which expand demand and reinforce the initial changes into cumulative growth. (For a discussion of some theoretical aspects, see Swan, 1962.)

9.9 The Role of Demand

In the production function approach of classical and neo-classical economics, the aggregate level of production in a country is determined by its productive capacity. But productive capacity only means potential production; how far this potential is realized depends on effective demand. The role of demand was neglected because of a belief in Say's law that supply creates its own demand. In neo-classical economics, Say's law is justified by arguing that the supply and demand for individual commodities are functions of their prices, and that these prices are flexible and speedily adjust to equilibrate supply and demand in each market, and hence to equate aggregate demand and aggregate supply. The adjustment of prices to clear all markets is explained by such devices as Marshall's assumption of instantaneous price movements, and Walras's auction and Edgeworth's recontract assumptions. On this argument, demand had no role in determining the volume of aggregate production, but only its composition.

The validity of Say's law was challenged by Keynes. He was specially concerned with the labour market, where he argued that changes in money wages in the face of disequilibrium were offset by changes in the price level, so that real wages were not sufficiently flexible to bring about full employment. He argued that, in the capital market, the volume of savings was determined by the level of income rather than the rate of interest, and that the rate of interest was determined by the supply and demand for liquidity, rather than by savings and investment. He therefore constructed an alternative model in which aggregate demand was partly exogenous and partly endogenous, the latter varying with the level of income. The fundamental equation of his model is the *ex ante* equality of aggregate demand and supply; from this, he showed how income and employment were determined by the exogenous component of aggregate effective demand. At low levels of exogenous demand, there may not be full employment or full utilization of productive capacity. There is a particular level of exogenous demand at which there is full employment; below it, there is unemployment; above it, there is inflation. The Keynesian model has been the basis of macro-economic policy in the DMEs since World War II and was a significant factor in their high levels of employment and rapid growth of incomes until the early 1970s. This was specially the case in such countries as West Germany and Japan, where effective demand was sustained by high levels of investment to repair extensive war damage and to catch up with advanced technology, and by rapid growth of exports. If effective demand was not sufficient to bring about full employment, increases in such elements of exogenous demand as government expenditures were used to increase output and employment in a multiplier process.

Although Keynesian policies have been widely applied with great success to raise employment and income in DMEs, they have been considered inapplicable to solve the problems of extensive unemployment in LDCs (see the influential article by Rao, 1952). It was assumed that, in the DMEs, policies to increase demand could expand employment because there was usually surplus capacity of other factors and because factor-proportions could be modified significantly. But with LDCs, it was argued that the stock of capital was fully utilized and that factor proportions were rigidly fixed; hence employment in these countries was determined by the stock of the cooperating factors, land and capital. Unemployment was due to the abundance of labour relative to other resources rather than lack of demand, and under these conditions, an increase in aggregate demand would only lead to inflation. However, there have been many examples of increases in output due to increases in demand even in the LDCs. For example, the growth of incomes in many LDCs in the nineteenth century and even in the post-war period has been attributed to the role of exports in providing a 'vent for surplus' (further discussed in Chapter 11). Another example is the rapid growth of industrial production in LDCs in the early phase of an import-substitution strategy; the rate of growth slackened as production in the newly set-up industries came up against the limitation of the home market.

One reason why Keynesian theory was thought not useful to study the role of demand in LDCs or to formulate policies lies in some of its special features. For example, Keynes argued that countries experienced unemployment or inflation according to whether exogenous demand was below or above the level required for full employment. Hence, Nurkse (1952, p.17) argued that the deficiency of market demand in LDCs

> is not a deficiency of 'effective demand' in terms of Keynesian economics. There is, as a rule, no deficiency of monetary demand; there is no deflationary gap. On the contrary, many of these countries suffer from a chronic inflationary pressure.

But since the early 1970s, the DMEs also have been suffering from 'stagflation', i.e. persistently high levels of unemployment together with high rates of inflation. Hence, there has been a revival of monetarist and cost-push theories in place of, or in addition to, the Keynesian theory of inflation.

Another special feature of the Keynesian theory is that it is a static one, in which the stock of the factors of production is taken as given. Therefore, it considers investment only as an element of effective demand. But investment plays a double role. In the short period, it increases effective demand as investment expenditures are incurred; in the long run, it increases productive capacity. In the historical experience of the DCs, investment was continually racing to catch up with advancing technology and led to a long period of rapid growth. Periodically, investment fell short of full employment levels and recovered thereafter, giving rise to trade cycles.

In the LDCs, the level of investment has been low. This has generally been attributed to the low rate of savings out of low levels of income. But Nurkse (1952, pp.5–6) has argued that it was primarily due to a weak inducement to invest:

> It may at first sight be surprising to hear that there can be anything wrong on the demand side of capital formation in underdeveloped countries. Can there be any deficiency in the demand for capital? Are not the backward countries, almost by definition, greatly in need of capital for the efficient use of their labour and for the exploitation of their natural resources? Is not the demand for capital in these areas tremendous? It may well be; and yet in terms of private incentives there is the difficulty that stems from the limited size of the domestic market in the early stages of a country's economic development. *The inducement to invest is limited by the size of the market.*

Especially in his advocacy of the balanced growth doctrine, (see Section 10.5 below), Nurkse assumed that investment was constrained by demand rather than supply factors.

> In my presentation balanced growth is an exercise in economic development with unlimited supplies of capital, analogous to Professor Lewis's celebrated exercise in development with unlimited labour supplies. (Nurkse, 1958, cited in Meier, 1976, p.642)

There is yet another way in which Keynesian theory is a rather special case of a more general situation of market disequilibrium. It assumes that it is only in the labour market that prices are too inflexible to bring about equilibrium of supply and demand; the market for goods is assumed to be in continuous equilibrium. This restrictive assumption has been relaxed in a new approach to output and employment that has been developed in some recent studies (e.g. Clower, 1965; Leijonhufvud, 1968, 1973; Barro and Grossman, 1976; Malinvaud, 1977). In this approach, disequilibrium due to rigidity of prices may occur in all markets, not only the labour market. It derives output and employment from the maximizing behaviour of individuals and hence provides some micro-economic foundations for macro-economic relationships. This approach may be briefly summarized as follows. (See Sundrum (1980) for a more detailed exposition.)

The central theme of this approach is that quantity adjustments occur much faster than price adjustments, and therefore it works out the way quantity adjustments take place in a model where all prices are fixed. If prices are fixed and not necessarily at their equilibrium levels, supply in a market may be greater than demand at the given prices, i.e. there may be excess supply; the transactions in such a market will be equal to demand and the market may be said to be demand constrained. Similarly, demand may be greater than supply, i.e. there may be excess demand, in which case, transactions are equal to supply, and the market is supply-constrained.

The most important point of the new approach is that desired purchases or sales in one market depend on the nature of disequilibrium in other markets. For example, the demand for labour by a firm depends on the market for its product. If the product market is in equilibrium, as assumed in neo-classical theory, the demand for labour will be given by marginal productivity of labour, when the product is valued at its equilibrium price. As Leijonhufvud (1976, p.97) has pointed out,

> it is one of the great achievements of general equilibrium theory to have shown that the vector of equilibrium prices conveys, in principle, all the information that each transactor needs to know in order to coordinate his activities with those of everybody else in the system.

But if the product price is fixed at a level at which the product market is not in equilibrium the demand for labour depends, not on the marginal productivity of labour, but on the quantity of the product that the firm expects to sell at the given price. In order to stress this distinction, demand and supply in a market based on the assumption of equilibrium in other markets are described as 'notional' functions; those based on disequilibrium in other markets are then described as 'effective' demand and supply functions. The demand and supply functions extensively used in neo-classical theory then correspond to the notional functions which express quantities as functions of prices, i.e. they are depicted on diagrams with price on one axis and quantities on the other. In contrast, the effective demand functions of disequilibrium theory express supply and demand in each market as functions of quantities, i.e. of the transactions in other markets, and have to be depicted in diagrams with quantities on both axes. The term 'effective' is particularly apt for these functions because this usage is already well-established in connection with demand backed by purchasing power. The interaction between markets has been explained by Leijonhufvud (1973, p.40):

> If the desired supply of labour exceeds employment, producers will be aware of the excess supply in labour markets but receive no valid signal indicating that the demand for wage-goods exceeds output. If desired supply of wage-goods exceeds current sales and output, workers are not informed that demand for labour exceeds employment. Even if the ratio of money wages to money prices comes out as the [general equilibrium] real wage, we may be caught in the vicious circle where the unemployed cannot make their consumption demand *effective* until they have sold their services for money, and producers with excess capacity cannot bid for labour until they have sold their goods— which the unemployed do not have the cash to purchase and so on. *This failure of the markets to transmit messages about desired transactions from one side to the other is what we mean by the phrase 'effective demand failure'.*

A simple example of the method of the new approach is the case where the economy is divided into two markets, a labour market and a goods market, and there is excess supply in both markets, i.e. transactions are determined by effective demand. Then, output and employment are determined as illustrated in Figure 9.3.

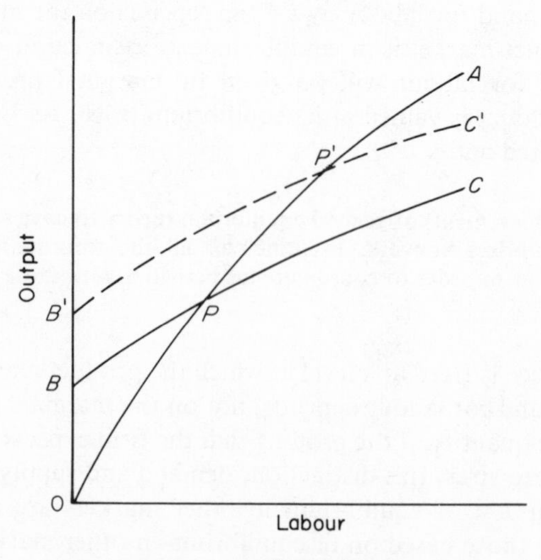

Figure 9.3

The curve OA represents the effective demand for labour as a function of the output of goods, where the point A may be chosen to represent full employment, and the curve BC represents the effective demand for goods as a function of employment. The two relationships then jointly determine output and employment at the point P, below the full employment level. If there is an increase in the effective demand for goods, e.g. by an increase in government expenditures, the curve BC shifts upward to B′C′, and output and employment increase to the point P′ by the multiplier process. The argument differs from Keynes' own theory in not assuming that the goods market is always in equilibrium, in which case the demand for labour is given by a downward-sloping marginal productivity curve, and employment can increase only with a fall in real wages; in the new approach, an increase in employment may occur even with a rise in real wages.

The final special feature of the Keynesian model to note is that it is a highly aggregative one in which all sectors producing consumer goods are lumped together. In the DMEs, agriculture has only a small share in total output. Most of the output comes from the industrial and service sectors; in these sectors, factors of production are more versatile and therefore they can be combined together for the study of the role of demand. But in LDCs, agriculture is a major sector of the economy; its product, mainly food, is less substitutable for the products of other sectors; the factors of production are less mobile between the agricultural and other sectors, especially between rural and urban areas which are highly specialized regarding these sectors of production. Therefore, consumption must be disaggregated to a greater extent in the LDCs for studying the nature of the constraints on growth.

To summarize, the new theoretical developments suggest that

> effective demand failures had to be perceived as a hitherto unrealized pervasive malfunction of price systems, casting grave doubts on the entire neo-classical vision of the self-regulating capabilities and *modus operandi* of the system. (Leijonhufvud, 1973, p.32)

Such effective demand failures may occur in LDCs just as much as in DMEs. Whether they occur or not cannot be decided only on the basis of whether there is inflation or not, for inflation may be due to factors other than excess effective demand, and the inflation that results from an increase of effective demand in the short run may be self-liquidating in the medium term. Especially when considering the medium term, the level of investment may be limited by the demand constraint of a weak inducement to invest. In the case of consumption, whether growth is limited by demand or by supply must be examined for each sector separately; such sectoral constraints are considered in Section 10.6.

CHAPTER 10

Production: Policy

10.1 Objectives of Production Policy

The great poverty in LDCs is ultimately due to the low level of their production. Such poverty is so serious that it impedes the full development of the human personality for a large proportion of the people. Therefore a major objective of policy must be rapid growth of production.

There is currently a considerable amount of controversy over economic growth as an objective of policy. (For a comprehensive review, see Arndt, 1978.) At first sight, it may seem self-evident that economic growth is a highly desirable objective of policy, and that faster growth is always to be preferred to slower growth. As Lewis (1955, p.421) put it,

> The case for economic growth is that it gives man greater control over his environment and thereby increases his freedom.

In the post-war period, pride of place has been given to a high rate of growth of national income in the so-called development plans of LDCs and the economic performance of DCs also has been judged by this criterion in the so-called growth-league tables. But recently, a number of doubts have been raised.

One line of argument is the distinction between what Scitovsky (1976) has called 'comforts'—the satisfaction of the basic needs of life, those involved in man's struggle with nature—which are limited, and 'pleasures' which go beyond these needs and are virtually unlimited. Most important among the latter are those which Hirsch (1977) has described as 'positional' goods, i.e. goods whose utility depends essentially on the position of some consumers *vis-à-vis* others, goods for which the demand has no limit. From a social point of view, the pursuit of such positional goods is self-defeating; what one person gains, others lose. In the analogy given by Hirsch, no one in a crowd of spectators can see better if all stand on tip-toes.

Another line of argument is based on the substantial costs of economic growth in social tensions, in depletion of scarce and exhaustible natural resources, in the congestion of excessive urbanization and in the deterioration of the environment, costs which are not accounted for in the conventional measures of national income, and which have to be balanced against greater material benefits. (For alternative measures of national welfare taking account of these costs, see Nordhaus and Tobin, 1972.) These costs have often been exaggerated by 'Doomsday' economists (see e.g. Meadows and Meadows, 1972; for a critique, see Beckerman, 1974). The real problem is that in many industrial countries, those benefitting from growth do not pay for the costs of these social diseconomies. Hence, growth may be pursued beyond the limits of social welfare, when 'growth-sensitive' persons and institutions, as Powelson (1972) has called them, become dominant and deeply embedded in the social fabric.

These doubts, however, are only relevant for the DCs. Because of the high degree of material affluence they have already reached, they have less need for economic growth as a means of further raising the standard of living. The doubts raised above apply particularly when economic growth is taken as an end in itself or as the preferred solution to other problems, such as unemployment, balance of payments problems, inflation, etc. Many of these problems involve the distribution of income. Hence, Hirsch (1977, p.7) pointed out that

> the compelling attraction of economic growth in its institutionalised modern form has been as a superior alternative for redistribution.

In the LDCs, where a large proportion of the population still lives in absolute poverty, rapid economic growth is needed, not as an end in itself but as a means to achieving an adequate standard of living for the mass of the population within a reasonable time. What standard of living they should aim at is for the people themselves to decide. This standard of living cannot be set at just above the level of absolute poverty, for such an austere standard is not likely to satisfy people for long.

Given the objective of a substantial increase in the general standard of living, we have next to consider how rapidly production should be increased to meet this objective. Some authors have argued that a minimum rate of growth is necessary; this is the big push argument. For example, Rosenstein-Rodan (1961, p.57) has argued that

> There is a minimum level of resources that must be devoted to a development program if it is to have any chance of success. Launching a country into self-sustaining growth is a little like getting an airplane off the ground. There is a critical minimum speed which must be passed before the craft can become airborne.

This argument for a big push approach is based on the balanced growth doctrine (see Section 10.5(c)) and on the indivisibilities in production, in demand and in the supply of savings. An alternative argument has been advanced by Leibenstein (1957), who related the required rate of growth to the rate at which the demographic clock is ticking in the LDCs, because small increases in living standards will only lead to population growth, while a quantum jump might reduce fertility and hence lead to an escape from the Malthusian trap.

Apart from the above considerations, it must be noted that the solution of the problem of mass poverty depends on the rate of growth over a long period. This is important because a policy of maximizing output or growth in each short period may not necessarily maximize the long-term rate of growth. As Schumpeter (1943, p.83) says,

> A system . . . that at every point of time fully utilises its possibilities to the best advantage may yet in the long run be inferior to a system that does so at *no* given point of time, because the latter's failure to do so may be a condition for the level or speed of long run performance.

Hence, in devising an appropriate strategy for LDCs, we must pay special attention to the long-term factors involved, even if this be at the expense of a short-term advantage.

Such a long-term perspective is specially needed in considering the rapid growth of production compared with other means of solving the poverty problem, such as redistributive policies. While a large proportion of people in LDCs are desperately poor, there are also small groups with a high standard of living, comparable to some of the richest people in DCs. Therefore, the solution to the poverty problem is sometimes sought in redistribution. Such policies are used in DCs to relieve some of their problems of relative poverty. But in the LDCs, the average level of production is so low that merely redistributing incomes alone will not go far towards relieving their much more massive problems of absolute poverty. To be effective, a large proportion of total income must be transferred from the rich to the poor, and this must be done repeatedly at great administrative and political costs. This is not to say that redistributive policies have no role to play, (see Chapter 14 for further discussion) but in the long run, faster growth of production is necessary to solve the poverty problem.

Growth of aggregate production will reduce poverty only if its benefits are widely distributed. This raises some of the most serious problems of policy, because some policy interventions to promote rapid growth may worsen the distribution of income, while others designed to improve distribution may reduce growth. But 'efficiency' and 'equity' need not always be in conflict, for there are policies which promote both efficiency and equity at the same time. Further, where there is a conflict, it is often one that occurs in the short run rather than the long. Therefore, in choosing among alternative policies, LDCs must give greater weight to those which involve less conflict between these objectives, and do so taking account of both the long-run and the short-run effects. It is from this point of view that we consider the instruments that governments can use for their production policy.

10.2 Instruments of Production Policy

The problems of production policy can be broadly classified as follows:

(a) how to increase the stock of productive resources rapidly relative to population and raise their productivity;
(b) how to combine these resources in producing individual commodities—the problem of the choice of techniques; and
(c) what combination of commodities to produce—the problem of the composition of output.

One aspect of the first problem which has received considerable attention in the literature which involves quite different considerations from others is the problem of reducing the rate of population growth; this problem is discussed in Section 10.3. The other two problems are discussed in Sections 10.4 and 10.5. The final section deals with each of the three major sectors of the economy. Before going into these topics, we consider some instruments of production policy in the present section.

In countries with a mixed economy, to which the present study is restricted, a great deal of productive activity is carried on in the private sector under the influence of market forces. Economics began its scientific career with the recognition of the systematic pattern underlying the working of market forces, so much so that the founder of economic science spoke of an invisible hand guiding individuals through market forces to promote the social interest. Elementary courses in economics to this day begin with extolling the efficiency of the market system and often end there. Some cases of inefficiency of the system are admitted, such as imperfect competition, increasing returns and externalities, but these are considered to be exceptional. It is not as fully appreciated nowadays as it was by the classical economists that free markets promote growth mainly through their 'creative' functions of encouraging innovative behaviour, i.e. in Landes's (1969, p.19) phrase, by multiplying the points of creativity. Instead the modern argument for freedom of markets rests more often on neo-classical theory which has been mainly concerned with the 'allocative' functions of markets. (For the distinction between the creative and the allocative functions of markets, see Section 8.4(a) above.) As Robinson, J. (1979, pp.20–1) puts it,

> The neoclassics claim Adam Smith as their patron because he was an advocate of laissez-faire. He believed in freeing the energies of self-interested action from limitations and restrictions by the state but he was not concerned with equilibrium; the famous invisible hand is not directing the allocation of scarce means between alternative uses, but guiding investment into the most advantageous channels and so promoting the growth of means to employ more labour and create more wealth.

The creative role of free markets is a powerful force for promoting growth; countries which have opted for a mixed economy should therefore not lightly interfere with this role of markets. The same, however, cannot be said about all aspects of the allocative role of markets. Neo-classical economics has evolved an elegant superstructure of theory to point out the virtues of resource allocation by free markets; this theory is based on a number of crucial assumptions, namely, the maximizing behaviour of individual producers and consumers, the efficiency of markets in bringing all buyers and sellers of each commodity together in an impersonal way, and the speedy adjustment of market prices to their equilibrium levels where supply equals demand.

These assumptions are not always satisfied, especially at the low level of development prevailing in LDCs. Individuals may not be maximizing their welfare, especially from a long-term point of view, for a variety of reasons such as the low level of education, the weight of custom and tradition, and other such social compulsions, the lack of infrastructure giving them access to modern technology, and the weakness of the economic institutions. This is most strikingly illustrated by the slowness in adopting new, and more productive, techniques which are already available in these countries. It may also be due to the fact that at their low level of income, individuals are unwilling to take the risks involved in experimenting with new techniques.

Secondly, markets in LDCs may be inefficient in bringing all buyers and sellers together. As discussed in Chapter 8, the extent of market participation is small, and even where there is wide participation, markets function in a highly personal way and are therefore often highly segmented, especially in the case of the factors of production. Further, even when markets are efficient in this sense, competition may be imperfect. The limited size of markets, the shortage of entrepreneurs and investment funds, and the pervasiveness of economies of scale often lead to monopolistic elements. Monopolies are often considered only from a distributional point of view but they should also be examined from a growth point of view. In some cases, they may promote growth because certain types of production may not be carried on at all without a monopoly. In other cases, monopolies may stand in the path of innovation (see Lewis, 1955, pp.94–101). Another weakness of markets, even when they are efficient, is that they may be highly unstable, both because of fluctuations in supply or demand and because the market itself may generate instability, for example, when there are lags in supply response. Such instability prevents more efficient long-term planning of production.

A third type of problem is that supply and demand for some important commodities may not be very elastic with respect to price changes and even when they are, market prices may not speedily adjust to the equilibrium levels at which supply equals demand. The first aspect has been stressed by the structuralist school of Latin American economists; they have argued that in LDCs the output of key commodities such as food for domestic consumption or of some commodites for export may not respond readily to changes in their relative prices, so that these commodities become serious bottlenecks to growth which cannot be removed by market forces alone (see, e.g., Diamand, 1978). The second aspect has been studied in the new theories of income and employment summarized in Section 9.9 above; it has been argued that this leads to extensive market failure to utilize resources fully.

Finally, it must be noted that even when all the assumptions of neo-classical theory are satisfied, what it has demonstrated is that market forces optimize production in a special sense. Firstly, this optimum is static in the sense of maximizing output from a given stock of resources, with given techniques and given consumer tastes and preferences. Secondly, what is maximized is output when its various components are valued at the relative prices which reflect the prevailing distribution of income. In short, markets function only in response to effective demand, and the composition of output and the techniques of producing it which reflect only consumer demand at a point of time may not necessarily be optimal from a social point of view.

The patterns of production resulting from the free play of market forces may be unsatisfactory from various points of view. From a distributional point of view, it may be felt that too little is produced of the goods consumed by the poor and too much of the luxuries consumed by the rich; this problem is discussed in Chapter 14. Again, concerning a country's foreign trade, it may be felt that too much of some commodities is imported or too little of some others is exported; such problems are discussed in Chapter 12. In the present section, we consider especially the growth problem, i.e. the extent to which market forces may fail to achieve the highest rate of growth that an economy is capable of.

In some countries at certain times, there may be such a fortuitous combination of circumstances that market forces lead to rapid growth. This was the case in Britain in the days of its industrial leadership when there was rapid technological progress combined with expanding markets. It was therefore not entirely an accident that the economic case for freedom of markets was most eloquently argued by British economists of the period. In other DMEs which were faced with British competition in industry, the governments had to intervene in markets, for example, by restricting imports and by providing credit and technical assistance to set up new industries; it was only after this initial period that further growth was left to market forces, and economists and political leaders of these countries emerged as champions of market freedom. The great increase in government interventions in these countries in recent times has been mainly motivated by distributional concerns.

In the post-war period, a small group of LDCs, known as outward looking countries or newly industrializing countries (NICs) has experienced rapid growth. This growth is often attributed to the working of free market forces and these countries put forward as salutary examples for other LDCs to follow. In fact, however, their growth was also due to a variety of deliberate government interventionist policies.

The fact that markets may fail to produce rapid growth does not necessarily mean that government interventions will always do so. Whether government interventions are more successful depends on the type of interventions and the efficiency and integrity with which they are carried out. However appropriate the interventions may be, they will not promote growth if they are not carried out properly. In fact, as pointed out in Section 8.4(a) above, the fear that governments will not act efficiently and honestly was one of the main reasons for Adam Smith's advocacy of market freedom. Thus, most LDCs have not achieved rapid growth in spite of extensive government interventions, because although such interventions have ostensibly been undertaken in the interests of rapid growth and a better distribution of income, they have actually been in the interests of particular sections of the population and the government bureaucracy concerned with their implementation, groups which are already well-off compared with the rest of society.

Partly because of the weaknesses of market forces in promoting growth and partly because of the type of government interventions and the way they have been implemented, these LDCs have failed to achieve the maximum possible rate of growth. One form of this failure is that available resources have not been fully utilized. The most glaring illustration of this failure is the extensive underemployment of labour. This is partly due to various institutional factors affecting the labour market, as a result of which the labour market is highly segmented and wages do not adjust to their full employment equilibrium levels (see Section 8.4(b) above). It is also partly due to technological factors affecting the choice of techniques (see Section 10.4 above). The problem is then compounded by some government interventions in the labour market.

The problem of underutilization also arises in the case of capital. LDCs are generally considered to be short of capital because of their low capacity to save. But the capital market is so undeveloped that it does not mobilize potential savings or allocate them to the most profitable investments as fully as possible (see Section 8.4(c)). Further, both in the historical period and in recent times, there has been considerable mobility of capital (see Section 11.2(d)). Some of this capital flowed into the LDCs but only to particular sectors, especially those with a strong export demand. In other sectors, the problem was rather a weak inducement to invest, as argued by Nurkse (see Section 9.9 above). Therefore, the available supply of capital is not being fully utilized.

In the post-war period, governments of LDCs have undertaken investments in the public sector but have not made full use of foreign capital. It is partly because of fears that debt-service charges may take up too high a proportion of export earnings. But around 1972, outstanding debt of LDCs was about 1.8 times annual exports, whereas in 1913, these ratios were about 2¼ for India, Japan and China; 4.8 for Australia, 5.2 for Latin America, and as high as 8.6 for Canada (see Lewis, 1978a, p.59). LDCs can therefore use foreign capital to a much greater extent to promote their growth, as was done in pre-war years by other countries. Failure to use foreign capital more fully is also based on the objective of self-reliance. However, LDCs face a very difficult task if they rely only on their own savings to achieve the maximum rate of growth that is technically possible. Therefore, they must plan to use foreign capital more fully at the least possible cost.

Another reason for the failure of market forces to achieve the maximum possible rate of growth rests on dynamic considerations, namely the interaction between increasing returns and effective demand. As Young (1928) argued (see Section 9.8 above), the historical experience of DCs was that, once economic growth begins, it continues by a process of cumulative circular causation due to this interaction. But without the initial impulse, an economy relying only on market forces may be locked into a low level equilibrium trap.

Two important ways in which market forces and the government interventions with these forces affect the rate of growth is through the choice of techniques and the composition of output. These topics are discussed more fully in Sections 10.4 and 10.5. It is there argued that market forces by themselves may not lead to rapid growth in LDCs. It is therefore possible to improve the situation by some interventions by governments if they are sincerely concerned to promote growth benefitting all sections of the population and if they have the political strength to do so. But it is also possible that government interventions may make things worse. The instruments of such interventions may be broadly classified as follows: (a) development policies; (b) state operation of productive activities; (c) quantitative regulations; and (d) price policies. In determining how these instruments should be used, the main criterion is the extent to which they modify the allocative consequences of market forces in a desired direction without hindering their creative functions.

The most important role of governments in bringing about rapid growth and also a more equal distribution of income in LDCs is to raise the level of development, as defined in Chapter 5, by the measures discussed in Chapters 6–8. These measures are the special responsibility of governments, as they will generally not be undertaken by the private sector, because of their substantial externalities. The previous chapters were mainly concerned with the long-term analysis and policies relating to these measures. But these measures can be phased in different ways in the short run, especially by varying their allocation to different sectors of the economy and different sections of the population. The allocation of development programmes to different sections of the population has its main effect on the distribution of income; it is therefore discussed in Chapter 14 below. Regarding different sectors of the economy, it is argued in later sections that there are particular sequences in the expansion of these sectors which are most conducive to rapid growth; especially crucial is the role of the agricultural sector in the early stages of growth. Development programmes must therefore be allocated to the various sectors accordingly; some particular implications are discussed in the following sections, especially Section 10.6, in relation to individual sectors. In countries which have not achieved high rates of self-sustaining growth, the overall pace of such development programmes has been slow and they have also been misallocated, giving much greater priority to the industrial sector in urban areas and neglecting the agricultural sector and rural areas.

Closely related to the development measures are the activities to promote technological progress to widen the range of techniques available to the private sector. In DCs, where there is a large pool of scientific and technological manpower and where there are many large enterprises which can afford to employ this personnel in research and development of new products and processes, much of the technological progress is undertaken by the private sector induced by demand and relative prices. There is much less endogenous technological progress of this kind in LDCs, while there are many possibilities for evolving new techniques and adapting old techniques to LDC needs. Therefore, there is considerable scope for governments to undertake such technological research and development, and its dissemination among producers by extension services.

We come next to the state operation of productive activities. The usual system of remunerating public servants does not generally give them sufficient incentives for efficiency in such productive activities; state enterprises are therefore generally less efficient than private enterprises. As a general principle, directly productive activities should be left to the private sector, and the burden of proof that certain activities are better carried on in state enterprises placed on those proposing such an arrangement. The argument usually advanced to justify state enterprises in LDCs is that the state should control the production of certain commodities which are strategic for growth —the so-called 'commanding heights' of the economy. In relying on this argument, we must consider a number of issues such as whether the particular commodities are indeed strategic; whether they cannot be more cheaply imported; whether the private sector is able and willing to produce them in the desired quantities, and whether the private sector can market these commodities at a reasonable price. Even if the private sector cannot or will not produce these commodities in the desired quantities or at the desired prices, it does not follow that they should be produced by state enterprises, for other instruments may be used, such as subsidies to induce adequate production or lower prices, and tax policy to prevent excessive profits. If after considering all these questions, it is still found necessary to have state enterprises, they must be run as efficiently as possible, for example, by running them as public corporations on commercial principles.

The third instrument often used by governments to influence production is quantitative regulation, such as quotas, prohibitions, quantitative allocation of inputs, and licensing of industrial production and investment. This is the least satisfactory method of influencing production because the main decisions about who should produce which goods are made by administrators who do not have complete information and who are exposed to the possibility of corruption; in other words, such regulations interfere with the creative functions of markets. As far as possible, attempts to influence the composition of output should be made through other instruments which make fuller use of the creative role of markets.

The final instrument at the disposal of governments is price policy, i.e. regulating prices so as to induce the desired allocation of resources. Often, price policy is pursued by the legal fixation of prices above or below the market level. Then, either there will be extensive black marketing to evade the legal prices or the excess demand and excess supply will have to be rationed by administrative action. A better method is to use taxes and subsidies to change prices in any desired direction, and ensure that these fiscal measures are fully implemented. An alternative is for the state to enter the market as buyer or seller so as to bring about the desired changes in prices.

10.3 Population Policies

From a simple statistical point of view, the rate of growth of per capita income can be calculated as the difference between the rate of growth of total income and the rate of growth of population. This relationship has, however, been used to make a sharp distinction between policies to slow down population growth on the one hand and policies to accelerate growth of total income. The belief that the former can be accomplished more easily than the latter has then given rise to much enthusiasm for population policies. In fact, however, as argued in Section 9.4 above, the factors involved are so tightly interwoven that policies cannot be separated in this fashion. Policies which concentrate only on slowing down population growth without at the same time influencing economic growth are not likely to be very effective. Further, even if they were effective, they would only increase the rate of growth of per capita income to a limited extent.

Population policies in this narrow sense have been mainly family-planning programmes. These programmes hope to slow down population growth by exhorting individual couples to practise contraception and reduce their fertility, and by assisting them with supplies and services to do so. There was so much confidence in their effectiveness that the official adoption of such programmes was sometimes made a condition for giving aid to LDCs. The effectiveness of these programmes has, however, proved doubtful. The rapid decline of fertility in such countries as Taiwan, South Korea, Hong Kong and Singapore was initially attributed to their family-planning programmes, but it now seems that fertility decline started before such programmes were mounted in these countries (see e.g. Hauser, 1973, p.238). Another example is the

Indian state of Kerala, where a substantial fertility decline started before any official family-planning programme got under way, and has instead been attributed to improvements in education and health facilities rather than to any significant increase in incomes (Nair, 1974). On the other hand, in countries which have remained at a low level of development, the implementation of official family-planning programmes over a considerable period has not had much effect in slowing down population growth significantly, as shown, for example, by the results of the latest censuses of India (1981) and Indonesia (1980). Such programmes may be useful in assisting families who have already reduced their desired family sizes, and hence in accelerating fertility decline after it has started, but are less effective in initiating a rapid decline of fertility in countries at a low level of development.

Another approach to population policies in the narrow sense has been the use of economic incentives for small families and disincentives for large families (see e.g. Enke, 1966). This approach assumes that fertility decisions in LDCs are already subject to conscious choice. This assumption is generally invalid in LDCs and therefore the policy based on it is not likely to be very effective.

Slower growth of population is, of course, highly desirable. It will facilitate the great task of modernization that these countries face. Growth of total income may not lead to a corresponding growth of population as assumed in Malthusian theory, but at the same time, it may not necessarily reduce population growth as envisaged in the demographic transition theory. The slogan that 'development is the best contraceptive' which was advanced by LDC delegates at the Bucharest World Population Conference in 1974 is doubtful if development is interpreted only as faster growth of total incomes; it is more likely to be true if development is defined as in Chapter 5, distinct from the concept of growth. In this sense, policies to promote development will increase the general standard of living, both by accelerating growth of incomes and by slowing down population growth.

The need to reduce population growth is one reason for giving high priority to development policies. It is a matter of great urgency because of the magnitude of population growth that LDCs face in the future. One factor involved is that, even if the age-specific fertility rates fall abruptly to the level of replacement, the age-distribution in LDCs is so highly concentrated in the child-bearing ages that population will continue to grow rapidly for a considerable time in the future. This tendency is known as the 'momentum' of population growth and is measured by the ratio of the ultimate stationary population to the population at the time of the fertility decline. Keyfitz (1971) has shown that this ratio is

$$\frac{be_0^0(R-1)}{\mu rR}$$

where b = birth rate; r = rate of natural increase; e_0^0 = expectation of life at birth and R = net reproduction rate, all measured before the decline of fertility, and μ is the mean age of child-bearing thereafter. This result shows the extent to which the ultimate size of population depends on the current demographic parameters. For example, with b = 41 per thousand, r = 22 per thousand, e_0^0 = 50 years, R = 2 and μ = 29 years, the momentum of population growth is 1.6, i.e. population will grow by 60 per cent even after age-specific fertility rates have fallen to replacement levels.

Another factor involved is the time taken, known as the 'braking distance' for fertility to be reduced. We must take account of the growth of population during this period. Ohlin (1967) has shown that, if the population growth rate takes T years to decline from g to $g-s$, the population thereafter will be higher than it would have been with an instantaneous drop in growth by a factor of $e^{sT/2}$; this factor shows the permanent legacy of the time taken to reduce fertility.

10.4 Choice of Techniques

One of the issues of production policy that has received much attention in the literature is the choice of techniques (for a recent survey, see Stewart, 1977). The controversy is mainly over the argument that the actual choice of techniques in LDCs is highly capital-intensive, i.e. that in producing various commodities, producers tend to choose techniques which require a high proportion of capital to labour. When the average capital-intensity of the chosen techniques is greater than the capital–labour ratio in the economy, some labour will be unemployed. Such a choice of techniques has therefore been considered inappropriate for LDCs where capital is scarce and labour abundant. Further, it has been noted that growth of employment is lagging behind growth of output, i.e. the productivity per worker is rising, especially in the industrial sector. This has been attributed to a steady increase in capital-intensity.

In order to understand the factors involved, we consider first the neo-classical model. In this model, it is assumed that there is available a continuous range of techniques which can be described by a smooth production function. Profit maximizing producers then make their choice from these techniques according to the commodity and factor prices they face. These prices are determined in efficient competitive markets so that all available resources are fully utilized and aggregate output is maximized. This model clearly cannot apply to LDCs with their extensive underemployment of labour. In the choice-of-techniques literature, such underemployment is explained in two ways. One is the failure of market prices to reach their equilibrium levels due to various institutional obstacles; the resulting underemployment is then described as 'institutional'. The other explanation is that LDCs do not have the wide range of techniques assumed in the above model and also that these techniques do not have enough flexibility in their factor proportions; underemployment due to these conditions is then described as 'technological' (see e.g. Eckhaus, 1955).

Most of the theoretical discussion has been concerned with the institutional factors affecting factor prices. Examples of these factors are the influence of custom and tradition in fixing wages; the 'high wage islands' of the modern sector maintained for political reasons, especially by large private and government enterprises; the unionization of labour in some sectors; the fixing of wages in the public sector as 'administered prices' not responsive to supply and demand, etc. Other institutional factors arise from government interventions. For example, the price of capital may be reduced for some producers below the equilibrium level by cheap credit and overvalued exchange rates for the import of capital goods, and the price of labour may be raised above the equilibrium level by minimum wage laws. Such institutional factors then lead to an excessive use of capital-intensive techniques. The ultimate solution suggested for such unemployment is then a policy of 'getting prices right' by eliminating such institutional obstacles to the working of market forces. If it is not possible to do this quickly, a system of taxes and subsidies is suggested (see e.g. Ahluwalia, 1973).

This approach to the problem raises a number of questions. Is there a full range of techniques available in LDCs with flexible factor proportions as assumed in the competitive model? How far is the choice of techniques influenced by relative factor prices? Is the choice of techniques the main cause of underemployment of labour in LDCs and of the tendency for growth of employment to lag behind growth of output?

To describe the actual situation in LDCs, the available techniques may be classified into two broad types: modern and traditional techniques, with a considerable difference between them in their factor proportions. Traditional techniques are those evolved over long periods of time by trial and error. They are usually suited to small-scale production of commodities generally consumed at low levels of income (see e.g. Bauer and Yamey, 1957, pp.118–22). In contrast, modern techniques have been evolved by the application of science to technology; they are usually suited to the large-scale production of commodities which are mostly consumed in LDCs at high levels of income. Traditional techniques are generally more labour-intensive than modern techniques but labour is mostly used in traditional techniques as a source of physical power, while it is used in modern techniques because of its skills. Therefore, the quality of labour used in the two types of techniques is quite different. In the long run, the objective of development is the use of human labour because of its skills rather than as a source of power. Hence, there is a steady substitution of modern for traditional techniques. In many LDCs, governments have followed policies to encourage the use of modern techniques. Such encouragement may be excessive in some cases; this depends on the trade-off between faster growth by adoption of these techniques in the long run and the unemployment they cause in the short run. Within each type, the range of techniques is extremely limited. Traditional techniques are usually those handed down from generation to generation and have become part of the customary ways of production, while modern techniques available to LDCs are often rigidly embodied in machinery.

As far as modern techniques are concerned, LDCs are technologically dependent on DCs. This is partly because the DCs are technologically more advanced; they have larger stocks of scientific and technological manpower and they are able to invest larger amounts in research and development of modern techniques. But it is also due to the fact that because of economies of scale, capital goods industries making machines which embody modern techniques are mostly located in the DCs. The result is that modern techniques are available to LDCs only in a highly capital-intensive form. One reason why modern techniques are so capital-intensive is simply that they are more efficient, i.e. they increase output so much that they use less labour and less capital to produce a unit of output (see, e.g., Kaldor, 1965, pp.98–9). Another reason is that, being mostly produced in the DCs, they reflect the scarcity of labour and the high wages relative to the cost of capital in those countries; hence the machines produced in these countries embody a considerable amount of 'automation', the substitution of mechanical devices for human labour. Partly because of this influence of high wages, technological progress in DCs tends to be predominantly of the type known as 'labour-augmenting' (see Bruton, 1976, for a mathematical result which separates the influence of the growth of wages and that of the nature of technological progress on capital-intensity).

Under these conditions, the influence of relative prices on the choice of techniques is likely to be limited, for a number of reasons. First, lowering the wages of unskilled labour which suffers from a higher rate of unemployment will not affect modern techniques which rely mostly on skilled labour. Second, even if wages are relatively low, capital-intensive techniques may be preferred because of the high transaction costs involved in employing and managing labour. Roumasset and Smith (1981), for example, have suggested that this is one reason for the recent rapid expansion of agricultural mechanization in the Philippines. Third, if available techniques use factors in rigid proportions, changes in relative prices will not affect their choice. Fourth, a more important problem than the rigidity of factor proportions is the limited range of modern techniques available. If at least two techniques of producing a commodity are available with widely differing factor-intensities, they can be combined to generate a wide range of average capital-intensities, but this cannot be done if there is only one technique available or if one technique is technically more efficient in the use of both labour and capital; then such a technique will be more profitable at all positive factor prices. Finally, so long as LDCs are technologically dependent on DCs, changing factor prices in LDCs will not influence the techniques available to them, because they are mostly evolved in the DCs.

So long as the range of techniques available in LDCs is limited, there is little they can do about making an appropriate choice to secure full employment of labour. This can only be done by making more use of traditional techniques and thus losing the advantage of the efficiency of modern techniques. A more promising solution is to extend the range of techniques available to include those which are more suited to the factor endowment of LDCs. This is not just a matter of taking on techniques which have become obsolete in the DCs just because they are less capital-intensive, for they may also be less efficient. What is needed is a set of techniques which embody the most efficient scientific methods in as labour-intensive a form as possible. This can be done partly by undertaking research in LDCs. In the DCs, the direction of technological progress may be induced by the prevailing factor prices because of their high level of scientific and technological development (see e.g. Binswanger *et al.*, 1978). But because of the lower level of development in the LDCs, the state may have to take a greater role in influencing the direction of technological progress. Another solution lies in the expansion of the capital-goods industries in LDCs, either individually or in cooperation, to produce capital equipment which embodies efficient methods in a more labour-intensive form than is available from the DCs (see Pack and Todaro, 1969).

We next go on to consider how far the choice of techniques is an important reason for the underemployment of labour. The fact that profitable techniques are only available in a highly capital-intensive form is clearly one reason. But there are also a number of other, more important, factors involved. One of the most important of these is the supply of wage goods, especially food. This has been put forcefully by Kaldor (1965, pp.98–9) thus:

> The amount of employment created outside agriculture looked at *in toto* is not primarily a matter of technology at all. What are the limits of wage employment in any country at any time? As many people as will not create an inflation. As many people as you have wage goods to pay for their work. So the total employment capacity of a country depends simply and solely on the supply of wage goods . . . it is food that is the primary factor and the size of the agricultural surplus is the vital factor which limits the wage labour force. That decides the wages a country can afford. When you realise this, then you see immediately that all this tremendous discussion about technology is really rather beside the point.

Given the limited range and rigid factor-proportions of the available techniques, the level of employment is also limited by the stock of capital. As argued in Section 10.2, the available sources of capital are not being fully utilized in LDCs, either for lack of demand or due to government regulations about the inflow of foreign capital. The level of employment and its growth can therefore be raised by making fuller use of available sources of investment funds.

Thirdly, the available techniques for producing individual commodities may have a limited range and rigid factor-proportions but they vary considerably among different commodities. For some commodities, these techniques are highly capital-intensive, whatever the relative factor-prices; they may therefore be described as capital-intensive commodities. Similarly, other commodities may be described as labour-intensive because the most profitable techniques for producing them are labour-intensive. Given this difference between commodities, the average capital-intensity for the economy as a whole depends on the relative shares of the two types of commodities in total output.

One circumstance affecting these shares is the nature of a country's foreign trade; this is discussed in Chapters 11 and 12, where it is argued that the extent to which LDCs can reduce the overall capital-intensity of production by exporting labour-intensive commodities and importing capital-intensive commodities is limited. The other factor affecting the overall capital-intensity is the distribution of income. The commodities mostly consumed by lower income groups tend to be more labour-intensive than those consumed by the upper income groups. Therefore, the more unequal the distribution of income, the greater the overall capital-intensity of production. An improvement in the distribution of income will therefore help to increase the demand for labour and hence reduce the extent of unemployment (see Chapter 14 for policies affecting the distribution of income).

The question of the choice of techniques as a means of expanding employment has been discussed in the literature mostly for the industrial sector in urban areas, perhaps because unemployment is most visible in these areas. But it is precisely in this sector that available techniques of production are strictly limited and there is little room for manoeuvre in the short run. On the other hand, the problem of underemployment of labour is more massive in rural areas and a more serious cause of absolute poverty. Also, there is more scope for expanding output and employment opportunities in the agricultural sector of these countries. In agriculture, all three factors of production—land, labour and capital—are important. Therefore techniques cannot be classified simply as capital-intensive or labour-intensive. The main problem in this sector is the scarcity of land. The DCs have managed to escape from this contraint to a considerable extent by using techniques using capital which Butt (1960) has described as 'mechanized' techniques in contrast to 'peasant' techniques which do not use capital in significant amounts. Capital used in agriculture has in turn been classified either as 'landesque' i.e. as a substitute for land or as 'labouresque', i.e. as a substitute for labour (see Sen, 1959). But these two forms are not necessarily exclusive. Capital can take one form or the other, or both, depending on the peasant techniques with which a mechanized technique is being compared. The peasant techniques themselves are constantly changing over time, becoming more and more labour-intensive as a result of growing population pressure on a limited area of land. Therefore, the extent to which a particular mechanized farming technique is land-saving or labour-saving or both also varies over time. In particular, the earlier a mechanized technique is introduced in the 'peasant calendar', the more likely it is to be labour-using and land-saving. The longer the investment of capital in agriculture is delayed in the agricultural sector, the more likely it is to be labour-saving and land-using (see Section 9.6).

The two aspects of capital in agriculture, i.e. its relation to land and to labour, explain the differences among DCs and the variation of techniques over time in these countries. They can also be used to explain the wide variation in labour-intensity of agricultural production among LDCs (see e.g. Ishikawa, 1978). The fact that some densely populated countries of Asia use less labour per hectare per crop and get less output per hectare than other countries is due to the amount and nature of capital used. Agricultural employment and output in the former countries can therefore be expanded considerably by investing more capital and adopting the techniques prevailing in the latter group of countries. (For a fuller discussion, see Booth and Sundrum, 1982.)

10.5 Composition of Output

Most of the discussion of the composition of output in the literature is about how it is determined at any point of time by the level of income at that time, and how growth of income leads to systematic changes in the composition of output on certain historical and cross-sectional patterns. In the LDCs, the reverse relationship of how the growth of incomes can be influenced by the composition of output is more important. As argued in Section 10.2 above, the way market forces allocate resources to different uses does not necessarily achieve the maximum possible rate of growth of production. We have therefore to consider what composition of output is most conducive to rapid growth.

One approach that is implicit in much of the literature and is also sometimes proposed explicitly is the imitative strategy, i.e. one of recapitulating the historical experience of DCs which achieved rapid growth in the past. Some weaknesses of this strategy were pointed out in previous chapters (see especially Section 1.2 and 9.3 above). Before following a historical pattern of development, we must consider in more detail why that pattern occurred, how far it was optimal at the time, and whether it will also be optimal under the conditions facing the LDCs in the future. Especially in connection with the composition of output, Ishikawa (1967, p.i) has shown in his detailed discussion of the problem in an Asian context that, as a result of differences in initial conditions,

> the experience of past economic development may not serve as a lesson to the contemporary developing countries.

He was particularly concerned with such differences in initial conditions as a higher population density, and a lower investment and lower productivity in agriculture, compared with the early stages of growth in the DCs. The past experience of DCs was one in which there was a steady transfer of labour and other resources from the agricultural to the other sectors. But in many LDCs, as he argues, it may be necessary to put more resources into the agricultural sector for some time in the future before that sector is able to release resources to other sectors.

Rather than merely imitating historical experiences, we must take account of the main relationships involved. Some theoretical studies of these relationships are therefore examined in this section as a basis for policy making.

(a) The Shadow Prices Approach

In this approach, it is recognized that markets in LDCs do not always function in the neo-classical manner in which actual market prices of goods and services reflect the satisfactions that consumers derive from them or the costs that producers incur in producing them. Such divergences of market performance from the neo-classical model are described as 'distortions', which may be due to the low level of development or to interventions by governments. The 'first-best' solution then is to improve the working of markets. To the extent that the results of market forces are unsatisfactory because of the unequal income distribution they produce, it is argued that they should be modified by non-distortionary measures such as lump-sum taxes and subsidies. But it may not be possible to achieve this solution in a reasonable time. Then, a 'second-best' solution is proposed for policy-making in which decisions are based on a set of 'shadow prices'. The idea is to select projects or choose techniques on the basis of costs and benefits measured in terms of such shadow prices rather than on actual market prices which are distorted. In the case of capital projects with costs and benefits spread over several years, the criterion usually recommended is the present value of the stream of net benefits (but see Sundrum, 1981a, for the advantages of the internal rate of return criterion from a long-term point of view).

These shadow prices are not the equilibrium prices that would prevail if all markets functioned efficiently and competitively. Instead, they are the prices which should be used to make decisions in particular cases, such as the appraisal of new projects, assuming that market distortions continue in the rest of the economy. The difference is brought out most clearly in the following method of determining shadow factor prices. Let p represent a vector of product prices and M the matrix of input–output coefficients corresponding to these product prices. Then the vector of actual factor prices w in a competitive situation is given by

$$w = M^{-1}p. \tag{10.5.1}$$

But p may be subject to a number of distortions, e.g. government interventions in foreign trade. In the O.E.C.D. *Manual* on project appraisal (Little and Mirlees, 1969), it is recommended that commodities should be valued at the prices at which a country can buy or sell them in international trade. If these prices are p^* and the corresponding matrix of input–output coefficients is M^*, then the first-best factor prices w^* will be

$$w^* = M^{*-1}p^* \tag{10.5.2}$$

But because the actual methods of production in the rest of the economy will not be affected by the decisions made on a marginal product, the second-best solution is to take the shadow factor prices for appraising the project as

$$w^{**} = M^{-1}p^{*}. \tag{10.5.3}$$

(For this interpretation, see Findlay and Wellisz, 1976.)

In general, shadow prices are derived by maximizing an objective function which is usually taken as the discounted present value of the stream of consumption benefits. To value these benefits, market prices are first adjusted to reflect the social point of view by some nationally chosen parameters described as 'weights'. These include weights for merit goods (i.e. goods whose value from a social point of view is considered greater than their valuation by individual consumers), weights for benefits accruing to different sections of the population, known as distributional weights, and weights for benefits occurring at different times, usually summarized by a social rate of time discount. The shadow prices of particular goods and services which enter into the costs or the benefits of projects are then derived from these weight parameters. We consider some examples.

One example is the *shadow price of investment* which the U.N.I.D.O. *Guidelines* (United Nations Industrial Development Organization, 1972) defines as

$$P^{\text{inv}} = \frac{(1-s)q}{i-sq} = 1 + \frac{q-i}{i-sq} \tag{10.5.4}$$

where i is the social rate of time discount—one of the weight parameters; q is the rate of return to capital, i.e. the marginal efficiency of investment, and s is the saving ratio. If the social rate of time discount equals the private rate and there is a perfect capital market, q will be equal to i, and P^{inv} equal to 1, i.e. a unit of investment has the same social value as a unit of present consumption. But if the social rate of time discount is less than the private rate or if the capital market does not function perfectly, investment is less than its optimal level as reflected in a marginal efficiency of investment greater than the social rate of time discount; then P^{inv} is greater than 1, i.e. a premium must be placed on funds allocated to investment rather than present consumption.

Another example is the *shadow wage rate*. As usually defined, this rate depends on the functioning of the labour market and the capital market. If the only problem is disequilibrium in the labour market, e.g. unemployment due to a market wage above the marginal product of labour, then the shadow wage rate should be taken as the marginal product of labour, leading to more employment than at the market wage. However, expanding employment in this way will increase wage incomes and reduce profits, and as a higher proportion is saved out of profits than out of wages, it will increase consumption at the expense of investment. This will not matter if investment has the same social value as consumption, but if not, i.e. if the shadow price of investment is greater than 1, an allowance for this divergence must be made in the shadow wage rate used for project appraisal. The solution proposed is

$$SWR = z + s_c(P^{\text{inv}} - 1)(w - m) \tag{10.5.5}$$

where m is the marginal product of labour in the project, z is the marginal product in the rest of the economy, w is the market wage that must be paid, and s_c is the rate of saving out of profits. If employment in a project is extended to the point where $m = SWR$, then we have

$$SWR = \frac{z + s_c(P^{\text{inv}} - 1)w}{1 + s_c(P^{\text{inv}} - 1)} \tag{10.5.6}$$

that is

$$SWR = w - \frac{(w - z)}{1 + s_c(P^{\text{inv}} - 1)} \tag{10.5.7}$$

i.e. the shadow wage rate will be less than the market wage both when P^{inv} is greater than 1 and when w is greater than z.

There are a number of problems in such a shadow price approach. It has been developed primarily as an aid to decentralize decision-making in the sense that once a central authority has laid down the shadow prices, other agencies can use them to make optimal decisions in the particular projects that concern them. In some cases, shadow prices can be fixed on general principles, e.g. as international prices in the case of traded goods. But in the typical case, shadow prices can be derived only from a complete optimization exercise, which already includes all the particular decisions. Hence, strictly speaking, there is no decentralization advantage in using shadow prices (Rudra, 1972). The only advantage is a computational one; in the language of linear programming, if the optimal allocation of resources is the primal problem, the shadow prices are the solution of its dual problem; the solution of the dual problem may sometimes facilitate the solution of the primal problem. In order to decentralize decision-making, i.e. to solve particular problems without solving all problems at the same time, shadow prices have to be derived by hunch or on the basis of highly simplified models. Such estimates are subject to a wide margin of error; their only effect is to make all decisions consistent with each other.

Second, there is a problem of implementation. Decisions in the public sector may be made on the basis of such shadow prices instead of market prices, but the public sector is only a small part of the economy of LDCs. Further, for most of the activities which are appropriate for the public sector, the benefits are not quantifiable (see e.g. Little and Mirlees, 1974, p.85). As argued in Chapter 5, the best strategy for development programmes is to provide them ahead of demand to stimulate directly productive activity in the private sector. In the case of directly productive activities, they will be decided by the private sector on the basis of actual market prices. A project may be highly desirable on the basis of shadow prices but unprofitable at market prices; then it will not be undertaken by the private sector. To induce the private sector to do so, the government must either subsidize the project or use taxes and subsidies to alter market prices so that they become equal to the shadow prices. A project may be profitable at market prices but undesirable at shadow prices; then, the government must prevent the project being undertaken by the private sector through administrative controls or other measures. Therefore the implementation of shadow prices involves extensive government interventions in the economy. Further, there is no reason why such interventions should be confined to particular projects. If the government intervenes widely in the private sector, it need no longer base such interventions on the second-best solution derived for particular projects.

Third, many of the causes of market distortions are the interventions by governments themselves. Therefore, as Corden (1974, p.401) argues,

> One must then be clear in one's mind why one expects a government to carry out and act upon a social cost–benefit analysis, while not being able to persuade it to impose first-best trade taxes.

(See also Sen, 1972).

Finally, shadow price formulae are mostly derived from highly simplified models. They are particularly weak in their estimates of the benefits flowing from various projects, especially in the public sector. In such cases, they are still useful for evaluating alternative methods of producing particular goods or providing particular services; their role is then one of comparing the cost-effectiveness of these methods. The process of carrying out a cost–benefit analysis is also useful in that it brings out all the factors that have to be considered and it forces us to quantify at least the quantifiable aspects of each problem. But it is also necessary to consider many other aspects which cannot readily be solved by this method. Two cases are considered below.

(b) Capital Goods and Consumer Goods

An important aspect of the composition of output is the division between capital goods and consumer goods. This aspect was intensely debated by Soviet economists in the 1920s, leading to the conclusion of Feldman (1928) that a large proportion of investment should be allocated to the capital-goods sector. The same conclusion was reached by Mahalanobis (1953) and used to formulate the Second Five Year Plan of India. There has been much criticism of the Feldman–Mahalanobis (FM) strategy as a whole (see, e.g., Bhagwati and Chakravarty, 1969) but to assess its strengths and weaknesses, we must distinguish three issues which are involved: (i) what should be the level of investment each year over a long period of time? (ii) should the capital goods required for the desired level of investment be produced domestically or imported? and (iii) what should be done to increase the domestic production of capital goods?

On the first issue, the aim of the FM strategy is to maximize the level of investment by maximizing the supply of capital goods. The strategy has been criticized on the ground that when investment exceeds voluntary savings, there will be underutilization of capital goods and excess demand for consumer goods, leading to inflation. The alternative proposed instead was that investment should be limited to the amount of savings that would be made each year, combined with policies to increase the rate of savings. If inflation is due to an excess of investment over savings, it may be desirable for the sake of monetary stability to make investment equal to savings, but in the interests of growth, this should be done as far as possible by raising the level of savings to the level of the maximum investment that is technically possible. In the Indian case, the slow growth of the economy has been attributed to the implementation of the FM strategy and forcing the pace of investment beyond the rate of savings. In retrospect, it appears more likely that the problem facing the Indian economy was a lack of demand. The FM strategy was followed for a short period coinciding with an import-substitution phase in industry (see Section 12.2 below). Thereafter, the strategy was not implemented as fully as before, partly due to conservative monetary policies. The result was that there was growing under-utilization of capacity in many industries, both in the capital goods and in the consumer goods sectors. The fact that capital goods cannot be consumed once they have been produced does not mean that the production of capital goods will promote growth; for this to happen, the capital goods must be fully utilized. A higher level of investment could have stimulated demand for both sectors and the economy could have achieved a higher rate of growth.

On the second issue, the FM strategy was in favour of the domestic production of capital goods rather than imports. In its early years, the Soviet Union had no choice. In the case of India, this strategy was criticized on the ground that resources should be allocated according to comparative costs, and hence that capital goods should have been imported in exchange for exports of consumer goods, i.e. according to an imitative strategy, because consumer goods had been given priority in the growth of other countries in the past. But at the time India did not have much prospect of increasing its foreign exchange receipts rapidly by expanding its traditional exports, both because of internal supply constraints and because of weak external demand. Instead, by its concentration on capital goods, it has greatly improved its comparative advantage in that sector and is now able to export these goods. Another criticism of the strategy was that as capital goods were more capital-intensive than consumer goods, the concentration on the former reduced the rate of growth of employment (see, e.g., Komiya, 1959). But using the composition of output to promote employment is a short-sighted view; in the longer run, the faster growth of investment by expanding the capital goods sector will expand employment more rapidly. Further, the domestic capital goods sector has been able to produce machinery embodying more labour-intensive techniques than were possible with imported capital goods.

Finally, on the third issue, the FM strategy took capital as the only constraint on the expansion of the two sectors. Therefore, attention was focussed on the proportion λ_k and λ_c of investment allocated to the capital goods and the consumer goods sectors respectively as the key parameters of policy. The growth of income Y_t was assumed to follow the relationship

$$Y_t = \left[Y_0 + I_0(\lambda_c\beta_c + \lambda_k\beta_k)\right]\left[\frac{(1 + \lambda_k\beta_k)^t - 1}{\lambda_k\beta_k}\right] \qquad (10.5.8)$$

(Mahalanobis, 1953), where β_k and β_c are the given output–capital ratios in the two sectors and I_0 is the initial level of investment. This shows that the higher the allocation of investment to the capital goods sector, the faster will be the growth of income. But whereas, under the conditions facing the Indian economy, maximizing the output of capital goods would have led to the most rapid growth of the economy, it is not necessarily true that the output of capital goods would always increase by allocating more investment to that sector. Instead, as Findlay (1966) has shown, there is an optimum allocation of investment to the two sectors which maximizes the output of capital goods; allocating a higher proportion of investment to the capital goods sector will mean a lower output of consumer goods, lower employment of labour in both sectors, and hence a lower output of capital goods also. The condition for investment allocation to maximize the output of capital goods is then given by

$$M_c = \frac{F_c}{w}M_l, \qquad (10.5.9)$$

where M_c and M_l are the marginal products of capital and labour in the capital goods sector, F_c is the marginal product of capital in the consumer goods sector, and w is the wage rate. This condition means that at the margin, the extra output of capital goods achieved by allocating an extra unit of investment to that sector must equal the extra output of capital goods that can be produced by allocating the extra unit of investment to the consumer goods sector and using the additional output of consumer goods to increase employment in the capital goods sector.

(c) The Balanced Growth Doctrine

The other important aspect of the composition of output is according to the major sectors of the economy. In order to ensure that an economy is growing as rapidly as its resources permit, the object of policy should be to push effective demand to the limit of potential supply. In the DMEs, it may be possible to do so by monetary and fiscal policies affecting all sectors because, in these countries, when aggregate demand equals aggregate supply, market forces may be sufficient to ensure equality of demand and supply in individual sectors. But in LDCs, factors of production are less mobile and less versatile, and the products of different sectors less substitutable for each other, so that individual sectors may be subject to different types of constraints. Hence, the composition of output has to be influenced by policy measures to relax the constraints on individual sectors to promote overall growth.

One such policy is the balanced growth strategy advocated by Rosenstein-Rodan (1943), Nurkse (1952) and Lewis (1955). In advocating this strategy, it is assumed that effective demand for each sector depends on the level of activity in other sectors (see Section 9.9 for the concept of effective demand). The problem then is to allocate the given resources among the sectors in such a way that there is adequate effective demand for the outputs produced with this allocation. It follows then that each sector should be expanded at a rate proportional to the income elasticity of demand for its product. As explained by Lewis (1955, pp.276–7):

> Suppose there is considerable innovation in the agricultural sector producing food for the home market. The result is either a surplus of food to sell to the towns, or a surplus of labour in agriculture seeking non-agricultural employment, or some combination of both. If manufacturing industry is growing simultaneously at the right rate, it can absorb both the surplus goods and the surplus labour. If it is not, the terms of trade will move against agriculture, and as there will be a surplus of farm labour as well as farm products, agricultural incomes will be depressed and further investment and innovation in this sector will be discouraged . . . Exactly the same difficulties arise if economic development is concentrated upon industrialisation to the neglect of agriculture, as happened in the USSR.

The reference to the terms of trade between agriculture and industry has given the impression that constant terms of trade are somehow desirable for their own sake; as an objective, this has been criticized by Findlay (1959). However,

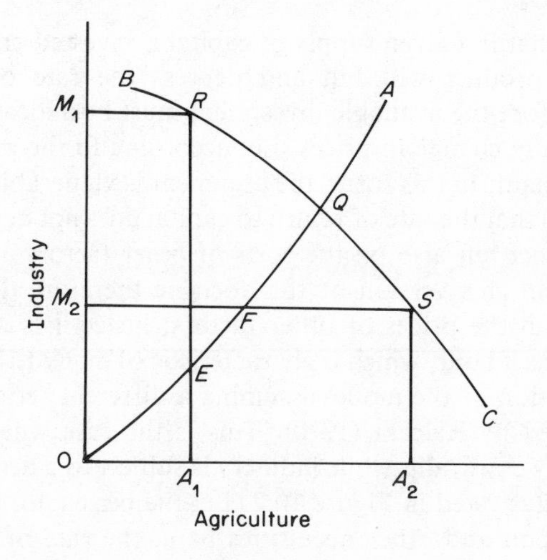

Figure 10.1

the terms of trade may not be very flexible in practice. It is then that the strategy becomes more relevant.

A simple diagrammatic exposition of the strategy is given in Figure 10.1. Here we consider the effective demand for agriculture as a function of industrial output and the effective demand for industry as a function of agriculture output. But with the economy divided into these two sectors, the two effective demand curves coincide and may be represented by the single curve OA in the figure. (This is generally known as the income–consumption curve.) The curve BC is the transformation curve between the two sectors and represents the common supply constraint. The allocation of resources to the two sectors depends on the point chosen on this curve.

Consider the point R where the allocation is biassed in favour of industry. With an agricultural output OA_1, the effective demand for industry is only A_1E; actual transactions are at E, leaving an excess supply of ER in industry. Similarly, consider the allocation S biassed in favour of agriculture. For industrial output OM_2, the effective demand for agriculture is only M_2F; actual transactions are at F, leaving an excess supply of FS in agriculture. Hence, the allocation which makes fullest use of available resources and thus maximizes the rate of growth is at the point Q, where OA intersects BC; at this point, the available resources are used to expand each sector at rates proportional to their income elasticities of demand.

Nurkse's version of the doctrine is based on the effects on the inducement to invest. He says (Nurkse, 1952, p.12) that:

> Balanced growth may be a good thing for its own sake, but here it interests us mainly for the sake of its effects on the demand for capital. It appears in the present context as an essential means of enlarging the size of the market and of creating inducements to invest.

The argument is that if a given supply of capital is invested only in one sector, the price of its product will fall and depress the rate of return to the investment; therefore the available investment must be allocated to all sectors so as to prevent any change in prices, i.e. according to the respective income elasticities of demand. In this form, the argument is vulnerable to the criticism of Sheahan (1958) that the rate of return to capital does not depend only on the price of the product but also on the costs of other factors and the extent of technical progress. This version of the doctrine therefore depends on there being no change in the prices of other factors; hence it is applicable to the situation of surplus labour, which is characteristic of many LDCs.

A dynamic version of the model assuming a different set of circumstances has been proposed by Kalecki (1970). This is the case where agriculture is subject to a supply constraint while industry is subject to a demand constraint. The situation is illustrated in Figure 10.2. Let the per capita income elasticity of demand for food and other necessities be μ, the rate of growth of total incomes be r, and the rate of growth of population be q. Then, the demand

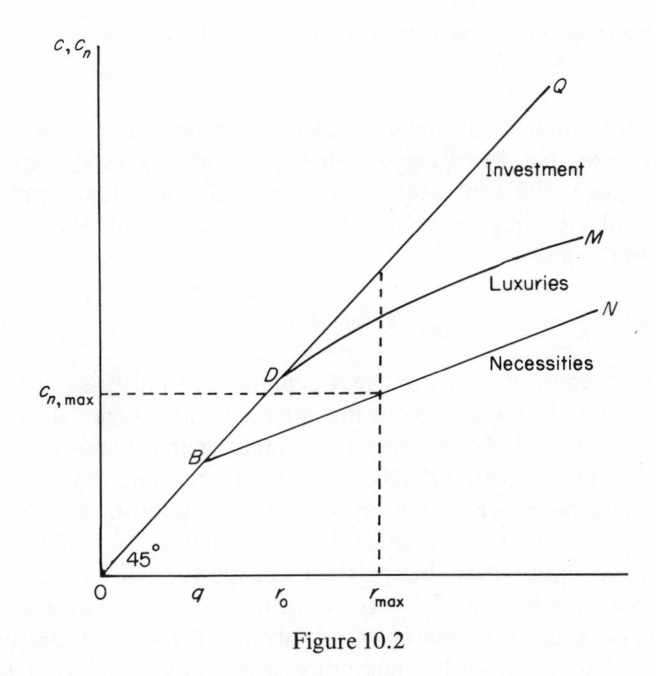

Figure 10.2

for necessities will grow at the rate c_n, given by

$$c_n = q + \mu(r - q) \tag{10.5.9}$$

For any given q, the relationship between c_n and r is shown by the line BN; this in turn determined the rate of growth of demand for other, luxury, commodities and investment goods. Suppose there is an upper limit $c_{n,\max}$ to the rate at which the supply of necessities, especially food, can be expanded. Then, the relationship BN can be used to determine the maximum overall rate of growth, $r_{\max}$. This assumes that there is no supply constraint on the expansion of non-essentials.

Kalecki himself used this model to study the problem of financing growth. Let the initial growth rate be r_0; in order to increase the overall growth rate beyond this level, a higher proportion of income must be channelled towards investment, and the investment ratio will generally increase with the rate of growth. When the requirements for investment are subtracted, we get the rate of growth of total consumption, c, as a function of r; this relationship is shown by the curve DM. The difference between c and c_n then represents the permissible rate of growth of luxury consumption. The task of fiscal policy is to tax higher income groups so as to keep the growth rate of luxury consumption within this limit. Attempts to have a higher rate of growth will involve taxation of lower income groups or an inflationary rise in prices to restrain the demand for necessities. Hence, on this argument, the key to 'financing' a more rapid growth is the removal of obstacles to the expansion of agriculture. (Kalecki, 1970, p.104)

In most simple models, the income elasticities of demand are assumed to be constant, for example, in fitting double-logarithmic regression equations to consumption data. But this assumption is invalid over a long term both on theoretical and empirical grounds. Theoretically, income elasticities must satisfy the condition:

$$\Sigma k_i \epsilon_i = 1 \tag{10.5.10}$$

where ϵ_i is the income elasticity of the ith commodity and k_i is the proportion of income spent on it. So long as the income elasticities are not equal to 1, the expenditure shares will change over time, and hence the income elasticities cannot remain constant. Empirically also it has been found that Engel curves, i.e. curves showing expenditures on various commodities as functions of income, in which income elasticities decline with the level of incomes, fit household expenditure data better than constant elasticity curves. Also, budget studies over time and across countries show a negative association between income elasticities and levels of income (Brown and Deaton, 1972, esp. p.1173). Therefore, each commodity goes through different stages; it starts being consumed at a 'tolerance' level of income; first it is a 'luxury' with an income elasticity greater than one and then it becomes a 'necessity' with a low income elasticity; finally it reaches a 'satiation' point when income elasticity is zero. Different commodities may therefore be arranged in a hierarchy according to the income levels at which they pass through these stages (see Cornwall, 1977, p.101 for a diagrammatic illustration). This hierarchical pattern indicates the changes in the composition of output required for rapid economic growth. These changes, however, may not always come about as a result of market forces alone. Then, they have to be brought about by deliberate policy. Some aspects of these policies are discussed below for the major sectors of the economy, taking account of the various supply and demand constraints on each of them.

10.6 Sectoral Policies

(a) The Agricultural Sector

The agricultural sector of LDCs produces two types of products. One consists of crops, mainly foodstuffs, produced largely by traditional methods on a small scale. Some of the output is exported but most of it is for domestic consumption; indeed much of it is produced on a subsistence basis and consumed by the producers themselves. This part of the agricultural sector is sometimes described as the peasant sector. The other type consists of foodstuffs and agricultural raw materials, often produced on a large scale in plantations by fairly modern techniques. Most of this output is produced for the market and exported to DCs; these products are therefore often described as cash crops. Because of the export orientation of these products, they are considered in the next chapter on international trade. The present sub-section is mainly concerned with the peasant sector, and particularly with food.

Typically, food is lowest in the hierarchical pattern described in the last section. At the low levels of income of the bulk of the population of LDCs, the income elasticity of demand for food, although less than unity, is still high; the demand for food therefore increases rapidly as incomes rise. Further, the demand also increases rapidly due to the high rates of population growth. Therefore, at this stage, a rapid growth of food supply is necessary for rapid overall growth. At high levels of income, the income elasticity of demand for food falls, and the rate of population growth slackens. Then, overall growth becomes largely independent of the growth of food supply, as it is now in the DCs. The role of the agricultural sector in moving countries from one stage to the other may therefore be considered as the historical mission of this sector.

Table 10.1 shows the levels of agricultural productivity in terms of wheat equivalents (see Hayami and Ruttan, 1971, Appendix A for the method of calculation) and the rates at which some modern inputs are used.

Table 10.1 Agricultural productivity, 1978 (tons of wheat equivalent)

Countries	Output per hectare	Area per male worker	Output per male worker	Output per capita	Fertilizer use per ha[a]	Tractors per 1000 ha[b]
DCs	0.93	49.7	46.3	1.58	115	25.4
N. America and Oceania	0.62	358.1	220.2	2.39	86	19.5
Western Europe	2.81	13.7	38.6	1.28	218	70.9
Japan	8.57	1.6	13.6	0.41	450	212.6
Eastern Europe and USSR	0.93	34.7	32.3	1.67	106	12.9
LDCs	0.59	4.7	2.8	0.49	39	3.6
Africa & Middle East	0.19	12.4	2.3	0.38	17	3.3
Latin America	0.48	19.0	9.1	0.93	44	6.3
Far East	1.58	1.4	2.2	0.40	33	1.7
of which China	1.55	1.6	2.4	0.53	94	5.6
World	0.74	7.7	5.7	0.79	75	14.0

Source: Compiled from data of F.A.O. *Production Yearbook, 1979*, and F.A.O. *Fertilizer Yearbook, 1979*, according to their classification of countries. (a) kg per ha of arable land and permanent crops; (b) number of tractors per 1000 ha of arable land and permanent crops.

Per capita output in the LDCs is less than a third of that in the DCs. The low output is the main cause of the low level of nutrition in the LDCs, the principal component of their poverty. A much smaller proportion of the labour force is engaged in agriculture in the DCs; the output per male workers in the DCs is sixteen times as high as in the LDCs, the area per male worker being ten times as large and the output per hectare about 60 per cent higher. The gap in the productivity of labour is higher in agriculture than in other sectors, and given the large share of the labour force in agriculture in the LDCs, accounts for most of the income difference between the two groups of countries. A rapid increase of productivity in the agricultural sector is therefore needed for that sector to fulfil its historical mission.

As shown in the table, the main component of the difference in the output per worker between DCs as a whole and LDCs as a whole is the difference in the area per worker. Given the high productivity of labour, a smaller labour force is sufficient to meet the demand for food in the DCs and therefore each worker has more land to cultivate and hence raises his productivity further. However, there are important differences among the DCs themselves. At one extreme, the countries of North America and Oceania have low yields per hectare, comparable to the LDCs, but this is compensated by large areas per worker. At the other extreme, Japan has a small area per worker, comparable to the most populous LDCs, but compensated by some of the highest yields in the world. The countries of western Europe are in an intermediate position.

There are also large variations among the LDCs. In Latin America, yields are about average but the area per worker is large; hence the output per worker is also high. Although area per worker is also quite large in the LDCs of Africa and the Near East, yields are much lower. China and the other LDCs of the Far East have the highest yields among the LDCs, but this is not sufficient to compensate for the intense population pressure in these countries, as shown by the small area per worker; therefore the output per worker is very low.

The main factors involved in agricultural growth in the post-war period are described in Table 10.2.

Food output in the DCs has been growing considerably faster than population, mainly through increases in yields. The productivity of labour in agriculture is generally lower than in other sectors (see Cornwall, 1977, Table 4.1, p.51 for a comparison of average incomes); therefore, the labour force in agriculture has been declining in absolute numbers, so that output per worker has been increasing at an even higher rate than total output. But the movement out of agriculture is not fast enough to equalize incomes; therefore they are maintained by various protective devices. The growth of yields is due to a rapid growth in use of fertilizers and the growth in output per worker to a considerable growth in use of machinery.

In the LDCs, output has been growing at about the same rate as population, and marginally faster than in the DCs. In the first half of the period considered, there was some increase in area cultivated, but in the second half, the growth of output was mostly due to increase in yields. The labour force engaged in agriculture has also been increasing with population growth, but the rate has declined in the latter half of the period. There has been a rapid increase in the use of fertilizers and of tractors, but because of the low base

Table 10.2 Growth of agricultural productivity, 1955–78 (annual percentage growth rates)

	DCs		LDCs	
	1955–1965[a]	1961/5–1978	1955–1965[a]	1961/5–1978
Growth of food output	2.3	2.8	3.0	3.0
Growth of output per ha	1.3	2.8	2.0	2.7
Growth of male agricultural labour	−2.4	−3.0	2.8	0.8
Growth of output per male worker	4.8	6.0	0.1	2.2
Growth of fertilizer consumption	5.8	5.8	11.9	12.1
Growth of agricultural tractors	5.9	2.7	8.9	7.6

Source: (a) compiled from data of Hayami and Ruttan, 1971, Table A-5; (b) compiled from data of F.A.O., *Production Yearbooks*, 1975 and 1979, and F.A.O., *State of Food and Agriculture*, 1979, Tables 1.12 and 1.13.

from which it started, it has not been the main cause of the increase in yields or in the output per worker. The increase in yields in the latter half of the period described above has been mainly due to technological progress, especially the introduction of the new high-yielding varieties of seed which have spread rapidly in the Asian LDCs.

In order to achieve faster overall growth and to relieve mass poverty in the LDCs, a more rapid growth of food supply is essential. In the post-war period, many LDCs have tried to achieve this objective by importing food from the DCs, often financed by aid. This option may still be available in the future for countries with rapidly expanding export earnings, such as the oil-exporting countries and the newly industrializing countries, but not for other LDCs. Therefore, for most LDCs, there must be a rapid growth in domestic production of food.

In the early post-war period, it was still possible to increase output by bringing in new land in some countries, but most LDCs have reached the limit of the land that can be cultivated under the prevailing technology. Once all available land is cultivated, there is a competition for the use of land between food and other crops, especially cash crops for sale to higher income groups and the non-agricultural sectors in LDCs, and for export to DCs. In this competition, the stronger demand for the cash crops may limit the area available for producing food for the lower income groups. Given the scarcity of land, the expansion of food production depends on raising the yield of land, following for example the experience of Japan. This is mainly a question of investing more capital in agriculture of a land-saving type and of technological progress to increase the productivity of capital used in this way.

Over a long period of time, the LDCs have been coping with the effects of population growth by adopting more and more labour-intensive peasant techniques, i.e. techniques with a limited use of capital, especially by increasing the frequency of cultivation (see Boserup, 1965, for a detailed discussion). There are great variations in the application of labour to land among the LDCs, with the lowest rates for a crop such as rice occurring in some of the most densely populated countries, such as those of South Asia (Ishikawa, 1981, p.2); in these countries, the rate of labour absorption at present has not reached the level attained in Japan in the mid-nineteenth century. One important reason for these variations lies in institutional conditions. Thus, countries with a high inequality in the distribution of operational holdings tend to rely on hired labour to a greater extent; as hired labour is generally employed only up to the point where the marginal product equals the wage, this tends to reduce the rate of labour absorption. In contrast, countries with a more equal distribution of land rely on family labour to a greater extent, applying such labour intensively up to the point where its marginal product is near to zero. The low absorption of labour in agriculture in some countries is also due to a high degree of segmentation and inefficient working of the labour market. The use of more labour in agriculture, which could be achieved by overcoming these institutional obstacles, is desirable not only to increase output more rapidly but also to provide productive employment to the large numbers of underemployed workers in rural areas; it is only by getting such employment that workers can earn the incomes to purchase the increase in output which more extensive use of labour may bring about.

Attempts to increase output by applying more labour to a limited area of land, however, will lead to rapidly diminishing returns. Therefore, LDCs must also try to overcome the scarcity of land by applying more capital in agriculture, i.e. by substituting mechanized for peasant techniques (see Section 9.6) as the DCs have done. Capital in agriculture can substitute both for land and for labour. Countries with an abundance of land relative to labour have mainly used capital in a 'labouresque' form, while countries with an acute scarcity of land have mainly used 'landesque' forms of capital (see Sen, 1959). As the main problem in most LDCs is land scarcity, while they have abundant labour, they have to adopt techniques in which capital is land-saving and labour-using. The best example of such capital is the extensive use of fertilizers combined with irrigation (see Booth and Sundrum (1982) for a fuller discussion).

Major irrigation works are part of the infrastructural facilities normally provided by governments. They are particularly important under tropical conditions and especially for rice cultivation, which is the main cereal crop of many LDCs. Hence, irrigation works were established from very early times. They have become even more important with the evolution of the new seed varieties, whose main characteristic is that they respond to high doses of fertilizers in the presence of a large and controlled supply of water. In 1978, 18.3 per cent of the arable land and area under permanent crops in LDCs was irrigated, compared with 7.9 per cent in the DCs; the irrigated area in the LDCs has been expanding at 2.0 per cent per annum in the LDCs in the period from 1961/5 to 1978, compared with 2.2 per cent in the DCs (F.A.O. *Production Yearbook*, 1979). Food production in the LDCs can be expanded more rapidly by faster expansion of irrigation facilities, which would also permit the greater use of fertilizers.

The private sector of agriculture has also to invest more capital to provide minor irrigation, to improve land and use fertilizers and other modern inputs. The extent to which intermediate inputs are used in agriculture is indicated by the value added in the sector as a proportion of total output; from estimates made by Hayami and Ruttan (1971, Table A-5, p.320) for 1960, intermediate inputs accounted for only 3 per cent of output in LDCs compared with 33 per cent in the DCs. The main obstacle to the flow of more capital to the private sector of agriculture in the LDCs is the imperfection of the capital market; the investment needs of most farmers are only met by the unorganized money market at high rates of interest, much higher than the rates in the organized money market serving the rest of the economy. At the same time, some of the larger farmers get their capital from organized money markets on such preferential terms that they invest in labour-saving capital, such as tractors.

For any given supply of productive resources, the growth of agricultural output depends on technological progress. For a long period, agricultural technology in LDCs in the production of food for domestic consumption remained stagnant, dominated by customary and traditional practices handed down from parents to children. Since the mid-1960s, there has been great progress in evolving new high-yielding seed varieties, mainly through the concentrated efforts of scientists in international research centres. However, there have also been problems in making full use of these technical advances. One is that the international varieties are not uniformly suitable in all countries and in all regions within countries. Therefore, they have to be supplemented by further national research efforts in individual LDCs to adapt these varieties to local conditions. The LDCs have increased their research expenditures in the post-war period but they are still inadequate; research expenditures as a percentage of agricultural output increased from 0.42 in 1951 to 1.62 in 1974 in the LDCs, compared with a rise from 0.88 to 2.25 in the DCs in the same period (Boyce and Evenson, 1975).

Even when more productive techniques have been developed in research centres, there is the problem of getting these techniques adopted by the farmers. Invariably, there is a large gap between the yields achieved in research centres and those actually obtained under field conditions. Part of this may be due to the better quality of land and the greater skills of the staff of the research stations. A part of the difference has also been attributed to the fact that farmers are more concerned with the economically optimum use of resources subject to the input and output prices they face, while the research stations often aim to get the technically maximum yields. However, most of the difference is probably due to the unfamiliarity of farmers with the new techniques; they have therefore to be assisted with extension services to a greater extent than in the DCs. The LDCs have been expanding their extension services but they are still inadequate. The expenditure on these services as a percentage of agricultural output increased from 0.52 in 1959 to 1.14 in 1974 in the LDCs, compared with a rise from 0.42 to 0.55 in the DCs in the same period (see Boyce and Evenson, 1975). While further increases in such services are desirable, they cannot completely compensate for the low level of development in the LDCs, especially the low level of education, the inadequacy of infrastructure and the weakness of the economic institutions serving the farm population of these countries.

Relaxing the various supply constraints described above is, however, not sufficient to induce a sustained growth of output; it depends also on demand factors. Three sources of demand may be distinguished; the export demand for cash crops, the demand for food and raw materials of the non-agricultural sectors, and the demand for food within the agricultural sector itself. The first two categories of demand have generally been strong and growing steadily, because of the rapid growth of incomes in the DCs and in the non-agricultural sectors of LDCs; the growth of export demand, however, has been very unstable because of the fluctuations of economic activity in the DCs. The demand for food within the agricultural sector has generally been weak, because of the extensive underemployment and poverty in that sector.

Most of the discussion in the literature has been about the role of the agricultural sector in relation to the non-agricultural sector. The agricultural sector has been expected to supply the non-agricultural sectors with their food requirements, to provide savings and foreign exchange, and to serve as the market for their growing output (see e.g. Johnston and Mellor, 1961). In particular, there has been great concern over extracting a growing marketable surplus from the agricultural sector. In the historical period, because of the slow growth of the marketable surplus under ordinary market forces, special policies were followed to extract a larger volume of such surpluses, such as high land and capitation taxes on the agricultural sector. Further, most of the research effort was directed to raising the productivity of cash crops for export; as the result was only to depress their prices in international trade, these efforts were largely misdirected from the national point of view of the LDCs (see Section 11.3(b)).

Up to about the later 1960s, the growth of agricultural output, especially the marketable surplus available for the urban areas, was severely constrained by supply factors and was subject to violent fluctuations due to weather conditions. Therefore, the LDCs were forced to import food to meet their urban demand. But during the 1970s, the progress of the new agricultural technology relaxed some of the supply constraints in many Asian LDCs. LDC net food imports continued to increase but mostly to countries outside Asia, whose share of such net imports increased from 38 per cent in 1970 to 62 per cent in 1978; this was mainly due to the growth of incomes in Latin America and the oil-exporting countries of the Middle East.

Although Asian countries have been able to meet the food demand of their urban areas more fully in recent years, there has been less progress in meeting the requirements of the rural areas, where there is still much malnutrition. Given the extremely high expenditure elasticities of demand for basic foodstuffs on the part of the rural poor, (see e.g. Mellor, 1978, Table 3 for some Indian estimates and Alderman and Timmer, 1980, Table 2 for Indonesian data) it seems plausible to argue that widespread malnutrition is primarily due to lack of purchasing power, and this lack of purchasing power is in turn due to the failure to find productive employment on a year-round basis. It is this lack of effective demand that Sen (1977) in his analysis of famines, has called a failure of exchange 'entitlements'. An increase in food production will thus not automatically increase demand, unless it is accompanied by increases in incomes for those with the greatest unsatisfied demand for food. This has been illustrated in recent years in the case of India, where increases in output due to the new agricultural technology have led to reduction of imports and the accumulation of stocks rather than to increases in consumption. What is needed therefore would seem to be further relaxation of the supply constraints on agricultural production through increased provision of irrigation, fertilizers, etc., on the one hand, and measures to increase the incomes of the poor such as promotion of employment in the agricultural and non-agricultural sectors on the other.

Those economists who have argued that it is 'distorted' domestic price incentives which are principally to blame for agricultural stagnation in LDCs say that increases in the prices of agricultural commodities (relative both to input prices such as fertilizers, and to non-agricultural prices generally) would increase output by making the utilization of such inputs more profitable (Schultz, 1978). But there is little evidence that aggregate agricultural output is very elastic with respect to price changes alone; it depends much more on the removal of the bio-physical constraints on production, as indeed Schultz and his colleagues also acknowledge. With output constrained by these factors, the role of price becomes primarily one of allocating a limited supply to different groups of consumers. With a very unequal distribution of urban incomes, the price of food will be pushed higher as upper income groups compete for a greater share of the supply, thereby reducing the consumption of the lower income groups. On the other hand, as far as rural income distribution is concerned, high food prices will mainly benefit the larger farmers who have the largest surpluses for sale to the market.

Because of these considerations, many LDCs have intervened to keep food prices low throughout the 1950s and 1960s, often relying on food imports obtained on concessional terms to reduce prices in times of domestic production downturns. These policies created the 'distortions' to which Schultz and his associates object. But in spite of the alleged price disincentives, cereal output increased in the latter part of the 1960s in many parts of Asia when the new seed-fertilizer technology was introduced. The growth rates were particularly impressive in those areas such as the Indian Punjab where the 'enabling' factors, particularly irrigation, were already in place. More recently, however, government food procurement prices have been allowed to rise; it has been argued in the Indian context that this increase has been largely because of the increased political strength of the large farmer lobbies (Mitra,

1977). This in turn has been a contributory factor to the slow growth of demand and the accumulation of stocks.

LDCs have thus been confronted with a dilemma in their food price policies. Should they keep prices high to induce output expansion or keep them low to help poor consumers? We have argued that higher prices alone are unlikely to be very effective in inducing growth of production, and lower prices will not encourage greater consumption if the poor still lack the means to buy food. Furthermore, increases in food prices are likely to lead to strong inflationary pressures in a situation where government cannot control the money supply. Therefore, LDCs should first aim to maintain stable food prices, supported by buffer stocks. At what level should the price be set? A possible guideline is as follows. The price of food should be set so that, when the prevailing wage rate is deflated by this price, a *fully employed* worker would be able to sustain his household at some stipulated 'minimum standard of consumption', including adequate nutrition, which may be taken as the poverty line.

Such a price policy would need to be combined with two further policies—one designed to bring about rapid growth of food production and the other designed to guarantee full employment to all workers at the prevailing wage. Policies to increase production relate to relaxation of the biophysical constraints on production, the expansion of research and extension services, and the implementation of needed institutional reforms. This has been achieved to some extent already, although the spreading of the new seed-fertilizer technology has been impeded by the failure of many governments to mobilize the resources needed to provide the enabling infrastructure, especially irrigation. To the extent that producers require a more favourable output-input price ratio in order to make investment in inputs such as fertilizers profitable, this should be achieved by subsidizing input prices.

However, much less has been done in any LDC as yet to achieve the other policy objective—the provision of full employment to all wishing to work at the prevailing wage. Some policy initiatives have been taken, such as the Employment Guarantee Schemes implemented in some parts of India, but generally speaking such programmes are small-scale and inadequately funded. Government employment creation schemes are not necessarily the only solution to the problem of providing jobs to an inadequately utilized labour force. In fact in many countries, both the objective of expanding agricultural output and the objective of expanding employment could be achieved simultaneously by increasing the use of labour in agriculture. In countries where the use of labour is below the level needed to achieve the maximum yield, a more intensive use of labour may be brought about by land reform measures to make operational holdings more equal. A movement towards greater labour intensity may also be triggered off by a short period of subsidizing the wage cost of hired labour to private employers.

(b) The Industrial Sector

Corresponding to the agricultural sector's large share of GDP and of the labour force in LDCs, the industrial sector of LDCs is very small. Table 10.3 shows some aspects of industry in LDCs in comparison with DMEs.

Table 10.3 Comparison of the industrial sector in LDCs and DCs, 1977 (LDC averages as percentage of DC averages)

Variable	Industry	Manu-facturing
Per capita industrial output	9.3	5.7
Percentage of labour force in industry	41.0	40.3
Productivity per worker	22.6	14.2

Source: United Nations, *Yearbook of National Accounts Statistics, 1979*; I.L.O., *Yearbook of Labour Statistics, 1978*

The productivity per worker in this sector of LDCs is very low compared with the DMEs, but the gap in productivity is smaller than in the agricultural sector. In Table 10.3, output and productivity are compared at the official exchange rate, which underestimates the purchasing power of LDC currencies. When an allowance is made for the exchange rate deviation, the gap in productivity becomes smaller. As a result of the low productivity and the low proportion of the labour force in industry, the LDCs with more than 70 per cent of the world's population produce only about 10 per cent of the value added in manufacturing.

The growth of the manufacturing sector in the post-war period is summarized in Table 10.4.

The output of the manufacturing sector in LDCs has expanded faster than in the DMEs, but the difference is only slightly greater than the difference in population growth rates. Most of the output expansion has been due to growth of employment, but with the labour force growing at nearly 3 per cent per annum, there has been little growth of the percentage of the labour force engaged in manufacturing. The growth of productivity per worker has been small and declining.

Apart from the small size of the manufacturing sector in LDCs, there is also a big difference between DCs and LDCs in the structure of the industrial sector and the composition of output, as shown in Table 10.5.

A large part of manufacturing value added in LDCs consists of the processing of food and agricultural products and of textile manufactures, while a large part in the DMEs consists of machinery and transport equipment. In the DCs, industrial production is mostly carried on in large factories using modern techniques, but in the LDCs, a considerable part of industrial activity is carried on in household and other small enterprises. In many LDCs,

Table 10.4 Growth of the manufacturing sector (annual percentage rates)

Growth rate of:		DMEs	LDCs	CPCs
Output	1955–66	5.3	7.3	9.4
	1966–78	3.7	6.6	8.4
Employment:	1955–66	1.9	4.4	3.8
	1966–78	0.3	4.7	2.2
Productivity:	1955–66	3.3	2.8	5.4
	1966–78	3.4	1.8	6.1

Source: 1955–66 United Nations, *Growth of World Industry, 1973;* 1966–78 United Nations, *Yearbook of Industrial Statistics, 1980*

Table 10.5 Structure of manufacturing sector, 1978

Percentage of value added in:	LDCs	DMEs
Food and agriculture	20.1	11.3
Textiles and clothing	13.0	7.4
Machinery and transport equipment	16.9	31.3
Chemicals	9.9	10.7
Other manufactures	40.1	39.3

Source: World Bank, *World Development Report*, 1981

the growth of large-scale production has been at the expense of small-scale production.

A significant aspect of the industrial performance of LDCs is the great diversity among countries, as shown in Table 10.6.

LDCs with one-fifth of the population account for two-thirds of the value added in manufacturing. Also countries with a larger share tend to have faster rates of expansion. Table 10.6 also shows the proportion of industrial output which was exported (the estimates are based on the countries for which data were available). On the average, LDCs exported 9.5 per cent of their industrial output, compared with 16.3 per cent in the DMEs; this proportion also tends to be higher for LDCs with a large share of value added.

The causes of the small size and the slow growth of the industrial sector in most LDCs can be divided into demand and supply factors. We consider first the demand factors. One reason why the demand for manufactures in LDCs has been small is simply that per capita income is low. At this low level of income, people spend most of their income on foods and little on other goods and services, and a large proportion of the labour force is engaged in agriculture. The demand for manufactures from the industrial sector itself is weak because the sector is small, while the demand from the agricultural sector is weak because most incomes are small due to the low productivity of labour in that sector. This is one of the reasons why the growth of the industrial sector depends on the prior development of the agricultural sector. Under the

Table 10.6 Distribution of LDCs according to industrial activity (in deciles of population arranged by per capita value-added)

Decile	Percentage of value added 1978	Annual growth rate of value added 1970–78 (%)	Exports as percentage of manufacturing output, 1978
1st and 2nd	3.35	2.94	5.6
3rd and 4th	5.21	4.75	7.6
5th and 6th	5.78	7.27	3.3
7th and 8th	18.51	7.72	3.8
9th	25.61	10.59	11.0
Top	41.54	6.08	21.2

Source: Calculated from data of World Bank, *World Development Report*, 1981

prevailing technology in LDCs, agricultural output and incomes are greatly affected by weather conditions. The extent to which industrial activity depends on the demand from the agricultural sector is then reflected by corresponding fluctuations in industrial production; this effect has been most intensively studied in India (see, e.g., Chitre, 1981).

Even when the average level of income is low, there is a small section with a high income who spend a higher proportion of that income on manufactures. Hence, the main source of domestic demand for manufactures comes from the upper income groups, especially in urban areas. But under the trade regime to which most LDCs were subject during the colonial era, this demand was mostly met by imports from the metropolitan countries which were industrially more advanced. Such industry as the LDCs had established previously, mostly in the small-scale handicraft sector, was destroyed by import competition in a process that has been described as 'de-industrialization' (for the Indian experience, see, e.g., Gadgil, 1948). The inter-war period was one of great disruption of world trade, as the DMEs went into a prolonged period of severe depression. For the LDCs, the consequence was a loss of export markets for many of their products and a sharp deterioration of their terms of trade; they could not therefore continue to import manufactures on the same scale as before. One result was that, of necessity, the beginnings of industrialization were established in LDCs in varying degrees. (For the Burmese experience see Spate, 1941.) In the post-war period, industrial growth was greatly influenced by the international trade policies of the LDCs; they are discussed in Section 12.2.

Turning now to some factors on the supply side, the LDCs have the advantage of abundant labour but have not been able to employ much of this labour in the industrial sector. One reason is the working of the labour market. Because of the segmentation between the urban and the rural sections of the labour market, the surplus labour of the agricultural sector has not been absorbed in the industrial sector. This is reflected in the wage level of the modern industrial sector being distinctly above the wage level in the rest of the economy even after allowing for the costs of transport, the higher cost of living in urban areas, and the difference in the quality of labour. Another reason is that increase in industrial employment requires an increase in the supply of basic goods especially food, and this is limited by the low productivity of the agricultural sector. As Lewis (1954, p.433) has explained:

> expansion (of the industrial sector) increases the demand for food in terms of capitalist products and so reduces profits. This is one of the senses in which industrialisation is dependent upon agricultural development; it is not profitable to produce a growing volume of manufactures unless agricultural production is growing simultaneously. This is also why industrial and agrarian revolutions always go together, and why economies in which agriculture is stagnant do not show industrial development.

The supply constraint which is most emphasized in the literature is that of capital. In fact, because of the rigid factor proportions of the prevailing technology, the shortage of capital is considered an important reason why industrial employment itself has been so small and growing so slowly. But, as argued above (see Section 10.2), the low level of investment is not primarily due to a supply constraint. Some countries have had high rates of savings without rapid industrial growth. The best example is the case of India in the 1970s; towards the end of this decade, the savings rate increased to over 20 per cent while there was only a low rate of industrial growth. Further, the LDCs have considerable access to foreign capital. In the pre-war period, foreign capital was concentrated in the extractive sectors. But in the post-war period, it has flowed in greater amounts to the industrial sector attracted by high profits due to the low wages in LDCs compared with the DCs. Data on a comprehensive basis are not available to compare wages in DCs and LDCs directly, but some indirect evidence is available from the data on the share of wages and salaries in value-added in manufacturing enterprises. According to the 1978 edition of the *Yearbook of Industrial Statistics* (United Nations, 1980), the weighted average of this share was only 29 per cent in LDCs compared with 48 per cent in the DMEs. This difference has been explained by Lewis (1969, p.32) as follows:

> Part of the reason why the share of capital is higher in low-wage than in high-wage countries is that machines cost more in the low-wage countries; they have to be imported from high-wage countries; are not so well maintained and have shorter lives. But judging by the willingness of private foreign capital to build factories in these countries we may also deduce that profits are higher in the low-wage than in the high-wage countries, over a fairly wide range of industries.

Shortage of capital cannot therefore be considered a serious constraint on industrial growth in countries which are willing to allow foreign captal into their industrial sectors. Some countries have restricted the flow of such capital, partly because they consider the costs to be too high and partly because of a wish to be more self-reliant.

Apart from the availability of foreign capital, most LDCs have channelled more domestic capital to the industrial sector in the post-war period. New financial institutions were set up to supply credit to industry on concessional terms. Foreign exchange was allocated to the industrial sector to import capital goods and intermediate products at a favourable exchange rate. In addition, most of the infrastructural expansion was biassed in favour of industry.

Neither labour nor capital has been a serious constraint on the growth of the industrial sector. We therefore consider how far the efficiency of these resources has been a constraint on industrial growth. Here we find a sharp contrast between two parts of the industrial sector of LDCs. One is the modern sector of large-scale production using modern capital-intensive techniques of production to produce goods, mostly consumed by the upper income groups. The other is a traditional sector of small-scale production, largely in cottage industries and household enterprises, using labour-intensive techniques to produce goods mostly consumed at lower levels of income. In comparison with the modern sector, the traditional sector is technically much less efficient. The traditional sector is able to co-exist with the modern sector because it uses more labour but employs it at low wages, and uses much less capital, often provided out of own savings. The modern sector uses much more efficient techniques, mostly embodied in equipment imported from the DCs; therefore in the case of goods produced in both sectors, the modern sector is steadily displacing the traditional sector, especially as it usually has more access to cheap credit. But the labour and management skills in the modern sector of LDCs is not as efficient as in the DCs. Therefore, LDCs are at a disadvantage in competing with the DCs, though the gap in productivity of labour in this sector is less than in other sectors.

Therefore, on the supply side, the main problem of the industrial sector is the level of efficiency. Industrial efficiency depends on many factors, especially those connected with the level of development, and the working of factor markets. The growth of efficiency is often considered to be a matter of time. In fact, however, it is more importantly a function of the size and growth of the sector itself. One way in which the size of the industrial sector affects its efficiency is through the competition of producers. This is the main contribution of the 'creative' function of markets. The growth of productivity achieved in this way has been described by Leibenstein (1966) as 'X-efficiency'. To achieve such efficiency, however, the competition must be neither too severe nor too weak. On the one hand, the competition of imports from the industrially advanced countries may be too severe to allow any industries to be established at all in the LDCs. On the other hand, if an industry is protected from import competition and consists only of a few domestic firms, these firms may enjoy such monopolistic or oligopolistic power that the competition among them is too weak to improve efficiency over time. Hence, in the early stages of industrialization, an LDC should promote only those industries in which the number of domestic firms is large enough for the competition among them to raise efficiency. Large countries are likely to have more such industries than small ones.

The other way in which the size and growth of the industrial sector affects its efficiency is through the dynamic internal and external economies of scale (see Section 9.8). These economies arise, not simply by the passage of time, but by the growth of output over time.

The fact that the efficiency of the industrial sector depends so heavily on its size means that there is a close interaction between the supply and demand constraints on industrial growth in the LDCs. Their essentially dynamic aspect poses a serious vicious cycle problem for the LDCs. When the industrial sector is small, it is relatively inefficient; for example, it cannot withstand import competition. When the efficiency is low, it cannot expand rapidly. Industrial growth depends on relaxing both supply and demand constraints together.

The process by which this was achieved in the DCs can be divided into two stages. In the first stage, there was a steady increase of industrial efficiency mainly through technological progress. At the same time, there was also rapid development of the agricultural sector. The growth of the agricultural sector was important in two ways. On the one hand, it supplied labour and food in increasing quantities to the industrial sector. On the other hand, it provided a market for the expanding output of the industrial sector. Therefore, as Habakkuk (1965, p.123) points out,

> All the successful nineteenth century industrialisations were accompanied in their early stages by an increase in agricultural output.

This process goes on until the agricultural sector has fulfilled its historical mission and is no longer a constraint on the rest of the economy.

The second stage is one in which the demand for manufactures comes from the industrial sector itself. Then, countries enter into a process of cumulative circular causation by an interaction between demand and supply factors. On the demand side, the process is propelled by an income elasticity greater than one. On the supply side, the main force is increasing returns to scale. The interaction between these two forces becomes the source of the self-sustaining growth of the DCs. An important feature of this stage is that the growth of productivity in the industrial sector spills over to other sectors; thus, the manufacturing sector becomes the 'engine of growth' (see Cornwall, 1977, chapters 6 and 7 for a fuller analysis).

In order to achieve self-sustaining growth at a high rate, the LDCs must eventually reach this second stage. Most of them are at present only in the first stage, and appear to be stuck there. We therefore consider the policies they have to follow at this stage. The most important is to give special attention to the interaction between the agricultural and the industrial sectors; this means giving high priority to the agricultural sector not only for its own sake but also for its effects on industrial growth. Then for any given rate of agricultural growth, they must seek to attain the maximum rate of industrial expansion consistent with it; attempts to force the pace of industrial growth beyond this will be futile.

When the overall rate of industrial growth is determined in this way, the LDCs have to consider the structure of the sector. At their present level of development, they cannot efficiently expand the industrial sector on all fronts. At this stage of industrialization, the balanced growth doctrine is most relevant in determining the balance between the agricultural and industrial sectors, as the demand for manufactures depends primarily on the agricultural sector. It is only in the second stage when the demand for manufactures comes mostly from the industrial sector itself, that this doctrine plays a greater role in determining the balance between different industries within the industrial sector.

At the first stage of industrialization, the LDCs have to concentrate on particular industries. One industry which deserves high priority is that which produces inputs for agriculture; examples are fertilizers, pesticides, materials for the expansion of irrigation, and some forms of agricultural machinery. Another type of industry deserving of high priority is the capital goods industry; the expansion of this industry will make the LDCs less technologically dependent on DCs and provide them with a wider range of techniques more suitable to their situation. In the case of consumer goods, they must give the highest priority to those for which the demand is large and likely to expand rapidly; these are the industries producing articles of mass consumption.

In pursuing these objectives, the most important instrument of policy that the LDCs can deploy is the allocation of development measures to the appropriate parts of the industrial sector. These are the special responsibility of governments. Some of the industries mentioned above are so strategic for growth, or are for other reasons unsuited to private sector investment, that they may have to be set up in the public sector as State enterprises. Apart from this, industrial policy has to be designed to make the fullest use of the creative functions of markets. One important method is that of indicative planning, i.e. providing information to prospective entrepreneurs about the most profitable lines of investment in the light of government's industrial strategy. In the past, however, LDCs have tended to regulate industrial expansion by a complex system of licensing and administrative controls. (For details, see Little, Scitovsky and Scott, 1970.) These controls were motivated by a number of considerations, such as a more equitable distribution of income, wider dispersion of ownership, greater regional balance, and self-sufficiency in strategic products. In the event, owing to the weakness of the administrative and political machinery, this approach failed to achieve even these objectives.

Finally, LDCs nowadays have to take account of the presence of many more industrially advanced countries than the DCs did in the early stages of their industrialization. Therefore, LDCs have also to use trade policies as an instrument of their industrialization; these are discussed in Section 12.2 below.

(c) The Services Sector

According to censuses and other surveys for the period around 1970, about 21 per cent of the labour force in LDCs was engaged in the services sector compared with about 51 per cent in the DCs (see Table 2.8 above). The fraction of the labour force in the services sector in LDCs is so low because such a high proportion is engaged in the agricultural sector. If we consider only the labour engaged in the non-agricultural sectors, we find that the proportions engaged in industry and in services were about the same in DCs and in LDCs. In contrast with the service sector's low share in the labour force, it has a rather large share in the GDP; around 1976, the proportion of GDP originating in this sector was about 41 per cent in LDCs compared with around 55 per cent in the DMEs (see Table 2.13 above). It therefore appears that the productivity of labour in the services sector as a ratio of that in DCs was about the same as in the industrial sector, and about double that in the agricultural sector (see Table 2.15).

These comparisons, however, are rather misleading. One reason is that labour in LDCs is not so highly specialized into the various sectors into which it is usually classified in labour force surveys mainly designed for the DCs. Another reason is that the services sector of LDCs shows a more marked dualism than other sectors. One, relatively small, part of this sector consists of highly educated persons working in public administration, in the financial and managerial sections of the modern sectors of industry and commerce, and in the professions such as medicine, law and engineering. The larger part of the sector consists of persons who are less educated and have low productivity; a considerable part of the sector consists of petty trading. Another considerable part of the sector consists of persons who perform service activities to earn a living for want of more productive employment; these service activities are therefore a form of 'disguised unemployment'.

A more puzzling feature is the service sector's high share in the GDP, considering the low average level of per capita income. The general pattern is for the output share of the sector to increase with per capita income. This is not primarily due to a quantitative increase in the demand for services as incomes increase, but rather due to a systematic change in relative prices. As Kravis *et al.* (1978, p.127) say:

> The positive association between the share of services in expenditure and per capita income that has been so widely commented upon reflects, if this cross-section sample of sixteen countries is typical, mainly a tendency for services to become more expensive as income rises rather than a tendency toward the consumption of relatively greater quantities of service. Services do increase with rising income but, if their prices did not rise, the service share would remain constant or even diminish. The sharp rise in service prices inhibits the increase in their consumption but not so much that their share of expenditure does not rise.

Such a price effect leads to a particularly strong tendency for the output share of the service sector to be highly correlated with per capita income. It is therefore all the more surprising that LDCs on the average have such a large share of GDP originating in the service sector. One reason is that the upper echelon of workers in the service sector of LDCs earn incomes very much higher than others. As Lewis (1976, p.32) says,

Modernisation depends on the creation of this modernising elite. Unfortunately this is an expensive group; relatively more expensive in the LDCs of this century than in the LDCs of the nineteenth century. There are two reasons for this. First, ever since the sixteenth century Western Europe has concentrated on producing university and secondary graduates in such numbers that 'clerks' have always been cheap; universal primary education was their lowest priority. Today's LDCs, however, with the exception of India, Egypt, and two or three others, neglected higher education until recently. They therefore had to import such people from abroad, and established traditional pay and status for these jobs far out of line with average incomes per head. The second reason is that this group is very highly mobile internationally. Racial and national prejudices have diminished, LDC nationals with high qualifications can find jobs almost anywhere. This limits the ability of their native countries to hold their salaries down to levels comparable with those of other groups who cannot enter a brisk international market.

There is also great diversity among LDCs. The output share of the service sector is quite low for many countries, especially the larger ones (see Chenery and Syrquin, 1975, p.176). The high average figure is due to a group of countries with relatively small populations and higher than average per capita incomes. Some of them, such as Hong Kong, Singapore and Lebanon, are highly specialized in service exports. Others are generally countries with a high inequality of income distribution; in these countries, the movement of labour out of agriculture in the post-war period has been absorbed in the service sector to a greater extent than in the industrial sector (see Booth and Sundrum, 1982).

As countries reach high levels of income and productivity in the commodity-producing sectors, the demand for food and even manufactures will decline. This process has been described as the 'de-industrialization' of the DMEs (see Cornwall, 1977, Chapter 9). Then the service sector has to play a greater role in absorbing labour and providing employment. The service sector is well suited to play this role because it is so labour-intensive, but workers in the service sector need more human capital than in other sectors. One of the problems of the service sector facing the DMEs is that many services have to be provided by the public sector. This raises complex questions of fiscal policy about the extent to which services should be subsidized out of general tax revenues. At the low levels of income in the early stages of growth in LDCs, the demand for services is likely to be low, unless the distribution of income is very unequal. Even then, the wages of most service workers are likely to be low. The productivity and wages of service workers can be increased faster by educational expansion. At the low level of education of LDCs, the limited supply of the more educated workers earn a disproportionately high income in some privileged employments, especially in the public sector and the modern sector. Such high incomes then inhibit the expansion of employment in other sectors. In order that the service sector can play a greater role in absorbing labour, a reform of the salary structure is more urgently needed here than in other sectors.

CHAPTER 11

International Trade: Analysis

11.1 Patterns of International Trade

The volume of international trade of most countries is much less than that of their internal trade but a large part of the development literature has been devoted to the international trade problems and policies of LDCs. This concern with international trade has been due to two main causes. Firstly, international trade has been the subject of very active policy on the part of LDC governments and also of much of the international debate between DCs and LDCs. Secondly, in the theoretical literature, the subject has been the main locus of the controversy over the merits of the free market system. These issues are discussed in this and the following chapter. In the present chapter, we begin with a survey of statistical data about the patterns of trade of DCs and LDCs, followed by a discussion of the causes and consequences of trade in the two following sections. Some information about the historical experience of international trade was given in Section 4.5; the present section gives more detail for the post-war period. Except where indicated otherwise, the statistical tables have been compiled from the data given in the *1979 Yearbook of International Trade Statistics* (U.N., 1980).

(a) Volume of Trade

In 1979, out of a world total of US$ 1627 billions of exports, 66 per cent originated in the DMEs, 25 per cent in the LDCs and 9 per cent in the CPCs. The DMEs thus accounted for the bulk of world trade. In fact, in 1970, their share of exports was even higher at 72 per cent; since then, their share declined and that of LDCs increased, mainly because of the rise in the price of the fuel exports of LDCs. Although the volume of exports of LDCs was much smaller than that of the DCs, it was a higher proportion of GDP; in 1977, exports as a proportion of GDP was over 20 per cent in LDCs, excluding the oil exporters, compared with 18 per cent in the industrialized countries (World Bank, *World Tables*, 1980, p.385).

(b) Direction of Trade

The direction of trade as between the three major groups of countries—DMEs, LDCs and CPCs—is summarized in Table 11.1. The bulk of world trade was among the DMEs. Similarly, the CPCs conducted most of their

Table 11.1 Direction of world trade, 1979 (percentages of world exports)

Exports: To	DMEs	LDCs	CPCs	World
From				
DMEs	48.4	14.5	3.3	66.2
LDCs	17.7	6.1	0.9	24.7
CPCs	2.7	1.7	4.7	9.1
World	68.8	22.3	8.9	100.0

trade among themselves. In contrast, the bulk of the exports of LDCs went to the DMEs and the bulk of their imports came from the DMEs. Further, there was a high degree of geographic concentration of the exports of LDCs (see e.g. Michaely, 1962, p.19); a high proportion of the trade of ex-colonial LDCs was with the former metropolitan country, with which they had built up strong trade relationships in the colonial era.

(c) Composition of Trade

The composition of exports of various groups of countries is summarized in Table 11.2. The typical pattern is that most of the exports of DMEs and CPCs

Table 11.2 Composition of exports, 1978 (percentage distribution of export values)

Commodity Groups	DMEs	OPEC	Other LDCs	CPCs	Total
Foodstuffs	10	2	26	9	11
Crude materials	7	2	15	8	7
Fuels	5	94	15	19	17
Primary products	22	98	57	36	36
Chemicals	10	—	3	5	7
Machinery etc.	37	—	10	30	29
Other manufactures	30	1	30	22	26
Others	2	1	—	8	2
Industrial products	78	2	43	64	64
Total	100	100	100	100	100

consist of industrial products, mostly machinery and manufactures, while the bulk of the exports of LDCs consists of primary products. Because of the major share of DCs in world exports, industrial products constitute the bulk of world trade. For the same reason, although primary products are a small proportion of DC exports, the volume of primary product exports of DMEs is greater than that of LDCs (excluding the OPEC), i.e. although the major exports of LDCs are primary products, the LDCs are not the major exporters of these products. LDCs (other than OPEC) export a considerable amount of industrial products; most of these exports, however, come from a small group of LDCs, as pointed out later, and consist mostly of light manufactures.

The share of primary products varies greatly in the trade between different groups of countries (Table 11.3). OPEC exports to other countries consist almost entirely of primary products, i.e. fuels. But even for other LDCs, most of their exports to DCs consist of primary products, while the share of industrial products is greater in the trade among themselves. Only about a fifth of DME exports were primary products. It is noteworthy that a considerable part of the exports of DCs to LDCs are primary products, mostly foodstuff exported to food-deficit LDCs.

Table 11.3 Share of primary products according to direction of trade, 1979 (percentage of exports)

Exports: To	DMEs	OPEC	Other LDCs	CPCs	World
From					
DMEs	23	11	17	20	21
OPEC	99	42	99	97	98
Other LDCs	57	47	47	86	57
CPCs	59	17	29	27	36
World	38	15	35	31	36

The foreign trade of countries can be classified into a useful set of categories proposed by Hirschman (1945). Writing X for exports and M for imports, with suffix p for primary products and m for industrial products, four categories may be distinguished as follows:

(A) Exchange of primary products for primary products, taken as twice X_p or M_p, whichever is smaller;
(B) Exchange of manufactures for manufactures, taken as twice X_m or M_m, whichever is smaller;
(C) Exchange of primary products and manufactures, taken as twice balance of trade in primary products or in manufactures, whichever is positive; and
(D) Exchange of commodities for invisibles, taken as the balance of commodity trade.

The shares of these categories in the trade of DCs and LDCs are shown in Table 11.4.

Table 11.4 Categories of trade of DCs and LDCs 1978 (percentages of total value of exports and imports)

Category	DCs	LDCs
A	27	29
B	62	23
C	10	47
D	1	1
Total	100	100

Most of the trade of DCs consists of category B, the exchange of manufactures for manufactures, while most of the trade of LDCs consists of category C, the exchange of primary products for manufactures, known as the 'traditional form of exchange'. This form of trade is even more dominant in the trade between DCs and LDCs, as shown in Table 11.5.

Table 11.5 Categories in the trade between DCs and LDCs (percentages of total value of exports and imports)

Category	1953	1960	1967	1970	1978
A	22	21	20	18	16
B	10	14	18	23	21
C	67	60	60	55	62
D	1	5	2	4	1
Total	100	100	100	100	100

The traditional form of exchange in this trade has been declining but very slowly. It may be noted that category A, the exchange of primary products for primary products in this trade, is quite considerable and has remained fairly constant; it consists mainly of the export of cash crops and mineral products by LDCs in exchange for foodgrains exported by DCs. The share of category B has doubled, but as mentioned earlier, this is due to the rapid growth of manufactured exports from a limited group of LDCs.

Another aspect of the composition of the trade of LDCs is the high degree of commodity concentration; for example, the top three commodities accounted for 59 per cent of total export earnings of LDCs in 1977, and was still 56 per cent when the oil countries were excluded (World Bank, *World Tables*, 1980, pp.414–19).

(d) Growth of Trade

The post-war period was one of a great expansion of world trade, faster even than the growth in the late nineteenth and early twentieth centuries, often considered the golden age of international trade. Between 1948 and 1979, world exports in real terms increased at 6.8 per cent per annum (7.6 per cent in DMEs and 5.2 per cent in LDCs). The rates of growth were quite uniformly high until the early 1970s, when they slackened, especially after 1973, because of the breakdown of the international monetary system and industrial recessions in many DMEs, following the rise in fuel imports. For a more detailed study, it is therefore useful to consider the 1960s and the 1970s separately.

The main features of trade in the 1960s were the following: (i) world exports increased at the phenomenal rate of over 8 per cent per annum in real terms; (ii) world exports of manufactures increased twice as fast as those of primary products; (iii) the exports of DMEs increased much faster than those of LDCs, thus further increasing their share of world trade; (iv) DME exports of primary products increased faster than those of LDCs, so that LDC share of these exports declined; (v) LDCs were able to increase their share of manufactured exports as their exports, starting from a low base, grew faster than those of DMEs; (vi) the exports of DMEs to other DMEs grew faster than their exports to LDCs, and this was true both in primary products and in manufactures; and (vii) the exports of LDCs to DMEs also grew faster than their exports to other LDCs; this was particularly so in primary products. The quantitative magnitudes are given in Table 11.6.

There were a number of significant changes in the 1970s. The rate of growth of world exports fell sharply but the exports of manufactures still grew nearly twice as fast as those of primary products. The exports of DMEs still grew faster than those of LDCs but the difference in growth rates declined slightly; the difference, however, widened in the case of primary products. LDCs continued their rapid expansion of manufactures exports, while the rates of growth in such exports fell, except to the LDCs. Exports to LDCs grew faster

Table 11.6 Growth of world exports (annual percentage growth rates in real terms)

Exports: To		DMEs	LDCs	Market Economies
From		(a) *1960–70*		
DMEs	T	9.3	6.0	8.6
	P	5.1	4.9	5.7
	M	11.3	5.9	8.2
LDCs	T	6.6	5.8	6.6
	P	4.7	3.1	4.5
	M	10.5	11.1	10.5
Market Economies	T	8.8	5.8	8.1
	P	5.7	4.7	5.5
	M	11.2	6.4	10.0
		(b) *1970–78*		
DMEs	T	5.4	8.6	6.1
	P	4.0	7.4	4.5
	M	5.9	8.7	6.5
LDCs	T	4.2	7.8	5.1
	P	1.4	4.8	1.9
	M	10.7	13.5	11.5
Market Economies	T	5.2	8.4	5.9
	P	3.2	6.3	3.7
	M	6.2	9.2	6.9

Note: T = total exports; P = primary products; M = industrial products

than to the DMEs. While the slackening in the growth rate of exports affected most DMEs, the two other major developments affected only a small group of LDCs, namely the growth of manufactured exports by the newly industrializing countries (NICs) and the growth of all kinds of imports by the OPEC countries.

(e) Terms of Trade

Table 11.7 summarizes the change in export price indices in the post-war period.

The main price trends of the 1960s may be summarized as follows: (i) This was a period of remarkable price stability in world trade; (ii) the price of DME exports increased faster than those of LDC exports; (iii) the terms of trade moved in favour of the DMEs and against the LDCs; (iv) the prices of primary product exports increased only at half the rate of those of manufactured exports; this was true of the trade in all directions and is the main explanation of the movement of the terms of trade against LDCs and in favour of DMEs; (v) the prices of primary products exports from DMEs to all destinations increased faster than those from LDCs to these destinations but the prices of manufactured imports of LDCs increased more slowly than those

Table 11.7 Annual percentage rates of change in export price indices of market economies

Exports: To		DMEs	LDCs	Market economies
From		(a) *1960–70*		
DMEs	T	1.5	0.9	1.4
	P	1.1	0.3	1.2
	M	1.4	1.1	1.3
LDCs	T	0.6	0.2	0.5
	P	0.1	0.1	0.1
	M	3.5	0.5	2.5
Market economies	T	1.3	0.8	1.2
	P	0.8	0.1	0.7
	M	1.5	1.1	1.4
		(b) *1970–78*		
DMEs	T	11.3	12.6	11.6
	P	13.7	13.1	13.6
	F	19.8	18.1	19.6
	NF	10.4	10.5	10.4
	M	11.0	12.5	11.4
LDCs	T	18.2	17.1	17.9
	P	18.4	18.5	18.4
	F	27.5	27.6	27.6
	NF	12.5	12.6	12.6
	M	10.5	11.0	10.7
Market economies	T	12.7	13.6	12.9
	P	16.6	17.2	16.7
	F	25.4	26.5	25.6
	NF	11.0	12.4	11.0
	M	11.0	12.4	11.4

Note: T = total exports; P = primary products; F = fuels; NF = non-fuel primary products; M = manufactures

of the DMEs. These results are based on indices of unit values calculated by the United Nations Statistical Office from trade data. Some other results have been provided by the World Bank and UNCTAD using market prices and are cited by Spraos (1980), indicating in one case an improvement of the terms of trade in favour of primary products (excluding petroleum).

The position changed dramatically in the 1970s, when the rate of inflation sky-rocketed in all countries. This was mainly due to the sharp increase in the price of oil. As a result, the prices of primary product exports increased faster than those of manufactures, and the price of LDC exports increased faster than those of DME exports. The terms of trade of LDCs improved considerably while those of DMEs declined but only slightly. The improvement of LDC terms of trade, however, benefitted only the small group of oil exporters. The other LDCs on the whole suffered more drastically from these changes because the rise in non-fuel primary products of these countries was only slightly higher than in their imports of manufactures but much less than the prices of their oil imports. A few of them, however, gained by expanding their exports (visible and invisible) to the OPEC countries.

(f) Summary

The 1970s were a period of great disturbances in world trade, with major changes in LDCs affecting relatively few countries. Therefore, in order to evaluate the main trends affecting the trade of the LDCs compared with the DCs, we summarize the experience of the 1960s instead. If, in this period, LDC exports had increased as fast as those of DCs, their value in 1970 would have been US $15.87 billions, or 30 per cent higher than it actually was. Table 11.8 shows a breakdown of this amount attributable to various factors.

Table 11.8 Factors affecting growth of LDC exports, 1960–70 (US $ billions)

Factor		Amount
(a)	Initial difference in composition of exports	13.67
(b)	Slower growth of primary product exports	1.05
(c)	Slower rise in prices of primary product exports	3.15
(d)	Faster growth of manufactured exports	−2.45
(e)	Slower rise in prices of manufactured exports	0.45
	Total	15.87

11.2 Causes of International Trade

(a) The Comparative Advantage Theory

Most of the theoretical study of international trade is based on the usual neo-classical assumptions of maximizing behaviour, efficient markets and equilibrium conditions, leading to what we have described as the production function approach. Much of it is highly static and based on special assumptions such as constant returns to scale. On these assumptions, in the absence of trade restrictions and after allowing for transport costs, a region will export those products which fetch a higher price in other regions and import goods which are cheaper in other regions. Such trade will go on until price differences (after allowing for transport costs) are eliminated. This explanation is just as applicable to the trade between regions within countries as to trade between countries. But why are prices different in different regions to begin with? These differences are due to a wide variety of reasons, such as differences in the availabilities of resources required to produce various goods, differences in the productivity of these resources, and differences in the way prices of goods and of factors of production are determined in the respective markets. If factors of production are mobile between regions and if their prices are determined in the same way in all regions, then they will move between regions until their prices are equalized; differences in commodity prices will then reflect only differences in the productivity of resources, i.e. in the 'absolute advantage' of different regions. In this case, if there are no differences in productivity, there will be no trade in commodities, only the movement of factors, i.e. the movement of factors will be a complete substitute for the trade in commodities.

International trade theory became a separate branch of economics when it was assumed that factors of production were completely immobile between countries and mobile within countries. If factors of production are immobile between countries, differences in pre-trade prices of commodities will reflect, not only differences in productivity of resources, i.e. absolute advantages, but also differences in factor endowments. Then a country may import goods in which it has an absolute advantage if it happens to have a greater absolute advantage in other goods, which are exported. This is the Ricardian theory of comparative advantage. If all goods are ranked according to their comparative advantage, the dividing line between what are exported and what are imported is determined by 'reciprocal demand' so that the total value of all exports equals the total value of all imports. This theory only explains relative prices. The absolute prices which govern actual trade are then explained by changes in the general price level brought about by monetary forces whenever there is an imbalance between the value of exports and of imports, as argued in Hume's theory of specie flows and its modern version, the monetary approach to the balance of payments.

The international trade theory of the classical economists took differences in comparative advantage as given and did not offer any explanation for these differences. Of the various possible reasons, such as differences in factor endowments, differences in technology, and differences in market institutions, the modern neo-classical theory of trade, at least in the simple versions most widely discussed in the literature, has concentrated on differences in factor endowments as the principal explanation of comparative advantages, following the seminal work of Hecksher (1919) and Ohlin, B. (1933). In order to highlight this aspect, the theory assumes away differences in technology and in institutions, and applies the neo-classical model of factor and goods price determination in competitive markets with full employment.

This theory has been most fully worked out in the highly oversimplified case of two countries trading in two commodities produced by two factors, the so-called 2 by 2 by 2 case. Then, for instance, the theory shows that wages of labour will be relatively low and the rate of profit relatively high in the labour-abundant, capital-scarce, country; that in such a country before trade, the price of the labour-intensive product will be relatively low and that of the capital-intensive product relatively high; and hence that the country will export the labour-intensive commodity and import the capital-intensive one. This theory is then used to explain why LDCs (the labour-abundant capital-scarce example) export primary products (assumed to be labour-intensive) and import manufactures (assumed to be capital-intensive). Such simple results do not always hold in the more complex model with more than two countries, goods and factors, which is discussed by Dixit and Norman (1980).

If the pattern of trade is indeed determined in this way, trade in goods will reduce international differences in the price of the immobile factors of production and therefore will act to some extent as a substitute for the movement of factors between countries. In fact, Samuelson (1948, 1953) proved that under the standard neo-classical assumptions, the trade in goods which proceeds until their prices are equalized in all trading countries will also equalize factor-prices completely under the simple condition that the number of traded goods produced in all countries (i.e. the case of no specialization) is greater than the number of immobile factors. However, this conclusion depends crucially on the assumption of identical, constant-returns-to-scale, production functions in all countries, without reversals of factor-intensities (see e.g. Hlaing, 1965). When some of these assumptions are relaxed, the trade in goods will reduce but not eliminate the differences in factor prices as Ohlin himself argued (see Samuelson, 1971). However, even when these assumptions are satisfied, it has been shown that the trade in commodities does not necessarily equalize the rate of profit in the trading countries (see Bliss, 1967). The rate of profit may still differ between countries according to their rates of time preference. Such differences then have an effect on trade patterns, because a country which has a comparative advantage in capital-intensive commodities at a low rate of profit may lose that advantage at a higher rate of profit (see Metcalfe and Steedman, 1972, 1972a; also Samuelson, 1973; Mainwaring, 1974).

The difference in factor endowments alone does not explain many of the most significant aspects of the international trade of LDCs. We therefore consider some other factors which have played a part.

(b) The Size of Countries

One of the factors affecting the extent of a country's participation in world trade is its size (see e.g. Lloyd, 1968). There are many ways of measuring the size of a country. The simplest is the geographical area within the national boundaries. Table 11.9 shows the relation between this measure and the exports of countries as a percentage of their GDP.

The tendency for trade ratios to decline with increasing size is quite strong in the case of DCs but much less so in the case of LDCs. This could be due partly to the weakness of geographical area as a measure of economic size. Therefore, Table 11.10 shows the effect of size as measured by population and per capita income.

The relationship of trade ratios to these measures of size is not very systematic when the data for all countries are put together but becomes much clearer when DCs and LDCs are considered separately. Then, a number of patterns emerge. First, the trade ratios of LDCs are generally higher than those

Table 11.9 Trade ratios and geographical size

Area (000 km²)	Exports as percentage of GDP (average of 1960 and 1977) DCs	LDCs
Below 100	34	25
100–500	23	24
500–1000	16	20
1000 and over	14	20

Source: World Bank, *World Development Report*, 1979

Table 11.10 Exports as per cent of GNP by population size and per capita income, 1970

Per capita income (US $)	Population (millions) Below 10	10–30	30–50	50–100	100 & over
(a) *DMEs*					
500–1000	15.3	12.3	7.4	—	—
1000–2000	17.4	7.1	—	15.3	9.8
2000 and over	27.2	21.5	—	16.0	4.3
(b) *LDCs*					
Below 100	31.4	8.3			4.7
100–300	17.6	21.4	12.0	15.5	6.9
300–500	35.3	16.7	4.6	6.2	—
500–1000	33.8	23.8	4.2	—	—
1000–2000	62.0	—	—	—	—
2000 and over	51.5	—	—	—	—
(c) *All countries*					
Less than 100	13.4	8.3	—	—	4.7
100–300	17.6	21.4	12.0	15.5	6.9
300–500	35.3	16.7	4.6	6.2	—
500–1000	29.7	16.8	5.8	—	—
1000–2000	22.3	7.1	—	15.3	9.8
2000 and over	28.0	21.5	—	16.0	4.3

Source: U.N., *Yearbook of International Trade Statistics*, 1974

of DCs in the same population and income size class. Secondly, trade ratios of countries in each income class tend to decline with increasing population. Thirdly, however, trade ratios of countries in the same population class tend to increase with rising per capita income. One consequence is that there is no simple relationship of trade ratios with the national income of countries, because a given national income may be due to a large population with a low per capita income, in which case the trade ratio will be low on both counts, or to a small population with high per capita income, in which case the trade ratio will be high on both counts.

In studying the effect of the size of countries (defined by GDP) on their trade ratios, we must guard against the purely statistical effect that the same volume of trade between a small and a large country will be a larger ratio of the GDP of the small country than of the large one. Therefore, in interpreting data on the difference in trade ratios of small and large countries, we must separate out the trade between countries of similar sizes and the trade between countries of different sizes. The difference in trade ratios relating to the trade between countries of different sizes will be greatly influenced by the purely statistical effect, while the difference in trade ratios relating to the trade between countries of similar sizes is more indicative of the economic effect of size on trade ratios. Some estimates of the two types of effects for the average of 1970 and 1971 are given in Table 11.11, by roughly dividing DCs and LDCs into small and large countries and decomposing the difference between their trade ratios (percentage of imports and exports to GDP) of small and large countries (column 2) into two parts, one arising from the trade between countries of similar size (column 3) and the other from the trade between countries of different sizes (column 4).

Table 11.1 Analysis of differences in trade ratios by size

Countries	Percentage difference in trade ratio	due to trade between countries of: similar size	different size
All countries	34.53	5.16	29.37
From DCs to DCs	32.03	4.40	27.63
From DCs to LDCs	9.94	7.37	2.57
From LDCs to DCs	19.10	0.99	18.11
From LDCs to LDCs	8.79	6.45	2.34

For all countries taken together, most of the difference in trade ratios is due to the statistical effect, but when we separate out different directions of trade, we find that there is a significant size effect on trade ratios in the trade to LDCs, as shown by the difference in the trade between countries of similar size.

The size relationship of trade ratios is a complex one. The lower trade ratios of countries with large populations is partly due to the larger geographic size of these countries; this relationship then follows from the assumption that international trade is of the same character as internal trade except that it is across national frontiers, for as Marshall (1919, p.25) pointed out:

> a small country has a larger frontier in proportion to her area than a large country of the same shape . . . the average distance of her people from the nearest foreign market is likely to be less.

Large countries are also more likely to have a greater variety of resources and are therefore likely to be self-sufficient in more commodities. Also, the demand from large populations can support a greater variety of domestic industries than small populations with the same per capita income (see Section 11.2(g) on the role of demand).

The tendency for trade ratios to increase with per capita incomes is particularly interesting because at one time it was thought that the contrary would be the case: this is the view underlying Sombart's 'law of the declining importance of foreign trade'. It was based on the idea that as all countries reach similar income levels, especially when they achieve comparable levels of industrialization, there would be less complementarity between them and hence less trade. In fact, however, at high levels of income and industrialization, there is more scope for economies of scale which is the major explanation of the large volume of trade among DMEs, one of the most striking features of the post-war pattern of world trade (on the role of economies of scale, see (f) below). In the case of LDCs, it is more likely that it is the high trade ratios which lead to high incomes.

(c) The Working of Factor Markets

In the neo-classical model, free trade in commodities equalizes their prices (apart from transport costs), and these prices then determine the prices of factors in efficient competitive markets. If the number of traded commodities produced in all countries is greater than the number of immobile factors, and if all countries have identical constant returns to scale production functions, the prices of the immobile factors are also equalized. There are a number of difficulties in applying this model to the trade between DCs and LDCs which are discussed in the following subsections, namely the mobility of factors (d); the role of technology (e); economies of scale (f) and the role of demand (g). In the present subsection, we consider one of the most serious weaknesses of this theory, namely its neglect of the institutional factors affecting factor markets.

One example is that many infrastructural services to production and even some directly productive services such as the provision of credit are provided by governments freely or at highly subsidized prices. Therefore, countries with more of these services are able to export products which use these services intensively to other countries where there is less of these services. This is one important reason for the comparative advantage of DCs vis-à-vis LDCs in manufacturing.

The most important example of the role of institutional factors in determining factor prices in LDCs is the case of labour. The productivity of most types of labour in LDCs is lower than in DCs, but wages are even lower, so that the labour cost per unit of output is lower in LDCs for many products. This is particularly true in the traditional sectors of LDCs where primary products are produced, and this is a major reason for the LDC specialization in such products. There are many types of institutional conditions which influence the level of wages in LDCs. Some of these were discussed in Section 8.4(b). In some sectors, the level of wages may be raised above the competitive level by political circumstances or the unionization of labour; this leads to slow expansion of these sectors. In others, it may be reduced below the competitive level by monopsonistic exploitation. Another important factor was pointed out by Lewis (1954) in his theory of unlimited supplies of labour; according to this theory, the low productivity of labour in producing food in the traditional sector leads to low wages in the modern sector.

The result is that, contrary to the neo-classical trade model in which commodity and factor prices are jointly determined in general equilibrium and in which, in small countries, international commodity prices determine domestic factor prices, the determination of prices in LDCs tends to follow the classical model; in this model factor prices are first determined by institutional and other long-term forces, and these in turn determine commodity prices according to their costs of production. Especially in the case of goods which are specific to the LDCs, this has important consequences for their terms of trade, which are considered below.

(d) Mobility of Factors

International trade theory starts off by assuming that factors are fully mobile within countries but immobile between countries. The concept of each country's factor endowment is based on this assumption. As argued in Chapter 8, factor markets are so highly segmented that there are severe restrictions to factor mobility within these countries. Capital is often only available at high cost to the traditional sectors of agricultural production, while the abundant labour of these sectors is unable to get industrial employment in the modern sectors.

On the other hand, there was, in historical fact, a considerable mobility of factors between countries. In former times, there was a larger international migration of people. The development of European settlements overseas in North America and Oceania was based on the migration of about fifty million people from Europe. Further, there was a migration of similar numbers from the densely populated countries of India and China to countries, especially LDCs, all over the world. It is only in recent times that the international movement of people has become a trickle as receiving countries have tightened up their immigration laws.

There was also a large movement of capital between countries. A large part of the capital accumulation in European settlements overseas and in LDCs was historically financed by foreign capital. Using his theory of the mechanization process, Butt (1954) analysed various phases in this process and their effects on trade and investment as follows:

Phase of accumulation	*Foreign trade and investment*
1. Beginning of capital accumulation and mechanization of industry A in country X.	None.

	Phase of accumulation	Foreign trade and investment
2.	Industry A in X fully mechanized and output greater than demand in X.	Trade begins. X exports A to Y in exchange for handicraft products.
3.	Industry A in X sufficient to meet demand in both countries. Mechanization in X moves to B and later industries in the sequence of mechanization. Prices of fully mechanized industries fall.	Trade expands. X exports A, B, . . . to Y in exchange for handicrafts. Terms of trade move in favour of Y.
4.	Service industry S mechanized in X.	X invests in S industry in Y (foreign investment in infrastructure)
5.	Capital accumulation begins in Y and is used to mechanize domestic production of goods previously imported from X.	Import substitution investment in Y.
6.	All industries in X fully mechanized.	X invests in non-service industries in Y.
7.	Final phase. Capital accumulation ceases.	Trade becomes unnecessary except for the products of natural resources. The country with the higher capital stock has higher income.

Historically, foreign capital flowed to LDCs to take advantage of the low level of wages in these countries in particular sectors, especially the sectors producing primary products which are specific to LDCs, such as the products of mines and plantations. Such a concentration of foreign capital in these sectors is an important reason for the specialization of LDCs in primary products.

There are still large amounts of capital seeking investment opportunities nowadays, especially from DMEs suffering from recessions in their economies and from OPEC countries which have large balance of payments surpluses as a result of the sharp rise in oil prices. But many LDCs have tended to restrict the inflow of foreign capital, partly because of the high cost of such capital and partly because they wish to be more self-reliant.

(e) The Role of Technology

Which commodities are cheap in a given country compared with other countries is not only a matter of the national endowments of resources but also of the productivity of these resources. The Ricardian theory explained trade by such productivity differences, but implied that these differences were mainly due to natural factors, such as climate. The simpler versions of the Hecksher–Ohlin theory, on the other hand, are based on identical production functions, which assume away differences in productivity. It is because of such an assumption that it explains trade in terms of differences in factor endowments.

In fact, however, the trade patterns of countries do not always conform to the factor endowment explanation. The best known example of this contradiction is the Leontief paradox (1954) which showed that the exports of the United States, which had an abundance of capital relative to its trading partners, were less capital-intensive than its imports, contrary to the predictions of the theory. This paradox is therefore explained by recognizing that the technological leadership of the United States in many products was a significant factor in explaining its trade with other countries. Attempts have then been made to extend the theory by including the level of technology, as reflected, for example, in the quality or skills of the factors of production, in the concept of factor endowments, but the theory loses its original simplicity, mainly because of the difficulty of quantitative measurement of the level of technology. Often, it is the level of technology which is deduced from the patterns of trade rather than the patterns of trade being explained by factor endowments. It also neglects many dynamic aspects of technological progress, such as the extent to which it is induced by the pattern of trade itself or the extent to which it occurs as the result of deliberate policies.

Technological factors have played a major role in determining the patterns of trade and specialization of LDCs. In the colonial pattern of development of these countries, a great deal of effort was devoted to developing primary production technology leading to their specialization in such products. There was much less emphasis on technological progress in manufactures or in commodities produced for domestic consumption, especially food. In the DCs, a considerable amount of technological progress in manufactures occurred as a result of their specialization in such products; there was little technological progress in this way in the LDCs and therefore they have remained dependent on imports of manufactures from DCs.

Some dynamic aspects of the diffusion of technology, especially among DCs, have been discussed in the theory of the product cycle (Vernon, 1966). A feature of recent trends in international trade has been that a country which develops and exports a new commodity, ends up by importing that commodity after some time. For example, in the early post-war years, the United States was an exporter of radios, but since then has been importing them, especially from Japan. This is a case of a country exporting a commodity when it has built up a technological superiority, and importing it when the new technology has diffused to other countries (see Posner, 1961; Hufbauer, 1965). During this period, the methods of production also change. In the early stages, a new product is produced on a small scale by sophisticated methods, requiring large inputs of skilled labour. When output expands beyond the requirements of the domestic market, it is exported by the innovating country. After some time, the methods of production are improved by a learning process, costs come down, the product is standardized, and as demand grows, the product becomes suitable for mass production requiring less skilled labour. At this stage, other countries begin their own production, and if their costs of unskilled labour are lower and if they can improve the methods of production further, these countries export the product back to the innovating country itself. This product cycle operates mostly among DCs. Where it reaches LDCs, it is usually the simpler processes and components that move to them.

(f) Economies of Scale

The explanation of many aspects of international trade in terms of the national endowment of resources is often crucially dependent on the assumption of constant returns to scale production functions. But as pointed out in Section 9.8, increasing returns to scale are pervasive in manufacturing industry. Because of such economies of scale, two countries may have the same factor endowments but if one country produces a commodity on a larger scale, it may be able to export that commodity to the other. This influence on trade patterns has important implications for analysis of some important features of international trade and policy towards international trade.

We have seen that one of the most striking features of post-war international trade is the large and growing volume of trade among the DMEs themselves, i.e. among countries which have similar national factor endowments. Most of this trade is in manufactures (category B in Table 10.5). Further, a large proportion of the trade in both directions consists of trade in the products of the same industry; such trade has been described as intra-industry trade (Grubel and Lloyd, 1975). A convenient measure of the extent of such trade for a country is

$$B = 100 - 100\,\Sigma \frac{|X_i - M_i|}{(X_i + M_i)}$$

where X_i and M_i are the country's exports and imports of the ith commodity at various levels of disaggregation. The results for a number of DCs and LDCs are shown in Table 11.12; the measures for DCs are based on a three-digit classification, while those for LDCs are based on a two-digit classification. We see that intra-industry trade constitutes a large part of the trade of DMEs and very little of the trade of LDCs. Further, during the period 1959–67, when the exports of 10 DMEs increased at an annual rate of 9 per cent, 80 per cent of this increase was accounted for by intra-industry trade (Grubel and Lloyd, 1975, p.42).

Intra-industry trade was much more important in the case of manufactures than in the case of primary products, as shown in Table 11.13. The explanation for the large volume of intra-industry trade in the case of manufactures is that such trade is mainly due to economies of scale, especially those based on the long production runs, which are more important in the case of manufactures than of primary products. This is a special case of the argument that specialization increases efficiency; it may be recalled that this was one of the main planks in Adam Smith's advocacy of free trade, i.e., that trade extends the market on which division of labour and its consequent growth of productivity depend.

Economies of scale also play an important part in the infant industry argument for protection; this argument is considered in Section 12.2.

Table 11.12 Extent of intra-industry trade (percentage)

DCs	Measure (1967)	LDCs	Measure (1962)
U.K.	69	Sri Lanka	4
France	65	India	8
Belgium & Luxemberg	63	S. Korea	5
Netherlands	56	Malaysia	12
U.S.A.	49	Pakistan	9
Canada	48	Philippines	2
Germany	46	Taiwan	15
Italy	42	Thailand	7
Japan	21		
Australia	17		
Average	48	Average	7

Source: Grubel and Lloyd, 1975, pp.39, 179.

Table 11.13 Extent of intra-industry trade, O.E.C.D. countries 1967

Commodity groups (SITC codes)	Measure
0. Food	30
1. Beverages	40
2. Crude materials	30
3. Fuels	30
4. Fats and oils	37
5. Chemicals	66
6. Manufactures	49
7. Machinery	59
8. Miscellaneous manufactures	52
9. Others, n.e.s.	55
Average	48

Source: Grubel and Lloyd, 1975, pp.31–35

(g) The Role of Demand

Finally, we consider the influence of demand factors on international trade. In most popular expositions of trade theory, markets are assumed to function efficiently to ensure that all resources are fully employed. Alternative patterns of production are then described by a transformation curve. Demand factors are introduced only in the form of the prices of various commodities, and the allocation of resources is determined by the point on the transformation curve where the marginal rate of transformation is equal to the relative prices which reflect the marginal rate of substitution in consumption. As we have seen, the assumptions on which this analysis is based are not always valid, especially in LDCs; hence demand factors play a major role in trade, not only by determining a point on the transformation curve, but also in determining how fully resources are utilized in the production of different commodities (see Section 9.9).

This role of demand is an important explanation of the rapid growth of primary product exports of LDCs after these countries were opened up to foreign trade by colonial powers. Previously, many of their resources, had not been fully utilized and were in surplus. The demand from the DCs for new products that could be produced with these resources, together with the technology and capital provided by the DCs, then led to fuller utilization of these resources. The subsequent specialization of LDCs in primary products was therefore due to an extension of the transformation curve due to the strength of demand, rather than just a movement along a fixed transformation curve. The possibility of exporting such commodities due to the foreign demand thus provided the LDCs with a 'vent for surplus', which was one of Adam Smith's main explanations of trade and his justification for the liberalization of trade (see Myint, 1958). In the case of manufactures, there was initially little demand in the LDCs because of their low incomes, and such demand as existed was met by imports from the DCs; in fact, it was the DCs which had a balance of trade deficit with the LDCs at the time and had to use various methods, including military intervention, to increase their exports to the LDCs. The lack of domestic demand was one reason why the manufacturing sector of LDCs did not expand in the historical period.

Another aspect of the role of demand has been studied by Linder (1961). His main thesis is that, to begin with, a country produces on a large scale those commodities for which there is a strong domestic demand. Its efficiency in producing some of these commodities as a result of economies of scale then reaches a point where they can be exported to other countries. As a country's per capita income rises, the demand for manufactures increases more than proportionately because the income-elasticity of demand for these commodities is greater than one; then, a larger number of such commodities become exportable. This is an important part of the explanation for the large volume of trade in manufactures among countries with a high per capita income (see Section 11.1), and for the large volume of intra-industry trade among them (see Section 11.2(f)).

In the 1970s, the DMEs have been facing great difficulties in maintaining levels of domestic demand to ensure full employment, and have been using trade policies to raise the level of demand. This is one explanation for the reversion to mercantilist policies, such as the scramble for exports and the rise in protectionism against imports, especially of labour-intensive products exported by LDCs.

11.3 Consequences of International Trade

The elementary theory of international trade is mainly concerned with the static aspects of the consequences of such trade, especially the extent to which it promotes the welfare of consumers with given tastes and preferences subject to given resource availability at a point in time, and argues that the gains from trade are maximized in all countries by free trade. Far more important than these static welfare effects has been the fact that the past pattern of trade between DCs and LDCs has led to intense specialization of LDCs in primary products and of DCs in manufactures and the dynamic consequences of trade on growth which have flowed from such specialization, and the unequal distribution of the gains from trade between these groups of countries. Some aspects of these consequences are discussed below.

(a) Trade and Growth

In the nineteenth century, the great expansion of world trade, brought about mainly by the revolution in transport, coincided with rapid economic growth in many countries. This historical experience gave rise to the view of international trade as the 'engine of growth'. This view, however, is misleading for a number of reasons. In the first place, the correlation between expansion of trade and rapid economic growth does not by itself show the direction of causation. In fact, it was due not only to the influence of trade on growth but also to the influence of growth on trade and the influence of the progress of development on both trade and growth, as rapidly growing countries increased their demand for imports from other countries.

Secondly, there was a difference in the growth trends of different groups of countries, corresponding to the two dynamic factors that Adam Smith had identified as the sources of growth from trade, namely his 'vent for surplus' argument and his increasing returns argument based on his dictum that division of labour depended on the extent of the market. The first factor tended to dominate in the LDCs and the second in the DCs, because of the nature of their specialization. In the LDCs, when they were opened up to world trade by the colonial powers, there was an expansion of their exports of primary products to the DCs as well as a rapid growth of their national incomes. But both these consequences were just different aspects of the same phenomenon, namely the exploitation of hitherto unused natural resources. In this case, trade led to growth by providing a vent for surplus. The growth, however, was not self-sustaining growth, for as the surplus was steadily exhausted, these countries also stagnated. The effect of trade on growth proved to be a once-over effect.

The growth effects of trade were more prominent among the European settlements overseas. These countries had a higher rate of growth than even the countries of Europe with which they traded. Further, this growth has continued to the present time. This was mainly due to the fact that simultaneously with the expansion of trade, there was also a high rate of development. As a result, they were able to get better prices for their primary products in international trade, and further, they were able to expand their industrial sectors and exploit the economies of scale in that sector. Therefore, Kravis (1970, p.859) has concluded that in their case:

> The mainsprings of growth were internal; they must be sought in the land and the people; and in the system of social and economic organisation . . . the term 'engine of

growth' is not generally descriptive and involves expectations which cannot be fulfilled by trade alone; the term 'handmaiden of growth' better conveys the notion of the role that trade can play.

In the post-war period, the idea of trade as the engine of growth has surfaced again because of the observation that some of the most rapidly growing LDCs, such as Taiwan, South Korea, Hong Kong and Singapore were 'outward looking' and greatly expanded their participation in world trade, while slow-growing countries like Indonesia in the 1950s, India and Burma were 'inward looking' (see, e.g., Myint, 1967). There have been many studies to establish the growth effects of trade in the post-war experience of LDCs based on high statistical correlations between rates of growth of GDP and of exports. But such correlations are partly due to the fact that, in the case of countries whose exports are a large proportion of their GDP, the increase of exports is a large part of the increase of GDP (see, e.g., O.E.C.D., 1968, p.17). Therefore, Kleimens (1980) considered instead the regression of the growth rate of output for domestic use (GDP minus exports) on the growth rate of exports, and found that the data were consistent with a weak version of the hypothesis that trade promotes growth, i.e. that the expansion of exports requires a less than commensurate withdrawal of resources from other uses. He also found that

> growth induced by trade liberalisation takes the form of a further expansion of exports rather than of the non-export component of GNP.

and that the data were also consistent with the reverse hypothesis that growth promoted trade.

(b) The Terms of Trade

How far a country benefits from trade depends not only on the volume of trade but also on the terms of trade. Prebisch (1950) and Singer (1950) argued that there was a secular tendency for the terms of trade to move against LDCs in their trade with DCs, mainly because the LDCs were specialized in primary products and the DCs in the manufactures, and because the terms of trade had deteriorated against primary products. There has been a great deal of controversy over the statistical evidence for this tendency. The most comprehensive review of this evidence is given by Spraos (1980) who concludes as follows:

> The relevant period covers the seventy years down to the Second World War. Over this period the evidence points to a deteriorating trend in the relative prices of primary products. Given the reservations which must be made about the quality of the evidence, there can be no finality about this conclusion, but it has been reached by examining one by one the main points adduced to question the inference of the deterioration and finding that they are contradicted or not confirmed by relevant material. The statistical

series chosen by Prebisch did, however, exaggerate the rate of deterioration—at worst by a factor of more than three.

The main issue discussed in the literature has been whether the terms of trade had deteriorated against primary products, whereas, at least according to classical economic theory, the operation of diminishing returns in primary production and increasing returns in industry would have led us to expect an improvement of these terms of trade. In fact, the terms of trade have been influenced considerably by demand factors, especially the demand for primary products in the DCs. Hence there have been great fluctuations in the terms of trade, and the results about the nature of the underlying trend have depended crucially on the choice of the period and the price index. For example, growth of DMEs in the post-war period led to a strong demand for primary products exported by the LDCs; for this period, Spraos (1980, p.126) concludes that

> though the relative price of the developing countries' primary products has had its ups and downs since the war, it has on average done quite well by the standard of pre-second-war decades, even when petroleum is excluded as a special case since 1973. So, while the deteriorating tendency cannot be decisively refuted, it is open to doubt when the record up to the 1970s is taken into account.

There have been a number of theoretical models of the behaviour of the terms of trade, each of which has stressed particular aspects of the demand and supply factors involved. For the case in which two countries were completely specialized in the production of two different commodities, Johnson, H. G. (1955) derived the result:

$$\hat{\theta} = \frac{\hat{Y}_1\epsilon_1 - \hat{Y}_2\epsilon_2}{\eta_1 + \eta_2 - 1} \tag{11.3.1}$$

where $\hat{\theta}$ is the change in the terms of trade of country 1; $\hat{Y}_i$ is the rate of growth of income, in country i, and ϵ_i and η_i are its income and price elasticities of demand for the product of the other country. This result focusses on the demand factors and shows that the terms of trade will move against the country whose rate of growth, weighted by its income elasticity of demand, is higher. There have thus been two influences in opposite directions on the terms of trade of LDCs in their trade with DCs. On the one hand, until recently, the DCs have grown faster than LDCs, thereby tending to improve the LDC terms of trade. On the other hand, the income elasticity of demand of the DCs for the produce of the LDCs has been lower than the income elasticity of demand of the LDCs for the produce of DCs. Findlay (1980) has given a dynamic extension of this model to derive a result for the terms of trade in terms of some fundamental determinants, such as the rate of population growth and of savings.

Hicks (1953) considered the case of no specialization, i.e. the case where two countries produced both an exportable and an importable commodity, and showed that technical progress will improve a country's term of trade if it occurs in the importable commodity and worsen them if it occurs in the exportable commodity. This result was extended by Findlay and Grubert (1959) who showed that

(1) Neutral technical progress in a commodity will improve a country's terms of trade if the commodity is the importable and worsen them if the commodity is the exportable;
(2) Technical progress in a commodity biased towards the factor in which the commodity is less intensive will improve the terms of trade if the commodity is the importable and worsen them if the commodity is the exportable; and
(3) Where technical progress in a commodity is biased towards the factor in which the commodity is more intensive, the effect on the terms of trade will depend on the extent of the technical progress and its factor bias. (For a formula showing the quantitative relationship, see Takayama, 1972, p.394.)

The nature of technical progress has had a great influence on the terms of trade of LDCs, because it was concentrated so heavily on the commodities exported by them; it occurred both in the LDCs and also in the DCs in the development of synthetic substitutes for the primary products they imported from the LDCs.

The most useful model for explaining the terms of trade of LDCs is that of Lewis (1954, 1969, 1978, 1978a) in which some commodities—which may be called the 'common' commodities—are produced in both a DC and an LDC, while other commodities—which may be called the 'specific' commodities—are produced only in one of the trading countries. In the Lewis model, the common commodities are exemplified by food, and the specific commodities by coffee in the LDC and by steel in the DC. The terms of trade between the countries therefore vary with the relative prices of coffee in terms of steel. The result is that technical progress in the LDC in its specific commodity, coffee, will worsen the terms of trade while technical progress in the common commodity, food, will improve them.

This result follows quite readily even from the neo-classical model of factor and goods pricing, such as that used in the factor-price equalization theory. According to that theory, given identical constant-returns-to-scale production functions, competitive markets and full employment, factor prices will be equalized in the trading countries so long as the number of common commodities is equal to, or greater than, the number of immobile factors. The most crucial assumption involved in this implausible result is that of identical production functions. The simplest way to relax this condition is to assume instead that the relative efficiencies of factors are the same in the production of all the common commodities. Then the two countries can be considered to have the same production function in 'efficiency units' of the factors, and the prices of factors in efficiency units will be equalized by commodity trade. These factor prices then determine the prices of the specific commodities produced only in one of the countries. It then follows that technical progress in the LDC in the common commodity, i.e. a rise in the relative efficiency of factors, will increase factor prices in natural units, raise the prices of its specific commodities, and improve its terms of trade. But technical progress in the LDC-specific commodity will not affect factor prices at all, as these are determined by the relative efficiency of factors in the common commodities; with unchanged factor prices, the technical progress in the specific commodity will only lower their prices and worsen the LDC terms of trade.

The above derivation is based on a neo-classical model in which factor and commodity prices are determined in general equilibrium. In Lewis' own exposition, it is derived from a classical model which is more applicable to LDCs. In classical theory, the chain of causation runs in one direction only, with certain long-term forces determining factor prices, and these, in turn, determining goods prices; demand enters only to determine the composition of output at these prices. In the dualistic theory of growth, the wage at which there is a perfectly elastic supply of labour is determined by the average productivity of labour in food production, in contrast to the neo-classical theory in which it is determined by marginal productivity. The prices of all commodities are then determined by the amount of labour required per unit of output multiplied by the wage rate. Hence, technical progress in food production will raise the wage rate; the rise in wages will raise the prices of specific commodities and improve the terms of trade. Technical progress in the specific commodities will reduce the labour required per unit of output without affecting the wage rate; therefore, the prices of these commodities will fall and worsen the terms of trade. As Lewis (1969, p.25) says,

> For the last eighty years the tropical countries have put practically all their agricultural research and extension funds and effort into trying to raise the productivity of export crops like cocoa, tea, or rubber and virtually no effort into food productivity. From their point of view, this effort was wholly misdirected.

The original statement of the Prebisch–Singer thesis emphasized the effect on the terms of trade of LDCs of the type of commodities they imported and exported, and the argument revolved around the conditions of marketing, highly competitive in the case of primary commodities and oligopolistic in the case of manufactures. In contrast, in the Lewis theory, the terms of trade depend not on the type of commodities but on the conditions in the trading countries which determine wages. Therefore, Lewis (1978a, p.16) says,

> If tea had been a temperate instead of a tropical crop, its price would have been perhaps four times as high as it was. And if wool had been a tropical instead of a temperate crop, it would have been had for perhaps one-fourth of the ruling price.

In a return to his 1950 paper, Singer (1975, p.59) also says,

Singer I assumed the centre/peripheral relationship to reside in the characteristics of different types of *commodities*, i.e. modern manufactures versus primary commodities. Singer II now feels that the essence of the relationship lies in the different types of *countries*.

A similar analysis is offered by Emmanuel (1972) who, however, attributes differences in wages to different degrees of exploitation of labour rather than to differences in labour productivity in food production. Further, while the Lewis theory is based on a single factor of production, labour, Emmanuel considers an additional factor, capital. With regard to capital, Emmanuel argues that the price of capital in LDCs is depressed below what it would otherwise have been by the high mobility of capital between countries. With the prices of capital brought to near equality in the trading countries by such mobility, the country with the lower wage rate sells its specific products at lower prices; this leads to what Emmanuel has described as 'unequal exchange'.

(c) Instability of Trade

The foreign trade of LDCs has been subject to great instability. The value of exports of a country or a commodity does not increase at a constant rate over time; the growth rate varies from year to year. In order to measure the degree of instability, therefore, we must separate the year-to-year variation into two parts—one due to the underlying trend shown by a steady rate of long-term growth, and the other to fluctuations around that trend. There are many ways of estimating the trend and many ways of summarizing the fluctuations around the trend, leading to different measures of instability. The simplest method is to estimate the trend as a linear function of time by some statistical method, and to measure the degree of instability as the average value of the fluctuations around that trend. The trend is sometimes estimated by the method of moving averages but this method absorbs some of the annual fluctuations into the trend and underestimates the degree of instability. When the trend is measured by the least squares method, and the fluctuations around the trend averaged by taking their root mean squares, the result, known as the standard error of estimate, expressed as a percentage of the average value, produces a convenient measure of instability; this measure was extensively used in the I.B.R.D.–I.M.F. joint study of commodity fluctuations (I.B.R.D.–I.M.F., 1969). According to that study, the export instability of different groups of countries was as shown in Table 11.14. The LDCs have had a much greater instability than DCs, and this has been true both in the volume of exports and in their unit values.

Table 11.15 shows the export instability in different groups of commodities exported by LDCs. The instability of unit values has been uniformly high for all groups of the primary products exported by LDCs, but the instability of

Table 11.14 Export instability of DCs and LDCs, 1953–63

Group (number of countries	Average index of instability:		
	Export value	Unit value	Export volume
DCs (14)	4.2	2.1	4.5
LDCs (37)	9.7	6.9	8.0
(a) Africa and Middle East (13)	9.3	6.4	8.7
(b) Latin America (11)	10.8	7.8	8.0
(c) Asia (8)	8.1	5.9	7.2

Source: I.B.R.D.-I.M.F., 1969, pp.41–59

Table 11.15 Export instability of LDCs according to commodities, 1953–65

Group (number) of commodities	Average index of instability:		
	Export value	Unit value	Export volume
Minerals (9)	12.5	9.3	5.9
Agricultural raw materials (9)	8.8	9.4	5.8
Foodstuffs (17)	13.8	9.0	13.1
(a) Tropical foods (4)	6.9	9.5	4.9
(b) Other foods (6)	18.1	9.8	15.8
(c) Oils and oil seeds (7)	14.2	8.1	15.6

Source: I.B.R.D.-I.M.F., 1969, p.56

export volumes has varied greatly, being high for foodstuffs and low for the mineral and agricultural raw materials. In the case of quantities, the world exports of individual commodities would naturally be more stable than the exports of particular countries, as fluctuations in the exports of one country will be offset to some extent by fluctuations in the exports of other countries. In his study of the instability of values of world exports of primary products compared with manufactures, Coppock (1962, p.35) came to the conclusion that

> contrary to widely held views, export proceeds were decidedly more stable for primary goods than for manufactured goods.

This conclusion is often cited in the literature, but it is due to an arithmetical error. In fact, the trade in primary products has been more unstable than the trade in manufactures, and the greater instability in the export earnings of LDCs compared with DCs has been due to the higher proportion of primary products in their exports.

Especially in the case of agricultural products, the major reason for the instability in export volumes is supply fluctuations, due to variations in weather conditions and other natural factors. It has also been due to demand fluctuations, as levels of activity varied in the importing DCs. These fluctuations in demand and supply in turn have led to a high instability in export prices, mainly because of the low elasticities of demand and supply. Attempts to identify other factors leading to instability of export earnings, such as geographical or commodity concentration of exports, have yielded inconclusive results (see e.g. Knudsen and Parnes, 1975). One possible link that has not been fully investigated is that of the rate of growth of exports itself (Table 11.16). This table suggests that countries tend to experience high export instability both when the export growth rate is above average and when it is below average.

Table 11.16 Rate of growth and instability of exports, 1953–65

Annual rate of growth of exports of countries	Average index of instability of export proceeds
Low (below 2.6%)	11.2
Medium (2.6–4.6%)	7.8
High (above 5.0%)	10.2
Average	9.7

Source: I.B.R.D.-I.M.F., 1969

For LDCs heavily dependent on export earnings for meeting the foreign exchange costs of their development and growth, the great instability of exports is a serious disadvantage. Such instability prevents the long-range planning of investments, both in the private and in the public sector. It also reduces the productivity of these investments if they are frequently disrupted by financial difficulties. According to some statistical studies, there is little correlation between export instability and various indicators of growth (see, e.g., MacBean, 1968). The results, however, are not conclusive because growth was also affected by many other factors which were not fully allowed for (see Maizels, 1968). The adverse effects increase disproportionately with sudden shortfalls in export earnings, as, for example, in the case of the cocoa exports of Ghana in 1965, or the export of rubber in Indonesia in 1961 which was an important cause leading to the great inflation lasting until 1966.

CHAPTER 12

International Trade: Policy

12.1 Interventions in International Trade

As pointed out in Section 10.2, economics as a science began with the vision of a self-regulating market system and stressed the advantages of a policy of laissez-faire over the mercantile system with its numerous state interventions with market forces. The change in attitudes was partly the result of a change in overall economic objectives, from increasing the economic power of the State to promoting overall economic growth. It was also due to the fortuitous circumstances of rapid technological progress and expanding markets that prevailed in Britain at the time and that gave her a special advantage in having free markets. This was particularly true in the case of international trade.

In other countries and at other times, however, governments have intervened with market forces, and they have done so more intensively in their international trade than in their internal trade. One reason was simply that it was administratively easier for them to do so. Most of the foreign trade of countries passed through a few sea-ports and other commercial centres. Most foreign exchange transactions involved in international trade have to be carried out through the well-organized banks established in the principal cities. Therefore, it has been relatively easy for governments to regulate and control international trade. In particular, when governments have wanted to raise more revenue, taxes on foreign trade—both imports and exports—have been resorted to because they are so much easier to collect than other taxes. Many government interventions with market forces have also been in response to political pressures from powerful vested interests; such pressures have often been particularly strong in connection with trade matters. In this chapter, we shall be concerned with policy interventions on the part of governments designed to correct what governments perceive as problems arising from international trade, i.e. undesirable commodity compositions of imports and exports, unfavourable terms of trade and imbalances in international payments. We must remember, however, that although such policies have the ostensible objective of correcting such national problems, they may in part be due to pressures from particular interest groups also.

Governments use a variety of instruments to intervene in international trade, such as taxes and subsidies, quantitative controls, adjustments of exchange rates, state operation of foreign trade, and the allocation of development measures to foreign trade activities. Some of these instruments, such as subsidies to exports and devaluation of the exchange rate, increase the volume of trade. More often, they take the form of taxing or otherwise controlling trade, which reduce the volume of trade below its free trade level.

In the inter-war period, the volume of trade was greatly reduced by extensive interventions in all countries, developed and less-developed. In the post-war period, the DMEs set about liberalizing their trade. They set up some international machinery in the form of the General Agreement of Tariff and Trade to negotiate and monitor such liberalization measures. This liberalization contributed to a great extent to the unprecedented growth of world trade up to the early 1970s. Since then, many DMEs have adopted restrictive policies as a result of the breakdown of the international monetary system and the emergence of persistent imbalances in international payments.

Historically, the LDCs were subject to a regime of free trade, especially with their respective metropolitan countries. In the post-war period, especially in the LDCs which achieved independence from colonial rule, the new national governments introduced a more intensive system of interventions with foreign trade as part of their efforts to promote development. Some aspects of these policies are discussed in this chapter.

12.2 Trade and Industrialization

Most discussions of international trade theory assume that the comparative advantage of countries in producing various commodities is fixed, and given by such immutable conditions as climate, geography or even the racial characteristics of people. Then, it is easily shown that, with the usual assumptions of neo-classical theory, free trade is the best policy in the sense of achieving the optimum allocation of resources which maximizes the satisfaction of given consumer tastes and preferences. It must be noted, however, that even when all these assumptions are satisfied, and welfare is maximized at a point of time, it does not necessarily follow that free trade will promote growth, except as a once-only effect, when, for example, a country is opened up to trade or when it shifts from restricted trade to a more liberal system. But these assumptions are not always satisfied; then some interventions in trade may become necessary for both allocation and growth objectives.

For example, one case of the failure of the assumptions of conventional trade theory, which has been discussed extensively, is Manoilesco's (1933) argument that wages are generally higher in the industrial sectors of LDCs than in their agricultural sectors, thereby restricting the former below its optimum level. He proposed that the industrial sector should be protected from foreign competition by tariffs on imports of manufactures. Modern neo-classical economists have, however, argued on the basis of welfare theory that it is better to correct this 'domestic' distortion by a wage subsidy to the industrial sector (see, e.g., Corden, 1974, pp.28–30). Another example is the case where a country has some monopoly power in its foreign trade. This is a case of a 'foreign' distortion, for which the solution proposed is a tax on imports; the amount of such a tariff is discussed in the theory of the 'optimum tariff' (see Corden, 1974, chapter 7).

These, however, are the static arguments for interventions with free trade. More important for growth are some dynamic considerations. The first point to note is that a country's comparative advantage is continually changing. Second, some of these changes in comparative advantage are due to the country's patterns of trade. Third, a country's comparative advantage can be changed by deliberate policy. It is through such changes that there is a significant interaction between trade and growth. The main policy issue facing LDCs concerned with growth is therefore how to change their comparative advantages in order to make the best of their trading opportunities. The problem was formulated quite clearly by Harrod (1963, pp.117–18) in his 'dynamized version of the law of comparative costs' as follows:

> What tradeable goods should be produced? There is a correct answer to this question, although one which it may be difficult to ascertain either by market forecast or by experience. Prior to the programme for expediting the provision of capital disposal and the growth of non-capital factors, there will have been a certain distribution of productive resources between exported goods and import-competing goods, including a null assignment to many types of imported goods. The provision of additional capital disposal and of non-capital factors should lower costs in the industries to which they are applied. The conjunction of more capital disposal and other high quality factors with a given quantum of common labour power will reduce costs over a certain range of increased output more in the production of some products than in that of others. The additional factor should be applied to the commodities of which the cost of production can be lowered more, over the range in which they can be lowered more. But that is just what is difficult to prognosticate. The introduction of additional capital disposal and other highly qualified factors may be regarded as *fertilizing* the productivity of common labour.

Having stated the problem so clearly, however, he goes on to say,

> I would suggest that it is *a priori* probable that the fertilizing effect of the increased supply of these factors will be greater (a) when there are certain specific natural resources that gave the pre-existing factors a comparative advantage, compared with other countries, and (b) in those lines of production to which pre-existing factors are habituated. If correct, this *a priori* assumption suggests that further endeavours should

be directed more strongly to industries producing exportable goods than to those making import-competing goods.

This *a priori* argument that comparative advantage will generally improve in a country's exportable sectors is a strange assumption to make. It is contrary to the historical experience of many DCs which were able to change their pattern of trade. Applied to the LDCs, it amounts to recommending that the 'traditional form of exchange' in which they specialize in primary products and import manufactures should continue in the future. However, the sectors of an economy in which comparative advantage can be improved depends on the nature of their production conditions and on the efforts made to increase productivity, rather than on whether they were previously importing or exporting sectors. At present, the productivity gap between DCs and LDCs is particularly large in the production of food for domestic consumption and of manufactures, rather than in the cash crops which form the bulk of exports from LDCs. Therefore, it is likely that the LDCs can improve their comparative advantage in food and manufactures more easily than in further raising productivity in cash crops.

One theory about the industrial sector is that changes in its comparative advantage occur naturally in the course of economic growth. For example, from his cross-section analysis of international data for the period 1952–54, Chenery (1960, p.644) concluded that:

> If a country has an increase in income with no change in comparative advantage, the analysis suggests that only about a third of the normal amount of industrialisation will take place. Changes in supply conditions, resulting from a change in relative factor costs as income rises, causes a substitution of domestic production for imports and to a lesser extent of factory goods for handicrafts and services. These supply changes are more important in explaining the growth of industry than are the changes in demand.

Similarly, Maizels (1963, p.14) summarized his findings thus:

> Industrialisation leads to increased real income per head and this in turn raises demand for manufactures per head (which rises 1½–2 times the rate of growth of real income per head). With the progress of industrialisation, the import content falls until a fairly mature level of industrialisation has been reached. The rate at which the import-content has fallen in the past is in the region of 40–60 per cent of the rate of increase in manufacturing production per head.

Based on these results, Chenery (1960) introduced the concept of the 'growth elasticity' of various types of manufactures, defined as the rate of growth of domestic production of each type of manufacture as a ratio of the rate of growth of national income. The concept is supposed to take account of both supply and demand factors and is therefore different from, and usually greater than, the income elasticity of demand for these manufactures. The concept, however, is based on cross-section analysis of data from DCs and LDCs together and, because of the 'double clustering' tendency in such data, only reflects the great contrast between DCs and LDCs in this respect. There is no single 'pattern of development' that explains the growth of industry in all countries, and individual LDCs have not experienced the rate of industrialization predicted by this model.

The actual rate of industrialization in individual countries has therefore to be analysed in more detail. Some of the factors involved were discussed in Section 10.6(b) above. They involve both demand and supply factors. These factors themselves are influenced by the nature of the foreign trade in manufactures. We now consider this relationship as it was reflected in the post-war experience of different groups of LDCs.

The main problem of the early stages of industrialization in LDCs is that, at their low level of income, the demand for manufactures is small, and because of the low level of efficiency, such demand as exists is met in a free trade regime by imports. Then, one of the ways in which industrialization can be speeded up is through the exports of manufactures. In Table 10.6, we saw that countries with a large per capita output of manufactures were also those which exported a high proportion of this output. In the period 1960–76, exports of manufactures from LDCs expanded rapidly, but most of this growth was confined to a few countries as shown in Table 12.1.

Table 12.1 Growth of LDC exports of manufactures, 1960–76 (average annual percentage growth rates)

Groups of LDCs	Share in total LDC exports, 1960	Growth rate
Countries specializing in exports of manufactures (Taiwan, South Korea, Hong Kong and Singapore)	42.0	17.8
Large semi-industrial LDCs (Brazil, Mexico and Turkey)	4.2	23.6
Countries emerging from primary specialization (Venezuela, Iran, Malaysia, Tunisia, Colombia, Ivory Coast, Morocco, Philippines, Thailand)	8.7	14.4
Large poor LDCs (Egypt, Indonesia and India)	45.1	3.4
Total	100.0	14.3

Source: Classification and growth rates from Chenery and Keesing (1979); export data from World Bank *World Development Report*, 1979.

One reason why a small group of countries achieved rapid growth of exports of manufactures and hence a rapid rate of industrialization is that they had undertaken a faster rate of development and allocated the development measures to the manufacturing export sector to a greater extent than other LDCs. It was also due to improvements in marketing channels, brought about at least in the initial stages by foreign entrepreneurs. At the time this group of countries expanded their exports of manufactures, they were also assisted by a high level and rapid growth of demand in the DCs. By the time other LDCs tried to emulate this experience, the DMEs went into a recession in the 1970s. The DMEs were then concerned to prevent the decline of their own industries, especially those producing labour-intensive products, in the face of competition of imports from LDCs, and therefore increased the levels of their protection against such imports. The reason for this rise in protection for already established industries has been described as the 'senescent industry argument' (Corden, 1974, pp.109–10).

The other way in which LDCs attempted to speed up their industrialization in the post-war period was by a policy of protection. They imposed high levels of import duties and even prohibited the import of some types of manufactures. In addition, they assisted domestic and foreign entrepreneurs to set up new industries by expanding infrastructure serving the industrial sector and by providing capital on special terms. The policy has generally been described as an 'import substitution' strategy, i.e. a strategy of substituting domestic production for imports, but it was also motivated by a desire to substitute one type of imports, namely capital goods, for another, consumer goods, in a situation of static foreign exchange receipts from exports and foreign aid. In fact, many of these countries assisted their industrial producers in importing capital goods by maintaining an overvalued exchange rate.

Such a policy of protection of manufacturing industry had been followed by some of the present-day DCs in the early stages of their industrialization to protect their new industries from the competition of imports from industrially more advanced countries, and this policy played a significant role in their subsequent economic growth. But when followed by the LDCs in the post-war period, these policies have not led to the same result for a number of reasons which we have to consider in some detail.

The theoretical justification of a policy of industrial protection is usually based on the 'infant industry argument'. According to this argument, a new industry set up in an LDC will not be efficient enough to compete with imports from the DCs under free trade. But if it is protected from such imports in its 'infancy', it will eventually become more efficient and then will no longer need the protection. Hence the main emphasis is on the temporary nature of the protection that is justified. Further, according to the Mill–Bastable test (see e.g. Corden, 1974, pp.265–8), protection is only justified in cases where the gain in efficiency is sufficiently great to balance the costs of protecting industry in its infancy.

The problem with this argument is that the growth of efficiency in an industry is not just a matter of the passage of time. For industries to become more efficient requires a number of other conditions both on the supply and the demand side. On the supply side, there must be a general improvement in the level of development, i.e. in such matters as education, infrastructure and institutions. Protection policy was accompanied by such improvements in the present-day DCs to a much greater extent than in the present-day LDCs. On the demand side, the demand for the products of the protected industries must be large enough to support a sufficient number of firms so that their competition will lead to an increase in their 'X-efficiency'. Also, this demand must grow rapidly enough to provide the benefits of dynamic economies of scale. What LDCs in the post-war period attempted to do was to expand their industrial sector on a wide front covering all the industries producing consumer goods which had previously been imported. The result was that the demand for each of them was too small to support many firms and their efficiency did not increase as a result of competition. Further, the products of these industries were mostly consumed by the upper and middle income groups, so that after a short initial phase of rapid expansion, the industrial sector came up against the limits of the home market and went into a severe recession in many countries. For a protectionist policy to be successful in promoting industrialization in the early stages of the development of LDCs, it has to be confined to particular products, especially those with a large and rapidly growing domestic demand, such as those described in Section 10.6(b).

12.3 Trade in Primary Products

In this section we consider the policies that LDCs can follow to deal with the two major problems that have affected their trade in primary products, namely the deteriorating terms of trade and the instability in export prices and earnings. In Section 11.3(b), it was argued that one major reason for the tendency for the terms of trade to move against LDCs was their highly competitive supply of primary products, especially by each country concentrating its research efforts to lower the costs of production of commodities specific to LDCs and by new producing countries entering the market. Therefore, any policy to keep the prices of these commodities at a remunerative level must be coordinated among the producing countries. This is the role of commodity agreements (see, e.g., Kaldor, 1962).

There have been many attempts to negotiate such agreements but they have generally failed. Negotiations for such agreements are usually started during periods of slack demand and low prices, but as soon as demand improves, the enthusiasm for pressing on with these negotiations and the willingness to make compromises wanes. One major problem has been that a number of new countries, especially in Africa, have emerged as major producers of some of the primary products which had been mostly produced by LDCs in Asia and Latin America. The earlier producers have therefore to concede some shares of the market to the newer producers. Under some circumstances, it is possible for a major producer to benefit itself as well as others by a unilateral reduction of supply. This possibility arises when the country's share of the market is sufficiently great. The technical condition is that

$$s > \frac{\epsilon + \eta}{1 + \epsilon}, \tag{12.3.1}$$

where s is the market share of the country, η is the price elasticity of world demand, and ϵ is the price elasticity of supply of the country's competitors.

This condition was satisfied in the case of the Brazilian supply of coffee and therefore the coffee agreement was successful in raising prices for many years. In most cases, however, commodity agreements can only be successful with greater cooperation of producing countries in their own long-term interest. The most successful example of such cooperation so far has been in the case of oil exports by the OPEC countries.

The second major problem of the trade in primary products has been its great instability both in prices and in export earnings of individual countries (Section 11.3(c)). Such inability leads to disruption of the development programmes of LDCs and makes it especially difficult for them to undertake long-term planning. Therefore, it is desirable for them to undertake measures to stabilize this trade. There have been many attempts to do so, mainly by setting up buffer stocks and buffer funds. Such attempts have so far not been very successful. One case where a buffer stock has had some success in stabilizing prices is that of tin, where a number of DCs were also interested. There have been two types of problems involved; one in securing agreement among producer and consumer countries in determining the band within which prices are to be stabilized, and the other in financing such buffer stocks.

In addition, there has been considerable confusion in the theoretical study of buffer stock arrangements. Such arrangements are primarily intended to stabilize prices, but stabilizing prices may adversely affect both the average level and the instability of export earnings. For example, with linear demand and supply functions, price stabilization by a buffer stock will increase total earnings if price instability is due to supply fluctuations and reduce them if they are due to demand fluctuations; in the more general case, the result also depends on the shapes of the demand and supply functions. The effect of price stabilization on the instability of earnings also depends on whether price instability is due to demand or supply fluctuations. Complete price stabilization will stabilize the earnings of producers completely in the case of demand fluctuations while supply is constant. In the case where demand is constant but supply fluctuates, complete price stabilization may reduce or increase the instability in earnings depending on the elasticities of supply and demand; for example, it can be shown that in the case of linear demand and supply functions, complete price stabilization will reduce earnings instability if

$$\eta < \frac{1 - \epsilon}{2}, \tag{12.3.2}$$

where η and ϵ are the price elasticities of demand and supply respectively. But even in the case where this condition is not satisfied, earnings instability can be reduced up to a point by partial as opposed to complete price stabilization (see Newberry and Stiglitz, 1979).

The above results are concerned with buffer stocks held to stabilize prices. In practice, stocks are held by individuals to maximize their profits from the price fluctuations. This is particularly true of traders in DCs which are not importers of some commodities, because they have greater financial resources to finance such stocks; the result may lead to greater price instability. In contrast, traders in producing LDCs are not able to hold such stocks, so that the LDCs suffer both from lower earnings and greater instability. If both producers and consumers hold stocks and operate them to maximize their respective profits, the result will be stable prices. This is the main advantage of an international buffer stock arrangement.

12.4 Balance of Payments

One of the most persistent problems of LDCs in the post-war period has been that they are frequently faced with a shortage of foreign exchange, especially of the currencies of the DCs. On the one hand, their export earnings have not been growing rapidly, particularly if they are mostly derived from primary products, and there has also been great instabilty in these foreign exchange receipts. On the other hand, their need for foreign exchange to pay for imports increases steadily and rapidly, as they try to accelerate the pace of their development and growth. It is partly to meet this problem that many LDCs choose an import-substitution strategy as far as consumer goods are concerned, in order to use more of their limited export earnings for the import of capital goods.

The shortage of foreign exchange has been considered one of the main constraints on growth in the LDCs. In fact, however, it is a reflection of a more deep-seated problem of structural rigidity in their economies. Thus, while the LDCs easily get into imbalances in their international payments, it is difficult for them to get out of these imbalances in a short period. The factors of production of their export products are highly specific and cannot be quickly shifted to other sectors in response to rapidly changing international conditions. Their demand for imports of consumer goods is determined by such long-term forces as their distribution of income. They are also highly dependent on the DCs for their capital goods; once they start on a major programme of investment, they cannot cut it back quickly without serious disruption. It is because their foreign trade transactions are determined by such long-term factors that, while a shortage of foreign exchange is a serious embarrassment for an ongoing investment programme, a sudden surplus of foreign exchange receipts does not necessarily lead to faster growth in the short period. This point is well illustrated by the experience of oil-exporting countries, which acquired such surplus from the rise in oil prices in the 1970s, and of such countries as India, which also have foreign exchange surpluses, namely from the remittances of emigrants to west Asian countries.

There is, therefore, a great difference between DCs and LDCs when it comes to dealing with balance of payments problems. When the International Monetary Fund was established soon after World War II to help countries suffering from such problems, it adopted a set of rules which were mostly suited to the circumstances of the DMEs. First, it laid down that countries should have a single unified exchange rate. Second, it was expected that the exchange rates should normally be pegged. Third, it provided that when countries get into balance of payments deficit, they could borrow from the IMF under a set of conditions. One of these conditions was that, if the deficit was due to a 'fundamental disequilibrium', the country concerned should devalue its currency. Another of these conditions was that the country should adopt fiscal and monetary policies to correct the causes of the disequilibrium in a rather short period. Hence, International Monetary Fund loans were usually given only for such short periods. These rules were framed with the circumstances of DMEs in mind, especially their highly developed fiscal and monetary systems which could deal with their foreign trade problems expeditiously. But when the same rules were applied to the LDCs, they gave rise to a number of problems.

First, there is the question of the appropriate rate of exchange. This is often thought of in terms of the purchasing power parity between the currencies of trading countries. In its absolute form, this is clearly invalid. It has been found that there is a systematic deviation of exchange rates from purchasing parities, much greater than the extent to which the actual exchange rates may differ from their equilibrium values. Further, these deviations increase with the difference in per capita income (see e.g. Kravis *et al.*, 1978). For example, in 1970, when the Indian rupee was considered to be overvalued at an official exchange rate of US $0.133, it is estimated to have had a purchasing power parity with the US dollar of US $0.444.

Such deviations of exchange rates from absolute purchasing power parities are usually explained by the presence of non-traded goods, especially services. If the differences in the productivity of resources are uniform in the production of all goods, then, according to the Heckshen–Ohlin–Samuelson theory, the equalization of the prices of traded goods will equalize the prices of factors in efficiency units and hence also the prices of the non-traded goods and services. Therefore, the exchange rate deviation of the currencies in LDCs has been explained by the argument that the DC–LDC productivity gap is smaller in the case of non-traded goods and services than in the case of traded goods. For example, Kravis *et al.* (1978, pp.127–8) say:

> The argument runs as follows: (1) International competition makes the prices of traded goods equal in all countries, (2) wages in each country's traded goods industries will depend upon the productivity of its labour in those industries, (3) the wages established in each country's traded goods industries will prevail in its non-traded goods industries as well, (4) productivity differentials are smaller in non-traded goods industries than in traded goods industries, (5) it follows that non-traded goods, of which services are a major component, will be relatively cheap in low-income countries. That is, low wages of low-income countries, established by their low productivity in traded goods production, extended to non-traded goods industries in which relatively better productivity produced low prices.

However, this is not the only way that the observed exchange-rate deviations of LDC currencies can be explained. Another possibility is that relative productivities are the same in both traded and non-traded goods industries, but wages are lower in the non-traded goods sector for various institutional reasons affecting the efficiency of factor markets, such as those which lead to the wage differentials between the modern and traditional sectors in the dualistic model of growth. Which explanation is true can only be decided by empirical research. Whatever the explanation, under prevailing conditions, the purchasing power parity theory in its absolute form does not provide any guidance for choosing the appropriate rate of exchange.

The purchasing power parity criterion is more often used in its relative form. Starting from a year in which the exchange rate is assumed to be appropriate, the usual approach is to vary it according to changes in purchasing power parity since the base year, i.e. according to the difference between rates of inflation in the trading countries. This approach also raises the question of choosing the base year in which the exchange rate may be considered appropriate. If any criterion is available to test the appropriateness of the exchange rate in the base year, it can also be applied to the current year as well.

The second major problem with the IMF approach is the insistence on a unified exchange rate. In DMEs, where resources move freely between sectors, such a policy may be useful in guiding the allocation of resources. But in LDCs, there is much less mobility of resources. Then, the internal structure of prices between sectors may be quite different from the external structure, and the two cannot be equated with a single exchange rate. It is for this reason that Kaldor (1964) supported the practice of multiple exchange rates that some LDCs have adopted. He was particularly concerned with promoting the expansion of industries. But the same problem has arisen in another way in some countries, as a result of sudden increases in their foreign exchange from oil exports. Then, the rate of exchange which brings about equilibrium in their balance of payments turns out to discourage exports of other commodities and to reduce incomes and employment in these sectors. This problem has arisen both in LDCs such as Indonesia and in DMEs such as Britain.

The third major problem with the IMF approach relates to the role of devaluation in dealing with balance of payments deficits. The effect of a devaluation on the balance of payments has been studied from various points of view. In the elasticity approach, the emphasis was on the extent to which exports were increased and imports reduced by devaluation as determined by the respective price elasticities of demand; this led to the Marshall–Lerner condition for devaluation to eliminate a balance of payments deficit. (See e.g. Robinson, J., 1949.) In the absorption approach, the emphasis is on the effects of devaluation on the difference between aggregate output and aggregate expenditure, which is taken as the counterpart of a trade deficit. Finally, the monetary approach to the balance of payments focusses attention on the fall in the real value of cash balances below its desired level resulting from a devaluation, which leads to reduced demand for goods and services as real cash balances are restored.

The effects of these factors is that, especially in LDCs, any favourable effect on the balance of payments that may result from a devaluation are usually short-lived. The main reason is that the rise in the prices of traded goods due to the devaluation may cause a general inflation leading to a rise in the prices of non-traded, domestic, goods as well. Then, the actual change in the relative prices of traded and non-traded goods, which Findlay (1973, Chapter 11) has called the 'effective rate of devaluation' will be less than the nominal rate. In course of time, this effective rate becomes smaller and the effects of devaluation on the balance of payments is dissipated. The consequence, as Kaldor (1964, p.187) argues, is:

> the periodic efforts of international authorities such as the IMF to secure an alleviation of the balance of payments problem of particular under-developed countries by the introduction of more 'realistic' exchange rates, however well intentioned, have proved misguided. In most of the cases, devaluation has been followed by a new wave of inflation which has swallowed up the stimulus to exports afforded by the devaluation, within a relatively short period.

Or as Lewis (1977, p.34) points out,

> An economy with weak control over its internal prices is likely to find itself on a treadmill, where devaluation raises domestic money incomes and prices, so setting off further devaluation, *ad infinitum*.

A more useful approach is to recognize that a given target for the balance of payments is only one among several objectives, others being full employment and rapid growth. At the same time, each of these objectives can be influenced by a number of instruments. In order to achieve all these objectives, an equal number of instruments must be used in a coordinated manner. One example that has been intensively studied is the case of using two instruments to secure both internal and external balance at the same time (see, e.g., Caves and Jones, 1973, Chapter 18). This means, on the one hand, that a balance of payments problem cannot be solved only by adjusting the exchange rate. On the other hand, a country's international payments can be balanced by any exchange rate, provided other changes, such as changes in the level or the distribution of incomes, take place.

The coordination of a number of policy instruments to meet several targets is difficult, especially when there is limited information about the levels of key variables and their relationships. Therefore, it would be convenient if each policy instrument could be 'assigned' to a particular objective. Then policy making can be decentralized among a number of specialized agencies, e.g. the exchange rate adjustment could be left to the central bank and the adjustment of government expenditure to the Treasury. For such an assignment to be successful, each instrument must be assigned to the target with respect to which it has a comparative advantage (Mundell, 1962; Turnovsky, 1978, p.211). When the problem is solved in this way, it may turn out that the exchange rate is not necessarily the most efficient instrument to assign to a balance of payments target (Turnovsky, 1978, p.233). There is a further complication. In the case of two instruments and two objectives, it is always possible to assign instruments in a common-sense way, i.e. according to a partial equilibrium analysis, but this is not always possible with more instruments and targets (Patrick, J. D., 1973).

In the past, in providing assistance to countries suffering from balance of payments deficits, the IMF has imposed conditions, such as reduced government spending and domestic credit, in addition to devaluation, in order to solve the balance of payments in a short time. The result has often been a deflation and reduced level of economic activity. In view of the great importance of growth in the LDCs, the conditions imposed should avoid such adverse effects and assistance should be provided over a longer period, in which the borrowing country can deal with the structural problems which led to the deficit in the first place.

12.5 A New International Economic Order

The foregoing analysis has pointed to a number of problems that LDCs face in the present international economic order, such as slow growth in their exports of manufactures to DCs, the declining terms of trade and the instability of their trade in primary products, and their access to financial assistance from such institutions as the IMF. In addition, there are problems that the LDCs face in their dealings with the large transnational corporations. The LDCs have therefore been concerned to bring about a new international economic order.

For a number of the problems arising from the present situation, the solution lies to some extent with the LDCs themselves, in such measures as promoting faster development in each country and greater cooperation among a number of countries. But for the problems discussed in this chapter, a solution also requires the cooperation of the DCs as well. For example, increasing the LDC export of manufactures requires lower protection in the DCs; improving the prices of primary products exported by LDCs requires the participation of DCs in commodity agreements; a more helpful stance of the international financial agencies requires the assent of the delegates of DCs who hold a majority vote in these institutions; and the regulation of the activities of transnational corporations require the support of DC governments.

It is to secure this cooperation that there have been a series of international meetings, known as the North–South dialogue. There is, however, little sign that these meetings are approaching any consensus of views or agreement as to practical actions. One reason may simply be that the DCs do not see any advantage for themselves in the proposed reforms and are unwilling to sacrifice what they perceive to be their own interests in the present international economic order. But another possible reason is that the DCs approach these issues with a theoretical framework which is inappropriate for dealing with them and which does not reflect the ways in which change in the present system can promote the growth and development of the LDCs. As Helleiner (1981, pp.541–2) argues:

> The 'theory' which lies behind dominant Northern approaches to North–South economic disputes is that of orthodox neoclassical economics. Although the modern literature of economics is rich in adaptations and elaborations of the core of the neoclassical 'paradigm', many of which attempt to bring it into closer touch with reality, it is its 'core' which exercises dominant influence. That core is based upon the assumption of individual, rational and well-informed actors interacting upon competitive markets in pursuit of their own self-interest . . . Approaching economic problems from a theoretical core of this character accustoms the analyst to treating important elements of reality as mere 'wrinkles' in the 'general case'.

To the extent that international negotiations depend on theoretical considerations, progress in the North–South dialogue towards a new international economic order will depend on a deeper analysis and a wider understanding of the problems of development of LDCs and of the economic relationship between them and the DCs.

In most elementary expositions of international trade theory, it is assumed that a country's comparative advantages are fixed and immutable; this assumption then leads to the policy conclusion in favour of free trade. In more advanced studies, it is recognized that comparative advantages may change over time but they are assumed to be the result of changes in national factor endowments, such as the accumulation of capital (see e.g. Stiglitz, 1970; Findlay, 1970); the policy conclusion of these studies is also in favour of free trade. We saw above how Harrod considered the case where changes in comparative advantages depend on how resources are allocated to various sectors but because of his *a priori* assumption that each country's comparative advantage in the future will continue to lie in the same sectors as in the past, he draws the policy conclusion that past patterns of trade should continue in the future. In the case of LDCs this means that the traditional form of exchange in which they specialize in primary products and depend on imports of manufactures from the DCs should continue. The underlying assumption about the likely changes in comparative advantage is, of course, pure speculation, as Harrod admits. It seriously underestimates the extent to which an LDC's comparative advantages are fossilized by such specialization and the extent to which it can improve its comparative advantage in manufactures by temporarily departing from the free trade pattern of specialization, with longer-run benefits in its growth prospects.

CHAPTER 13

Distribution of Income: Analysis

In previous chapters, we were mainly concerned with the level, sectoral composition and growth of aggregate national income or product of countries, and the factors influencing these variables. But if we are interested in the standard of living of the mass of the population, we must also consider how total income is distributed among persons and households. In most elementary expositions, the analysis of income distribution is divorced from that of aggregate income, and carried out in terms of quite distinct factors, often of a political nature. However, there is a close interaction between the growth of total income and its distribution; the growth of income influences, and is also influenced by, its distribution, and these interactions are influenced by various development factors. Therefore the distribution of income must be given a central place in development economics. The present chapter is devoted to the analysis of income distribution, especially at a low level of development, while some policy aspects are discussed in the next chapter. In the present chapter, we first summarize the available statistical data in Section 13.1 and review the main conclusions of the literature in Section 13.2. These conclusions are mostly derived from historical generalizations and statistical patterns, with little theoretical analysis. Therefore, some theoretical suggestions are offered in Sections 13.3 to 13.5. These sections deal with the effects of growth on distribution. In the final section, we consider how the distribution of income in turn affects economic growth.

13.1 Some Statistical Data

In trying to understand the forces influencing income distribution in a country, we shall be particularly concerned with the ways these forces operate through economic factors, interpreted broadly to include the institutional conditions in an economy. For this purpose, the most useful data are the incomes of people in various economic categories; such categories include groups divided according to their ownership of property—industrial capital or agricultural land; people whose incomes are mainly in the form of wages, such as landless labourers in agriculture, divided according to conditions of employment; and people using different techniques of production. Unfortunately, there is little detailed information available about the incomes of such categories. (For rough estimates of average incomes in some of these categories in an LDC, see I.L.O. 1972, Table 25, p.74.) Most often, the available data only show the distribution of income among groups classified according to their incomes, and a few demographic, industrial and occupational categories.

There are many serious problems in comparing the data on income distribution from different countries or even different surveys in the same country. In some cases, the data refer to the distribution among individuals or income earners; in others, they show the distribution among households. As household sizes usually vary considerably between income classes, the two types of distributions are not comparable. Households are sometimes classified according to their total incomes and sometimes according to their per capita incomes. The concept of income itself is not well defined, especially in LDCs, where much economic activity is undertaken on a subsistence basis; therefore, in some cases, the data show the distribution of consumption expenditures rather than incomes. In most cases, the data refer to incomes or expenditures in a relatively short period, such as a few months or a year, during which the survey was conducted.

The data on income distribution from different countries can only be compared subject to these differences in methods of collection. Some recent data compiled by the World Bank (Jain, 1975) are summarized in Table 13.1 for DCs and LDCs. It is generally assumed that the distribution of income varies systematically with the average income level of countries. One such pattern is shown in Table 13.2.

The distribution of income described by these tables is usually summarized by calculating a measure of inequality from them. There are many measures of inequality that can be calculated (see Kakwani, 1979). One of the most convenient is the Gini-index, which is related to the relative mean difference of statistical distributions. It varies from 0 in the case of complete equality to 1 when all income is received by one person, a case which might be considered as one of maximum inequality. It has a particularly simple geometrical interpretation. From data of the type given in tables 13.1 and 13.2, we can draw a curve, known as the Lorenz curve, showing the relationship between the cumulative relative frequency of persons with incomes below various levels, and the cumulative relative amounts of the incomes accruing to them.

Table 13.1 Distribution of income by decile groups (percentage of total income)

		LDCs			
Decile	DMEs	Total (a)	Africa & Middle East	Latin America	Asia
		(a) Households			
0–10	2.1	1.7	1.4	1.3	2.5
10–20	3.9	2.8	2.2	2.4	3.8
20–30	4.9	3.7	3.2	3.2	4.6
30–40	6.0	4.6	4.0	4.3	5.6
40–50	7.2	5.7	5.1	5.3	6.6
50–60	8.5	7.0	6.5	6.7	7.9
60–70	10.2	8.8	8.4	8.6	9.5
70–80	12.5	11.4	11.0	11.4	11.8
80–90	16.0	15.9	15.7	16.4	15.5
90–95	10.4	11.4	11.6	12.2	10.5
95–100	18.3	27.0	30.9	28.3	21.7
Total	100.0	100.0	100.0	100.0	100.0
Gini-coefficients	0.382	0.490	0.539	0.522	0.410
		(b) Income Recipients			
0–10	1.8	2.2	1.9	1.3	3.5
10–20	3.6	3.4	2.6	2.7	4.8
20–30	4.8	4.2	3.3	3.7	5.5
30–40	5.9	5.0	4.0	4.6	6.3
40–50	7.0	6.0	5.0	5.8	7.2
50–60	8.4	7.1	6.2	7.1	8.1
60–70	10.0	8.7	7.7	8.8	9.5
70–80	12.3	10.8	10.1	11.3	11.1
80–90	16.0	14.6	14.3	15.6	13.9
90–95	10.6	10.1	10.4	11.0	8.9
95–100	19.6	27.9	34.5	28.1	21.2
Total	100.0	100.0	100.0	100.0	100.0
Gini-coefficients	0.401	0.468	0.545	0.502	0.357

Source: Jain, 1975 (a) The figures in each region are weighted averages, but that for all LDCs is the simple average of those for the three regions.

The Gini-index is then just twice the area between such a curve and the diagonal. The index also has a simple economic interpretation; it is the proportion of total income that must be transferred from the rich to the poor to make all incomes equal, when each transfer is weighted by the number of persons across whom it is made.

The Gini-index of inequality for various groups of countries was shown in Table 13.1. Table 13.3 shows how this index varies with per capita income in the cross-section of countries.

Table 13.2 Distribution of income of countries according to per capita income, c 1965

Per capita GDP (US $)	Number of countries	Decile groups: 0–20	20–40	40–60	60–80	80–95	95–100	Total
Below 100	9	7.0	10.0	13.1	15.4	21.4	29.1	100.0
101–200	8	5.3	8.6	12.0	17.5	31.6	24.9	100.0
201–300	11	4.8	8.0	11.3	18.1	25.7	32.0	100.0
301–500	9	4.5	7.9	12.3	18.0	27.4	30.0	100.0
501–1000	6	5.1	8.9	13.9	22.1	24.7	25.4	100.0
1001–2000	10	4.7	10.5	15.9	22.2	25.7	20.9	100.0
2000 & over	3	5.0	10.9	17.9	24.1	26.3	16.4	100.0

Source: Paukert (1973)

Table 13.3 Gini-index of countries by per capita income

Per capita income (US $)	Average value of Gini-index
Below 150	0.441
150–299	0.472
300–499	0.493
500–999	0.479
1000–2499	0.384
2500 & over	0.380

Source: Jain, 1975

This table shows a tendency for income inequality to increase with per capita income up to a point and to decline thereafter, i.e. an inverted U-shaped pattern in the relation between income inequality and per capita income. Countries in the middle-income ranges are usually the LDCs in which incomes are rising rapidly compared with those in the low or the high income ranges; the data therefore suggest that high levels of inequality are particularly associated with a state of rapid transition. Kuznets (1966) has suggested that the U-shaped pattern may also have occurred in the historical experience of many DCs over time.

The distribution of income of a country cannot be adequately summarized by a single figure, such as an index of inequality. Two countries may have the same Gini-index but their income distributions may be very different. For this to occur, their Lorenz curves must intersect. Therefore, we must consider the shapes of their Lorenz curves as well. A convenient measure of this aspect of income distribution is the skewness of the Lorenz curve (see Kakwani, 1979, Chapter 17); a positive skewness indicates a large share of total income accruing to the middle income groups and a negative skewness indicates a low share of these groups. There is a great difference in the skewness of Lorenz curves between DCs and LDCs; Kakwani (1979, p.385) found that a sample of

33 LDCs, with only one exception, had negatively skew Lorenz curves, while a sample of 17 DCs, with only two exceptions, had positively skew Lorenz curves.

We next consider the extent of poverty in LDCs. The most convenient measure of the extent of poverty is the proportion of the population living below a specified poverty line. There are two ways of defining the poverty line. In DMEs, it generally refers to the line dividing off about 10 to 15 per cent of the population at the bottom of the income scale, who are poor because they are somehow left out of the normal functioning of the economic system. Such people include the handicapped, the aged and the unemployed. The poverty line defined in this way is a relative concept and varies among these countries and over time according to their per capita income; the extent of poverty is thus a reflection of income distribution rather than of the average income of countries. In LDCs, however, the concept of the poverty line is usually defined in absolute terms, for example, as the income level just sufficient to purchase the minimum requirements of nutrition, clothing and shelter. The extent of poverty based on such a poverty line then varies inversely with the average income of countries and directly with the inequality of distribution. Some idea of the rate at which the extent of poverty varies with average incomes and with inequality of distribution is given in Table 13.4; in this table, the poverty line is taken as a *per capita* income level of US $80 which corresponds to the 40th percentile income of India in 1975. The table summarizes the data of 36 LDCs.

Table 13.4 Percentage of population with per capita income below US $80: 36 LDCs — 1975

Classification of countries	Extent of poverty (%)
(A) Per Capita Income: US $	
Below 150	45
150–299	19
300–499	11
500 and over	5
(B) Gini-index of Inequality	
Below 0.4	7
0.41–0.50	23
0.51–0.56	18
0.57 and over	33

Source: Ahluwalia *et al.*, 1978, Table 1, p.7 and Appendix Table 1, p.38

Poverty may also be interpreted in terms of malnutrition; for example, as the proportion of people below 1.2 times the basic metabolic rate; by this test, about a quarter of the population of LDCs are undernourished (see United Nations, *World Population Trends and Policies*, 1979).

The above data have been mainly concerned with a static aspect of income inequality based on the distribution of income at a point of time. It is this aspect which economists have focussed on. Sociologists, on the other hand, have been more interested in the dynamic aspect, particularly in the way individuals are able to change their relative economic position depending on their social mobility. The distribution of income can be compared to the positions of individuals on a ladder; the static 'snapshot' picture of inequality given, for example, by a Lorenz curve, corresponds to the steepness of the ladder and the number of individuals standing at various heights. The dynamic aspect refers to the movement of people up and down the ladder. The dynamic aspect is also important, especially from a political point of view. This is because a highly unequal distribution of income at a point in time, i.e. a steep ladder, may be more easily tolerated and may even be preferred if it is combined with a high degree of social mobility, which offers individuals at the bottom of the ladder a better chance of moving up. Thus, for example, static inequality is greater in the United States than in Great Britain, but it is often claimed that this is compensated by greater social mobility in the United States. Unfortunately, there is little information on this aspect of inequality in LDCs. A recent discussion of the dynamic aspects of income inequalities is given in Adelman and Whittle (1979).

13.2 Factors Affecting Income Distribution

Theories concerning income distribution were at the heart of classical economics; as Ricardo (1952, Vol. VIII, pp.277–8) claimed in a well-known statement,

> Political economy . . . should rather be called an enquiry into the laws which determine the division of the produce of industry among the classes who concur in its formation.

Marx's economic analysis was also deeply concerned with the distribution of income. But theoretical interest in distributional questions dwindled with the rise of neo-classical economics, which was primarily interested in the allocation of resources and the level and growth of total national income. Most studies of distribution were mainly concerned with deriving statistical relationships rather than with theoretical analysis. In the case of DMEs, one result of such studies was the attempt to find a fairly standard pattern of income distribution, such as that given by Pareto's law, i.e. a pattern in which the logarithm of the cumulative percentage of the population above a certain income level is a linear function of the logarithm of that income. Another result was Kuznet's historical generalization of an inverted U-shaped relationship between inequality and income over time, referred to above.

A number of such statistical studies of income distribution in LDCs have been made in recent years. The usual approach in these studies is to use regression analysis of international cross-section data to identify the national characteristics which are associated with various degrees of income inequality. An example of this approach is that of Ahluwalia (1976). He found that the cross-section pattern also showed an inverted U-shaped relationship between inequality and per capita income, but no evidence that faster growth led to higher inequality. He also found that inequality was positively correlated with the non-agricultural share of production and the educational level of the population and negatively correlated with the rate of growth of population; he concluded that

> the operation of these processes appears to explain some of the improvement in income distribution observed in the later stages of development, but they do not serve to explain the marked deterioration in the earlier stages.

Using a rather different approach also based on cross-section data, Adelman and Morris (1971a, 1973) found a number of national characteristics associated with inequality. For example, the higher the school enrolments, the smaller the inequality and the larger the income shares of the lower and middle income groups; the greater the national resource endowment of countries, the greater the inequality and the larger the income shares of the top five per cent; the greater the government's share in total investment, the lower the income share of the top groups; the greater the degree of economic dualism, the greater the inequality; and the greater the opportunities for political participation, the lower the inequality. On the basis of this analysis, they conclude that,

> once a sharply dualistic development pattern has been initiated, further economic growth actually *reduces* the share of the lowest 60 per cent. Faster growth, when accompanied by improvements in economic institutions, tends to redistribute income away from the two extremes of the income distribution towards the families in the 60–95 per cent income brackets. The more dynamic the economy, and the more malleable its institutions, the larger is the share of the middle income groups. However, the more rapid economic growth also increases the proportion of income accruing to the upper 20 per cent, even though it decreases the share of income of the upper 5 per cent. The effect of economic growth in the share of the lowest 20 per cent is not very systematic, but there is an indication that better growth performance tends to lower the share of the poorest households. (Adelman and Morris, 1971a, p.37)

The statistical methods used to derive these conclusions are somewhat unorthodox and have been sharply criticized by Little (1976).

These studies have been mainly concerned to identify the factors influencing the level of inequality at a point of time in a cross-section of countries, especially the level and growth of income. But the level and growth of income are not at all related to changes in income inequality over time, about which data are available for a smaller number of countries. Such data are shown for 16 LDCs in Table 13.5. These countries appear to be about equally divided between those in which inequality increased and those in which it declined. There is no difference between the relatively rich (with per capita income over

Table 13.5 Changes in income inequality: selected LDCs

Country (type of distribution)	Year	Gini-Index	Per capita income 1969: US $	Annual growth rate of GDP (%)
India (Hb)	1960	0.473	100	4.5
	1967/8	0.478		
Sri Lanka (Hb)	1963	0.450	100	5.0
	1973	0.350		
Pakistan (Hb)	1963/4	0.387	100	4.7
	1970/1	0.330		
Indonesia (Pc)	1970	0.346	100	8.3
	1976	0.346		
Thailand (Hb)	1962/3	0.410	170	4.8
	1968/9	0.470		
Philippines (Hb)	1961	0.513	230	5.4
	1971	0.494		
South Korea (Hb)	1966	0.342	230	9.3
	1971	0.360		
Taiwan (Hb)	1966	0.330	310	6.8
	1974	0.300		
West Malaysia (Hb)	1957/8	0.436	320	9.4
	1970	0.518		
Colombia (IR)	1960	0.525	350	6.2
	1970	0.562		
Brazil (IR)	1960	0.590	350	6.9
	1970	0.647		
Peru (EAP)	1961	0.612	480	5.4
	1970/71	0.594		
Costa Rica (Hb)	1961	0.521	510	6.8
	1971	0.445		
Mexico (Hb)	1963	0.555	640	7.6
	1969	0.583		
Hong Kong (Hb)	1966	0.490	750	9.3
	1971	0.410		
Singapore (IR)	1966	0.480	840	9.3
	1973	0.460		

Source: For Gini-Index, Jain, 1975; Sundrum, 1979.
For per capita income and growth rates Chenery *et al.*, 1974; U.N., *Yearbook of National Accounts Statistics* (various years)

Notes: Hb = households; Pc = per capita income; IR = income-recipients; EAP = economically active population

US $310) and the relatively poor; inequality seems to have increased in half the number of countries in each group and declined in the other half. Also, when the sample is divided into a fast-growing (with growth rate 6 per cent and over) and a slow-growing group, each group is again divided about equally between those in which inequality increased and those in which it declined.

The main weakness of cross-section studies of the factors affecting income distribution is that they assume that all countries are following the same path, whereas in fact there are many differences among countries. To avoid this problem, an alternative approach may be used to estimate the effect of various factors on inequality, using data from different sub-groups of the population within individual countries. In this approach, the overall inequality in a country is decomposed into two parts. The population is divided into groups according to a particular variable; then the inequality between groups is a measure of the inequality due to that variable, which may then be compared with the inequality within groups, as a measure of the effect of all factors other than that variable. The more significant the effect of a variable on inequality, the greater will be the between-group component of inequality compared with the within-group inequality, when the groups are classified according to that variable. Table 13.6 shows the between-group and within-group components of the Gini-index for certain variables in a few countries for which recent data are available.

Table 13.6 Decomposition of Gini-Index of inequality

Variable/country	Between group	Within group	Total
1. *Age*			
Philippines (1971)	0.089	0.479	0.483
Thailand (urban, 1968–9)	0.042	0.414	0.422
Thailand (rural, 1968–9)	0.042	0.466	0.471
USA (1970)	0.110	0.359	0.364
2. *Household Size*			
Indonesia 1964–5	0.065	0.350	0.403
Indonesia (8 cities, 1968–73)	0.073	0.326	0.362
Thailand (urban, 1968–9)	0.055	0.397	0.422
Thailand (rural, 1968–9)	0.040	0.485	0.471
Philippines (1971)	0.132	0.466	0.484
USA (1970)	0.228	0.357	0.364
3. *Education*			
Philippines (1971)	0.232	0.477	0.483
Indonesia (8 cities)	0.223	0.446	0.503
USA (1971)	0.154	0.214	0.364
4. *Sources of Income*			
Philippines (1971)	0.301	0.437	0.498

Sources: USA: Bureau of Census, 1973; Philippines, Bureau of Census and Statistics, 1973; Thailand, National Statistical Office, 1969; Indonesia, Central Bureau of Statistics, 1964–65, 1968–73.

An individual's income varies with his age, increasing up to a point and declining thereafter in his retirement. Hence, even if all persons had the same life-time patterns of earnings, i.e. if there were no inequality in life-time incomes, there would be a certain amount of inequality among individuals in their annual incomes in a given year because of differences in their ages. The US data give incomes of individual earners by age and these show that a considerable part of overall inequality is due to age differences. Data for LDCs only show household data by age of heads of households; these data show much smaller inequality due to age compared with other factors. Although the data are not strictly comparable, the substantial difference suggests that inequality due to age differences is much smaller in these LDCs than in DCs.

When considering the distribution of household incomes, part of the inequality is due to the variation in household sizes and would remain even if every member of the population had the same income; the extent of this inequality is shown in Table 13.6 by the between-group component when households are classified by size. In a DC like the United States, the component due to differences in household size is large. But in LDCs, this component is reduced by the fact that households with larger average incomes are also the larger households.

The component due to education is much more significant in LDCs than in DCs, partly because of the inequality of educational opportunities in LDCs and partly because of the greater income differentials between educational classes. Data about different sources of income, such as wages, profits and rents, are available only from the Philippines; the inequality between incomes from different sources is found to be very high.

One of the most characteristic features of LDCs is the income disparity between the urban and rural sectors, or between the agricultural and non-agricultural sectors. Even allowing for a difference in the cost of living of as much as 50 per cent, the disparity in sectoral incomes is considerable in most LDCs, as shown in Table 13.7. Generally, the inequality in the urban and non-agricultural sector is higher than in the rural and agricultural sectors. But there is also quite a high inequality even within the rural areas.

It is sometimes argued that economic growth in LDCs in the post-war period has not only worsened income distribution but also that the absolute incomes of the lower income groups have declined. For example, Adelman and Morris (1973, p.192) say

> the frightening implication of the present work is that hundreds of millions of desperately poor people throughout the world have been hurt rather than helped by economic development.

Also, Chenery *et al.* (1974, p.xii) say,

> It is now clear that more than a decade of rapid growth in underdeveloped countries has been of little or no benefit to perhaps a third of their population.

Such conclusions are misleading mainly because they are derived from cross-sectional analyses; while many LDCs have had rapid growth, most of the people who have not benefitted are in the large LDCs like India, which have experienced little growth, a point which has been stressed by Little (1976) in his critique of both these works.

Table 13.7 Inequality within and between sectors

Country (Year)	Relative disparity	Gini-coefficient National	Urban	Rural
Bangladesh (66/7:a/c)	0.486	0.342	0.399	0.334
Brazil (70:c)	1.045	0.641	0.596	0.578
Colombia (70:b)	0.730	0.562	0.552	0.476
Costa Rica (71:f)	0.730	0.445	0.418	0.367
Honduras (67/8:f)	1.415	0.619	0.501	0.486
India (67/8:f)	0.329	0.478	0.465	0.477
Indonesia (69/70:e)	0.398	0.347	0.332	0.347
South Korea (71:f)	0.565	0.360	0.338	0.310
Malaysia (70:f)	0.863	0.518	0.508	0.476
Malaysia (70:b)	0.683	0.513	0.521	0.473
Philippines (71:f)	0.815	0.494	0.458	0.466
Philippines (71:a)	0.522	0.494	0.474	0.470
Philippines (71:e)	0.745	0.323	0.316	0.254
Sri Lanka (69/70:f)	0.655	0.377	0.410	0.352
Sri Lanka (73:b)	0.323	0.309	0.399	0.373
Taiwan (72:a)	0.194	0.284	0.274	0.294
Thailand (68/9:f)	1.577	0.432	0.329	0.388
Tunisia (61:d)	0.810	0.509	0.444	0.460
Uganda (70:a)	0.478	0.401	0.398	0.266

Sources: Jain, 1975. (a) for agricultural and non-agricultural sectors; (b) for income recipients; (c) for economically active population; (d) per capita income; (e) expenditures; (f) households.

Note: Relative disparity refers to the difference between urban and rural incomes as a ratio of the national average.

In contrast, Ahluwalia (1976) concluded that

> The cross section results do not support the stronger hypothesis that the deterioration in relative inequality reflects a prolonged absolute impoverishment of large sections of the population in the course of development.

In fact, even in countries where income inequality has increased and the income *share* of the lower deciles has declined, there has been some improvement in the income level of the poor. This is illustrated by the case of urban Java in the period 1970–76, where evidence from household expenditure surveys suggests that, although inequalities increased sharply in the six-year period, all decile groups experienced some improvement in income (Sundrum, 1977). In Table 13.8 the changes which took place in urban Java are compared with those in Taiwan, where income inequality declined.

It is clear that, first, the overall income growth rate was higher in Taiwan than in urban Java, and second, that the poorest deciles benefitted more than the richest ones from this growth.

The experience of urban Java in the period 1970–76 is similar to that of Brazil during the decade of rapid growth in the 1960s. Fields (1977, p.579) concludes:

At minimum the widely held notion that 'the richest got rich at the expense of the poor' receives no support in the data examined here. To the contrary, the poor in Brazil clearly *did* share in a decade of economic development. Some poor were lifted out of poverty. For those left behind, their incomes grew at least as rapidly as those in the non-poor. At the same time, the very rich also got richer than before, in both absolute and relative terms.

In contrast to the rapidly growing economies such as Indonesia and Brazil, the experience of India was that the incidence of rural poverty 'cannot be characterised as showing either a trend increase or decrease' in the period 1956–57 to 1973–74. Ahluwalia *et al.* (1979, p.39) says:

What we observe is a pattern of fluctuation, with the incidence of poverty falling in periods of good agricultural performance and rising in periods of poor performance. This is precisely what one would expect given the importance of weather-induced variations in Indian agriculture, and the lack of any strong growth trend.

Table 13.8 Percentage increases of income by income deciles

Deciles	Urban Java 1970–76	Taiwan 1964–72
Poorest 10%	22	109
10–20%	22	98
20–30%	30	91
30–40%	26	87
40–50%	28	83
50–60%	30	83
60–70%	36	81
70–80%	45	78
80–90%	55	71
Richest 10%	81	53
Total	49	88

Sources: Sundrum, 1977: Fields, 1977

It has generally been argued that the close relationship between income level and inequality found by Kuznets in the historical experience of the DCs also applied to LDCs. Although Oshima's study of the post-war experience of Asian countries did not produce results consistent with the Kuznets results (Oshima, 1970, p.29ff), Ahluwalia argues on the basis of a cross-sectional study of countries that 'there is some confirmation of the hypothesis that income inequality first increases and then decreases with development' (Ahluwalia, 1974, p.17). Such a relationship has even been used to project changes in income distribution in the future (e.g. World Bank, 1978, p.33) and thus to derive the conclusion that even under optimistic assumptions 'elimination of absolute poverty in the low income countries by the end of the century seems impossible' (World Bank, 1978, p.33).

But the data reviewed above show that there is no simple relationship between income levels and inequality or between growth of income and changes in inequality. Apart from the level of income, there are many other economic, institutional and historical factors which influence the nature of income distribution. Some of these factors are amenable to policy influences so that what happens in the future depends to some extent at least on the nature of the policies followed by individual countries.

This point has been well made by Ranis in his note on Taiwan in Chenery *et al.* (1974, pp.285–90). According to Ranis, Taiwan may constitute an exception to the 'prevailing U-shaped relationship between growth and distribution over time.' He says (p.285) that the Taiwanese experience

> thus points to the possibility that there may be no necessary conflict in other countries, even in the short-term, between growth and income distribution. The generally observed U-shaped relationship must be viewed as not inevitable in nature but subject to control by man.

In this section, we have reviewed some studies which have sought to identify the factors affecting income distribution mainly by statistical methods, especially the association of income inequality with the level and growth of income. These studies are mostly of the 'measurement without theory' type. What is needed for a deeper understanding is a set of theoretical models applicable to differing conditions prevailing especially in LDCs. Some useful models are discussed in the following sections.

13.3 The Traditional Society

Income distribution in traditional societies is largely determined by non-economic factors, which have been intensively studied by sociologists and anthropologists. This does not mean that incomes are equally distributed in these societies; in fact, there may be great inequality. The main feature of the distribution of incomes in traditional society is that it depends greatly on the social hierarchy and the division of society into rigid social classes. This means that there is little social mobility to allow individuals to improve their relative economic position over time. Persons born in particular classes have a limited range of occupations they can enter. In each occupation, earnings are determined by social custom and traditional practice. There are very limited opportunities for individuals to learn new skills and move to different occupations. At the same time, there is a much greater provision for collective ownership and use of some resources. For example, a part of the village land is traditionally left for grazing by cattle belonging to all members of the village. Individuals enjoying any piece of good fortune tend to share it with all members of society in lavish feasts. There is much labour provided on the basis of exchange between households. A particularly widespread practice is to give all members of a village the right to share in the harvest work, the wages of the group being traditionally fixed at a specified fraction of the output. Also there are rules to provide for the poorest members of society, so that no one is allowed to become destitute. This aspect of traditional society has been described as 'shared poverty' by Geertz (1963). Many such traditional influences on income distribution have survived in LDCs in various degrees and some aspects of the distribution of income in these countries can only be explained in terms of these influences.

13.4 The Classical Determinants

In the course of time, traditional systems governing economic transactions break down, giving way to more impersonal transactions made through markets. Commercialization has in all countries led to economic growth. In some countries, especially DCs, it also led in course of time to a reduction in economic inequality. But the same process currently occurring in some LDCs increases inequality. This is because of the breakdown of the traditional safeguards against destitution.

In the commercialized economy, the prices of goods and of factors are determined by market forces. The incomes of individuals depend on their ownership of productive resources and the prices these resources fetch in the market place, so that the distribution of income is a by-product of production. This system was intensively studied by the classical economists; therefore these influences on income distribution may be called the classical determinants. The classical economists identified ownership of the factors of production with distinct social classes, such as workers, landlords and capitalists. They also evolved theories showing the 'natural' levels of the prices of factors of production as a result of long-term forces. Hence they were able to apply their theory of the functional distribution of income to explain the distribution of income among social classes. This model may not be appropriate to explain income distribution in the DCs. As Johnson, H. G. (1964, p.177; also 1973, Chapter 17) argued, the classical distinctions between the factors of production has worn threadbare as the stock of capital has increased and become greatly mixed up with other factors of production, so that 'the time has come to sever the link with the classical attempt to identify categories of income with the distinctively different kinds of productive factors.' He therefore proposed a generalized capital approach to the theory of distribution in the DCs. In the LDCs, however, the stock of capital is still very low and the distinction among the various factors of production is still important as a significant influence on income distribution. Most people in LDCs own only their untrained labour and earn low incomes because wages are low. Most of the land is owned by a minority who earn high incomes from the rents of their properties.

The classical economists also had a dynamic theory of changes in income distribution over time, but this theory did not take full account of the effects of the accumulation of fixed capital. In order to include these effects as well, the classical theory has been modified by Butt (1974). His model helps to trace out a number of possibilities for changes in income distribution over time resulting from population growth and capital accumulation; a brief summary follows here.

The rate of population growth increases with per capita income up to a point and declines thereafter, in accordance with the demographic transition theory. Per capita income (y) increases so long as the rate of capital accumulation (R_C) exceeds that of population growth (R_L). Under the same condition, the rate of profit declines until it becomes zero, as explained in his theory of the mechanization process (Section 9.6). One possibility is illustrated in Figure 13.1. In this case, to start with there is no capital but abundant land; hence there are no profit or rent incomes. Inequality is small, being due only to differences in effort and family size. As capital accumulates, profit incomes accrue to the relatively few who own capital and introduces a major source of inequality. The pattern is illustrated in Figure 13.2; in this figure, the curves represent the average

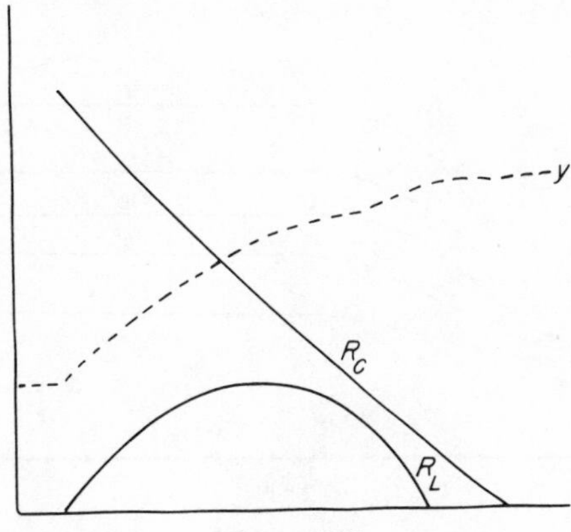

Figure 13.1

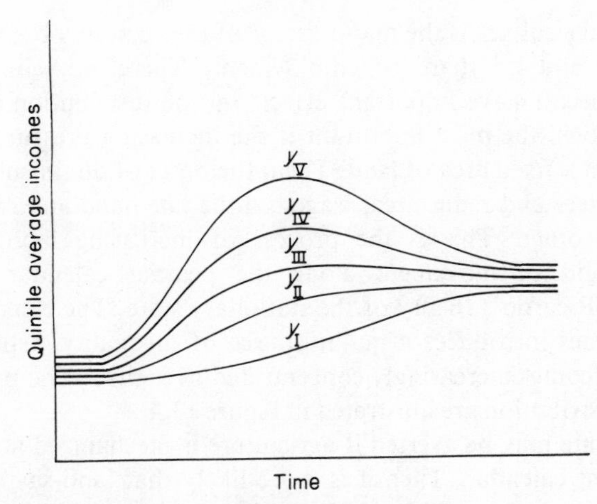

Figure 13.2

incomes of various income classes. Eventually the rate of profit falls faster than the accumulation of capital and profit incomes decline. Finally, when profit incomes disappear with the 'euthanasia of the rentier' inequalities fall back to their original level. This pattern then leads to an inverted U-shaped relationship between income and inequality, such as that observed in the historical experience of DMEs.

It is, however, possible that the process is interrupted if at any time the rate of capital accumulation becomes equal to that of population growth, and the economy get stuck in a 'spreading stationary state', and from that point onwards, per capita income remains constant and the pattern of income distribution is as illustrated in Figure 13.3. This may explain the relative stability of highly unequal income distributions in some LDCs.

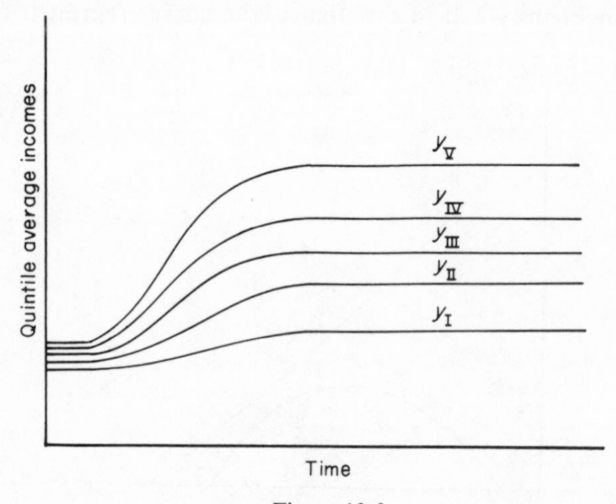

Figure 13.3

In LDCs, agriculture is the major sector of the economy both in its share of total output and its share of employment. Therefore, conditions in the agricultural sector have important effects on the distribution of income. Of these conditions, the most important is the increasing pressure of a growing population on a fixed area of land. Then, the onset of diminishing returns will raise food prices and reduce real wages on the one hand and raise the rent of land on the other. This is the process of increasing labour-intensity of cultivation and of movement along the peasant calendar (Section 9.6) envisaged in Ricardo's theory of the stationary state. The emergence and rise of rent incomes introduces a major source of inequality, especially as land ownership becomes increasingly concentrated over time. The probable effects on income distribution are illustrated in Figure 13.4.

This outcome may be averted if agriculture is mechanized at an early stage of the peasant calendar. Then it is more likely that land-saving mechanized farming techniques in which capital substitutes for land will be profitable and

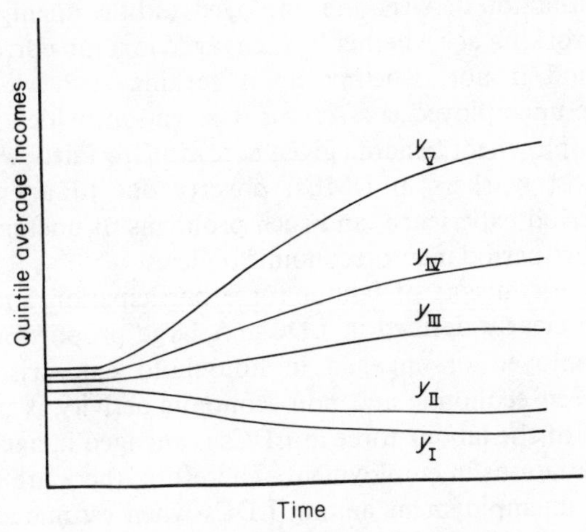

Figure 13.4

the introduction of such techniques will act as a brake on the growing scarcity of land and the rise of rent incomes. This is what happened in some DCs, most notably Japan, but has not happened to a great extent in the LDCs.

This model is very useful in highlighting the effects of population growth and capital accumulation on the distribution of income through changing factor prices. As far as these effects operate, the difference in income distribution between DCs and LDCs can be explained in terms of the different stages they have reached in the dynamic process analysed by Butt. This, however, is useful only as a first approximation. For a more complete analysis, we must consider some other aspects as well. One of the most important in LDCs is the relation between income distribution and the degree of employment of labour, discussed in the following section.

13.5 Poverty and Unemployment

The above analysis assumes the full employment of resources, especially labour. In LDCs, especially the more densely populated ones, there is a great deal of unemployment and underemployment of labour. One reason for such widespread underemployment is population pressure, arising from the rapid growth of population and the labour force in the post-war period. A second reason is that the proportions in which factors can be combined in production are very rigid in the techniques available in the LDCs (see Section 10.4). Finally, it is due to the inefficient functioning of the labour market (see Section 8.4(b)).

Such underemployment of labour has been considered the main cause of poverty in LDCs. This is true to a great extent but the relationship between the two problems must be considered carefully. In DMEs, there is a fairly clear concept of the type of work a person is qualified to do, so that it is possible to make a clear distinction between the employed and the unemployed by asking each person of working age whether he is engaged in a job corresponding to his qualifications and if not, whether he is seeking such work. On such a definition, to be unemployed is a serious deprivation, which is only partially relieved by unemployment benefits given according to fairly well-defined legal criteria. For most workers in DMEs, poverty due to unemployment is a relative short-period experience, and such problems of unemployment can be dealt with by short-period macro-economic policies.

In contrast, the concepts of labour force participation and of unemployment are not so clearly defined in LDCs. A large proportion of the labour force is self-employed or engaged in household enterprises, so that the distinction between economic and non-economic activity is blurred. Also, a large proportion of the labour force in LDCs is engaged in agriculture with its wide seasonal variations in employment. Therefore, there are great variations in the extent of unemployment among LDCs when estimated by the survey procedures evolved in the DMEs. Table 13.9 shows the results for a few Asian LDCs.

Table 13.9 Unemployment rates in Asian LDCs (percentages)

Category	Philippines Aug. 1972	Java 1971	Malaysia 1967/8	Thailand 1973	Sri Lanka 1969/70
Total	6.1	8.8	6.6	0.4	13.4
By sex: male	5.7	7.5	5.7	0.6	10.9
female	7.0	11.5	9.1	0.2	20.9
By age: under 25	12.4	13.4	15.5	0.6	35.6
over 25	3.6	7.1	2.5	0.3	3.4
By region: urban	10.8	12.5	10.1	1.3	17.3
rural	4.0	8.2	5.5	0.3	12.6
By education:					
below secondary	5.4	8.4	4.8	0.3	7.3
secondary & above	13.3	13.7	15.3	2.0	22.6

Source: National censuses and labour force surveys.

Some general patterns may be noted. In many of these countries overall unemployment rates are rather low. This, however, is mainly a consequence of the absence of unemployment benefit schemes; therefore most people cannot afford to be unemployed and have to do some work, however low their productivity and however ill-suited they may be to such work. Unemployment rates are generally higher for females than for males, as women previously engaged in household activities tend to enter the wage labour force and seek employment in larger numbers than there are jobs for them. Unemployment is mainly concentrated among young workers and new entrants to the labour force, and is then a reflection of their aspirations for well-paid jobs and their unwillingness to accept such jobs as may be available; in course of time, these aspirations are revised downwards and the unemployment rate drops dramatically. Unemployment rates are higher in urban than in rural areas. One reason is that there is less scope for household employment in urban areas. A much higher proportion of the more educated workers report themselves as unemployed than the less educated; generally this is not so much because of their higher level of education as because they are young and can depend on their families while waiting for better-paid jobs to turn up.

The difficulty of identifying the problem of unemployment statistically in LDCs complicates the relationship between poverty and unemployment. Because measured rates of unemployment were found to be low, there has been a tendency to identify the poor as unemployed in what has been described as an 'income approach to unemployment'. (Turnham and Jaeger, 1971, pp.68–71) This approach has been followed by the country studies of unemployment organized by the I.L.O. For example, Seers (1970), p.378) says of the report on Colombia that,

> We came to see poverty and unemployment, not as different problems, but as different aspects of the same problem.

The Philippines report (I.L.O., 1974, p.7) made a rough 'guesstimate of total unemployment (i.e. open unemployment plus an inadequate income measure of underemployed) in the vicinity of 25 per cent.' But as Sen (1975, p.38) says,

> To identify unemployment with poverty seems to impoverish both notions since they relate to two somewhat different categories of thought.

In DCs, the unemployed are identified as those who are 'idle' (i.e. doing no work or less than normal hours of work); they are then found to be 'willing' to do more work and also to be relatively 'poor'. But in the LDCs, there is much less overlap among the people with these three characteristics (see e.g. Raj Krishna, 1973 for data from an Indian survey). First, those who are visibly unemployed, especially the better-educated young workers in urban areas, often come from well-off families and are not necessarily poor. Second, many who report themselves to be employed in the usual labour force surveys are poor because they are engaged in low-productivity activities and often have to work long hours to make a living; they have been described as the 'working poor' (I.L.O., 1972). Finally, there is a large group of desperately poor people, especially landless labourers in agriculture, who work for wages for only a few weeks in a year, usually as casual workers at times of peak demand for labour; the rest of the year, their position is best described as 'disguised unemployment'. Such persons are not fully reflected in the usual statistics of unemployment but they are the group for whom the connection between poverty and unemployment is closest. (See Visaria, 1981, for a discussion of the linkages between casual labour, unemployment and poverty in the west Indian states of Gujerat and Maharashtra.)

13.6 Distribution and Growth

So far, we have considered the effects of growth on the distribution of income. But income distribution also has some effects on growth; some of these effects are discussed in this section. To economists relying on the production function approach, the most obvious link between income distribution and economic growth is the rate of saving. The usual conclusion is that the more equal the distribution of income, the lower will be the saving ratio and hence the rate of growth of income. This conclusion is derived from two assumptions, one that the saving ratio is the principal constraint on growth, and the other that the propensity to save increases with the level of income. Some reasons why domestic savings are not the main constraint on growth were discussed in Section 9.5. Further, the second assumption, which is generally true, is not a sufficient condition for reaching the conclusion that the saving ratio will be reduced by a more equal income distribution. This can be seen by a simple counter-example; if the marginal saving ratio is constant and greater than the average, the propensity to save will increase with the level of income, but for any constant marginal saving ratio, the volume of savings will be independent of the distribution of income. The necessary condition to ensure the conclusion is that the propensity to save must increase faster than the level of income (technically, by a mathematical theorem known as Jensen's inequality, the curve showing the volume of savings as a function of income must be convex from below). But this condition is not always satisfied in LDCs. The usual estimates of savings often include amounts invested in the construction and purchase of residential houses, but these assets are more appropriately considered as durable consumer goods than as productive assets. They are an example of the conspicuous consumption on which much of the incomes of richer people in LDCs are spent.

There is another link which is often used to argue that greater equality of income distribution will affect economic growth adversely; this is the effect on incentives. According to this view, an unequal distribution of income is necessary to provide incentives for greater effort in the supply of labour and for a more rapid supply of the technical and entrepreneurial skills needed for growth. Hence, the more unequal the distribution of income, i.e. the steeper the income ladder, the greater the incentives and the faster the growth. It is true that if all incomes were equal irrespective of effort and skill, there would be no incentives to supply more effort and to use skills more productively. But the question of how much incentive is needed for the purpose is a complex question; the amount of incentives needed depends on prevailing social valuation of individual performances. In many countries with great income inequality, high incomes are not always derived from greater effort or better use of skills, but rather from an unequal distribution of property and unequal access to political influence. Therefore, we have to discount the effect of inequality on growth on this account.

In the neo-classical economic models, it is assumed that markets work efficiently and bring about equilibrium of demand and supply by speedy adjustments of prices. On this view, the productive resources of an economy are always fully employed. Then, the distribution of income will have no effect on the utilization of these resources and hence on the level and growth of incomes. The distribution of income will only affect the composition of output. But, as we argued in Section 9.2 above, such models are not very realistic in their assumptions about market behaviour; a substantial part of the productive resources both in DCs and in LDCs are not utilized because of effective demand failures. Then, the distribution of income will have important effects on the degree to which resources are utilized and hence on the level and growth of national income.

For example, if the resources which are most underutilized are those which are needed to produce goods and services demanded by the poorer sections of the community, while those needed to produce goods demanded at high income levels are in scarce supply, then a more equal distribution of income might in fact increase the utilization of resources and hence raise the level and growth of national incomes. Opinion is divided on the role of demand in the historical experience of DCs, with some writers claiming that modern economic growth originated in Britain because of a more even distribution of wealth there than in other countries of Europe (Landes, 1969, pp.47–50) and others denying that it took hold only in countries 'sufficiently egalitarian in their income structure for their masses to be in a position to buy all the new commodities which the revolution could produce' (Lewis, 1978, p.30). However, regarding the current position in LDCs, some estimates made in the draft of the Indian Fifth Five-Year Plan (Government of India, Planning Commissions, 1973, Vol.I, p.28) indicate that a more equal distribution of income might lead to faster growth, because the sectors with the fastest growth potential are also those most constrained by lack of effective demand. If it is the case that a more equal distribution of income accelerates growth in LDCs, then there will be a basis for a cumulative process: faster growth leading to greater equality and greater equality in turn leading to faster growth. The challenge to policy-making in LDCs is to guide the economy along such a process.

CHAPTER 14

Distribution of Income: Policy

14.1 Government Policies and Income Distributions

In a free enterprise system without government policy interventions with market forces, the distribution of income is determined by the classical determinants, namely, the national stock of the factors of production, the way this stock is distributed among households, the extent to which it is utilized for production, and the prices at which the factors are sold or the productivity with which they are employed. In countries at a low level of development, the consequence is widespread poverty and a high inequality of income distribution, both because the stock of capital and land is low relative to labour, so that profits and rents are high relative to wages, and further because the ownership of land and capital is more highly concentrated than labour. This is the price that countries in the early stage of their growth pay in opting for the market system in the expectation that this system will lead to a rapid growth of income. It is the poor who bear the main burden of this choice. The price paid by them is all the greater if markets do not work efficiently and are obstructed by weak and traditional institutions, because such institutional barriers to the efficient working of markets not only reduce the rate of growth below its potential but also reduce the social mobility through which the poor can improve their lot by dint of their own efforts. Therefore, there is frequently a case for some policy intervention to ameliorate their poverty in the course of economic growth. In this section, we consider policies which may modify the distribution of income and the various factors which influence governments in formulating and implementing such policies.

The economic policies of governments have been mainly discussed in the literature from the point of view of their effects on aggregate national income. Most of these policies, however, also affect the distribution of income, making the incomes of some people higher, and of others lower, than they would otherwise have been. Hence governments are under constant pressure from particular interest groups to implement policies benefitting them. How far the sum total of all policies affects the overall distribution of income depends on various factors.

First, it depends on the political pressure exerted by the interest groups. In particular, it depends on the efforts of the large majority of people in LDCs, who depend only on their labour to make a living and who are left poor as a result of the way market forces work in these countries. Where there are free elections to political office, the poor should have greater representation in government because of their sheer numbers but in practice, their representatives are either too weak to support policies to help those who have elected them or succumb to other interests after they are elected. It is sometimes argued that the grinding poverty of this group, especially when faced with the affluence of a relative minority of others, will lead them to active political efforts, and even violent revolutionary action, to remedy their position by getting governments to change their policies or by changing the governments themselves. The civil unrest that has taken place in countries such as Bangladesh and Sri Lanka and more recently in Iran is often cited as evidence for this view, but these disturbances have not been primarily triggered off by the really poor. It is more likely that political discontent arises, not when there is great and persistent distress, but rather when conditions begin to improve for some groups, but the improvement does not spread fast enough to other groups to satisfy their newly awakened aspirations (see e.g. Hirschman, 1973). As Galbraith (1980) suggests, there may be a sense of resignation on the part of the poor, who then become politically apathetic; the case for measures to improve their lot has then to be advanced by other groups interested in their welfare. In contrast, people who are already better off are much more articulate in pressing for further improvements in their positions.

Second, even when all sections of the population exercise an equal pressure on governments to follow policies in their favour, the outcome depends on the extent to which governments respond to the pressures from different groups. This is primarily a matter of the nature of the political system, particularly the extent to which governments are elected on a democratic basis and depend on popular approval for their re-election. But even within a democracy, leaders who have done little to help the majority of the people tend to get re-elected for other reasons such as their charisma or their campaign efforts; this is particularly the case in LDCs where a large proportion of people are poor and illiterate or have only limited education. In the case of authoritarian governments, their reaction depends much more on the preferences of the rulers. It is often argued that, because political leaders generally come from the better-off sections, they will be particularly responsive to the pressures from these sections, and that this is also true of the higher levels of the bureaucracy who have considerable influence on the formulation and implementation of policies. If this were always so, there would have been little improvement anywhere in the distribution of income as a result of government policies. But in fact governments composed of members of the so-called 'ruling class' have brought about significant reforms in some countries in some periods, especially in the past history of DCs. There can be no simple generalizations on how governments are selected and once selected, how they function in economic affairs; these complex questions cannot be pursued here.

Third, the distributional impact of the government depends on the economic strength of the government. A government may be highly motivated to improve the distribution of income in favour of the poor but not very effective in doing so because it lacks financial resources or administrative capacity, while governments with greater financial ability have much greater impact one way or the other. The latter case is best illustrated by the OPEC countries whose governments collect a large fraction of the national income as revenue without an elaborate fiscal system; their position has been described by Katouzian (1978, p.349) in his analysis of the situation in Iran:

> the state has become the exclusive fountain of economic and social power; a power, moreover, which is independent of the productive effort of the community . . . the most clear line of demarcation between different social categories is not so much their common relations with the means of *production* but their common relations with the means of *consumption*, i.e. the state. Social stratification then becomes a function of economic dependency upon the state.

Another OPEC country in which the government is economically powerful and exercises a decisive influence on the distribution of income is Indonesia; according to the data for the 1970s, increases in incomes of various social groups were found to be inversely related to their distance from the seat of political power (see Sundrum and Booth, 1980).

Finally, the impact of the distributional policies of governments depends on their efficiency, i.e. the extent to which the policies, once formulated, are implemented so as to achieve their objective. This is the area in which the economist as economist can make the greatest contribution. Therefore, the rest of this chapter will be concerned with what governments *can* do, if they are so minded, to improve the effectiveness of their policies relating to income distribution. Section 14.2 deals with the objectives of policy and Section 14.3 with the instruments that may be used.

Before going into the objectives and instruments of policy in detail, it is worth making one general point about distributional policies. As noted above, there are many factors which limit the effectiveness of government policies to influence the distribution of income in a significant way. These obstacles are particularly serious in the short period. Governments can hope to make a significant impact on income distribution only in the long run. Therefore the objectives of distributional policies, and the deployment of instruments to achieve these objectives, must be planned with a long time frame in view. Whether any particular government will survive throughout this long period is, of course, another issue.

14.2 Objectives of Policy

The distributional objectives of policy in LDCs can be broadly divided into two parts, namely the reduction of absolute poverty and the reduction of income inequality. These are distinct objectives but they are often confused in the literature. This is mainly because of the confusion between the concepts of absolute poverty and relative poverty. The concept of poverty in DCs is mainly defined in relative terms, i.e. as the level of income which separates about 10 to 15 per cent of the population in the lower income groups from the rest; the poverty line so defined then varies with the average income of the population and varies between countries and over time. It is then an aspect of the overall distribution of income. Absolute poverty, on the other hand, depends on the lack of adequate quantities of food, clothing, shelter and the basic amenities of life. The extent of absolute poverty is much less influenced by the inequality in overall income distribution. Absolute poverty may be widespread either with a high or a low income inequality. It is more likely to be influenced by the average level of income of LDCs. Therefore, we discuss the two objectives separately.

(a) Reduction of Absolute Poverty

The widespread extent of absolute poverty is one of the most serious problems of LDCs. In fact, it is often considered to be the main aspect of the problem of underdevelopment, but as we have argued in Chapter 5 it is useful to distinguish the two concepts and to view development as one among several instruments for the relief of poverty.

The first step is to define the concept of absolute poverty so that its complete eradication in a reasonable period of time becomes a clear-cut objective of policy. It is usually thought of in terms of a minimum standard of living which can be determined by physiological standards, but short of the needs for bare survival, there are no objective criteria for defining the minimum requirements of life. For example there is a great deal of controversy going on in India about the minimum requirements of nutrition (see e.g. Sukhatme, 1978, 1981; Srinivasan, 1977; Dandekar, 1981; Rao, 1981) which smacks of a veterinarian debate about the proper feeding of domestic animals. Then there is the problem of a variety of needs that must be considered. The usual way of getting over these difficulties is to define poverty in terms of a per capita income level. This is how, for example, the Indian Planning Commission in 1962 defined the minimum standard of living in terms of certain items of consumption such as food, fuel and light, clothing and shelter, as well as services such as health, sanitation, safe drinking water and education, and then translated into a level of income sufficient to meet such requirements. Too much, however, must not be claimed for this approach, as, for example, Streeton and Burki (1978, p.413) do when they say:

> One way out of this conceptual impasse is to identify a core of basic needs. The emphasis on a few needs does not mean that others are neglected. It does mean that at the level of income required to meet the core needs, the households would also satisfy other needs. A definition of core basic needs in very poor societies proves to be surprisingly robust, so that counting deficiencies for different items of the basket yields approximately the same number of people.

How far a single measure, such as the level of income, leads to the same results as others depends on the cut-off points chosen for the other needs and on the wide variations in expenditure patterns to be found in different countries and different regions within large countries. These approaches to the definition of poverty largely mistake the purpose of such a definition as an aid to policy making. They seem to be based on the view that the objective of policy is to raise the lower income groups up to the poverty line and leave them there. If an economy grows and if its income distribution does not worsen drastically in the process, these groups of people will eventually reach any specified poverty line. The problem is that the alleviation of poverty in this way may take too long. The real objective of policy in regard to poverty is to reduce the period involved in alleviating poverty by giving it the highest priority in the process of economic growth. It is only then that this distributional objective can be used to make a difference in government's policies.

To follow a policy for relieving poverty means that the efforts needed for this purpose must be made the first charge on government's material, intellectual and administrative resources. It is therefore unavoidable that the definition of the poverty line is itself a matter of political judgment rather than of physiological considerations. Once this principle is accepted, the minimum standard of living has to be defined in terms of what governments propose to do in various areas of policy. For example, a definition in terms of a minimum level of income would become appropriate if governments seriously thought in terms of income redistribution, while a definition in terms of nutrition would be more appropriate for a policy of food distribution and one in terms of education for a policy of education. It is only in this way that the definition of policy objectives in this area becomes an active aid to implementation. Otherwise, such objectives remain passive indicators to monitor progress of policies largely unrelated to their objective.

(b) Reduction of Income Inequality

It has become fashionable in much recent writing to bemoan the high inequality of incomes in many LDCs and to call for a reduction of income inequality as an important objective of policy. However, the problem is not always thought through to its logical conclusion. For example, if a more equal distribution is preferred to a less equal distribution, then it follows that the best situation is one of a completely equal distribution. Apart from the serious problems of defining what is meant by equality for individuals differing widely in their personal circumstances such as age, sex, health, education and family obligations, a certain amount of inequality is implicit in any mixed economy which relies on market incentives for private effort. Hence, we must also consider the relationship between income equality and other objectives such as economic growth (see Section 13.6). Just as a very equal distribution might reduce incentives for effort, a very unequal distribution might also affect growth by its effects on demand. One objection to a highly unequal distribution of income is that it leads to an excessive concentration of economic power. If by an excessive concentration of economic power is meant only the unequal distribution of income, it does not add anything to the argument against inequality. But if it means that great wealth leads to adverse economic effects because of its monopolistic tendency, we should also consider measures other than distributional policies to deal with this problem.

In discussions of equality as a policy objective, much of the attention is focussed on the distribution of income at a point of time. This is only the static aspect of income distribution. Equally important is the dynamic aspect of social mobility (see Section 13.1). When this is taken into account, a more suitable policy objective is that defined by Lewis (1969a, p.56) as follows:

> If one is concerned with incentives for effort, as any serious thinker must be, the emphasis rests naturally on equality of opportunity rather than equality of reward. The latter survives only in the form of a concern to eliminate extremes from both ends of the income scale. Equality of opportunity centres these days on trying to ensure that every young person shall have equal access to the fullest education from which he can benefit and thereafter equal access to every job irrespective of tribe, class, race, or religion. If incomes were based only on opportunity the result would be poverty for the handicapped and the unlucky, and riches for the talented or the lucky. Here the sentiment for the equality of incomes comes in to cut off both ends.

14.3 Instruments of Policy

We now examine some broad strategies or instruments of policy that have been proposed or used for improving the distribution of incomes and consider how far each will be useful for promoting the two objectives distinguished above.

(a) Growth of National Income

The growth of national income has always been taken as one of the main objectives of policy, but when some changes in income distribution were recognized to be important for the social and political health of a nation, the growth of national income came to be recognized as an instrument for attaining other more fundamental objectives, including those of income distribution. There are two views on the matter. One view is simply that growth of national income will improve the distribution of income; this view is nowadays caricatured as the 'trickle down' theory. The other view is that economic growth by itself may not improve the distribution of income but it is only when the national income grows rapidly that other policies to improve the distribution of income will be successful, i.e. that growth is a necessary but not a sufficient condition for a better distribution of income.

It is obvious that when the national income of a country grows and if the distribution of income improves in the sense of becoming more equal or at least does not worsen, the extent of poverty will diminish. This raises two issues for policy: one is whether growth worsens the distribution of income so much as to offset its direct effect on the extent of poverty and the other is whether, even if growth does not have such adverse effects on distribution, the feasible rates of growth will reduce the extent of poverty sufficiently rapidly.

Radical political economists have been urging for some time that, in the words of Griffin and Khan (1978),

> development of the type experienced by the majority of third world countries, in the last quarter century has meant, for very large numbers of people, increased impoverishment.

i.e. that a growth strategy actually increases the extent of poverty. The case of India is often cited to prove the point but India has not been conspicuous for the rapidity of its economic growth and there is no evidence of any trend in levels of poverty in India since the 1950s (see Ahluwalia *et al.*, 1978, for a review of the evidence). It is more likely that there has been a steady decline in the proportion of the total population who may be considered poor in LDCs as a whole, with considerable variations among individual countries, but that, because of the slow growth of total incomes and the rapid growth of populations, the decline in this proportion has been so slow that the numbers of poor people in LDCs have not declined significantly and may even have increased.

The relationship between economic growth and inequality of income distribution is more complex. Unfortunately most of the literature has been concerned to derive some simple relationships between these variables. Most of these studies are based on Kuznets' (1966) historical generalization that in the past history of the DCs, inequality first increased and then declined in the course of development. The same pattern is constantly being rediscovered in cross-section studies of countries at different levels of income at present. One of the most comprehensive of these is the study of Ahluwalia (see Section 13.2); his regression equations have been used to determine the precise level of per capita income at which income inequality will stop increasing and start declining, and to project the size of the poor population on various assumptions of future rates of economic growth. But the past changes in income inequality and the present variations in inequality among countries have been influenced by many factors other than per capita income. As Srinivasan (1977, p.15) puts it,

> It would be wrong, therefore, to interpret the curve and the projections from it as representing some sort of 'iron law' of development.

Instead the process of growth must be studied in more detail. For example, Lewis argues that growth takes place in enclaves, surrounded by traditional activities, and hence that

> development must be inegalitarian because it does not start in every part of an economy at the same time. (Lewis, 1976, p.26)

The overall impact of growth starting in an enclave depends on how it affects other parts of the economy.

> In a developed society, these benefits would spread swiftly and surely, but this may not happen in a traditional society. (Lewis, 1976, p.27).

Hence,

> in practice, the inegalitarianism of the development process derives not so much from failure to trickle down vertically as from the failure of horizontal spread from the enclaves to the traditional sectors.

We have to conclude that growth is an essential condition for the relief of poverty but for poverty to decline rapidly, growth must not only be more rapid than it has been in the past but must also be accompanied by a decline in the inequality of income distribution. We cannot rely on overall growth alone to bring about a reduction of income inequality. Therefore, we consider other policy instruments that may be used.

(b) Development

One weakness of the debate over how far growth promotes equality from a policy point of view is that growth depends on so many circumstances outside the direct control of governments that it cannot be properly considered an instrument fully available to governments in their distributional policy. We therefore turn to the role of development as we have defined it in Chapter 5, which is much more specifically the responsibility of government and over which they have much greater control.

In Section 13.4, we considered how the distribution of income was affected by the classical determinants, which were also involved in the growth process. These factors are particularly decisive in the LDCs at their low level of development. Their effects on income distribution are less significant in the more developed societies, where income distribution is much more equalized by the development factors. There, high levels of education and infrastructure and the efficient working of economic institutions dwarf the effects of differences in the ownership and prices of directly productive assets, such as land and capital, so that even those deriving their incomes from their labour alone have a high standard of living.

These development factors are often described as 'social services provided by governments' as if they were only ways of supplementing the consumption of individuals. But they are even more important as ways of expanding the opportunities of individuals to raise their productive capacities. A rise in the general level of development is therefore directly related to the goal of equality of opportunity and the dynamic aspect of income distribution involved in social mobility. It is through its effects on raising the productive capacity of individuals that development promotes faster growth by facilitating the absorption of new technology. Therefore, when growth is accelerated by rapid development, there is less of a conflict between growth and equality than when growth occurs through other factors.

However, until a high level of development is achieved, the process of raising this level is the source of increasing inequality, especially in its early stages. The very process which promises a high degree of equality in the long run becomes an unequalizing force in the intermediate stage. This effect is best illustrated by the example of education. As we have seen, one of the major sources of inequality in LDCs is the great differences in educational qualifications. Educational expansion increases inequality in its early stages for a number of reasons. First, if the educational facilities available at a given time are not sufficient to provide for all children of school-going age, some children will benefit while others do not, thereby contributing to inequality between them in their later lives. Second, the effect on inequality depends on how the limited educational facilities are allocated to different sections of the population. In practice, as Streeten and Burki (1978, p.415) say,

> Public services like education, health and housing tend to be not only inadequate in total but also concentrated in the cities and pre-empted by the middle and upper income groups.

Such inequality of educational opportunity therefore reinforces the inequality due to shortage of facilities. For education to play a stronger role in promoting greater equality, it must not only be expanded rapidly but in the early stages, a larger share of the public provision of educational facilities must be allocated to the poorer sections of the society. Third, the effect of a given difference in educational qualifications is accentuated by the large differentials in incomes of educational categories prevailing in LDCs (see Section 6.2). These effects are also to be found in the case of infrastructure and economic institutions, and account for much of the high level and substantial increase in inequality found in some LDCs in the early stages of their development.

(c) Regulation of Prices

One type of policy that governments have sought to follow on distributional grounds is the regulation of prices. The real income of a household depends on the prices of the goods and services it buys and the prices of the productive services it sells. Therefore, in order to benefit the poor, governments have tried to fix the maximum price of the goods mainly consumed by the poor below their market levels, and minimum prices of the productive services mainly supplied by the poor, especially labour, above their market levels.

In following this approach, however, governments must take account of its effects on consumption and production. Here, we must distinguish two cases according to whether market forces are functioning efficiently or not. By the efficient functioning of market forces, we mean the situation in which supply and demand are responsive to prices, and prices adjust speedily to bring about equilibrium of supply and demand. In the case where markets may be assumed to function efficiently, high prices of some commodities indicate that their supply is low relative to their demand, and the function of the high prices is to induce a larger supply and a smaller demand in the future. Similarly, the low price of some factors of production indicates that their demand is low relative to their supply, and the function of the low prices is to induce a larger demand and a smaller supply in the future.

Under these circumstances, one of the most serious problems facing any attempt to regulate prices is to make such a policy effective. If maximum prices are fixed below their maximum equilibrium level, demand will be greater than supply; some buyers will be willing to pay higher prices and will seek to evade price regulation. Similarly, if minimum prices are fixed above market equilibrium levels, supply will be greater than demand; some sellers will be willing to take lower prices and evade the price regulation. Therefore regulated prices by themselves will lead to black markets and the corruption of officials appointed to enforce them. To make them effective, there must be a system of rationing the excess demand or supply that results from such price regulations. Alternatively, there must be a system of taxes and subsidies which is rigorously enforced.

Suppose price regulations are somehow made effective. Then, they will affect production in the future. A typical example is the case of rent controls. Any attempt to keep down house rents by legislation will lead to a fall in the rate of housing construction, and exacerbate the shortage of housing, which led to the problem of high rents in the first place. Another example is the case in which food prices are kept low in the interests of poor consumers, leading to slower growth of production.

Next we consider the case where markets are not functioning efficiently in the sense described above. For example, the price of a commodity or service may be low not because there is a large supply relative to demand but because of imperfect competition, such as a monopsony; the price is then lower than it would have been in an efficient competitive market. Then, a regulation of the price may help the sellers without adverse effects on production. A good example is the case of minimum wage legislation. In the case where the labour market is functioning efficiently, fixing the wage above the equilibrium level causes unemployment and raises the incomes of the employed at the expense of those who become unemployed. But in the case where employers behave monopsonistically, such wage regulation may increase wages and employment at the same time. The problem, however, is the difficulty of enforcing minimum wage laws. In most cases, such laws are effectively enforced only in the public sector and in the modern sector where labour is organized and wages are already higher than in the rest of the economy. Therefore, price regulations are rarely likely to be effective by themselves; in order to be effective, they must be supplemented by other policies affecting the structure of production and employment, so as to be consistent with the regulated prices.

One of the most serious dilemmas facing LDCs concerns the appropriate policy towards food prices. On the one hand, governments wish to keep food prices low because it will help poor consumers who spend a large proportion of their incomes on food. On the other hand, they would like to keep food prices high, partly to induce producers to expand supplies and partly because of the political power of the large farmers who supply the biggest share of the marketable surplus. As proposed in Section 10.6(a), a useful guideline is to keep the price of food sufficiently low in relation to the wage level so that a fully employed person will be able to buy enough food to maintain himself and his family at the minimum standard of living until such time as supplies are large enough to force prices to a lower level still. Having fixed food prices in this way, the policy must be supplemented by two other types of measures. One is to expand employment, through programmes such as employment guarantee schemes, so that all workers willing to work for the minimum wages have the employment opportunity to do so. The other is to stimulate production by measures other than output price incentives, for example, by subsidizing capital and modern inputs used in that sector, and by giving the food sector higher priority in the allocation of development measures.

A related problem in the case of food prices is that of instability. Food production, especially in LDCs, is highly variable over time, because it depends so greatly on weather fluctuations. Hence there are periodic shortfalls and gluts. During a glut, the market price falls drastically as demand is very inelastic; such price declines then lead to diversion of land to other crops leading to high food prices in the next season. During a shortfall, prices rise dramatically; the relatively rich are able to maintain their consumption of food, as expenditure on food is a small fraction of their incomes. The main brunt of the shortfall is borne by the poor. In many LDCs, even a temporary shortfall of food output leads to a cumulative process of inflation. The stabilization of food prices is therefore highly desirable but this cannot be done just by price regulation. One way of making a regulated stable price effective is to support it with a buffer stock scheme. This appears to be the main role of the Agricultural Prices Commission and the Food Corporation of

India, and of the BULOG (rice procurement) agency of Indonesia. Another possible solution is to augment supplies during a shortfall by imports. This policy has been followed by many LDCs in the past decade. Often, such food imports from DCs were financed by foreign aid, for example, the PL 480 aid of the United States. Such food aid has sometimes been criticized as disturbing the price system and interfering with incentives to expand production, but to the extent that imports are used only to meet temporary shortfalls, their function is to relieve the hardship that falls mostly on poor consumers and to prevent prices rising rather than to depress them below normal levels.

(d) Structure of Production

The structure of production and the distribution of income are related in two ways. One relationship is based on the influence of the distribution of income on the structure of production through the patterns of expenditure of people at different income levels. Consider two societies with the same total endowment of resources, and the same consumer tastes and preferences, but with different distributions of income. Then, the greater purchasing power of the rich in the more unequal society will channel more resources to the production of goods mainly consumed by the rich, and less resources to the production of goods mainly consumed by the poor. The structure of production will thus reflect the distribution of income.

The other relationship is based on the influence of the structure of production on the distribution of income, through the way incomes are generated in different sectors of the economy. The major sectors of the economy in most LDCs differ considerably in the way the total income generated in each sector is distributed among the different income groups, depending on the factors of production which are highly immobile within each sector, the techniques of production, and the institutional factors affecting the working of factor markets. The overall distribution of income is more unequal, the greater the disparity between sectors and the greater the share of the sector with the more unequal intra-sectoral distribution. In most LDCs, average incomes are higher in the modern, industrial, sector than in the traditional, agricultural, sector. It was generally believed that incomes are more unequally distributed within the modern sector than within the traditional sector but some recent empirical studies have shown that in some LDCs, the distribution of incomes derived from agriculture may be very unequal, mainly because of the high concentration of land ownership and the inefficient working of labour markets, while incomes may be more equally distributed in the modern sector, mainly because of the service employment given by upper income groups.

Given these two relationships arising from the behaviour of individuals in the respective markets, they jointly determine both the structure of production and the distribution of income. In order to modify the situation determined in this way by market forces, governments may follow one or both of two approaches. They may attempt to influence the structure of production by using other instruments within their control or they may attempt to influence the distribution of income. Either approach will lead to a new result for both the structure of production and the distribution of income. The first of these approaches is discussed in the present sub-section and the second in the next sub-section.

Most so-called development plans consist largely of production plans based on measures to influence the mobilization and allocation of resources. High priority is given to achieving high rates of growth of production and to altering the structure of production to achieve this objective. But in some cases, planners have also been concerned to modify the structure of production to improve the distribution of income. This approach was most explicitly and comprehensively followed in the approach paper for the Indian Fifth Five Year Plan. The method used was to assume a more equal distribution of income, derive the corresponding patterns of demand, and draw up programmes of public investment and other public policies to bring about changes in the structure of production to match the changes in demand. For example, as poor people spend a higher proportion of their incomes on food than rich people, the assumption of a more equal distribution of income (see Booth *et al.*, 1980 for a mathematical statement) implied a more rapid expansion of the agricultural sector than would have been the case if the distribution of income had remained constant.

But this line of argument follows only one of the two relationships connecting the structure of production with the distribution of income, namely, the relationship based on patterns of expenditure. The impact of policy interventions in the structure of production on the distribution of income will, however, depend also on the other relationship based on how incomes are distributed within individual sectors. Then, it is by no means certain that efforts to increase the production of goods mainly consumed by the poor will necessarily improve the distribution of income. For example, if the incomes generated in the agricultural sector are more unequally distributed than in other sectors, the expansion of the agricultural sector relative to other sectors may actually increase overall inequality. Sinha *et al.* (1979) have found that this would indeed be the case in a simulation model they constructed for the Indian economy, because of the great inequality of the distribution of incomes generated in the Indian agricultural sector. Hence, under these conditions, policies operating only through the structure of production may not be sufficient to bring about any desired change in the distribution of income.

Another example of how the distribution of income is affected by the structure of production arises in the case of a dualistic pattern of growth. In LDCs, there is usually a fairly sharp differentiation between a low-income traditional sector and a high-income modern sector. The disparity between these sectors is a significant component of overall income inequality. Then, the effect of growth on inequality depends on whether growth occurs mainly by expanding the modern sector or by modernizing and raising incomes in the traditional sector. If inequality in the modern sector is high relative to the traditional sector, the modernization of the traditional sector will reduce overall inequality continuously, but if growth occurs only by the expansion of the modern sector, it is more likely that inequality will increase to begin with and decline only thereafter.

(e) Redistribution of Incomes

Even in the case where economic growth leads to a more equal distribution of income, the favourable effects on distribution may appear only slowly in the institutional circumstances prevailing in the LDCs. In order to attain distributional objectives faster, one possible approach is that of redistributing incomes. We consider some aspects of this approach, namely the methods, the magnitude and the duration of an income redistribution strategy.

The simplest method is one of cash transfers, through the fiscal system, for example, by progressive taxation and welfare payments. This is the policy followed by the DMEs, but even with their highly developed fiscal system, the overall redistributional impact of fiscal policy seems to be rather small. The amount of redistribution needed to make a significant impact on poverty and inequality in LDCs is very large, and with their much weaker fiscal machinery, it is unlikely that they will be able to cope with the administrative problems of taxing the rich and giving cash transfers to the poor in an efficient and honest manner. There is also the serious problem of identifying the poor deserving of financial assistance; if this has to be done by going through records of their incomes and assets there will be massive opportunities for corruption. Therefore, some LDCs have adopted the method of assisting the poor by enlarging their employment opportunities, for example, by providing guaranteed employment at a wage corresponding to some specified minimum standard of living. This method has the advantage of providing a simple means of identifying the beneficiaries as those who are willing to work for the basic wage. It also has the advantage that the labour mobilized in this way can be used for productive purposes. In many schemes, such labour is used only for infrastructural works in the public sector; in this case, projects are not often formulated in sufficient numbers to use all the available labour productively and are often not of a high technical quality. It may be useful to consider ways of inducing the private sector to use this labour for more directly productive activities at least in some specified activities, such as land improvements, which may not be carried out otherwise. Of course, the approach through such employment creation will only be useful for dealing with those whose poverty is due to lack of adequate employment.

As against the above method of reaching the poor through the process of generating or transferring incomes, some other alternatives have been widely discussed in the recent literature. One is the allocation of the social services normally provided by governments, such as education, health and water supply, and housing, to the poor in greater quantities than has been done hitherto. These social services are generally thought of as contributing to the consumption benefits of the poor, but in fact most of them are valuable because they increase the productive capacity of the poor, and then become part of the development measures discussed in subsection (b) above.

Some other alternatives have been discussed by many writers under the title of the 'Basic Needs' (BN) approach. There is great variation in the interpretations of this approach by different authors. Perhaps the clearest statement is that of Streeten and Burki (1978). They say that

> BN gives high priority (attaches considerable weight) to meeting specified needs of the poorest people, not primarily in order to raise productivity (though additional production is necessary), but as an end in itself . . . BN emphasises *supply management*, especially for the period of transition, so that increases in the incomes of the poor are not neutralised by increases in the prices of the goods and services on which they spend these increments, or increases in their productivity are not neutralised by lower money incomes; the basic needs targets are not just desirable consumption goals but carry implications about changes in the structure of production, its growth, and its accrual to the poor . . . BN implies certain limits to the unrestricted exercise of consumer's demand in the market.

A significant feature of this approach is that it calls for action to change both the distribution of income and the structure of production at the same time. However, it appears to envisage a redistribution of income carried out in kind. As Srinivasan (1977, p.18) points out:

> The basic needs approach does not rely solely on income generation or transfers, and places primary emphasis on the production and delivery to the intended groups of the basic needs basket through 'supply management' and a 'delivery system'. It can be argued that by selective direct interventions in the production and distribution process (rather than through creating purchasing power in the hands of those who need it and expecting them to consume the basic needs basket), the basic needs approach may lead to the provision of basic needs to people at much lower levels of aggregate income per head than would otherwise be possible.

This approach raises the question of how the political willingness to implement it can be brought about, but this is a problem which also arises in other approaches to distributional policy. The problems specific to this approach are essentially problems of implementation, such as how to deliver the goods included in the basic needs basket in an efficient way, and how to ensure that once delivered, the recipients do not sell them in the market for cash additions to their incomes.

One of the great concerns in many discussions of redistributive policies is that they may have adverse effects on growth. Thus, in some simple simulations of a dynamic model of growth and distribution, Chenery *et al.* (1974, Chapter 11) found that in the long run, aggregate income will be reduced by redistribution of both investment and consumption; in the case of the latter, not only will total income be reduced to a greater extent, but the poor will also be worse off. Therefore, there has been great interest in a strategy of redistribution with growth. This strategy was first spelt out in the I.L.O. report on Kenya (I.L.O., 1972). As Jolly (1976, p.44) summarizes it, one of its four main elements was the maintenance of rapid growth and another was 'The stabilisation for some years of the incomes of the richest 10 per cent of the population'. This approach is therefore one of setting a ceiling rather than a floor to incomes. It was presumably adopted in the hope that the freezing of incomes of those who are already very well off would somehow be politically more acceptable than taxing a larger group of moderately well-to-do people, but the logic of this argument is difficult to follow, especially when it is also assumed that growth can be maximized while the top incomes are frozen. In any case, the resources that can be mobilized by this strategy are unlikely to make a significant impact on poverty in most LDCs. In fact, a greater contribution can probably be made by changing the existing allocation of public expenditures. In some LDCs, even poor ones like India, public expenditure is already about a fifth of GNP. Earmarking a specific percentage of GNP, say 5 per cent, as the amount that should be used exclusively for poverty relief through the budget is one means of assigning a high priority to this objective. It may also assist governments in planning their expenditures more efficiently.

One of the most awkward problems in combating poverty solely through the redistribution of incomes is that such redistributions may have to be repeated indefinitely. In studying this problem, it is useful to distinguish two concepts of income distribution, namely the distribution of income arising from the production process itself which may be described as the primary distribution, and the distribution as modified by transfers, which may be described as the secondary distribution. Income redistribution from the rich to the poor will certainly make the secondary distribution more equal than the primary distribution. If, in the process, the structure of production itself is modified, there will be an effect on the primary distribution also. Then, the need for repeated redistributions may be obviated if the effect is to make the primary distribution more equal.

There have been a number of studies of how a certain amount of income redistribution carried out for some years will affect the structure of production and through it, the primary distribution in subsequent years. In the study of India by Sinha *et al.* (1979) it was found that a redistribution of income might actually worsen the primary distribution of income. This was mainly because the income transfers from the rich to the poor increased the demand for food and hence the size of the agricultural sector, but as the incomes generated in this sector were more unequally distributed than in other sectors, the expansion of the agricultural sector worsened the overall primary distribution of income. In some Latin American countries, on the other hand, a large proportion of the poor were engaged in the services sector, providing services to the upper income groups. Then, it was found that a redistribution of income away from the rich reduced their expenditures on services and, by affecting the employment opportunities of the poor, again worsened the primary distribution of income. In their study of Colombia, Ballentine and Soligo (1978, p.706) found that their model simulations

> provide no support for the hypothesis that the poor tend to consume goods and services produced with factors of production owned primarily by the poor while the rich consume goods and services produced with factors owned by the rich. Rather it appears that a unit of expenditure by any of the three income groups has roughly the same impact on the distribution of income. Differences which show up work perversely so that expenditures by the poor tend to increase factor earnings by the rich more than those of the poor, and *vice versa*. Thus, the second-round effects of a change in the distribution of income induced by a tax-transfer scheme are small and work in the opposite direction from the initial redistribution.

The study of the effects of income redistribution on the primary distribution of income is still in its early stages and greatly limited by the lack of sufficient reliable data. The preliminary findings suggest that the effects may be perverse and, even if not actually perverse, may be small. Therefore, for a lasting impact on distribution without the need for continuous transfers, we have to consider other approaches as well. One of these which is likely to have a more lasting effect is the redistribution of productive assets, considered below.

(f) Redistribution of Assets

One of the most important causes of the unequal distribution of incomes in LDCs is the unequal distribution of assets; ownership of assets in limited supply, and which therefore earn high rewards, like land and capital, is highly concentrated, while labour which is in abundant supply, and is provided by a majority of persons, earns a low wage. Further, there is an obvious cumulative interaction between the distribution of income and the distribution of wealth. A highly unequal distribution of wealth leads to inequality of income distribution, because income from property accrues only to the owners of these assets. In turn, unequal distribution of income leads to increasing inequality in asset ownership as richer people save more and acquire more of the existing assets from poorer people; at the same time they also acquire a disproportionate share of newly created assets.

A redistribution of productive assets is therefore a powerful method of improving the distribution of income. While redistributions of income have to be carried out year after year to maintain a desired distribution of income, the same objective can be achieved by a once-for-all redistribution of assets. Hence, asset redistribution will have fewer effects on growth than income redistribution.

These advantages of a policy of redistributing assets, however, will be realized more fully if the new owners are able to utilize these assets as productively, or more productively, than the old owners. Therefore, an important question to consider is how to choose as beneficiaries those most competent to make productive use of the redistributed assets. One solution that has been followed in the case of industrial capital in some DMEs is to encourage the participation of workers in ownership and management; this approach is less likely to have a significant effect in the LDCs because the organized industrial sector in these countries is so small. In the LDCs, the most promising case for asset redistribution is that of agricultural land.

The ownership of land is very unequally distributed in LDCs, as shown in Table 14.1. Because of the weakness of the market for leasing land, there is usually little difference between the inequality in owned and in operated holdings (Raj, 1970). Such a high inequality in the ownership and operation of

Table 14.1 Index of land concentration

Country (Year)	Gini-Index
Argentina (70)	0.873
Brazil (60)	0.845
Colombia (60)	0.865
Greece (61)	0.597
India (60)	0.607
Indonesia (73)	0.556
Iran (70)	0.624
Japan (60)	0.473
Pakistan (60)	0.607
Philippines (60)	0.580
Spain (62)	0.832
Taiwan (60/1)	0.474
Turkey (63)	0.611

Source: World Bank, *Land Reform* (1975)

land affects not only the distribution of incomes derived directly from the land but also has effects on the incomes derived from employment on the land and on the productivity of the land. It has been found almost universally that employment per hectare and yield per hectare declines as farm size increases. As Berry and Cline (1979, pp.131–4) conclude from an intensive analysis of data from six LDCs,

> the small farm sector makes better use of its available land than does the large farm sector, largely through applying higher levels of labor inputs (family labor) per unit of land.

From the inverse relationship of employment and output to farm size, it is sometimes argued that land reform will *always* increase total employment and output, but this result depends on who the beneficiaries are. In the case where land is redistributed only among the present operators, this inverse relationship is not sufficient to ensure an increase of employment and output; for this to happen, the rate at which employment per hectare and output per hectare decline with increasing farm size must exceed a critical limit. (More precisely, from the probability theorem known as Jensen's inequality, the necessary condition is that employment and output *per farm* as a function of farm size must be convex from below.) Employment and output will certainly increase if large farms are broken up into smaller farms and distributed to landless agricultural labourers. In this case, it will usually be necessary to assist the new operators with financial and technical assistance in cultivating the land. It is therefore important that land reform programmes identify the potential beneficiaries carefully, determine the size of farm that will assure them the minimum standard of living, and, on the basis of these considerations, determine the ceiling on land ownership, above which land is to be taken over and redistributed.

PART IV

The Financing of Development

CHAPTER 15

Planning and Financial Policies

The previous chapters were concerned with the changes that must occur in the LDCs in order to promote development in the long run, and to accelerate growth and improve income distribution in the medium term while these countries are still at a low level of development. Many of these changes are the responsibility of governments. Therefore, in the present chapter, we consider ways in which governments can discharge this responsibility efficiently. Most governments in LDCs have followed various methods of planning; some problems with existing planning techniques and ways in which they can be improved are discussed in Section 5.1. Development ultimately depends on changes occurring in the economy in real terms, but there are some serious financial problems in bringing about as fully as possible all the real changes that an economy is capable of. The financial policies of governments must, however, be considered in the development context; otherwise there is the danger of underestimating what can be achieved in real terms and of letting financial contraints reduce the actual rate of growth and development below what is feasible. The problems of external finance are discussed in the next chapter. In this chapter, we consider two aspects of domestic finance, namely fiscal policy in Section 15.2 and monetary policy in Section 15.3.

15.1 The Role of Planning

(a) Advantages of Planning

In the early post-war years, the concept of planning was often identified with extensive government control over the economy as in the socialist countries, which are still generally described as 'centrally planned countries'. Although the conceptual difference between planning and government control is more widely recognized nowadays, the two concepts are still confused with each other in practice, especially when plans are drawn up and theoretical studies of planning made for mixed economies as if the government had more control over the economy than it really has.

The essence of planning has been well brought out in the definition of Dror (1963, p.50) as

> a process of preparing a set of decisions for action in the future directed at achieving goals by optimal means.

By looking ahead and looking at problems as a whole, planning helps to make better decisions. This advantage of planning is well illustrated by the story of the dog and its master. Suppose a man is walking along a straight road and his dog runs towards him from a point off the road. If the dog always runs in the direction in which it sees its master, it will trace out a curved path and take a long time to catch up with him. However, there is a straight line path along which it will catch up with him sooner. (For a mathematical analysis, see Allen, 1938, pp.431–3) This example shows how a more efficient path of travel in the future can be derived if the objective is well defined and if the laws governing the motion of the system are known. Similarly, the 'turnpike' theorems of economics (see, e.g., Dorfman *et al.*, 1958, Chapter 12; also Frisch, 1970) show that the problem of achieving a distant objective can be solved more efficiently by considering it as a whole rather than by breaking it up into a number of separate, short-term, problems. According to these theorems, every production system has a growth path along which the movement of the economy is most rapid. Then, to move from any starting point to a distant objective, it will be quicker to go first towards this 'turnpike' path of the production system and then, when we are near the objective, move away from this path to the goal, just as we use turnpike roads in long distance driving. When the production system is a simple one with constant parameters, its turnpike is a balanced growth path known as the von Neumann ray. It has been shown that the more distant the objective, the closer the optimum solution is to the path along which the economy is most productive.

The main advantage of planning in this sense of advance decision-making is that it leads to more efficient decisions about future actions. Once a plan is formulated and announced by a government, it has further advantages. First, it helps to coordinate the activities of various government agencies among themselves. Second, the decisions that government proposes to make will help individuals in the private sector to formulate their own plans. If the government's plan includes a road in a particular place, it will influence people to locate their shops or factories along that route. If the government proposes to introduce a particular new technology, it will induce people to take advantage of it. In most LDCs, the greatest enemy of planning by the private sector is uncertainty about government actions. Therefore, the more this uncertainty is reduced by government planning, the more the private sector also can extend its plans into the future. Third, a plan by a government informs other governments and international agencies about its proposed actions so that, for example, it can be the basis for foreign aid.

These advantages of planning depend on the commitment to implement the decisions in the plan. An optimal plan ceases to be optimal if some parts of the plan are implemented while others are not. A sub-optimal plan which is implemented may be better than an optimal plan which is not. For example, an optimal education plan might include a decision to expand primary education in one period and at the same time increase teacher training to cope with the increased enrolment at the secondary level that will result from the primary expansion. But if primary enrolment is expanded but not the training of secondary school teachers, then the quality of secondary education in the future will suffer. If a government makes plans which are not realized, a problem of credibility arises; the private sector will not believe in or act upon future plans.

The term 'plan', however, is used to describe many statements of proposed actions which are not seriously intended to be implemented. As Lewis (1966, p.13) put it,

> plans differ so much in structure and content that the title 'Development Plan' no longer conveys a meaning.

Sometimes, such documents only describe projections of the probable future pattern of growth made by technical experts as a background or perspective against which the government makes its own decisions. This is useful but does not have the advantages of advance decision-making of plans to which the government is committed. Often ambitious plans are made just as the means of negotiating for more aid. In fact, some aid agencies, including the World Bank, insist on countries producing plans before even starting negotiations for aid. This is illogical, for no country can make plans with a firm commitment to implement them if it does not even know how much aid it will get.

In the rest of this section, we shall consider only planning in the sense of advance decision-making. When so considered, planning has some important implications which are not always fully appreciated. We consider some of these implications below.

(b) The Coverage of Plans

It is often assumed that the more widely a plan covers the economy, the better it is. That is why many plans have macro-economic targets such as growth of the GNP, agricultural output, employment and so on. Of course, in arriving at decisions about future government actions, planners must consider the likely repercussions on, and from, all sectors of the economy. But this does not mean planning the entire economy; indeed it cannot mean this as governments in most LDCs operate within a mixed economy. In order to produce a plan with a commitment to action on which others can rely, planners must restrict themselves to areas within their control. The issues involved have been so well stated by Dandekar, V. M. (1967, pp.10–11; reproduced by permission of The Indian Society of Agricultural Economics) in his discussion of agricultural planning that it is worth quoting him at some length:

A plan is a plan in the true sense of the term when it is essentially a plan of action on the part of one who makes the plan. In the present context, if a government has prepared the plan, it must be a plan of action by government and other public authorities. The reason why our plan for agricultural development is not a plan in the true sense of the term is that it is not essentially a plan for state action. It is much more or much less than that. In fact, it covers many fields and areas over which the government has little authority to make decisions or initiate action. Consequently, many targets set out in the plan lack real meaning, validity and sanction. Take for instance our target of agricultural production, crop by crop. Admittedly, this is a matter primarily governed by millions of individual farmers. It is not therefore very meaningful to fix plan targets in this field. For instance, a plan target in major irrigation, in the sense of creating a certain irrigation potential, has a clear meaning, but the plan target for minor irrigation, as it includes investment decisions of individual farmers in digging of wells, etc., is not equally meaningful. The targets for production of nucleus or foundation seed of improved varieties are meaningful; but the targets for bringing certain acreage under improved seed are a fiction. Targets of production and input of chemical fertilizers are meaningful, but the targets of organic manures and green manuring are worse than fiction—they deserve to be dumped into a compost pit. Nevertheless, we have been planning in terms of these targets, because our plans include not only plans for government action but also our expectations and hopes as to how the millions of farmers would respond to these actions. I think it is essential to make a distinction between the two, and distinguish planning from speculative thinking about the future, and plan targets from statistical projections or economic forecasts. I am not saying that speculative thinking about the future and informed projections and forecasts are not useful. Such projections or forecasts are valid and useful even in a completely unplanned economy. They should certainly be useful in a planned or partially planned economy. But they are not valid plan targets because they lack sanction. Let me therefore suggest that our plans for agricultural development should be confined to those fields and those items over which the government has authority to make decisions and initiate action and that our plan targets should be in terms of state action.

Let me then ask: What is it that the state can do in respect of all such items in which the ultimate decisions lie with the farmers? As I see it, there are three functions which the state can perform in this sphere. They are (1) to educate and improve the farmer as a farmer; (2) to reorganize the production apparatus in agriculture so as to enable the farmer to take better care of his land and water resources; and (3) to create appropriate institutions in order to improve the decision-making in agriculture. These are the three functions which the state can perform in this sphere and these should constitute the essential elements of the district and block-level programmes for agricultural development. The first is a task of education. The second is a task of much detailed work on the ground. The third is a political task. We have neglected all three because of a mistaken belief that we could achieve the production targets directly without bothering to improve the man, to improve the land and to improve the institutions governing the relation between man and land.

As we have seen in earlier chapters, there are a number of very important measures which are the special responsibility of governments; these are particularly the development measures discussed in Chapters 6–8. It is such measures which are most suitable contents of a government plan.

(c) The Planning Horizon

A plan is a decision about future actions; it is a method by which governments can make better decisions about these actions. But when we make decisions in advance, we surrender a certain degree of manoeuvrability because the future is uncertain. It means crossing bridges before we come to them, shooting at the enemy before seeing the whites of their eyes. Therefore, just because a five year plan is better than a one year plan, it does not mean that a twenty year plan is better than a five year plan. While the advantages of advance decision-making increase with the period over which it is carried out, the costs also increase; therefore there is an optimum period of advance decision-making which should be taken as the planning horizon.

The optimum period of advance decision-making, however, varies with each problem. In the case of what we have described as development activities, especially education and infrastructure, the optimum planning horizon is long, a matter of decades rather than years. There are strong interrelations over time in these activities of government; different levels of education and different aspects such as enrolments, school building and teacher training, as well as different types and location of infrastructure, have to be coordinated. In the past, the expansion of education and infrastructure have been designed in response to the demand for them based on the current evolution of the rest of the economy, but as argued in Chapters 6 and 7, a better strategy is for governments to provide them ahead of demand and as a means of stimulating the rest of the economy. Further, these are the activities largely within the control of governments. Therefore these are the sectors most eminently suitable for long-term planning. There is one difficulty about long-term planning, namely, that in democratically governed LDCs, the life of a party in power is usually limited to four or five years, which is perhaps one reason why most plans are restricted to this medium term. Long-term planning therefore raises the question of how a party in power can make decisions binding future governments. But even in such countries, there are political decisions and constitutional provisions covering periods beyond the tenure of the existing government. The sectors which are to be planned on a long-term basis must be those where there is a widespread consensus about targets and for which a constitutional sanction is obtained. An example is the provision in the Indian constitution to establish universal primary education within ten years of independence. The failure to achieve this target was due to a lack of commitment, rather than to a political difficulty, because the same party was in power in India throughout this period.

At the other extreme is financial planning—the balancing of government receipts and expenditures, and macro-economic management, the balancing of aggregate demand and supply. These are the areas most fraught with uncertainty in the long run, and over which the governments of LDCs have little control. It is useless for governments to pretend that they can forecast their revenues even for as long as five years. As a result when the targets of five year plans are not realized, it is usually blamed on the failure of projected resources to materialize. Further, when it becomes clear that the required resources are not forthcoming, the plan gets pruned in a most unplanned way. In between the long-term horizon needed for most development activities and the short-term horizon inevitable for financial planning is the implementation of major projects which can be planned for a medium term period of about five years.

Because the optimum planning horizon varies with different activities, it is not advantageous to synchronize the plans for all such activities within the framework of a single five year plan. Such medium-term plans have become very popular in LDCs, perhaps in unconscious imitation of the practice in socialist countries, but in these countries the governments have much greater control over the economy and they also have a much clearer picture of what they wish to achieve over the long period. When applied to the LDCs, they have been less successful. Hence, Singh, T. (1974, p.93) who drafted a number of Indian Five Year Plans, concluded that:

> It can be seen now that because of the compulsions associated with each of them, five year plans have set a constraint upon thought and analysis in a sphere which called for fundamental changes in the organisation of society and of the economy.

The appropriate solution lies in having plans of different horizons for different activities. It is sometimes proposed that the planning horizon should be extended by the method of a rolling plan. According to this proposal, a plan is made for, say, five years but is revised every year. However, from the point of view of a plan as a commitment to action, this is really not a five year plan at all, but just a series of annual plans.

So far, we have been mainly considering the economic aspects of the planning horizon. In addition, there are other advantages of a political nature in a longer planning horizon (see Lewis, 1966, p.149). Suppose a country starts out to make a five year plan and invites agencies in different sectors and regions to submit projects to be included in the plan. Some of these projects will have to be rejected because they are not sound. But even the projects left after this screening process may overcrowd the five year plan and cost more than the government can afford to spend in the next five years. Then, the duration of the plan may be extended. The conflict over whether project A in one part of the country or project B in another should be included in the plan, a very real conflict in practice, gives way to the compromise of extending the period over which both projects are implemented. Of course, this advantage can be achieved only if the plan is credible and consists of firm commitments which the population at large is confident will be carried out.

(d) The Contents of Plans

The aspect of planning which has received most theoretical attention is the consistency of plans. This is, of course, an important consideration. The provision of, say, teachers, buildings, equipment and places in different grades of the educational system in any year must be consistent with the numbers who will be qualified to enter those grades in that year. Different types of transport infrastructure must be consistent with each other, and so on. The problem, however, is that the criterion of consistency is applied in areas where it is neither feasible nor even necessary, as in financial and macro-economic exercises. The task of planning is excessively complicated by the demand for such consistency. As Lewis (1966, pp.16–17) puts it,

> The principal danger of a macro-economic exercise lies in its propensity to dazzle. The more figures there are in a plan, produced by an army of professionals who have laboured mightily to make them consistent, the more persuasive the Plan becomes. Attention shifts from policy to arithmetic. Consistency can be mistaken for truth. Revision is resisted. Yet the Plan is not necessarily right because its figures are mutually consistent.

The method of planning largely in financial terms is dangerous because financial consistency emphasizes certain objectives which are not very important and which may in fact detract from the rate of growth and development. For example, one such objective is that of equilibrium of individual markets. On this interpretation, planning economists set themselves the goal of ensuring a balance of supply and demand in these markets. Hence, for instance, they spend a lot of time and effort in projecting consumer demands rather than seeking the most fruitful production possibilities. Elaborate calculations are then made with input–output tables to estimate the direct and indirect requirements of various industries to meet the final demand, themselves based on doubtful projections of the overall rate of growth. Such exercises rarely allow for price changes in adjusting demand and supply or for foreign trade. But during a period of rapid change, it will not be possible to maintain continuous equilibrium at stable prices; in fact, it is disequilibrium which propels the economy forward and changes in prices have a part to play in the process.

An even more serious problem is that plans are mainly drawn up in financial terms at a high level of aggregation. Often financial provisions are made for projects which have not been worked out in real terms. The weakness of this approach has been described by Kaldor (1964a, pp.299–300, 303) in connection with the preparation of the Indian Third Five Year Plan, as follows:

> When I look at the various preliminary papers drawn up in connection with the new Plan, my main reaction is one of increasing scepticism as to the adequacy, or even the appropriateness, of looking at the problem of resource mobilisation mainly in financial terms . . . This approach is appropriate to 'advanced' economies like the U.K. and the U.S.A. but it is not appropriate to under-developed countries like India. The important differences as I see them are due to two factors: (i) in the 'advanced' countries, the only important bottleneck on increased investment, at any rate for medium-range periods, is manpower. Hence, deficit financing is inflationary if, and only if, the economy is at full employment or nearly full employment; (ii) in the 'advanced' countries sums of money made available for particular purposes can be appropriately used to indicate a corresponding supply of goods and services which are required for the particular objectives aimed at. The reason for this is that, granted a certain period of adjustment, the market mechanism is capable of adapting the production pattern to any given pattern of final demand. In countries like India, this technique can be very misleading in both directions—both in thinking that the required (domestic) resources will automatically be forthcoming if sufficient money is made available through the 'normal' sources of taxation, the profits of public enterprises, and borrowing in the open market; and also in thinking that there is a clear limit beyond which expenditure covered by deficit financing will not cause any increase in production but will merely lead to inflation.

When so much attention is paid to consistency in financial terms, the objective of monetary stability takes precedence over growth; the size of plans is mainly thought of as the amount of money to be spent, and determined in the light of estimated savings and other financial resources. But estimates of savings are notoriously unreliable and tend to be based on *ex post* data of the past; they tend therefore to be conservative and fail to realize the full potential for growth and development that an economy is capable of. A better alternative is that urged in a document of the Indian Planning Commission (1964) which says:

> The right approach is to investigate closely the nature of the problem to be tackled, the concrete tasks to be carried out, the physical resources, skills and organisational efforts to be mobilised for the purpose. If these appear to be operationally feasible, it should be possible to devise policies by which the finance can be found to facilitate the process of mobilisation of the real resources.

The ultimate constraints on growth and development in LDCs are the real resources and the administrative limits of government actions. It should be the object of financial planning to promote growth and development to the limits set by these constraints.

(e) Decentralization of Planning

Because the typical plan has come to be a sophisticated technical exercise, it has become more and more a job done by professional economists, and if the economists of a country are not expert enough in planning techniques governments usually call in foreign experts who know even less of the country they are planning for. But if plans are to be credible commitments to future action, they must be made by the political leaders of a country—those with the power to make decisions. Many published plan documents make strange reading, as if they have been written by a small group of intellectuals or backroom boys to be read by ministers; they are full of criticisms of government actions in the past and of exhortations to do better in the future.

This does not mean that planning should only be done by the central government of a country. Usually, it is the central government which employs all the most expert economists in the country; therefore it is often said that the central government has to do all the planning because the lower levels of government do not have the required expertise. As a result, plans concentrate on macro-economic exercises and frequently do not even specify the individual projects on which funds are to be spent. However, the success of a plan does not depend so much on the brilliance of the technical methods employed in drafting it but rather on a knowledge of how the economy works and what can be done to develop it. Therefore, the lower levels of government, who know local problems and local conditions best, have a contribution to make.

The decentralization of planning does not mean that local planning units should become small replicas of the national planning commissions. One problem is that local planning units do not know what funds and other resources are available when they start planning, or they start planning in a hurry to match the funds they are allotted from the centre. Another problem is that, though local planning units may know the conditions and problems in their areas better than the central planning agency, they may not know the full technological possibilities of solving them. Therefore the best procedure is to have an iterative interaction between the local and the national units. This process may start with enunciation of some guiding principles of planning by a central agency, dealing not with financial allocations, but with broad guidelines as to technology, education, infrastructure, urbanization and the solution of particular problems of production. These guidelines are then used by local planning units to draw up a development perspective in each local area in the form of specific projects based on the guidelines laid down by the centre and on the intimate knowledge of local conditions. At this stage, the development programme is not broken up into five-year-plan packages. The development perspectives of local areas are then sent to the provincial or state level to be screened and coordinated with each other and assembled into a development perspective for the province or the state. The provincial or state development perspectives are then sent to the national planning agency to be further screened and coordinated and combined with national projects. After arriving at a national perspective of development, the central planning agency will make a tentative proposal to incorporate it into plans of various types. These proposals are then sent down to lower-level planning units for modification as necessary. The plan proposals approved by the local areas are then assembled at the centre and finally confirmed as the nation's development plan.

15.2 Fiscal Policy

If LDC governments are to achieve faster growth and accelerated development, they must modify the way existing resources are used and mobilize more resources for development purposes. This imposes a heavy financial burden on their governments. Friendly governments of more affluent countries can relieve some of this burden by giving foreign aid but, so far, such aid has contributed only a small part of the needs of most LDCs. In raising domestic resources for government expenditure on development, LDCs cannot usually borrow much domestically because of their weak financial institutions and cannot rely heavily on deficit financing through money creation because of the danger of inflation which can easily get out of control (see Section 15.3). Therefore, they have to rely mostly on the tax revenues they collect.

In a sample of 24 LDCs, the average percentage of taxes to GNP was 11.8 in 1953–55 and increased to 16.3 in 1972–76, while in the same period the average percentage for 15 DMEs increased from 26.2 to 36.2 (see World Bank, *World Development Report, 1980*, Table 6.1, p.73). While the tax ratio increased at the same rate in both groups of countries, the average ratio in LDCs has remained only about 45 per cent of that in DMEs. Towards the end of the 1970s, the average ratio for a larger sample of 72 LDCs had increased to 18.5 per cent (see I.M.F., *Government Finance Statistics Yearbook, 1980*).

The tax ratios that the LDCs inherited before they embarked on their post-independence development efforts were influenced by historical factors. It is therefore particularly important to see how they have managed to increase these ratios with growth of incomes since then. A convenient measure of such changes is the tax elasticity, i.e. the percentage increase in tax revenues as a ratio of the percentage increase in GDP. This elasticity can also be interpreted as the ratio of the marginal tax ratio to the average. Apart from indicating that tax revenues are increasing rapidly in the course of income growth, a high elasticity also means that countries may have greater tolerance for deficit financing, which will then have fewer inflationary effects for a shorter period. In a study of 33 countries, mostly less-developed, for the period 1960–65, the tax elasticity ranged from 0.52 in Nigeria to 3.70 in India. The average tax elasticity was 1.31; with the average tax ratio at that time of 13 per cent, this implies a marginal tax ratio of only 17 per cent (see U.N., 1970).

Before discussing the factors affecting tax performance, we consider the patterns of public expenditure and receipts.

(a) Patterns of Public Expenditure

Table 15.1 shows a comparison of the patterns of public expenditure by function between DMEs and LDCs (excluding the oil-exporting countries) according to the latest data available.

Table 15.1 Patterns of public expenditure by function, c.1977 (percentages of total expenditures)

Function	DMEs	LDCs
Defence	7.4	13.4
Education	9.6	14.9
Health	8.6	6.4
Social Security	40.0	7.3
Housing and community services	3.1	4.6
Economic Services	14.5	25.9
of which: agriculture etc.	4.1	7.5
roads and transports	6.7	9.0
Others	16.8	27.5
Total	100.0	100.0

Source: For DMEs, I.M.F., *Government Finance Statistics Yearbook 1980*; for LDCs, World Bank, *World Tables, 1980*

The main difference between DMEs and LDCs is the large share of social security payments in the former. For some purposes, a more useful classification is by economic type. Some recent data on such a classification are summarized in Table 15.2.

Table 15.2 Patterns of public expenditure by economic type, c.1977

Economic type	DMEs	LDCs
Current expenditure on goods and services	30.4	48.1
Capital expenditure	10.0	23.1
Transfers	57.0	16.2
Others	2.6	12.6
Total	100.0	100.0

Source: I.M.F., *Government Finance Statistics Yearbook, 1980*

From this table, we see a further difference, namely, that LDCs spend a much higher percentage of their public expenditure on capital account than the DMEs, but because public expenditure as a proportion of GDP was so much smaller in LDCs than in DMEs, this meant that, as of the mid-1970s, the contribution of the central government to capital formation was about the same ratio to GNP in both groups of countries, i.e. around 4 per cent.

(b) Composition of Public Revenues

Table 15.3 summarizes the latest available data on the composition of public revenues in DMEs and LDCs (excluding the oil-exporting countries). The most notable difference between DMEs and LDCs is that the former rely mostly

Table 15.3 Composition of public revenues, c.1977 (percentages of total revenues)

Type of revenue	DMEs	LDCs
Taxes on income and profits	34.2	21.8
Social security receipts	26.6	9.7
Property taxes	2.0	2.0
(a) Direct taxes	62.8	33.5
Taxes on production and internal trade	26.3	21.2
Taxes on international trade	3.2	30.7
(b) Indirect taxes	29.5	51.9
Other revenues	7.7	14.6
Total	100.0	100.0

Source: I.M.F., *Government Finance Statistics Yearbook, 1980*

on direct taxes, while the latter rely mostly on indirect taxes, especially taxes on foreign trade.

(c) Tax Performance

The proportion of GNP that a country collects as public revenue is often used as a criterion of economic performance. However, the fiscal policies of countries should be judged not only by the amount of revenues they collect, but also by the way they collect these revenues and the purposes for which they spend the proceeds. The purposes for which public revenues are to be used influences the willingness of people to pay taxes and the effort that governments make to collect them.

When the patterns of expenditure are taken into account, we find a qualitative difference between DCs and LDCs. In the DCs, most of public expenditure is used for current consumption. Hence, the tax ratio in these countries is a reflection of the community's choice between private goods and public goods. In the past, the tax ratio of the DCs has been increasing, but there is no particular merit in this; it simply reflects the growing preference for public over private goods. In recent years, there has in fact been a popular movement, much publicized in the United States and elsewhere, in favour of 'small government' and voters have supported parties who advocate a reduction in taxation. As has already been pointed out, a high proportion of government expenditure in the DMEs is for transfers, and the 'small government' movement in these countries reflects resentment on the part of the better off against high levels of welfare payments.

There is in fact little difference between LDCs and DMEs in the ratio of government capital formation expenditure to GNP. Obviously, such capital expenditures in the LDCs play an important role in promoting development and faster growth in these countries. In addition, as argued in Chapter 14, it may be essential for LDCs to earmark a certain proportion of GDP, say 5 per cent, for fiscal policies designed to provide basic needs for the poorest sections of society. The criterion which is therefore most appropriate for judging fiscal performance in LDCs is the extent to which they mobilize resources for public capital formation and for the needs of poverty relief. This in turn depends on the total amount of revenues collected and the extent to which they are channelled to these purposes rather than to administrative expenditures.

In the past, much of the success in increasing tax collection in LDCs has been frustrated by the growth in current government expenditures, as pointed out by Please (1967, 1970) and Krishnamurty (1968). The trend noted by these writers for the 1960s has continued in the 1970s. Between 1970 and 1977, general government consumption increased at an annual rate of 8.5 per cent in LDCs; as a share of GDP, it increased from 11.9 to 13.1 per cent (World Bank, *World Tables, 1980*). The ability of LDCs to finance development and poverty relief depends not only on their ability to raise more tax revenue, but also on the economy they exercise in their administrative expenditures.

While the expenditure side of the budget has been largely neglected, most of the large literature on fiscal performance of LDCs has tended to discuss only tax performance. Even on this topic, however, much of the literature has adopted a rather narrow focus. The performance of countries in collecting tax revenue should be judged, from a policy point of view, not just by their 'success' in collecting a particular target amount of revenues, but also by the extent to which their success or failure is due to the 'effort' they put in. The distinction has been well put in an UNCTAD study of the measurement of development effort (U.N., 1970, p.1), thus:

> One country may succeed virtually without effort, because of some windfall such as the discovery of rich oil resources. Another may fail notwithstanding intense effort, because of unfavourable circumstances beyond its control. The problem is to find quantitative indicators that would clearly identify what is good fortune in the case of the one and misfortune in the case of the other.

A similar distinction differentiates the concept of a country's 'taxable capacity' which is based on factors not directly amenable to policy, from the extent to which such taxable capacity is actually realized. One way of defining taxable capacity is the amount that people are able to pay in taxes. The simplest measure of taxable capacity from this point of view is per capita income. On this basis, the DMEs collect a higher proportion of their national income as revenues than LDCs simply because they are richer. Tax ratios in LDCs are also associated with their per capita income levels but the relationship is rather weak, as shown in Table 15.4.

However, what the people of a country can afford to pay in taxes depends not only on per capita income but also on the extent to which the incomes of

Table 15.4 Tax ratios of LDCs, c.1977

Per capita income (US $), 1977	Number of countries	Unweighted average of Tax Ratios to GNP (%)
Under 200	14	14.7
200–400	17	18.4
400–600	13	19.1
600–800	5	17.4
800–1000	9	20.1
1000 & Over	14	20.4
Total	72	18.5

Source: Compiled from data of World Bank, *World Tables, 1980*

various groups are above a minimum consumption level. As Kaldor (1962a, p.227) says:

> The taxation potential of a country depends on the excess of its actual consumption over the minimum essential consumption of the population.

The concept of minimum essential consumption cannot be defined very precisely but some approximate measure can be used, as illustrated by the following example given in the World Bank's *World Development Report, 1980* (p.73):

> Take India as an example; its taxable surplus may be defined as all income above the poverty line (defined there as the income of the fortieth percentile in the distribution of income). On this basis India's taxable surplus in 1975 was 41 per cent of aggregate income; the ratio of taxes to taxable surplus therefore was 34 per cent—comparable with the tax-to-GNP ratios of industrialized nations.

An alternative approach to the concept of taxable capacity that has been much used by studies in the I.M.F. Fiscal Affairs Department is based on a composite indicator including not only GNP per capita but also such other variables as the percentage share of mining in GDP and the share of exports in GNP (see, e.g., Chelliah, Baas and Kelley, 1975, p.191). These studies usually judge tax effort or tax performance of an individual country by deriving through regression analysis some norm or standard from the experience of a large sample of countries. This procedure can be criticized on two grounds. First, the use of a composite indicator including not just an indicator of ability to pay (GNP, perhaps adjusted for incomes below the poverty line) but also indicators of easy availability of tax 'handles' such as a large mining sector, seems to confuse two rather separate issues. It is one thing to say that a particular country has a low tax/GNP ratio because it is poor, and another thing to say that this ratio is low because it lacks administratively convenient tax handles. In principle, a dollar of income is the same whether it comes from agriculture or from mining; the fact that most countries find, for political and administrative reasons, that it is 'hard' to tax agriculture and 'easy' to tax mining should not be allowed to obscure this basic point.

A second reason why these studies of tax performance based on regression analysis are misleading is that the average performance of a sample of countries does not necessarily show the potential that a particular country is capable of. Bolnick (1978, p.75) has pointed out that most tax effort studies

> are actually hybrid measures which confuse (i) the differences in performance relative to desires and (ii) differences in desires themselves across countries.

There is no doubt that some countries are more efficient in their tax administration than others, i.e. a greater part of their success in meeting a particular norm of tax-to-GNP ratio is due to effort rather than luck. But at the same time other countries may be far more efficient in their expenditure and be able to achieve a given ratio of government capital formation to GDP with a much lower tax-to-GNP ratio. On balance, though, it is probably true to say that virtually all LDCs could in fact collect more tax revenue than in fact they do from that part of the population above the poverty line, and that they could spend a higher proportion of available revenues on productive investment rather than on current administration.

Apart from any deficiency of taxable capacity, the tax administration of LDCs is weak; they have therefore tended to concentrate on administratively convenient ways of raising revenues. This explains the large share of indirect taxes, especially taxes on foreign trade, in their total revenues. Because of the weakness of tax administration, there is widespread tax evasion in many LDCs, and because of such evasion, governments have tended to raise the tax rates on those from whom they can be collected, thereby exacerbating the problem of evasion. In the agricultural sector, until recently, revenue was mainly collected in the form of land taxes, but as these ancient taxes got eroded by inflation, the agricultural sector virtually escaped taxation in most LDCs. Most incomes earned in this sector are too low to be taxed but where the larger farmers earn incomes comparable to those in other sectors, they should be taxed on the same basis. (For a proposal for agricultural taxation in India, see Raj, 1972.)

15.3 Monetary Policy

Elementary expositions of economics generally follow the classical dichotomy between 'real' forces and 'monetary' forces. In this approach, the real forces of supply and demand determine the composition of output and the relative prices of goods and services, while monetary forces based on the quantity of money determine the general price level. In other words, money is treated as a 'veil' over real economic phenomena. Changes in the general price level brought about by changes in the quantity of money would have no effect on the economy in real terms because relative prices would be constant. But, even on this view, it is felt that changes in the general price level may cause some inefficiency because they would make economic calculations over time more difficult due to a 'money illusion', i.e. the tendency of some people to take changes in absolute prices of individual goods and services at their face value rather than in real terms. Therefore, a stable value of money, i.e. a stable price level came to be given a high priority as an objective of monetary policy.

Closely related was the objective relating to the balance of payments. If inflation of prices occurred faster in one country than in another, then the country with the faster inflation would become less competitive in international trade, its exports would fall, its imports rise, and the balance of payments situation would deteriorate. In the days of the Gold Standard under which the exchange rate between currencies was fixed, a deterioration of the balance of payments led to an outflow of bullion; in Hume's theory of specie flows, this would reduce the quantity of money and the price level, and thus restore equilibrium in the balance of payments. With the abandonment of the Gold Standard but with a free market in foreign exchange, equilibrium in the balance of payments would be restored by a depreciation of the exchange rate. But when the exchange rate increasingly came to be managed by monetary authorities, the maintenance of a balance of payments position also came to be an important objective of monetary policy, to be attained by such instruments as control of the money supply and adjustment of the exchange rate.

In practice, however, changes in the quantity of money and the ways they are brought about have significant effects on real variables such as the aggregate level of production and employment, and the composition of output, and on relative prices of goods and services. For example, when banks create credit and lend to investors, resources are transferred from consumption to investment, and the economy is enabled to grow faster. If the economy is already fully employed, such an increase in money supply will cause inflation in the short run but the inflation will be liquidated in the long run with the growth of output. Hence, there will be a conflict between the monetary objective of stable prices in the short run and the 'real' objective of faster growth in the long run. If the economy is underemployed to begin with, there may not even be an inflation in the short run, just an increase in employment and output. Because of the interrelations between monetary and real forces influencing the economy, monetary policy cannot be 'assigned' only to the monetary objectives of price stability and balance of payments equilibrium. Instead, countries should pursue all their objectives by a combination of policy instruments (ideally the same number as there are objectives). In case there is a conflict between objectives, it is desirable, especially in LDCs that, as Kaldor (1980, p.87) has argued,

> policies which strengthen the 'real' economy, i.e. output, employment, capital formation and the rate of economic growth—ought to be given higher weight than 'monetary objectives' such as a lower rate of inflation and a stronger balance of payments.

It is from this point of view that we now examine the inflationary experience of LDCs and the monetary policies relating to it in the post-war period. Table 15.5 shows the rates of inflation in LDCs and DMEs in this period. In the 1960s, the DMEs had low rates of inflation, less than 5 per cent per annum; the three countries with inflation rates over 20 per cent were the countries of temperate South America. In that period, most LDCs also had low rates of inflation but there were a number with rapid inflation. It was therefore generally felt that the LDCs were particularly prone to inflations, due to financial mismanagement. But in the 1970s, the DMEs also found themselves having high rates of inflation, many at double-digit rates. Inflation is therefore not peculiarly an LDC phenomenon.

Table 15.5 Distribution of countries according to rates of inflation

Annual percentage rates of inflation	1960–70		1970–79	
	DMEs	LDCs	DMEs	LDCs
Below 5	15	62	—	3
5–10	6	9	12	25
10–20	1	5	11	38
20 & Over	3	2	4	11
Total	25	78	27	77

Source: World Bank, *World Development Report, 1981*

There is currently a great deal of controversy over the causes of the high rates of inflation that most countries have been experiencing. The main theories on the subject may be broadly classified into three groups. First, there is the revival of the classical quantity theory of money in the form of the monetarist theory, mainly due to the work of Milton Friedman. This theory is ultimately based on the concept of a stable demand function for money to be held in cash balances. The amount that people wish to hold in such balances is determined by the opportunity cost, i.e. the returns from holding assets in other income-yielding forms, on the one hand, and by expectations of future changes in the real value of cash balances on the other. In most statistical estimates of this demand function for money, the expected rate of inflation is proxied by the current rate of inflation, so that the demand function gives a relationship between the quantity of money and the current rate of inflation. Given such a relationship, changes in the quantity of money determine the rate of inflation. The second theory is the Keynesian theory that explains inflation as the result of an excess of aggregate demand over aggregate supply. The third explanation is the cost–push theory in which a rise in costs, for example wages, leads to a rise in prices which in turn leads to a further rise in wages and so on in a cumulative wage–price spiral. Such a process depends on workers and capitalists trying to maintain what they feel to be their 'just' shares of aggregate income, when these shares are incompatible with each other.

In practice, all these forces have an influence on inflation; inflations in particular countries at particular times have been due to one or the other of these factors. These forces, however, have different speeds of action, some acting rapidly and therefore being more powerful in the short run, while others act more slowly and have their full effect only in the long run. Also, we must distinguish different phases of an inflationary process. The factors which start an inflation may be different from those which keep it going after it has started, just as the operation of igniting a match stick is different from the process which keeps it burning. The Keynesian factors of aggregate demand and supply act most speedily and are particularly relevant in explaining how an inflation gets started, e.g. by an increase in aggregate demand or a fall in aggregate supply. An increase in aggregate demand may be due to an increase in consumer or export demand, or an increase in private or public investment financed by credit creation by banks or, as is more often the case in LDCs, by an increase in money supply by the monetary authorities. An increase in aggregate demand will increase output without much inflation if there are idle resources, but there will be inflation if resources are already fully employed. Therefore, at the start, it is often a case of either inflation with full employment, or increased employment with stable prices, as Keynes himself argued, but not both. The origin of inflations in LDCs is often due to a fall in aggregate supply, e.g. harvest failures. Hence, during the short period in which an inflation starts, there may or may not be an increase in money supply. Even if there is an increase in money supply, its effects on inflation depends on whether there is full employment of resources to begin with or not.

Once an inflation starts for any reason, other factors determine whether it keeps going or not (Lewis, 1964). The typical case of continuing inflation is the cost-push inflation with a spiral interaction between costs and prices; it is then a reflection of incompatible income claims. For inflation to continue in this way, there must be an increase in money supply, but the inflation itself sets up strong forces to increase the money supply. For example, the banks would be willing to lend more funds for investment as money costs go up with the inflation, so long as the investments remain profitable in real terms. In LDCs it is more often the case that an inflation, once started, forces governments to create money, which keeps the inflation going. This is because government revenues increase in nominal terms with inflation but its expenditures increase faster, so that government has to create money to finance its deficit. This was the main cause for the continuance of rapid inflation in Indonesia in the period 1961–65 (see Sundrum, 1973). Hence, once an inflation has started, an increase in money supply is often the result, rather than the cause, of its continuation. In this phase, when the continuation of inflation is due to cost-push factors, aggregate demand may be equal to, or even less than, aggregate supply. This explains why in this phase inflation may coexist with unemployment, a situation generally described as 'stagflation'.

Finally, there is the influence flowing from the quantity of money to the level of prices operating through the money demand function, i.e. the inverse relationship between inflationary expectations and the quantity of money which people wish to hold in their cash balances. This influence is likely to be particularly slow in its action and to take a long period to become fully effective. The adjustment of cash balances to price expectations will occur faster under conditions of hyper-inflation; the empirical relationships observed under such conditions are therefore likely to reveal the underlying money demand functions more closely (see Cagan, 1956). The inverse relationship is also observed in periods of milder inflation and then identified with the money demand function; however, it is more likely that such a relationship reflects either the effect on prices of an increase in aggregate demand brought about by an increase in money supply or the effect of inflation on the quantity of money supply.

We now consider the policy implications of the above analysis. Among the various objectives of policy, LDCs must give the highest priority to development and faster growth, while a lower priority attaches to the purely monetary objectives of price stability. Some degree of price stability is necessary to promote rapid growth; a high rate of inflation may have serious adverse consequences on economic growth. This does not mean, however, that prices should be completely stable. For example, it has been advocated that there should be a gradual rise in the value of money corresponding to the rate of technological progress (see, e.g., Robertson, 1953, Part III, Chapter 2). Also, Samuelson (1958) has argued that money is one of the instruments by which society allocates consumption to different generations; on this basis, he has shown that a socially optimum allocation implies a rise in the value of money at a rate equal to the steady rate of population growth, a result that would follow with a constant supply of money. A question of special importance for LDCs is the extent to which governments can obtain command over resources by inflationary money creation. This question has been analysed by Friedman (1971) and Mundell (1971), assuming conditions of steady rates of inflation; then they showed that the fraction of GDP that governments can acquire by inflation will increase with the rate of inflation up to a point and then decline, i.e. there is a maximum amount of resources that governments can acquire by inflation, as illustrated by the curve SS in Figure 15.1. For some plausible values of parameters, it is found that at this maximum point, only a small amount of resources can be acquired and the rate of inflation required is so high that there is a real danger of inflation getting out of control. This analysis is concerned with the case of steady rates of inflation. A more relevant question is the relationship during a transitional period of a once-over increase in money supply. Then, the relationship between the rate of inflation and the amount of resources that governments can acquire is likely to be as shown by the curve TT in Figure 15.1, i.e. the amount of resources will decline continuously with the rate of inflation. However, in the transitional period, governments may be able to acquire more resources than that shown by the maximum point of the SS curve for steady rates of inflation. (See Sundrum, 1976a, for a mathematical statement.)

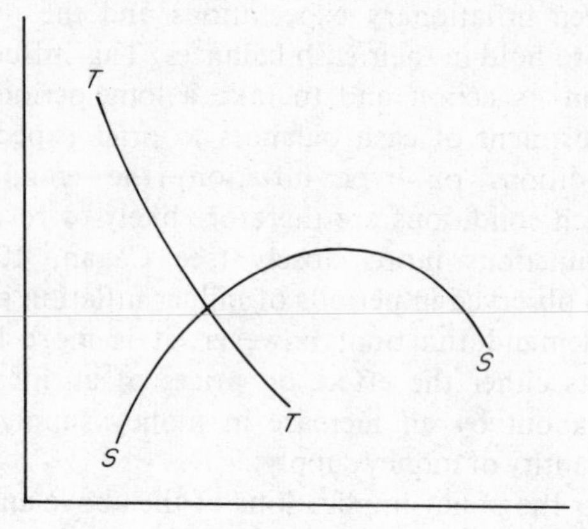

Figure 15.1

Attempts to finance development by inflationary methods are therefore likely to be unsuccessful in the long run. The amount of resources that can be mobilized in this way will be very little considering the rate of inflation involved; attempts to raise more resources will lead to inflation getting out of control. But a certain amount of inflation is inevitable when any significant amount of re-allocation of resources is involved. As Johnson, H. G. (1965, pp.281–2) said,

> (Though) a policy of deliberately promoting development by inflationary means is likely to retard rather than foster economic growth, a moderate degree of inflation—specifically, inflation at an annual percentage rate that can be counted on the fingers of one or at most two hands—is likely to be an inevitable concomitant of a development process that seeks efficiently to mobilise an economy's resources for economic growth.

When inflation leads to economic growth in a short period, as, for example, when it is used to employ unemployed labour in improving rural public works and increasing agricultural production, it is likely to be self-liquidating (see Lewis, 1954, pp.422–6).

Once an inflationary process has got under way, LDCs face the problem of stopping its continuation because rapid inflation leads to adverse effects on growth and distribution. Governments are particularly concerned with the worsening situation of the balance of payments and therefore seek financial assistance from the I.M.F. The I.M.F. then offers loans to meet the balance of payments deficits but usually on a short-term basis because of the revolving nature of its own funds, and on conditions imposed by the I.M.F. designed to repay the loans in a short period. These conditions usually involve a devaluation of the currency. In addition, they generally also involve policies to reduce the growth of money supply. But the inflation may not have been due to excessive growth of money supply. Further, the governments of LDCs do not usually have effective instruments to control the money supply. Attempts to control money supply more tightly then involve reduction of government expenditures or bank lending for investment. Then, the net result is to restore monetary stability at the cost of economic growth.

A more appropriate method of controlling an inflation in an LDC without sacrificing economic growth is to give an adequate amount of assistance to deal with the balance of payments deficit over a longer period of time. This was, in fact, the approach followed by the I.M.F. in its assistance to Indonesia in the period 1966–68, which resulted in one of the most remarkable cases of the speedy control of inflation without reducing the rate of growth and, in fact, raising it (see Grenville, 1981).

CHAPTER 16

Development Aid

16.1 Volume and Distribution of Aid

The present chapter deals with what the DCs can do to help the LDCs promote their development. The rich countries have recognized their international responsibility to provide such aid since the end of World War II; the flow of such international aid is indeed one of the historically distinguishing features of this period. It has been described by White, J. (1967, p.13) thus:

> Towards the end of the 1950s, the nations of North America and western Europe found themselves drifting into what was probably the most ambitious collective enterprise that a group of nations had ever undertaken. The ultimate aim of the enterprise was quite simply, in one prolonged effort, to eliminate from the earth those evils of material privation which had throughout history been regarded as the ineradicable marks of an imperfect society.

The result of this was a steady flow of aid from the rich to the poor countries. A certain amount of it was channelled through the United Nations multilateral institutions, especially the newly set up International Bank for Reconstruction and Development (the World Bank) and the International Monetary Fund. Most of it was given on a bilateral basis. The aid effort of the DMEs was coordinated by the Organisation of Economic Cooperation and Development (OECD) through its Development Assistance Committee (DAC)

Table 16.1 Net flows of official development assistance (ODA) from DAC countries

Period	Amount (US $ billions) —annual average	Percentage of GNP of DAC countries	Index of real volume (1961 = 100)
1950–55	1.9		
1956–59	4.0		
1960–64	5.8	0.52	105.1
1965–69	6.6	0.41	102.7
1970–74	8.8	0.33	104.0
1975–78	15.5	0.33	118.5

Sources: 1950–59: Pearson *et al.*, 1969, p.378; 1960–78: O.E.C.D., *Development Cooperation* (various years).
Note: The index of real volume of aid was derived from the nominal amounts using the GNP deflator of donor countries.

which has been carrying out annual reviews providing much of the data on aid flows. The data are summarized in Table 16.1.

There was a significant increase in the late 1950s and after more than a decade of stagnation, again in the mid-1970s. There has been a steady increase in the share of multilateral agencies; the proportion of DAC aid channelled through these agencies increased from 5.8 per cent in the 1950s to 16.5 per cent in 1970 and 27.7 per cent in 1975.

Official development assistance includes both grants and loans. Strictly speaking, there is an aid element in loans only to the extent that the loans are made on concessional terms, i.e. below commercial rates of interest. The concessional element of a loan is usually calculated as the difference between the face value of a loan and the discounted value at the market rate of interest of the scheduled repayments as a fraction of the face value. There has been a steady improvement in the terms of aid; grants as a proportion of ODA increased from 55 per cent in 1967 to 69 per cent in 1975, and the concessional element of ODA grants and loans increased from 75 to 89 per cent in the same period.

Individual donors have allocated most of their bilateral aid to LDCs with whom they have special historical and political ties. British aid has been directed mostly to Commonwealth countries and French aid to French-speaking African countries. Japan has concentrated its aid in Asia while a large part of American aid has gone to Latin America, to countries on the periphery of the communist world, and to areas of great political tension such as Taiwan and South Korea which received a large volume of American aid at a critical period of their development. Table 16.2 summarizes some aspects of the distribution of aid.

The unequal position of donors assisting different LDCs and the variety of motives for giving aid have meant that there is little relationship between the distribution of aid and the needs of recipients. The per capita level of aid and

Table 16.2 Distribution of DAC aid, 1969–72 (annual averages)

Per capita income of recipients (US $)	1971 Population (millions)	Aid: (a)	(b)	(c)	(d)	(e)
Below 100	780.8	2.1	2.2	27.5	97.5	7
100–199	401.4	4.5	3.0	16.1	88.5	5
200–399	236.8	9.2	3.2	13.2	84.9	7
400–799	230.3	1.8	0.3	2.4	95.6	6
800 & Over	63.2	10.4	0.9	3.3	81.6	3

Notes: (a) per capita aid in US $; (b) aid as percentage of recipient GDP; (c) aid as percentage of recipient imports; (d) grant element of ODA (percentages); (e) debt-service ratio (percentage).

Source: U.N., *Journal of Development Planning*, No. 10, 1976, Tables 1, 7, 8 and 10.

Table 16.3 Per capita aid by population size, 1969–71

Population of recipient (millions)	Number of countries	Per capita aid US $	Aid as percentage of imports	Aid as percentage of GDP
Below 4	36	14.71	19.98	6.95
4–10	22	6.38	19.59	4.23
10–20	13	4.10	15.16	2.64
20–50	12	3.35	9.19	1.51
50–120	6	3.06	20.11	2.37
Over 120	1[a]	1.72	31.86	1.60

Source: Edelman and Chenery, 1977.
Note: (a) India.

the percentage of aid to GDP tend to increase with the level of income of recipients, but aid as a percentage of imports and the grant element of aid are higher for the poorer countries. There is a more systematic relationship between per capita aid and the population size of countries (Table 16.3).

Table 16.4 Sectoral allocation of aid, 1975–78 (averages of annual percentages)

Sector	DAC aid	World Bank group
Agriculture	9.5	20.3
Industry	5.8	16.3
Power		19.3
Transport and communication	15.2	27.1
Education	10.7	3.7
Others	58.8	13.3
Total	100.0	100.0

Sources: O.E.C.D., *World Bank Annual Reports* (various years).

The smaller the country in population size, the higher the per capita aid it gets and the higher the percentage of aid to its GDP, while aid as a percentage of imports is fairly constant. Thus, India with its large population receives very little aid per capita, although she is one of the poorest countries.

The sectoral allocation of the bilateral aid from DAC countries and from the World Bank Group for the period 1975–78 is shown in Table 16.4.

16.2 Effects of Aid

(a) Aid and Growth

By the end of World War II, most of the European countries and Japan, which had been involved in the war, had suffered severe damage to their economies. Only the United States emerged with a highly efficient and productive economy, and provided massive financial assistance to the other countries to reconstruct their economies. A total sum of US $13 billion was disbursed to the European countries in the space of four years. The results were dramatic. Because these countries were highly developed to begin with, in the sense we have adopted of having a full complement of technical skills, infrastructure and institutions, a brief injection of capital was sufficient to set them back on a path of self-sustaining growth.

From this experience with the war-damaged DCs, it was expected that aid would also have a prompt and significant effect on growth in the LDCs. It was generally assumed that the poverty of LDCs was primarily due to their lack of capital and that the role of aid was to finance the import of capital goods from the DCs. On this basis, an estimate of aid requirements was made by a UN Expert Group (United Nations, 1951). It estimated the annual investment needs of LDCs in two parts; an amount of US $4 billion for agriculture (being 4 per cent of the combined LDC national incomes—1 per cent for research and extension and 3 per cent for agricultural investment) and US $15 billion for industrialization, calculated at the rate of US $2500 per worker to shift 1 per cent of the labour force annually from agriculture to non-agriculture. The Group expected that the annual investment of US $19 billion in LDCs would increased their national income by 2½ per cent per year, and with population growth estimated at 1¼ per cent annually, 'per capita national income might rise annually by about two per cent (*sic*)' (United Nations, 1951, p.78). The UN Expert Group estimated the annual domestic savings in LDCs at US $5 billion (5.4 per cent of their national income). A certain part of the capital requirements was expected to come from private foreign investment. For the remainder, which worked out to about US $9 per head of LDC population, they recommended a balance between loans and grants as follows:

> The World Bank should set itself to reach, within five years, some such target as an annual rate of lending of not less than $1 billion a year to the underdeveloped countries.

There remains an important obstacle to lending which it is not within the power of the Bank to remove. This is the fact that the amount that can profitably be invested at a four per cent rate of interest depends on the amount which is being spent at the same time on improving social capital, and especially on public health, on education and on roads and communication. Most of them [the under-developed countries] do not have the money required for these purposes, and they cannot borrow it. We, therefore, urge most strongly that some mechanism be created for transferring from the developed to the under-developed countries, by way of grants-in-aid, a sum of money which should increase rapidly, reaching a level of about $3 billion a year. This would be equivalent to rather less than one per cent of the national income of Western Europe, Australasia, the United States and Canada (United Nations, 1951, pp.84–5).

In the event, however, the effect on the growth of LDCs of the aid that actually flowed to them was disappointing and quite different from the effects of the Marshall Plan aid to Europe. A study of 51 LDCs for the period 1960–65 showed little correlation (0.16) between GDP growth rates and per capita official aid, much lower than the correlation (0.71) between GDP growth rate and growth rates of export earnings (OECD, 1968, pp.126–7).

There were a number of reasons for this disappointing result. First, the volume of aid given to the LDCs was very little, much lower than that given for reconstruction of war-damaged DCs in per capita terms. Even the estimates of the UN Expert Group were based on rates of population growth lower than those which actually eventuated. There appeared to be a threshold in the growth effects of aid. In small amounts, aid will not affect the growth rate or the investment rate but by contrast a massive injection will do so.

The cases of Taiwan, Korea, Puerto Rico and Greece are clear examples of foreign capital inflow raising the domestic investment rate when it is in large enough doses. (Singh, S. K., 1975, p.181)

Second, there was a big difference between the DCs which received aid and the LDCs. Unlike the DCs, the LDCs did not have a skilled labour force, adequate modern infrastructure and efficient economic institutions. This reduced the ability of LDCs to use capital productively; it has been described as the 'absorptive capacity of capital', i.e. the amount of capital that can be invested at a given rate of return, but the factors determining any country's absorptive capacity are precisely those which we have described as fundamental to the concept of development. The absorptive capacity of capital in fact refers to a country's ability to absorb *directly productive* capital, but the concept has been used to determine the amount of aid that a country can benefit from. But if aid is used to promote development as we have defined it, it will increase a country's capacity to absorb directly productive capital.

Third, as shown in Table 16.4, a certain amount of aid was used to improve education, infrastructure and institutions but their effects on growth was limited for a number of reasons. The main reason was that the effects on income growth of improving these elements of development will only materialize in the long run. These effects were further reduced by the fact that the amount allocated for these purposes was small, that it was concentrated on physical infrastructure using material that was imported from the donors, and that it was not accompanied by corresponding measures that could only be taken by the recipient countries themselves.

(b) Aid and Savings

The relationship of aid to growth was based on the expectation that each dollar of aid would lead to a dollar increase in imports and in investment over what they would otherwise have been. It is a difficult problem to determine whether this was in fact the case. Using regression equations fitted to international cross-section data, Chenery and Syrquin (1975, p.132) found that a unit increase in external capital was associated with an increase in investment of 0.45 units and with an increase in imports of 0.43 units. But part of the explanation may simply be that in many cases, aid was given to offset sudden declines in export earnings or increases in requirements of consumer imports (Papanek, 1972).

Nevertheless, aid was expected to have a significant effect on savings. This was spelt out most clearly by Rosenstein-Rodan (1961a):

> Aid should continue not until a certain income level is reached in under-developed countries but only until these countries can mobilise a level of capital formation sufficient for self-sustaining growth . . . The foreign capital inflow mobilised by international action should be within the limits on the one hand of technical absorptive capacity, and on the other hand of the capacity to repay of under-developed countries. While the first limit should preponderantly determine the amount of aid, the second limit should largely determine the method of financing it. Where the capacity to repay in low income under-developed countries is below their absorptive capacity, a proportion of aid will have to be given in grants on 'soft loans'.

On this basis, the required volume of aid was estimated at US $5.7 billion annually in 1961–66, the same amount again in 1966–71, and US $3.8 billion in 1971–76, with the percentage of grants and soft loans being 75, 66 and 50 per cent respectively in the three periods.

This model assumes that capital is the main constraint on growth and that it promotes growth through a stable capital–output ratio. The role of aid is to supplement savings to achieve a target rate of growth. Further, it assumes that the savings ratio increases with the level of income, so that when income has reached a sufficiently high level, domestic savings will be sufficient to sustain growth at the target rate. Therefore, it concludes that aid will be needed for a finite period. On these assumptions, the objective of self-sustaining growth becomes the same as that of achieving a particular income level.

(c) Aid and Foreign Exchange

Aid implies a transfer of resources from the donor to the recipient; when aid is given across national boundaries, it takes the form of foreign exchange. But aid is often identified with the supply of foreign exchange itself.

> The chief source of trouble among these dubious concepts is the convention of measuring development assistance in terms of net financial flows from developed to developing countries, and including in these flows a heterogeneity of tied and untied official cash grants and loans on concessional terms, food aid and private foreign investment, including export credits. These items have widely differing real values, in terms of net contribution of real resources to development, from both the donor and the recipient point of view. In particular, it is sheer fiction to pretend that private foreign investment involves a loss to the developed countries whose firms undertake it, for which credit is due as for official cash grants. The same is true of food aid whose real function is to dispose of unwanted agricultural surpluses generated by domestic price support policies. (Johnson, H. G., 1970, pp.18–19)

An attempt has been made to give a theoretical justification to the notion that aid promotes growth in the recipient countries by increasing the supply of foreign exchange, just as it does by supplementing savings, in the 'two-gap' analysis (Chenery and Strout, 1966). According to this theory, LDCs suffer from two gaps, a domestic gap between savings and investment and a foreign exchange gap between imports and exports. When the two gaps are unequal, the recommendation is for aid to fill the larger gap. It is then argued that in many LDCs, the foreign exchange constraint is more severe than the savings constraint. One interpretation is that, if the relationships of the two gaps to the rate of growth are as shown in Figure 16.1, the growth rate r_f determined by the foreign exchange constraint is lower than r_s, that determined by the savings constraint. In that case, aid in an amount equal to the foreign exchange gap at r_s will enable the recipient country to raise its rate of growth beyond r_f to that which is possible given only the savings constraint. The more usual interpretation is that the foreign exchange gap at a target rate of growth is greater than the savings gap and therefore the target rate of growth r_t can only be achieved if aid is sufficient to fill the larger gap in foreign exchange. As drawn, the result depends crucially on the rate of growth chosen as the target. If such a target is chosen and aid is given equal to the foreign exchange gap, then part of it will be used for consumption (Findlay, 1971). The figure shows that there is a rate of growth r_e at which the two gaps are equal, and if aid is to help countries to achieve the maximum growth possible, it should be equal to the common value of the two gaps at this rate of growth.

One consequence of treating aid as an addition to the supply of foreign exchange is that aid and trade are taken as alternatives to each other. Since the mid-1960s, perhaps because LDCs were not hopeful of an increase in the volume of aid, they have been demanding trade concessions from the DCs. Because of the opposition of vested interests, the DCs have resisted these demands, preferring aid paid out of their general revenues as the soft

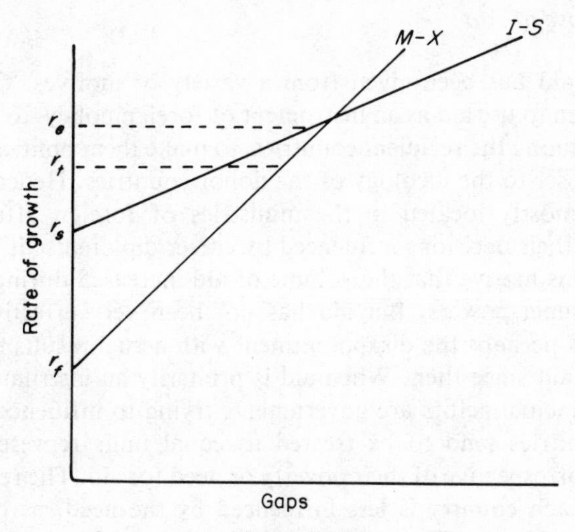

Figure 16.1

option. However, aid and trade are not real alternatives. The benefits of trade concessions accrue primarily to the producers and traders of export commodities in LDCs. The amount of such benefits is relatively small (Johnson, H. G., 1967). Trade concessions from the DCs are useful in improving the conditions of world trade between DCs and LDCs, but they are not a substitute for an increased flow of aid for development purposes.

16.3 Aid Policies

There has been a great deal of debate in the north–south negotiations between DCs and LDCs about a new international economic order. The debate has covered a wide range of issues, such as more aid to LDCs, freer access to DC markets for LDC exports of primary products and manufactures, measures to stabilize the foreign trade of LDCs, regulation of the transfer of technology, a code of conduct for multinational corporations, and more control of international economic agencies by LDCs. For a recent review of these issues, see the report of the Independent Commission on International Development Issues (1980), commonly known as the Brandt report. However, most of these proposals do not go to the heart of the problems arising from the old international economic order (Lewis, 1978a). These are essentially the problems arising from what we have defined as the low level of development of the LDCs. In order to deal with them, the LDCs need much greater access to long-term aid aimed primarily at promoting such development. Some of the ways in which aid can promote the development objectives more fully than in the past are discussed in this section.

(a) The Purpose of Aid

International aid has been given from a variety of motives. One important motive has been to use aid as an instrument of foreign policy, to win or at least keep friends among the recipient countries, to make them politically stable and bring them closer to the ideology of the donor countries. Hence, national aid agencies are mostly located in the ministries of foreign affairs of donor countries and their decisions influenced by career diplomats. It was under the influence of this motive that the volume of aid increased during the cold war between the super-powers. But aid has not been very effective in winning friends. It was perhaps the disappointment with actual results that led to the stagnation of aid since then. When aid is primarily an instrument of foreign policy, the principal actors are governments trying to influence one another. Recipient countries tend to be treated as equal units represented by their governments, irrespective of their poverty or need for aid. The result is that the aid given to each country is less influenced by the need, as determined by population or poverty. Thus, the amount of aid per head of population in recipient countries tends to vary universely with their population (Table 16.3). Another consequence of the foreign policy interest in aid is that much of it is given on a bilateral basis, involving costly aid administrations duplicating work among themselves and vis-à-vis the multilateral institutions.

Another motive behind aid has been to promote the exports of donors to recipients. One effect has been the prevalence of tied aid. This practice reduces the real value of aid as recipients have to pay higher prices when restricted to purchase from a particular country. For example, in a pioneering study, Haq (1965) estimated that the excess cost of the tying of aid received by Pakistan was at least 14 per cent of total aid; similar estimates were found in later studies of other countries (UNCTAD, 1967).

The most important motive for aid giving, however, is the humanitarian one born out of the moral obligation to the rich to help the poor. The emergence of large-scale international aid to the LDCs is basically due to this motive, although the other motives have influenced the ways aid has been distributed and administered. The case for more aid and more effective use of aid rests ultimately on an appeal to the humanitarian motive and in demonstrating that aid can indeed relieve poverty. The humanitarian motive has been the basis of charitable assistance to relieve immediate distress in the case of famines and natural disasters at all times, within and between nations. But while acute distress due to these causes occurs only occasionally and is amenable to assistance over relatively short periods, the LDCs suffer from a chronic condition of mass poverty. Therefore, what distinguishes international aid in the present period is that it is now addressed to helping LDCs, not just to relieving present poverty, but to remedy the underlying causes of such poverty. The problem of achieving this objective as rapidly as possible is the main challenge facing aid policy.

Aid alone cannot solve the problem of mass poverty in the LDCs. Much depends on the efforts of the people and the governments of the LDCs themselves, as described in earlier chapters. By its very nature, international aid suffers from two limitations in meeting this challenge. First, aid can only take the form of resources transferred from one set of countries to another. Secondly, a large part of it consists of transfers between governments; 'the participants in the charitable transfer are not individuals but nation-states jealous of their sovereignty' (Johnson, H. G., 1972, p.143). The root causes of mass poverty cannot be overcome by donor governments simply handing sums of money to recipient governments. To be successful, the transfer of resources must be based on a theory of the causes of mass poverty.

In the early post-war years, the theory that inspired the aid relationship was that mass poverty was due to the low national incomes of LDCs, due in turn to the absence of some 'missing components'. The search for these missing components identified a number of candidates, including shortage of capital, shortage of foreign exchange, low level of education, rapid population growth, weakness of the agricultural sector, etc. Therefore, the role of aid was seen as remedying each of these factors, the fashions in opinion changing briskly at every annual conference on the subject. In practice, however, much of the flow of aid was used to expand the modern sector, especially the industrial sector in urban areas, and to provide the infrastructure for that purpose (Table 16.4), because this is what the recipient governments wanted to do anyway. Most of the poor, however, were in the traditional sectors and in the rural areas. Therefore, although national incomes of LDCs increased in some cases quite rapidly, not necessarily due to aid, there was little impact on mass poverty.

There has been a change of emphasis in the 1970s. Nowadays, the emphasis is on providing aid so that it directly reaches the poor in LDCs. More can certainly be done in this way. An example is the proposal for the third U.N. Development Decade for the 1980s to provide drinking water supply to all people in the LDCs. As Patel (1971, p.308) has argued,

> Linking aid to projects with a predominantly social rather than economic content might generate more warmth and a broader based appreciation of the benefits of aid. When one builds houses and clears slums rather than sets up industries, the points of conflict on issues of economic policy are minimised, and the dialogue on overall performance gets automatically divorced from particular acts of assistance.

But there is a limit to the extent to which mass poverty can be relieved by the public provision of such consumption services. Beyond that are measures to increase the incomes earned by the poor by raising their productive capacity.

It is in this respect that the analysis of the previous chapters becomes relevant to aid policy. Ultimately, the solution of the problem of mass poverty is the development of the LDCs, as this concept was defined in Chapter 5, i.e. by promoting education and infrastructure and improving institutions. As argued in Section 14.3(b), mass poverty can be relieved by implementing these development measures as rapidly and as equitably as possible. This cannot be done by international aid alone, but international aid can greatly help the LDCs to achieve the objective of poverty eradication, if it is addressed specifically to these development measures. This approach has important implications for aid policy which are discussed in more detail below.

(b) The Conditions of Aid

Once the purpose of aid is established, the next problem is to ensure that aid is used for that purpose. This is the function of performance conditions for aid. When the purpose of aid was seen primarily as supplementing domestic savings to promote growth, these performance conditions revolved around the savings rate of recipients. The key concept was that of matching aid with self-help.

A marginal rate which is higher than the average rate of savings is the main lever of a development program and should be the principal condition of aid to underdeveloped countries. (Rosenstein-Rodan, 1961a, p.82)

Economic growth depends on a great many institutional and psychological factors, but in terms of finance, which is the chief province of foreign aid, it depends on adequate expenditures on public services and on capital formation. Taken together, and excluding defense, public expenditure and gross capital formation together should absorb at least 30 per cent of gross domestic product, leaving 70 per cent for personal consumption. In less developed economies public expenditure and capital formation absorb nearer 20 per cent, and consumption takes 80 per cent. The financial condition for self-sustaining growth can therefore be put starkly, if not precisely, by saying that the share of consumption must fall from 80 per cent to 70 per cent of gross domestic product. When you allow for the increased consumption taken up by population growth, and the per capita increase as well, I judge that the ratio of consumption should not fall by more than one-half-of-one per cent per year, so that a fall from 80 per cent to 70 per cent should take twenty years. The essence of my proposal is that the amount of foreign aid should be tied to success in achieving this objective. (Lewis, 1964a, p.22)

A number of performance conditions were proposed along these lines. Apart from the assumption that savings are the main constraint on growth, the weakness of these criteria is that they are based on past performance and that the result is to use aid to reward success which may be due to a variety of factors not necessarily connected with conscious policy effort on the part of the recipient. If the main object is to ensure the efficient use of aid,

It should be made clear to any country for which a [consultative] group is being set up that the group's concern with the recipient's performance is not confined to a review of progress, but extends also to consideration of future policy. Since future policy is likely to be the principal determinant of the level of future requirements, and since the level of aid available is itself likely to affect future policy, the group clearly cannot be debarred from effectual discussion of policy by, for instance, considerations of national sovereignty. The time for the group to discuss a five-year development plan—to take the most conspicuous example—is not after it has been published but while it is still under consideration. (White, J., 1967, pp.208–9)

When it appeared in the mid-1960s that the volume of aid was unlikely to increase significantly, attention shifted to elaborate country reviews of economic performance to improve the allocation and effective use of aid. These reviews covered all aspects of government policies, covering not only the use of aid funds, but of domestic resources as well. But aid is essentially a transaction between the people of rich countries and those of the poor, and governments are only the intermediaries in this transaction. The aid-giving process is not particularly well-served by broad-ranging reviews of all government policies:

> Such a recipe for international intervention or even involvement on an extensive scale cannot suit the realities of the second half of the twentieth century . . . the strident style of performance-oriented aid diplomacy smacks of neo-colonialism to many in the developing world. There is something awkward about punishing ordinary people for the temporary aberrations of their leaders. Performance for a society can only be judged over the long pull—no society can be free from upsets and stresses and strains from time to time. The style that is most likely to suit the decade of the seventies is not one of intervention or even involvement but of duty done without too much fuss or subsequent bother. And it is doubtful if most of the voters in the affluent countries have an appetite for detailed reviews and judgments about distant countries, the inner logic of whose development they neither comprehend nor wish to comprehend. (Patel, 1971, p.308)

What is needed, therefore, is a more specific agreement between donor and recipient about future policy regarding the use of aid. This is the rationale behind project aid as distinct from programme aid.

> The only requirement imposed by the specific project provision of the Articles is that, before a loan is made, there shall be a clear agreement both on how the proceeds of the loan are to be expended and on what the loan is expected to accomplish. (World Bank, 1969)

Also, as the U.N. Expert Group recommended (United Nations, 1951, p.85),

> We do not suggest that aid should be given unconditionally to under-developed countries. This would not be wise. Each grant should be linked to a specific function, and there should be international verification that the funds are used only for the purpose for which they have been granted.

Project aid has been criticized, because it has often suffered from a fallacy of misplaced concreteness, i.e. it has been given mostly for physical constructions and also to cover only the foreign-exchange costs of projects. Recipient countries have therefore been demanding more aid in the form of programme aid. But, in principle, project aid is a way of ensuring that the purposes of aid are examined carefully beforehand by donor and recipient alike and that aid is used for the agreed purpose. The principle of project aid is essentially that of supervised credit, which has been successful and widely accepted in the case of agricultural loans.

However, there is the difficulty even with project aid, arising from the fungibility of financial resources, that the *actual* purpose for which aid is used may not be the *ostensible* purpose for which it is given.

> If the project to which aid is ostensibly tied is a 'high priority project' which would in any case have been part of the recipient's plan, and which he otherwise would have undertaken with his own money, then obviously the aid given enables the recipient to release his own money from project A (which is now aid financed), continue with project B, C and D, which he financed with his own money, the utilize his money now released from project A in order to add a new project E to his original development plan or expenditure schedule. This could mean that the donor of aid ties his aid to project A, studies it minutely and satisfies himself that it is technically sound and economically right, while in reality—as distinct from appearance—his aid may go into project E, which he may know nothing about, which he does not study, and which may be neither technically sound nor economically right, nor generally the kind of thing that the aid donors would want to support. (Singer, 1965, pp.539–40)

There is certainly this limitation of project aid in principle; it is, however, a limitation which is inherent in international aid. Any method of avoiding such diversion of funds would require such extensive international intervention in domestic policies of recipients as to be unacceptable. Further, the diversion of funds is likely to be relatively small in practice, if aid is more deliberately tied to the kind of development measures described in Chapters 6–8. It is precisely because such measures have not been vigorously pursued in the LDCs that there has been so little impact on mass poverty in these countries in the past three decades. It is only by spelling out these measures in, and getting a consensus for, a list of specific projects as particularly aid-worthy, and allocating aid to these projects, that faster progress can be achieved in meeting the challenge of aid policy more successfully in the future.

(c) Volume and Distribution of Aid

The above conditions for aid have important implications for the volume and allocation of aid. In the current negotiations between DCs and LDCs, the target for aid has been laid down primarily in terms of the principle of ability to pay, for example, total transfers at 1 per cent of the GDP of donors and official aid as 0.7 per cent, rather than according to need for, and utilization of, aid by recipients. Further, the allocation of aid has been mainly on the basis of political, especially foreign policy, considerations leading to a very inequitable distribution among recipients.

But once it is agreed that aid should be given for specific development projects as defined above, there is a better alternative for determining the volume and allocation of aid. The volume of aid would be determined by the amount that each recipient country is willing and able to use according to these conditions. Much therefore depends on the recipient country. As the influential Indian journal, the *Economic and Political Weekly* observed editorially (July 5 1980)

The inflow of external assistance, in both gross and net terms, has shown a noticeable decline since 1975–76. The principal reason for the slowing down of the inflow of aid is the slow progress of the development projects for which the aid has been meant, because of lack of domestic financial and real resources and administrative failings. So instead of aid being the constraint on development, it is utilization of available aid which has been limited by the insufficiency of the development effort.

The above proposal implies that the amount of aid that is given for a particular project should not be limited to its foreign exchange component but to whatever amount is needed to permit the recipient government, given its circumstances, to implement it. The result would be that the progress of development in LDCs would be relieved of the financial constraint, as far as this can be done by international aid. The allocation of aid among recipients would depend primarily on the recipients, rather than on the political preferences of the donors. In particular, it would have the effect of increasing the flow of aid to the least developed among the LDCs. The targets for aid will be based, not simply on the capacity of donors or the needs of recipients, but on the extent to which the aid promotes development.

Although aid on this proposal is primarily oriented towards the development objective, it is possible to reconcile it with the other motives behind aid. A large proportion of the aid of individual donors is given bilaterally for foreign policy considerations, because if given through the multilateral institutions, their contribution to particular recipients becomes anonymous when merged with other funds. But it may be possible to combine the political advantages of liberal aid with the economic advantages of aid administration by the multilateral institutions, if individual donors use the multilateral institutions as 'executive agents' for the aid given to particular recipients. One of the problems arising from the foreign policy interest is the inequitable allocation of aid among recipients. Therefore, there should be greater international coordination of aid flows among recipients as there now is for the distribution among donors. Similarly, the balance of payments concerns of donors has led to extensive tying of aid. When an individual donor unties its aid, it may suffer some balance of payments effects, but these effects are likely to be less if all donors do so together (Bhagwati, 1967).

(d) Terms of Aid

The financial resources the LDCs get from the World Bank and a considerable part of the bilateral aid from individual donors are in the form of loans. If the LDCs increase the pace of their development, this loan component of aid will also increase in the future. Therefore, we must consider the extent to which the development of LDCs can be financed by borrowing.

Commercial banks usually measure the creditworthiness of their clients by their income or wealth; this approach has also been extended to the case of loans to governments, whose creditworthiness is measured by the amount of outstanding debt to total income, or more usually by the proportion of annual debt-service payments to export receipts, known as the debt-service ratio. In the case of private borrowers, this measure of creditworthiness is really a rough indication of willingness to repay. In the case of government borrowers, the willingness to repay loans depends so much on political factors that it is a matter for political judgment. From an economic point of view, the main consideration in lending to governments is their ability to amortize the loan on agreed terms.

Sometimes the case for soft loans or grants to a country is made on the grounds that it is not 'creditworthy' for commercial loans, i.e., it will not be able to make the interest and capital repayments. This argument seems to imply that there are no viable projects in these countries, and that the country is not 'developable'. It is clearly preferable to base an argument for soft loans simply on the fact that a country is poor, rather than introduce spurious notions of creditworthiness. In principle, any loan is justified if the returns from investing in it are sufficient to repay the loan on the terms on which it is borrowed; this depends on how the proceeds of the loans are used. But in the case of foreign loans borrowed by governments, there are some other problems.

The volume of debt is of no significance if the loans have been invested economically. By 'invested economically' I mean that the loan must add more to national income than it costs. But I also assume that the economy is able to translate extra income into foreign exchange: to convert it into tax revenues if the loan is for a public purpose, and to convert these revenues into foreign exchange. I also assume that enough of this extra income accrues within the lifetime of the loan, i.e., that one is not borrowing on short-term to finance long-term investment. Given these conditions, a loan is not a burden but a blessing; the larger the debt burden, the better off the country will be. (Lewis, 1978a, pp.60–1).

Given the share of the increase of national income that governments can mobilize to meet debt service, there is a limit to the rate of interest at which it can borrow, known as the critical rate of interest (see Hayes *et al.*, 1964, p.171). Most of the discussion about the debt-service burden has been concerned with the ability of borrowing countries to convert their savings into foreign exchange. Therefore, the ratio of debt or debt-service changes to exports has generally been used to limit lending. This approach is unsatisfactory for a number of reasons. First, this ratio has not been very high in LDCs, compared with the historical experience of other countries. We have already drawn attention to the very high historical rates of borrowing relative to exports undertaken by Latin America, Australia and Canada (see Section 10.2 above).

Second, this approach discriminates against countries whose exports are small and are expanding slowly.

Such an approach is unfair to the larger countries, which, because of their geographical diversity, import very little. India, for example, needs to import only about 5 per cent of national income, and on any such rule of thumb is permitted a maximum debt charge of 1.7 per cent of national income. The error in this approach is that it assumes that a country with relatively small imports must also have relatively small exports. But if India's debt charges came to 5 per cent of national income, why should she not meet her obligations by importing 5 per cent and exporting 10 per cent of her national product? If debt limitations are to be imposed, they should be in terms of national income and not trade. (Lewis, 1978a, p.63)

Third, this approach relates the amount that a country can borrow to the amount of its exports in a relatively short period. If funds are borrowed for development purposes, they will help the country to repay only in the long run. Therefore, such loans must be made for a sufficiently long period. If, for any reason, this cannot be done, there must be arrangements for rolling over loans by incurring new debt to pay off old debts.

To relieve the development process in LDCs of any financial constraint, they need a large volume of funds now. If the amount they can borrow on currently available terms is unduly limited by their current ability to service the loans, there is considerable advantage in using a part of grant aid to make up the difference and borrow a larger amount. (This is the proposal known as the Horovitz plan.) Ultimately, the amounts that LDCs can usefully borrow depends on how the funds are used and not on the purely financial criteria discussed above.

Bibliography and Author Index

Figures in square brackets refer to pages where each article or book is cited.

Abramovitz, M. (1956) 'Resources and output in the U.S. since 1870', *Amer. Econ. Rev. Pap. & Proc.* **46**, 5-23. [148]

Adelman, I. and Morris, C. T. (1971) *Society, Politics and Economic Development* (Baltimore, Johns Hopkins Press). [78]

Adelman, I. and Morris, C. T. (1971a) 'An Anatomy of Income Distribution Patterns in Developing Countries', *Development Digest*, **9**(4), 24–37. [249]

Adelman, I. and Morris, C. T. (1973) *Economic Growth and Social Equity in Developing Countries* (Stanford, Stanford University Press). [249, 252]

Adelman, I. and Whittle, P. (1979) *Static and Dynamic Indices of Income Inequality* (Geneva, World Employment Programme WEP 2–23/WP 74). [248]

Adler, J. (1965) *Absorptive Capacity: the Concept and its Determinants* (Washington, Brookings Institution). [145]

Ahluwalia, M. S. (1973) 'Taxes, Subsidies and Employment', *Quar. Jour. Econ.* **88**, 393–409. [170]

Ahluwalia, M. S. (1974) 'Income inequality: some dimensions of the problem', in Chenery, H. B. et al. (1974), pp.3–37. [254]

Ahluwalia, M. S. (1976) 'Inequality, poverty and development', *Jour. Dev. Econ.* **3**, 307–42. [249, 253]

Ahluwalia, M. S. *et al.* (1978) *Growth and Poverty in Developing Countries* (Washington, World Bank Staff Working Paper No. 309). [247, 270]

Ahluwalia, M. S. (1979) ''Growth and poverty in developing countries', *Jour. Dev. Econ.* **6**, 299–341. [28, 254]

Ahmed, B. and Blaug, M. (eds) (1973) *The Practice of Manpower Forecasting* (Amsterdam, Elsevier). [96]

Alderman, H. and Timmer, C. P. (1980) 'Food policy and food demand in Indonesia', *Bull. Indonesian Econ. Studies* **16**(3), 83–93. [191]

Allen, R. G. D. (1938) *Mathematical Analysis for Economists* (London, Macmillan). [106, 286]

Arndt, H. W. (1954) 'Economic development: some lessons of Australian experience', *Weltwirtschaftliches Archiv.* **73**(1), 162–70. [54]

Arndt, H. W. (1955) 'External economies in economic growth', *Econ. Record* **31**, 192–214. [150]

Arndt, H. W. (1978) *The Rise and Fall of Economic Growth* (Melbourne, Longmans Cheshire). [158]

Arndt, H. W. (1981) 'Economic development: a semantic history', *Econ. Dev. and Cultural Change* **29**, 457–66. [74]

Arndt, H. W. and Sundrum, R. M. (1975) 'Regional price disparities', *Bull. Indonesian Econ. Studies.* **11**(2), 30–68. [121]
Arrow, K. J. (1962) 'The economic implications of learning by doing', *Rev. Econ. Studies.* **29**, 155–73. [148]
Arthur, W. B. and McNicoll, G. (1975) 'Large scale simulation models in population and development, what use to planners', *Pop. and Dev. Rev.* **1**, 251–66. [140]
Atkinson, A. B. and Stiglitz, J. E. (1980) *Public Economics* (London, McGraw-Hill). [99]
Bairoch, P. and Limber, J-M. (1968) 'Changes in an industrial distributions of the world's labour force by region, 1880–1960'. *International Labour Rev.*, **98**, pp.311–336. [44]
Ballentine, J. G. and Soligo, R. (1978) 'Consumption and earnings patterns and income distribution', *Econ. Dev. and Cultural Change* **26**, 696–708. [280]
Barro, R. J. and Grossman, H. I. (1976) *Money, Employment and Inflation* (Cambridge, Cambridge University Press). [5, 155]
Bauer, P. T. (1971) *Dissent on Development* (London, Weidenfeld and Nicolson). [21]
Bauer, P. T. and Yamey, B. S. (1957) *The Economics of Underdeveloped Countries* (Cambridge, Cambridge University Press). [66, 144, 170]
Beckerman, W. (1974) *In Defence of Economic Growth* (London, Jonathan Cape). [159]
Bereday, G. Z. F. and Lauwerys, J. A. (1967) *Educational Planning* (World Yearbook of Education) (London, Evans Brothers). [84]
Bernardelli, H. (1952) ''New Zealand and Asiatic migration', *Pop. Studies.* **6**, Pt.I, 39–54. [58]
Berry, I. and Cline, W. R. (1979) *Agrarian Structure and Productivity in Developing Countries* (Baltimore, Johns Hopkins Press University Press). [281]
Beteille, A. (1969) *Caste, Class and Power* (Berkeley, University of California Press). [122]
Bhagwati, J. N. (1967) 'The tying of aid', reprinted in J. Bhagwati and R. S. Eckhaus (eds) *Foreign Aid* (London, Penguin Books). [319]
Bhagwati, J. N. and Chakravarty, S. (1969) 'Contributions to Indian Economic Analysis: A Survey', *Amer. Econ. Rev.* **59**(4), Pt. 2, Supplement, 2–73. [178]
Bhatt, V. V. (1978) *Interest Rates, Transaction Costs and Financial Innovation* (Washington, Domestic Finance Study No.49). [125]
Bicanic, R. (1962) 'The threshold of economic growth', *Kyklos* **15**, 7–28. [145]
Binswanger, H. P. and Ruttan, V. W. (1978) *Induced Innovation* (Baltimore, Johns Hopkins Press). [172]
Birnberg, T. B. and Resnick, S. A. (1975) *Colonial Development* (New Haven, Yale University Press). [58, 103]
Blaug, M. (1974) *Education and the Employment Problem in Developing Countries* (Geneva, I.L.O.). [84]
Blaug, M. (1979) 'Economics of education in developing countries', *Third World Quarterly* **1**(1), 73–83. [91]
Blaug, M., Layard, P. R. G. and Woodland, M. (1969) *The Causes of Graduate Unemployment in India* (London, Allen Lane, The Penguin Press). [94]
Bliss, C. J. (1967) 'Review of collected scientific papers of Paul A. Samuelson', *Econ. Jour.* **77**, 338–45. [211]
Bliss, C. J. and Stern, N. (1978) 'Productivity, wages and nutrition', *Jour. Dev. Econ.* 331–98. [122]
Boeke, J. H. (1953) *Economics and Economic Policy of Dual Societies* (Haarlem, Tjeenk, Willink & Zoon). [113]
Bolnick, B. R. (1975) 'Tax effort in developing countries: what do regression measures really measure?' in Toye, J. F. J. (ed.) *Taxation and Economic Development* (London, Frank Cass) Chapter 3. [299]

Booth, A., Chaudhri, D. P., and Sundrum, R. M. (1980) *Income Distribution and the Structure of Production* (Canberra, Australian National University, mimeograph). [276]
Booth, A. and Sundrum, R. M. (1976) 'The 1973 Agricultural Census' *Bull. Indonesian Econ. Studies* **12**(2), 90–105. [121]
Booth, A. and Sundrum, R. M. (1982) *Labour Absorption in LDC Agriculture* (Canberra, Australian National University, mimeograph). [133, 174, 188, 201]
Boserup, E. (1965) *The Conditions of Agricultural Growth* (London, Allen and Unwin). [140, 187]
Boserup, E. (1970) *Women's Role in Economic Development* (New York, St Martins Press). [78]
Boyce, J. K. and Evenson, R. E. (1975) *Agricultural Research and Extension Programs*, New York, Agricultural Development Council). [189–90]
Braidwood, R. J. (1952) *The Near East and the Foundations of Civilization* (Eugene Oregon, Oregon State System of Higher Education). [50]
Brown, A. and Deaton, A. (1972) 'Models of consumer behaviour', *Econ. Jour.* **82**, 1145–1236. [184]
Brown, H. (1975) 'Population growth and affluence: the fissioning of human society', *Quar. Jour. Econ.* **89**, 236–46. [32]
Bruton, H. (1976) 'Employment, productivity and income distribution', in Cairncross, A. and Puri, M. (eds) *Employment, Income Distribution and Development Strategy* (New York, Holmes and Meier) pp.71–89. [171]
Butt, D. M. B. (1954) 'A model of trade and accumulation', *Amer. Econ. Rev.* **44**, 511–29. [215–6]
Butt, D. M. B. (1960) *On Economic Growth* (Oxford, Clarendon Press). [145–8, 173]
Butt, D. M. B. (1974) *Economic Development and Income Distribution: A Model Illustrated* (Canberra, Australian National University, mimeograph). [256–9]
Butt, D. M. B. (1978) *On Economic Man* (Canberra, Australian National University Press). [5, 113]
Cagan, P. (1956) 'The monetary dynamics of hyperinflation', in Friedman, M. (ed.) *Studies in the Quantity Theory of Money* (Chicago, University of Chicago Press) pp.25–117. [303]
Caldwell, J. (1976) 'Towards a restatement of demographic transition theory', *Pop. and Dev. Rev.* **2**(3–4), 321–66. [139]
Caves, R. E. and Jones, R. W. (1973) *World Trade and Payments* (Boston, Little, Brown and Co.). [240]
Chaudhri, D. P. (1968) 'Education and Agricultural Productivity in India' (unpublished Ph.D. thesis, Delhi University). [67]
Chelliah, R. J., Baas, H. J., and Kelley, M. R. (1975) 'Tax ratios and tax effort in developing countries', *I.M.F. Staff Papers* **22**, 187–205. [298]
Chenery, H. B. (1960) 'Patterns of industrial growth', *Amer. Econ. Rev.* **50**, 624–54. [232]
Chenery, H. B. and Keesing, D. B. (1978) *The Changing Composition of Developing Country Exports* (Washington, World Bank Staff Working Paper No.314). [233]
Chenery, H. B. and Strout, A. M. (1966) 'Foreign assistance and economic development', *Amer. Econ. Rev.* **56**, 679–733. [312]
Chenery, H. B. and Syrquin, M. (1975) *Patterns of Development 1950–1970* (London, Oxford University Press). [135–6, 142, 201, 311]
Chenery, H. B. *et al.* (1974) *Redistribution with Growth* (London, Oxford University Press). [77, 250, 252, 255, 278]
Chitre, V. (1981) *Growth Cycles in the Indian Economy, 1951–75* (Pune, India, Gokhale Institute of Politics and Economics, mimeograph). [195]
Clark, C. (1940) *Conditions of Economic Progress* (London, Macmillan). [132]
Clower, R. W. (1965) 'The Keynesian counterrevolution: a theoretical appraisal',

in Hahn, F. H. and Brechling, F. P. R. (eds) *The Theory of Interest Rates* (London, Macmillan) pp.103–25. [155]

Clower, R. W. *et al.* (1966) *Growth without Development* (Evanston, Illinois, Northwestern University Press). [74]

Coale, A. J. (1973) 'The demographic transition reconsidered', in *Report of International Population Conference, 1973* (Liege, I.U.S.S.P.) Vol.1, pp.53–72. [139]

Coale, A. J. and Hoover, E. M. (1958) *Population Growth and Economic Development in Low-Income Countries* (Princeton, Princeton University Press). [140]

Coppock, J. B. (1962) *International Economic Instability* (New York, McGraw-Hill). [227]

Corden, W. M. (1974) *Trade Policy and Economic Welfare* (Oxford, Clarendon Press). [151, 178, 231, 234]

Cornwall, J. (1977) *Modern Capitalism* (London, Martin Robertson). [7, 141, 148, 150–1, 184, 186, 198, 201]

Dandekar, V. M. (1967) 'Presidential address', *Indian Jour. Agr. Econs.* **22**, 7–23. [288–9]

Dandekar, V. M. (1981) 'On measurement of poverty', *Econ. and Pol. Weekly* **16**, 1241–50. [267]

Dandekar, K. and Sathe, M. (1980) 'Employment guarantee scheme and food for work programme', *Econ. and Pol. Weekly*, **15**, 707–13. [123]

Davis, K. (1969) *World Urbanisation 1900–70*, Vol.I (Berkeley, University of California Press). [109–10]

Davis, K. (1972) *World Urbanisation 1950–70* Vol.II (Berkeley, University of California Press). [108–9]

De Wit, Y. B. (1973) 'The Kabupaten programme', *Bull. Indonesian Econ. Studies*, **9**(1), 65–85. [123]

Demeny, P. (1968) 'Early fertility decline in Austria–Hungary: a lesson in demographic transition', *Daedalus* No.97, 502–22. [138]

Denison, E. F. (1967) *Why Growth Rates Differ* (Washington, D.C., The Brookings Institution). [152]

Denison, E. F. and Chung, W. K. (1976) *How Japan's Economy Grew So Fast* (Washington D.C., The Brookings Institution). [152]

Diamond, M. (1978) 'Towards a change in the economic paradigm through the experience of developing countries', *Jour. Dev. Econ.* **5**, 19–53. [163]

Divatia, V. V. and Bhatt, V. V. (1968) 'On measuring the pace of development', *Reserve Bank of India Bulletin* **1968** (April), 1–10. [78]

Dixit, A. and Norman, V. (1980) *Theory of International Trade* (Cambridge, Nisbet). [211]

Dore, R. (1976) *The Diploma Disease* (London, Allen and Unwin). [89–93]

Dorfman, R., Samuelson, P. A., and Solow, R. M. (1958) *Linear Programming and Economic Analysis* (New York, McGraw-Hill). [286]

Dror, Y. (1963) 'The planning process', *Inter. Rev. Administrative Science* **29**(1), 46–58. [286]

Durand, J. D. (1967) 'The modern expansion of world population', *Proc. Amer. Phil. Socy.* **3**(3), 136–59. [39]

Eckhaus, R. S. (1955) 'The factor proportions in underdeveloped countries', reprinted in Agarwala, A. N. and Singh, S. P. (eds) *The Economics of Underdevelopment* (London, Oxford University Press) pp.348–80. [169]

Edelman, J. A. and Chenery, H. B. (1977) 'Aid and income distribution', in J. N. Bhagwati (ed.) *The New International Economic Order* (Cambridge, Mass., M.I.T. Press), Chapter 2. [308]

Eltis, W. (1971) 'The rate of technical progress', *Econ. Jour.* **81**, 502–24. [148]

Emmanuel, A. (1972) *Unequal Exchange* (New York Monthly Review Press). [8, 226]

Encarnacion, J. (1974) 'Fertility and labour force participation, Philippines, 1968', *Philippines Rev. of Business and Economics* **11**, 113–44. [135]
Enke, S. (1966) 'The economic aspect of slowing population growth', *Econ. Jour.* **76**, 44–56. [168]
Fei, J. C. H. and Ranis, G. (1964) *Development of the Labor-Surplus Economy* (Homewood, Ricard D. Irwin). [55]
Feldman, G. A. (1928) 'On the theory of growth rates of national income—I' in Spulberg, N. (ed.) *Foundations of Soviety Strategy for Economic Growth* (Ithaca, Cornell University Press, 1964) 174–99. [178]
Fields, G. S. (1977) Poverty, inequality and development: acceleration or exacerbation?' (Center Discussion Paper No.260) (New Haven, Yale University Economic Growth Center). [253–4]
Findlay, R. E. (1959) 'International specialization and the concept of balanced growth, comment'. *Quar. Jour. Econ.*, **73**, 339–46. [181]
Findlay, R. E. (1966) 'Optimal investment allocation between consumer goods and capital goods', *Econ. Jour.* **76**, 70–83. [180]
Findlay, R. E. (1970) 'Factor proportions and comparative advantage in the long run', *Jour. Pol. Econ.* **78**(1), 27–34; reprinted in Findlay, R. E., *International Trade and Development Theory* (New York, Columbia University Press, 1973) Chapter 7. [242]
Findlay, R. E. (1971) 'The "Foreign Exchange Gap" and growth in developing economies', in Bhagwati, J. N., Jones, R. W., Mundell, R. A., and Vanek, J. (eds) *Trade, Balance of Payments and Growth* (Amsterdam, North-Holland) pp.168–82. [312]
Findlay, R. E. (1980) 'The terms of trade and equilibrium growth in the World economy', *Amer. Econ. Rev.* **70**, 291–9. [223]
Findlay, R. E. and Grubert, H. (1959) 'Factor intensities, technical progress and the terms of trade,' *Oxford Econ. Papers* **2**, 111–21. [224]
Findlay, R. and Wellisz, S. (1976) 'Project evaluation, shadow prices, and trade policy', *Jour. Pol. Econ.* **84**, 543–52. [178]
Fisher, A. G. B. (1935) *The Clash of Progress and Security* (London, Macmillan). [132]
Fisk, E. K. (1975) 'The response of nonmonetary production units to contact with the exchange economy', in Reynolds, L. G. (ed.) *Agriculture in Development Theory* (New Haven, Yale University Press) pp.53–83. [120]
Foster, P. J. (1966) 'The vocational school fallacy in development planning', in Anderson, C. A. and Bowman, M. J. (eds) *Education and Economic Development* (Chicago, Aldine) pp.142–66. [87]
Frank, A. G. (1967) *Capitalism and Underdevelopment in Latin America* (New York, Monthly Review Press). [8, 59]
Friedman, M. (1971) 'Government revenue from inflation', *Jour. Pol. Econ.* **79**, 846–56. [303]
Frisch, R. (1970) 'Econometrics in the World of today', in Eltis, W. A., Scott, M. F. G., and Wolfe, J. N. (eds) *Induction, Growth and Trade* (Oxford, Clarendon Press) Chapter 11. [286]
Gadgil, D. R. (1948) *The Industrial Evolution of India in Recent Times* (Calcutta, Oxford University Press). [195]
Galbraith, J. K. (1980) *The Nature of Mass Poverty* (London, Penguin Books). [113, 265]
Ganguli, B. N. (1965) *Dadabhai Naoroji and the Drain Theory* (Bombay, Asia Publishing House). [59]
Geertz, C. (1963) *Agricultural Involution* (Berkeley, University of California Press). [256]
Gerschenkron, A. (1962) *Economic Backwardness in Historical Perspective* (Cambridge, Mass., Belknap Press). [55, 124]
Gerschenkron, A. (1963) 'The early phases of industrialisation in Russia: afterthoughts

and counterthoughts', in Rostow, W. W. (ed.) *The Economics of Take-Off into Sustained Growth* (London, Macmillan) pp.151–69. [57]

Goldsmith, R. W. (1969) *Financial Structure and Development* (New Haven, Yale University Press). [124]

Gomulka, S. (1971) *Inventitive Activity, Diffusion and the Stages of Economic Growth* (Aarhus, Aarhus University). [149]

Government of India, Ministry of Education (1966) *Education and National Development* (Report of the Education Commission) (New Delhi, Government Publications). [92]

Government of India, Planning Commission (1974) *Draft Fifth Five Year Plan* (New Delhi, Planning Commission). [263]

Grenville, S. (1981) 'Monetary policy and the formal financial sector', in Booth, A. and McCawley, P. (eds) *The Indonesian Economy during the Soeharto Era* (Kuala Lumpur, Oxford University Press) Chapter 4. [305]

Griffin, K. and Khan, A. R. (1978) 'Poverty in the Third World: ugly facts and fancy models', *World Development* **6**, 295–304. [270]

Griliches, Z. (1957) 'Hybrid corn: an exploration in the economics of technological change', *Econometrica*, **25**, 501–22. [149]

Grubel, H. G. and Lloyd, P. J. (1975) *Intra-Industry Trade* (London, Macmillan). [150, 218–9]

Habakkuk, H. J. (1965) 'Historical experience of economic development', in Robinson, E. A. G. (ed.) *Problems in Economic Development* (London, Macmillan) Chapter 6. [198]

Haq, M. (1965) 'Tied credits: a quantitative analysis', in Adler, J., and Kuznets, P. (eds) *Capital Movements and Economic Development* (London, Macmillan). [314]

Harberger, A. C. (1959) 'Using the resources at hand more effectively', *Amer. Econ. Rev.*, **49**, 134–46. [73]

Harberger, A. C. (1966) 'Investment in man versus investment in machines: the case of India', in Anderson, C. A. and Bowman, M. J. (eds) *Education and Economic Development* (Chicago, Aldine) pp.11–50. [94]

Harbison, F. H. and Myers, C. A. (1964) *Education, Manpower and Economic Growth* (New York, McGraw-Hill). [92]

Harris, J. R. and Todaro, M. P. (1970), 'Migration, unemployment and development: a two-sector analysis', *Amer. Econ. Rev.* **60**, 126–42. [106]

Harrod, R. F. (1963) 'Desirable international movements of capital in relation to growth of borrowers and lenders and growth of markets', in Harrod, R. F. and Hague, D. (eds) *International Trade Theory in a Developing World* (London, Macmillan). [231–2]

Hasan, I. (1976) 'Rice marketing in Aceh', *Bull. Indonesian Econ. Studies*, **12**(3), 77–94. [120]

Hauser, P. M. (1973) 'Population criteria in foreign aid programs', in Wogaman, J. P. (ed.) *The Population Crisis and Moral Responsibility* (Washington D.C., Public Affairs Press) pp.233–51. [167]

Hawtrey, R. G. (1937) *Capital and Employment* (London, Macmillan). [145]

Hayami, Y. and Ruttan, V. W. (1971) *Agricultural Development: An International Perspective* (Baltimore, Johns Hopkins Press). [185, 187, 189]

Hayes, J. P., Wyss, H., and Husain, S. S. (1964) 'Long run growth and debt servicing problem: projection of debt servicing burden and the conditions of debt failure', in Avramovic, D. (ed.) *Economic Growth and External Debt* (Baltimore, Johns Hopkins Press) pp.154–192. [320]

Hecksher, E. F. (1919) 'The effect of foreign trade on the distribution of income', reprinted in Ellis, H. S. and Metzler, L. A., *Readings in the Theory of International Trade* (Philadelphia, Blakiston). [210]

Heer, D. (1966) 'Economic development and fertility', *Demography* **3**, 423–44. [138]

Helleiner, G. K. (1981) 'The Refsnes seminar: economic theory and north-south negotiations', *World Development*, **9**, 539–55. [242]
Henry, L. (1961) 'Some data on natural fertility', *Eugenics Quarterly*, **8**(2), 81–91. [140]
Hicks, J. R. (1953) 'An inaugural lecture', *Oxford Economic Papers*, **5**, 117–35. [223]
Hicks, J. R. (1969) *Theory of Economic History* (Oxford, Clarendon Press). [51]
Hicks, J. R. (1977) *Economic Perspectives* (Oxford, Clarendon Press). [65]
Higgins, B. H. (1956) 'The "Dualistic Theory" of Underdeveloped Areas', *Econ. Dev. and Cultural Change*, **4**(2), 99–115. [113]
Hirsch, F. (1977) *Social Limits to Growth* (London, Routledge and Kegan Paul). [71, 159]
Hirschman, A. O. (1945) *National Power and the Structure of Foreign Trade* (Los Angeles, University of California Press). [205]
Hirschman, A. O. (1958) *The Strategy of Economic Development* (New Haven, Yale University Press). [98, 104]
Hirschman, A. O. (1973) 'The changing tolerance for economic inequality in the course of economic development', *Quar. Jour. Econ.* **87**, 544–66. [265]
Hlaing, A. (1965) *An Economic and Statistical Analysis of Economic Development of Burma under British Rule* (University of London Ph.D. thesis). [211]
Horvat, B. (1958) 'The optimum rate of investment', *Econ. Jour.* **68**, 747–67. [145]
Hufbauer, G. C. (1965) *Synthetic Materials and the Theory of International Trade* (London, Duckworth). [217]
Hutchinson, T. W. (1978) *On Revolutions and Progress in Economic Knowledge* (Cambridge, Cambridge University Press). [118]
I.B.R.D.–I.M.F. (1969) *The Problem of Stabilization of Prices of Primary Products* (Washington, D.C., I.B.R.D. and I.M.F.). [226–7]
I.L.O. (1972) *Employment, Incomes and Equality* (Geneva, I.L.O.). [122, 244, 261, 279]
I.L.O. (1974) *Sharing in Development* (Geneva, I.L.O.). [121, 261]
Indian Planning Commission (1964) *Notes on Perspective of Development 1960–61 to 1975–76* (New Delhi, Planning Commission). [292]
Ishikawa, S. (1967) *Economic Development in Asian Perspective* (Tokyo, Kinokumiya Bookstore). [174]
Ishikawa, S. (1978) *Labour Absorption in Asian Agriculture* (Bangkok, A.R.T.E.P.). [173]
Ishikawa, S. (1981) *Essays on Technology, Employment and Institutions in Economic Development* (Tokyo, Kinokuniya Company). [188]
Jain, S. (1975) *Size Distribution of Income* (Washington, D.C. World Bank). [244–6, 250, 253]
Jeffreys, H. (1973) *Scientific Inference* (3rd edition) (Cambridge, Cambridge University Press). [134]
Johnson, E. A. G. (1970) *The Organization of Space in Developing Countries* (Cambridge, Mass., Harvard University Press). [108]
Johnson, H. G. (1955) 'Economic expansion and international trade', *Manchester School* **23**, 95–112. [223]
Johnson, H. G. (1964) *Money, Trade and Economic Growth* (2nd edition) (London, Allen and Unwin). [256]
Johnson, H. G. (1965) 'Is inflation the inevitable price of rapid development or a retarding factor in economic growth', reprinted in Johnson, H. G. *Essays in Monetary Economics* (London, Allen and Unwin, 1969) Chapter 9. [304]
Johnson, H. G. (1967) *Economic Policies towards Less Developed Countries* (Washington, D.C., Brookings Institution). [313]
Johnson, H. G. (1970) 'Pearson's "grand assize" fails', *Round Table* **60**, 17–25. [312]

Johnson, H. G. (1972) 'The "crisis of aid" and the Pearson Report', in Byres, T. J. (ed.) *Foreign Resources and Economic Development* (London, Frank Cass), 135–54. [315]

Johnson, H. G. (1973) *The Theory of Income Distribution* (London, Gray-Mills Publishing). [256]

Johnston, B. F. and Mellor, J. (1961) 'The role of agriculture in economic development', *Amer. Econ. Rev.* **51**, 566–93. [190]

Jolly, R. (1976) 'Redistribution with growth', in Cairncross, A. and Puri, M. (eds) *Employment, Income Distribution and Development Strategy* (New York, Holmes and Meier) pp.43–55. [279]

Kakwani, N. C. (1979) *Income Distribution: Methods of Analysis and Applications* (Washington D.C., World Bank). [244, 246–7]

Kaldor, N. (1957) 'A model of economic growth', *Econ. Jour.* **68**, 591–624. [148]

Kaldor, N. (1961) 'Capital accumulation and economic growth' in Lutz, F. A. and Hague, D. C. (eds) *The Theory of Capital* (London, Macmillan). [148]

Kaldor, N. (1962) 'Stabilising the terms of trade of under-developed countries', reprinted in Kaldor, N. (1964) *Essays on Economic Policy* Vol.II (London, Duckworth) pp.112–130. [235]

Kaldor, N. (1962a) 'The role of taxation in economic development', reprinted in Kaldor, N. (1964) *Essays on Economic Policy* Vol.I, pp.225–254. [298]

Kaldor, N. (1964) 'Dual exchange rates and economic development', reprinted in Kaldor, N. (1964) *Essays on Economic Policy*, Vol.II (London, Duckworth), pp.112–130. [239–40]

Kaldor, N. (1964a) 'Problems of the Indian Third Five Year Plan', reprinted in Kaldor, N. (1964) *Essays on Economic Policy*, Vol.II (London, Duckworth), pp.299–305. [291–2]

Kaldor, N. (1965) 'Remarks' in Robinson, R. (ed.) *Developing the Third World* (Cambridge, Cambridge University Press, 1971) pp.98–99. [171–2]

Kaldor, N. (1972) 'The irrelevance of equilibrium economics', *Econ. Jour.* **B 82**, 1237–55. [119]

Kaldor, N. (1980) 'Memorandum', in Treasury and Civil Service Committee *Memoranda on Monetary Policy* (London, H.M.S.O., 1980) pp.86–130. [300]

Kalecki, M. (1970) 'Problems of financing economic development in a mixed economy', in Eltis, W., Scott, M. F. G., and Wolfe, J. N. (ed.) *Induction, Growth and Trade* (Oxford, Oxford University Press), pp.91–104. [182–4]

Kalecki, M. (1976) *Essays on Development Economics* (New Jersey, N.J., Harvester Press). [145]

Kamarck, A. M. (1977) *The Tropics and Economic Development* (Baltimore, Johns Hopkins Pres). [21]

Katouzian, M. A. (1978) 'Oil versus agriculture', *Jour. Peasant Studies* **5**, 347–69. [266]

Kay, G. B. (1975) *Development and Underdevelopment: A Marxist Analysis* (London, Macmillan). [8]

Keyfitz, N. (1971) 'The momentum of population growth', *Demography*, **8**, 71–80. [168]

Keyfitz, N. (1975) 'How do we know the facts of demography', *Pop. and Dev. Rev.* **1**, 267–88. [138]

Keynes, J. M. (1919) *Economic Consequences of the Peace* (London, Macmillan). [143]

Kindleberger, C. P. (1965) *Economic Development* (2nd edition) (New York, McGraw-Hill). [75]

Kirk, D. (1971) 'A new demographic transition?', in National Academy of Science, *Rapid Population Growth* (Baltimore, Johns Hopkins) pp.123–47. [138]

Kleimens, E. (1980) *Exports and Growth: Evidence and Interpretation* (Canberra, Australian National University, mimeograph). [222]

Knudsen, O. and Parnes, A. (1975) *Trade Instability and Economic Development* (Lexington, D.C., Heath & Co.). [228]

Komiya, R. (1959) 'A note on Professor Mahalanobis' model of Indian economic planning', *Rev. Econ. and Stat.* **41**, 29–35. [179]

Kravis, I. B. (1970) 'Trade as a handmaiden of growth', *Econ. Jour.* **80**, 850–72. [221–2]

Kravis, I. B., Kenessy, Z., Heston, A., and Sumers, R. (1975) *A System of International Comparison of Gross Product and Purchasing Power* (Baltimore, Johns Hopkins). [28]

Kravis, I. B., Kenessy, Z., Heston, A., and Summers, R. (1978) *International Comparison of Real Product and Purchasing Power* (Baltimore, Johns Hopkins). [28, 200, 238]

Krishnamurty, K. (1968) *Savings and Taxation in Developing Countries: An Empirical Study* (Washington, D.C., World Bank Staff Working Paper No.23). [297]

Kuznets, S. (1957) 'Quantitative aspects of the economic growth of nations: Part 2. Industrial distribution of national product and the labour force', *Econ. Dev. and Cultural Change* **5** (Supplement), 3–111. [132]

Kuznets, S. (1966) *Modern Economic Growth* (New Haven, Yale University Press). [14, 42, 246, 270]

Kuznets, S. (1972) 'The gap: concept, measurement, trends', in Ranis, G. (ed.) *The Gap Between Rich and Poor Nations* (London, Macmillan) 3–43. [46]

Kuznets, S. (1973) 'Modern economic growth: findings and reflections', *Amer. Econ. Rev.* **53**, 247–58. [70]

Kuznets, S. (1975) 'Fertility differentials between less-developed and developed regions: components and implications', *Proc. Amer. Philosophical Soc.* **119**, 363–96. [139]

Landes, D. S. (1969) *The Unbound Prometheus* (Cambridge, Cambridge University Press). [52, 54, 119, 161, 263]

Leibenstein, H. (1957) *Economic Backwardness and Economic Growth* (New York, John Wiley). [160]

Leibenstein, H. (1966) 'Allocative efficiency versus X-efficiency', *Amer. Econ. Rev.* **60**, 392–415. [197]

Leijonhufvud, A. (1968) *On Keynesian Economics and the Economics of Keynes* (Oxford, Oxford University Press). [155]

Leijonhufvud, A. (1973) 'Effective demand failures', *Swedish Jour. of Econ.* **75**, 27–48. [155–7]

Leijonhufvud, A. (1976) 'Schools, paradigms, revolutions and research programmes', in Latsis, S. (ed.) *Method and Appraisal in Economics* (Cambridge, Cambridge University Press, 1976) pp.65–108. [155]

Leontief, W. W. (1954) 'Domestic Production and Foreign Trade: The American Capital Position Re-examined', *Economia Internazionale*, **7**, 9–38. [216]

Lewis, W. A. (1954) 'Economic development with unlimited supplies of l abour', *Manchester School* **22**, 139–91. [143, 196, 215, 224, 304]

Lewis, W. A. (1955) *Theory of Economic Growth* (London, Allen and Unwin). [112–4, 120, 137, 141, 158, 162, 181]

Lewis, W. A. (1958) 'Unlimited labour: further notes', *Manchester School* **26**, 1–32. [143]

Lewis, W. A. (1964) 'Closing remarks', in Baer, W. and Kerstenetzky, I. (eds) *Inflation and Growth in Latin America* (Homewood, R. D. Irwin) pp.21–33. [302]

Lewis, W. A. (1964a) 'Allocating foreign aid to promote self-sustained economic growth', in Society for International Development, *Motivations and Methods in Development and Foreign Aid* (Washington, D.C. S.I.D. 1964) pp.20–33. [316]

Lewis, W. A. (1966) *Development Planning* (London, Allen and Unwin). [103, 287, 290–1]

Lewis, W. A. (1968) 'Education and economic development', *Social and Econ. Studies* **10**, 113–27. [97]

Lewis, W. A. (1969) *Aspects of Tropical Trade 1883–1965* (Stockholm, Almqvist and Wiksell). [58, 196, 224–5]

Lewis, W. A. (1969a) *Some Aspects of Economic Development* (Accra, University of Ghana). [117, 269]

Lewis, W. A. (1970) *The Development Process* (New York, United Nations Centre for Economic and Social Information). [75]

Lewis, W. A. (1972) 'Reflections on unlimited labour', in Marco, L. E. di (ed.) *International Economics and Development* (New York, Academic Press) pp.75–96. [143]

Lewis, W. A. (1976) 'Development and distribution', in Cairncross, A. and Puri, M. (ed.) *Employment, Income Distribution and Development Strategy* (New York, Holm and Meier) pp.26–42. [200–1, 271]

Lewis, W. A. (1976a) 'The diffusion of development', in Wilson, T. and Skinner, A. S. (ed.) *The Market and the State* (Oxford, Clarendon Press). [5, 6–7, 58–9]

Lewis, W. A. (1977) 'The less developed countries and stable exchange rates', in I.M.F., *The International Monetary System in Operation* (Washington, I.M.F. 1977) pp.33–44. [240]

Lewis, W. A. (1978) *Growth and Fluctuations* (London, Allen and Unwin). [51, 53, 54, 69, 107, 144, 224, 263]

Lewis, W. A. (1978a) *The Evolution of the International Economic Order* (Princeton, Princeton University Press). [54, 57–8, 165, 224–5, 313, 320–1]

Lewis, W. A. (1979) 'The dual economy revisited', *Manchester School* **47**, 211–29. [143]

Linder, S. (1961) *An Essay on Trade and Transformation* (Uppsala, Almqvist and Wiksell). [220]

Little, I. M. D. (1976) 'Review of Adelman and Morris' *Economic Growth and Social Equity in Developing Countries*, and Chenery *et al. Redistribution with Growth*', in *Jour. Dev. Econ.* **3**, 99–106. [249, 252]

Little, I. M. D. and Mirlees, J. A. (1969) *Manual of Industrial Project Analysis in Developing Countries*, Vol.II (Paris, O.E.C.D.). [175]

Little, I. M. D. and Mirlees, J. A. (1974) *Project Appraisal and Planning* (London, Heinemann). [177]

Little, I. M. D., Scitovsky, T. and Scott, M. (1970) *Industry and Trade in Some Developing Countries* (Paris, O.E.C.D.). [199]

Lloyd, P. J. (1968) *International Trade Problems of Small Nations* (Durham, N.C. Duke University Press). [211]

Lockwood, W. W. (1954) *The Economic Development of Japan* (New Jersey, Princeton University Press). [55]

Lowrey, G. H. (1978) *Growth and Development of Children* (Chicago, Yearbook Medical Publishers). [75–6]

MacBean, A. (1968) *Export Instability and Economic Development* (Cambridge, Mass., Harvard University Press). [228]

McGranahan, D. V., Richard-Proust, C., Sovani, N. V., and Subramanian, M. (1972) *Contents and Measurement of Socioeconomic Development* (New York, Praeger). [78]

McKinnon, R. A. (1973) *Money and Capital in Economic Development* (Washington, D.C., The Brookings Institution). [124–5]

Maddison, A. (1970) *Economic Progress and Policy in Developing Countries* (London, Allen and Unwin). [72]

Mahalanobis, P. C. (1953) 'Some observations on the process of growth of national income', *Sankhya* **14**, 307–12. [178, 180]

Mainwaring, L. (1974) 'A neo-Ricardian analysis of international trade', in *Kyklos* **27**, 537–53. [211]

Maizels, A. (1963) *Industrial Growth and World Trade* (Cambridge, Cambridge University Press). [232]

Maizels, A. (1968) 'Review of MacBean's export instability and economic development', *Amer. Econ. Rev.* **58**, 575–80. [228]

Malinvaud, E. (1977) *The Theory of Unemployment Reconsidered* (Oxford, Blackwell). [155]

Manoilesco, M. (1931) *The Theory of Protection and International Trade* (London, P. S. King and Son). [231]

Marshall, A. (1919) *Industry and Trade* (London, Macmillan). [213]

Marshall, A. (1925) *Memorials* (ed. Pigou, A. C.) (London, Macmillan). [67]

Marshall, A. (1961) *Principles of Economics* (two-volume variorum edition) (London, Macmillan). [65, 95, 150]

Marx, K. (1969) *Collected Works* (Moscow, Progress Publishers). [7]

Marx, K. and Engels, F. (1848) *The Communist Manifesto* (London, Lawrence and Wishart). [7]

Meadows, D. H. and Meadows, D. L. (1972) *The Limits to Growth* (New York, Universe Books). [159]

Meier, G. M. (1976) *Leading Issues in Economic Development* (3rd edn) (New York, Oxford University Press). [155]

Mellor, J. W. (1978) 'Food price policy and income distribution in low-income countries', *Econ. Dev. and Cultural Change* **27**, 1–26. [191]

Metcalfe, J. S. and Steedman, I. (1972) 'Re-switching and primary input use', *Econ. Jour.* **82**, 140–57. [211]

Metcalfe, J. S. and Steedman, I. (1972a) 'Heterogeneous capital and the Heckscher-Ohlin theory of trade', in Parkin, M. and Nobay, R. (eds) *Essays in Modern Economics* (London, Longman) pp.51–9. [211]

Michaely, M. (1962) *Concentration in International Trade* (Amsterdam, North Holland). [203]

Millikan, M. F. (1970) *A Strategy of Development* (New York, United Nations Centre for Economic and Social Information). [73]

Minhas, B. S. (1974) 'Rural poverty, land distribution and development strategy', *Indian Econ. Rev.* reprinted in Srinivasan, T. N. and Bardham, P. K. (eds) *Poverty and Income Distribution in India* (Calcutta, Statistical Publishing Society) pp.252–63; 397–416. [121]

Mitra, A. (1977) *Terms of Trade and Class Relations* (London, Frank Cass). [191–2]

Mundell, R. A. (1962) 'The appropriate use of monetary and fiscal policy for internal and external stability', *I.M.F. Staff Papers* **9**, 70–9. [240]

Mundell, R. A. (1971) *Monetary Theory* (California, Goodyear Publishing). [303]

Musgrave, R. A. (1969) 'Provision for social goods', in Margolis, J. and Guiton, H. (eds) *Public Economics* (London, Macmillan) pp.124–44. [105]

Myint, H. (1954) 'An interpretation of economic backwardness' reprinted in Myint (1971), Chapter 3. [74]

Myint, H. (1958) 'The "classical theory" of international trade and the underdeveloped countries', reprinted in H. Myint (1971), Chapter 5. [58, 220]

Myint, H. (1960) 'The Demand Approach to Economic Development', *Rev. Econ. Studies*. **27**, 124–32. [104]

Myint, H. (1962) 'The Universities of southeast Asia and economic development', reprinted in Myint, H. (1971), Chapter 9. [88]

Myint, H. (1964) *The Economics of Developing Countries* (London, Hutchinson). [114]

Myint, H. (1965) 'Education and economic development', reprinted in Myint, H. (1971), Chapter 8. [69]

Myint, H. (1967) 'The inward and outward-looking countries of southeast Asia', reprinted in Myint, H. (1971), Chapter 12. [222]

Myint, H. (1969) 'Trade, education and economic development', reprinted in Myint, H. (1971), Chapter 11. [93]

Myint, H. (1971) *Economic Theory and the Underdeveloped Countries* (Oxford, Oxford University Press). [332]

Myrdal, G. (1968) *Asian Drama* (3 volumes) (New York, Pantheon). [21, 152]

Myrdal, G. (1970) *The Challenge of World Poverty* (London, Allen Lane). [116–7]

Nabseth, L. and Ray, G. F. (eds) (1974) *The Diffusion of Industrial Processes* (Cambridge, Cambridge University Press). [148–9]

Nair, P. R. G. (1974) 'Decline of birth rates in Kerala', *Econ. and Pol. Weekly* **9**, 323–36. [168]

Neher, P. A. (1971) *Economic Growth and Development* (New York, John Wiley). [73]

Newberry, D. M. G. and Stiglitz, J. E. (1979) 'The theory of commodity price stabilisation rules', *Econ. Jour.* **89**, 799–817. [236]

Nordhaus, W. and Tobin, J. (1972) *Economic Growth* (New York, National Bureau of Economic Research). [27, 157]

North, D. C. and Thomas, R. P. (1973) *The Rise of the Western World* (Cambridge, Cambridge University Press). [111, 113, 115]

Notestein, F. W. (1945) 'Population — the long view', in Schultz, T. W. (ed.) *Food for the World* (Chicago, University of Chicago Press). [137]

Nurkse, R. (1952) *Problems of Capital Formation in Underdeveloped Countries* (London, Oxford University Press). [99, 103, 154, 181–2]

Nurkse, R. (1958) 'The case for balanced growth', in Meier, G. M. (ed.) *Leading Issues in Economic Development* (Oxford, Oxford University Press) (1976) pp.640–3. [154–5]

Nurkse, R. (1961) 'Further comments on Professor Rosenstein-Rodan's paper', in Ellis, H. S. and Wallich, H. C. (eds) *Economic Development in Latin America* (London, Macmillan) pp.74–78. [102–3]

O'Brien (1975) *The Classical Economists* (Oxford, Clarendon Press). [119]

Ohlin, B. (1933) *Interregional and International Trade* (Cambridge, Mass., Harvard University Press). [210]

Ohlin, G. (1967) *Population Control and Economic Development* (Paris, O.E.C.D.). [140, 169]

O.E.C.D. (1968) *Development Cooperation* (Paris, O.E.C.D.). [222, 310]

O.E.C.D. (1971) *The Conditions for Success in Technological Innovation* (Paris, O.E.C.D.). [149]

Oshima, H. (1970) ''Income inequality and economic growth: the postwar experience of Asian countries', *Malayan Econ. Rev.* **15**, 7–41. [254]

Owen, W. (1964) *Strategy for Mobility* (Washington D.C., The Brookings Institution). [99–100, 102–3]

Pack, H. and Todaro, M. (1969) ''Technological transfer, labour absorption and economic development', *Oxford Econ. Papers* **21**, 395–403. [172]

Papanek, G. F. (1972) 'The effect of aid and other resource transfers on savings and growth in less developed countries', *Econ. Jour.* **82**, 934–50. [311]

Parnes, H. S. (1962) *Forecasting Educational Needs for Economic and Social Development* (Paris, O.E.C.D.). [92]

Patel, I. G. (1971) 'Aid relationship for the seventies' in Ward, B., D'anjou, L., and Runnals, J. D. (eds) *The Widening Gap* (New York, Columbia University Press) pp.295–311. [315, 317]

Patrick, H. T. (1966) 'Financial development and economic growth in underdeveloped countries', *Econ. Dev. and Cultural Change* **14**, 174–89. [124]

Patrick, J. D. (1973) 'Establishing convergent decentralised policy assignment', *Jour. Inter. Econ.* **3**, 37–52. [241]

Paukert, F. (1973) 'Income distribution at different levels of development: a survey of evidence', *Inter. Labour Rev.* **108**, 97–125. [246]

Pearson, L. B. *et al.* (1969) *Partners in Development* (New York, Praeger). [73, 307]

Please, S. (1967) 'Saving through taxation: mirage or reality', *Finance and Development* **N 4**(1), 24–32. [297]

Please, S. (1970) 'The "Please effect" revisited' (I.B.R.D. Economics Dept Working Paper No.82) (Washington D.C., I.B.R.D.). [297]

Polanyi, K. (1958) 'The Economy as Instituted Process', in Le Clair, E. E. and Schneider, H. K. (eds) *Economic Anthropology* (New York, Holt, Rinehart and Winston, 1968), Chapter 8. [120]

Polya, G. (1954) *Induction and Analogy in Mathematics* (Princeton, Princeton University Press). [5]

Posner, M. V. (1961) 'International trade and technical change', *Oxford Econ. Papers.* **31**, 323–41. [217]

Powelson, J. P. (1972) *Institutions of Economic Growth* (Princeton, Princeton University Press). [159]

Pratten, C. F. (1971) *Economies of Scale in Manufacturing Industry* (Cambridge, Cambridge University Press). [150]

Prebisch, R. (1950) *The Economic Development of Latin America and its Principal Problems* (New York, U.N.). [222]

Psacharapoulos, G. (1973) *Returns to Education* (Amsterdam, Elsevier). [85]

Raj, K. N. (1969) 'Investment in livestock in agrarian economies', *Indian Econ. Rev.* **4**, 1–33. [114]

Raj, K. N. (1970) 'Ownership and distribution of land', *Indian Econ. Rev.* **5**, 1–42. [121, 281]

Raj, K. N. (1972) *Direct Taxation of Agriculture* (CDS Working Paper No.11) (Trivandrum, Centre for Development Studies). [299]

Raj Krishna (1973) 'Unemployment in India', *Indian Jour. Agr. Econ.* **28**, 1–23. [261]

Rao, V. K. R. V. (1952) 'Investment, income and the multiplier in an underdeveloped economy', reprinted in Agarwala, A. N. and Singh, S. P. (eds) *The Economics of Underdevelopment* (London, Oxford University Press) pp.205–18. [153]

Rao, V. K. R. V. (1981) 'Measurement of poverty: a note', *Econ. and Pol. Weekly*, **16**, 1433–6. [267]

Reynolds, L. G. (1977) *Image and Reality in Economic Development* (New Haven, Yale University Press). [72, 130]

Ricardo, D. (1952) *Collected Works*, Vol. 8 (London, Macmillan). [248]

Robertson, D. H. (1953) *Lectures on Economic Principles* (London, Fontana Library). [303]

Robinson, E. A. G. (1953) *The Structure of Competitive Industry* (Cambridge, Cambridge University Press). [150]

Robinson, J. (1949) 'The foreign exchanges', reprinted in Ellis, H. S. and Metzler, L. A., *Readings in the Theory of International Trade* (Philadelphia, Blakiston) pp.83–103. [239]

Robinson, J. (1962) *Economic Philosophy* (London, Penguin Books). [7]

Robinson, J. (1979) *Aspects of Development and Underdevelopment* (Cambridge, Cambridge University Press). [162]

Rosenberg, N. (1974) 'Science, innovation and economic growth', reprinted in Rosenberg, N., *Perspectives on Technology* (Cambridge, Cambridge University Press, 1976), Chapter 15. [149]

Rosenstein-Rodan, P. N. (1943) 'Problems of industrialization of eastern and southeastern Europe', *Econ. Jour.* **53**, 202–11. [181]

Rosenstein-Rodan, P. N. (1961) 'Notes on the theory of the "big push" in Ellis, H. S. (ed.) *Economic Development of Latin America* (London, Macmillan) pp.57–73. [160]

Rosenstein-Rodan, P. N. (1961a) 'International aid for underdeveloped countries', *Rev. Econs and Stats.* **43**, 107–38. [311, 316]
Rostow, W. W. (1960) *The States of Economic Growth* (Cambridge, Cambridge University Press). [54, 57, 73, 132]
Rostow, W. W. (1975) *How It All Began* (London, Methuen). [53, 152]
Roumasset, J. and Smith, J. (1981) *Population, Technological Change, and Landless Workers; The Extent of the Market is Limited by Specialization* (East–West Center Working Paper 81-6) (Hawaii, East–West Center). [171]
Rudra, A. (1972) 'Use of shadow prices in project evaluation', *Indian Econ. Rev.* **7**, 1–15. [177]
Ruttan, V. W. (1978) 'Induced institutional change', in Binswanger, H. P., and Ruttan, V. W., *Induced Innovation* (Baltimore, Johns Hopkins University Press), Chapter 12. [116]
Samuelson, P. A. (1947) *Foundations of Economic Analysis* (Cambridge, Mass., Harvard University Press). [5]
Samuelson, P. A. (1948) 'International Trade and the Equalisation of Factor Prices', reprinted in *Collected Papers* (1966) Vol.2, Chapter 67. [211]
Samuelson, P. A. (1953) 'Prices of factors and goods in general equilibrium', reprinted in *Collected Papers* Vol.2, Chapter 70. [211]
Samuelson, P. A. (1954) 'The pure theory of public expenditure', reprinted in *Collected Papers* (1966) Vol.2, Chapter 92. [99, 303]
Samuelson, P. A. (1958) 'An exact consumption–loan model of interest with or without the social contrivance of money', reprinted in *Collected Papers* (1966) Vol.1, Chapter 21. [303]
Samuelson, P. A. (1969) 'Pure theory of public expenditure and taxation', reprinted in *Collected Papers* (1972) Vol.3, Chapter 172. [99]
Samuelson, P. A. (1971) 'Ohlin was right', reprinted in *Collected Papers* (1977) Vol.4, Chapter 254. [211]
Samuelson, P. A. (1973) 'Deadweight loss in international trade from the profit motive', reprinted in *Collected Papers* (1977) Vol.4, Chapter 253. [211]
Samuelson, P. A. (1974) 'Analytical notes on international real income measures', reprinted in *Collected Papers* (1977) Vol.4, Chapter 210. [28]
Schmookler, J. (1966) *Invention and Economic Growth* (Cambridge, Mass., Harvard University Press). [148–9]
Schultz, T. W. (1964) *Transforming Traditional Agriculture* (New Haven, Yale University Press). [66]
Schultz, T. W. (ed.) (1973) 'New economic approaches to fertility', *Jour. Pol. Econ.* **81**, 514–64. [139]
Schultz, T. W. (1978) *Distortions of Agricultural Incentives* (Bloomington, Indiana University Press). [191]
Schumpeter, J. A. (1934) *The Theory of Economic Development*, Cambridge, Mass., Harvard University Press). [76, 124]
Schumpeter, J. A. (1939) *Business Cycles* (two volumes) (London, McGraw-Hill). [76]
Schumpeter, J. A. (1943) *Capitalism, Socialism and Democracy* (London, Allen and Unwin). [7, 160]
Scitovsky, T. (1976) *The Joyless Economy* (New York, Oxford University Press). [159]
Seers, D. (1969) 'The meaning of development', *Inter. Dev. Rev.* **11**(4), 2–6. [74]
Seers, D. (1970) 'New approaches suggested by the Colombia employment programme', *Inter. Lab. Rev.* **102**, 377–89. [261]
Sen, A. K. (1959) 'The choice of agricultural techniques in underdeveloped countries', *Econ. Dev. and Cultural Change* **7**, 279–85. [173, 188]
Sen, A. K. (1970) 'Crisis in Indian education', in Chaudhuri, P. (ed.) *Aspects of Indian Economic Development* (London, Allen and Unwin). [90]

Sen, A. K. (1972) 'Control areas and accounting prices; an approach to economic evaluation', *Econ. Jour.* **82**, 486–501. [178]

Sen, A. K. (1975) *Employment, Technology and Development* (Oxford, Clarendon Press). [261]

Sen, A. K. (1977) 'Starvation and exchange entitlements', *Cambridge Jour. Econ.* **1**, 33–59. [191]

Shaw, E. S. (1973) *Financial Deepening in Economic Development* (New York, Oxford University Press). [125]

Sheahan, J. (1958) 'International Specialisation and the Concept of Balanced Growth', *Quar. Jour. Econ.* **72**, 183–97. [182]

Singer, H. W. (1950) 'The distribution of gains between investing and borrowing countries', *Amer. Econ. Rev. Papers and Proc.* **11**, 473–85. [222]

Singer, H. W. (1965) 'External aid: for plans or projects', *Econ. Jour.* **75**, 539–45. [318]

Singer, H. W. (1975) *The Strategy of International Development* (London, Macmillan). [226]

Singer, H. W. and Ansari, J. A. (1977) *Rich and Poor Countries* (London, Allen and Unwin). [75]

Singh, S. K. (1975) *Development Economics* (Lexington, D.C., Heath & Co.). [10, 143–4, 310]

Singh, T. (1974) *India's Development Experience* (Delhi, Macmillan Co. of India). [290]

Sinha, R., Pearson, P., Kadekodi, G., and Gregory, M. (1979) *Income Distribution, Growth and Basic Needs in India* (London, Croom Helm). [276, 279]

Smith, A. (1776) *The Wealth of Nations* (Cannan edition, 1961) (London, University Paperbacks). [51, 67, 74–5]

Solow, R. M. (1957) 'Technical change and the aggregate production function', *Rev. Econ. and Stats.* **39**, 312–20. [148]

Solow, R. M. (1962) 'Note on Uzawa's two-sector model of economic growth', *Rev. Econ. Studies* **29**, 48–50. [141]

Spate, O. H. K. (1941) 'Beginning of industrialization in Burma', *Econ. Geography*, **17**, 75–92. [195]

Spraos, J. (1980) 'The statistical debate on the net barter terms of trade between primary commodities and manufactures', *Econ. Jour.* **90**, 107–28. [208, 222–3]

Srinivasan, T. N. (1977) 'Development, poverty and basic human needs: some issues', *Food Research Institute Studies* **16**, 11–28. [267, 271, 278]

Stewart, F. (1977) *Technology and Underdevelopment* (London, Macmillan). [169]

Stigler, G. J. (1975) *The Citizen and the State* (Chicago, University of Chicago Press). [118]

Stiglitz, J. E. (1970) 'Factor price equalization in a dynamic economy', *Jour. Pol. Econ.* **78**, 456–88. [242]

Stiglitz, J. E. and Uzawa, H. (1969) *Readings in the Modern Theory of Economic Growth* (Cambridge, Mass., M.I.T. Press). [141]

Stoler, A. (1977) 'Garden use and household economy in rural Java', *Bull. Indonesian Econ. Studies*, **16**(2), 85–101. [122]

Streeten, P. and Burki, S. J. (1978) 'Basic needs: some issues', *World Development*, **6**, 411–21. [268, 272, 278]

Sukhatme, P. V. (1978) 'Assessment of adequacy of diets at different income levels', *Econ. and Pol. Weekly* **13**, 1373–84. [267]

Sukhatme, P. V. (1981) 'Measuring the incidence of undernutrition: a comment', *Econ. and Pol. Weekly* **16**, 1034–6. [267]

Sundrum, R. M. (1973) 'Money supply and prices: a reinterpretation', *Bulletin. Indonesian Econ. Studies* **9**(3), 73–86. [302]

Sundrum, R. M. (1976) 'The statistical study of fertility', *Malayan Econ. Rev.* **21**(2), 36–48. [139]

Sundrum, R. M. (1976a) 'Transitional dynamics of deficit financing', *Indian Econ. Rev.* **9** (new series), 193–203. [303]

Sundrum, R. M. (1977) 'Changes in consumption patterns in urban Java', *Bull. Indonesian Econ. Studies* **13**(2), 102–16. [253–4]

Sundrum, R. M. (1978) 'Application of David Butt's theory of growth to the allocation of investment', *Econ. Record.* **54**, 78–93. [148]

Sundrum, R. M. (1979) 'Income distribution 1970–77' *Bull. Indonesian Econ. Studies.* **15**(1), 137–41. [250]

Sundrum, R. M. (1980) 'New approaches to income and employment theory', *Australian Econ. Rev.* No. 49, 23–8. [155]

Sundrum, R. M. (1981) *Dynamics of Agricultural Investment* (Canberra, Australian National University, mimeograph). [148]

Sundrum, R. M. (1981a) *Present Value and Rate of Return Criteria* (Canberra, Australian National University, mimeograph). [175]

Sundrum, R. M. and Booth, A. (1980) 'Income distribution in Indonesia: trends and determinants', in Garnaut, R. G. and McCawley, P. T. (eds) *Indonesia: Dualism, Growth and Poverty* (Canberra, Australian National University) pp.455–86. [84, 266]

Swan, T. W. (1962) 'Circular causation', *Econ. Record* **38**, 421–6. [152]

Takayama, A. (1972) *International Trade* (New York, Holt Rinehart and Winston). [224]

Temin, P. (1967) 'A time series of patterns of industrial growth', *Econ. Dev. and Cultural Change* **15**, 174–82. [46]

Tinbergen, J. and Bos, H. C. (1964) 'A planning model for the educational requirements of economic development', in O.E.C.D. *The Residual Factor and Economic Growth* (Paris, O.E.C.D.) pp.147–69. [93]

Tun Wai, U. (1977) 'A revisit to interest rates outside the organized money marts of underdeveloped countries', *Banca Nazionale del Lavoro*, No.122, 291–312. [125]

Turnham, D. and Jaeger, I. (1971) *The Unemployment Problem in Less-Developed Countries* (Paris, O.E.C.D.). [261]

Turnovsky, S. (1978) *Macro-economic Analysis and Stabilization Policy* (Cambridge, Cambridge University Press). [240–1]

United Nations (1951) *Measures for the Economic Development of Underdeveloped Countries* (New York, U.N.). [309–10, 317]

United Nations (1963) *Population Bulletin No.7* (New York, U.N.). [23, 32]

United Nations, (1964) 'Plant size and economies of scale', in *Industrialisation and Productivity Bulletin No.8* (New York. U.N.) pp.53–61. [150]

United Nations (1970) *The Measurement of Development Effort* (New York, U.N.). [294, 297]

United Nations (1973) *Determinants and Consequences of Population Trends* (Second Edition) Vol.1 (New York, U.N.). [137]

United Nations (1975) *Poverty, Unemployment and Development Policy* (New York, U.N.). [120]

United Nations Industrial Development Organization (1972) *Guidelines for Project Evaluation* (New York, U.N.). [176]

Vaidyanathan, A., Nair, K., and Harris, M. (1979) *Bovine Sex and Species Ratios in India* (Trivandrum, Centre for Development Studies, Working Paper No.108). [114]

Vernon, R. (1966) 'International investment and international trade in the product cycle', *Quar. Jour. Econ.* **80**, 190–207. [217]

Viner, J. (1953) *International Trade and Economic Development* (Oxford, Clarendon Press). [64]

Visaria, P. (1981) 'Poverty and unemployment in India: an assessment of recent evidence', *World Development* **9**, 277–300. [261]

White, B. (1976) *Production and Reproduction in a Javanese Village* (New York, Columbia University Ph.D. thesis). [122]

White, J. (1967) *Pledged to Development* (London, Overseas Development Institute). [306, 316]

Wilber, C. K. and Jameson, K. P. (1979) 'Paradigms of economic development and beyond', in Jameson, K. P. and Wilber, C. K. (eds) *Directions in Economic Development* (London, University of Notre Dame Press). [7, 59]

World Bank (1978) *World Development Report, 1978* (Washington, D.C., World Bank). [254]

Yotopoulos, P. A. and Nugent, T. B. (1976) *Economics of Development* (New York, Harper and Row). [42, 66]

Young, A. (1928) 'Increasing returns and economic progress', *Econ. Jour.* **38**, 527–42. [150–2, 165]

Youngson, A. J. (1967) *Overhead Capital* (Edinburgh, Edinburgh University Press). [98–9]

Subject Index